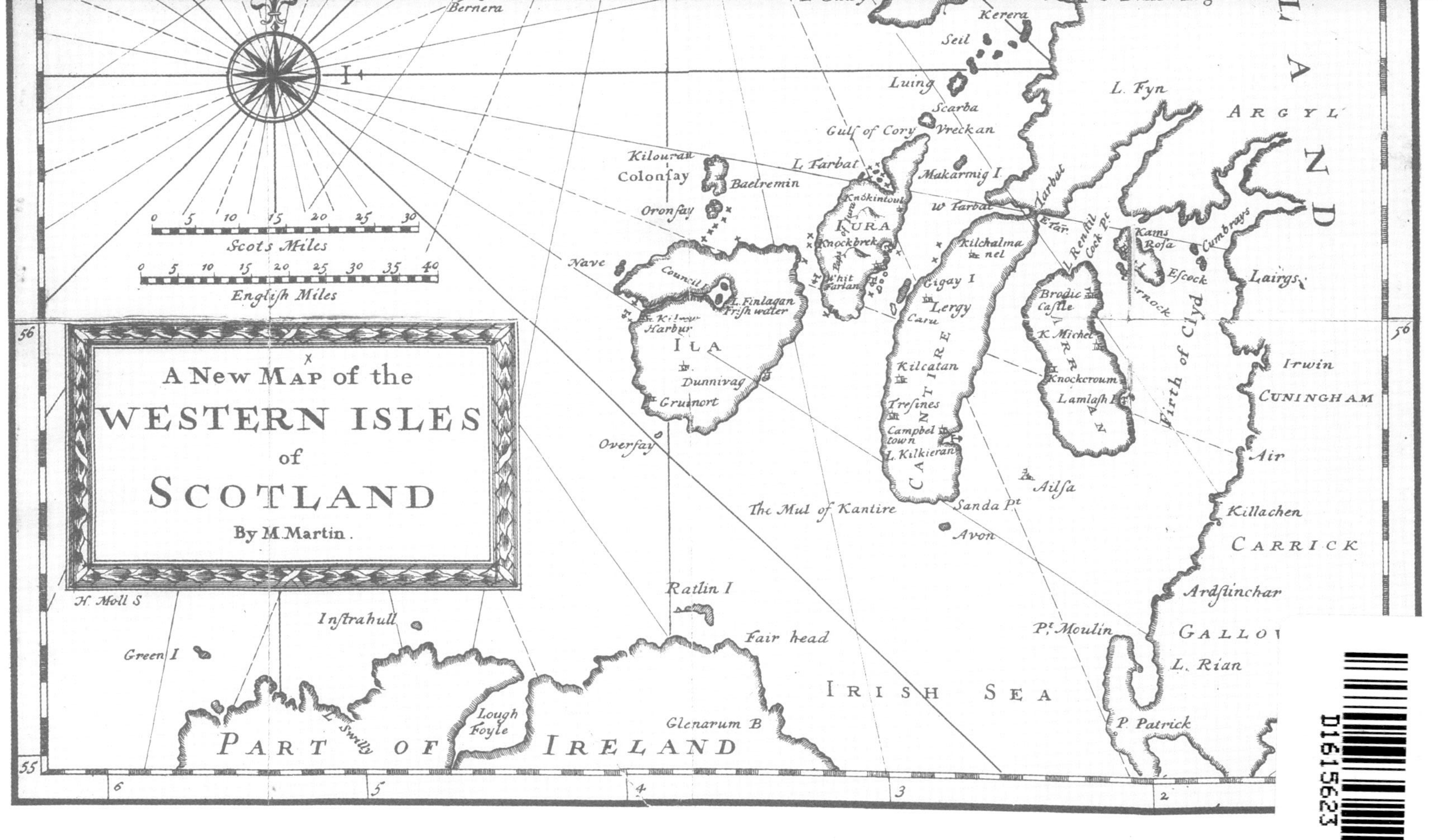
A New Map of the
WESTERN ISLES
of
SCOTLAND
By M. Martin.
H. Moll S
Scots Miles
0 5 10 15 20 25 30
English Miles
0 5 10 15 20 25 30 35 40
Bernera
Kerera
Seil
Luing
Scarba
Gulf of Cory
Vreckan
L. Fyn
ARGYL
N
D
Kilouran
Colonsay
Baelremin
Oronsay
L. Farbat
Makarmig I.
W Tarbat
Tarbat
Knokintout
IURA
Knockbrek
Whit Farlan
Nave
Council
L. Finlagan Frish water
Harbur
ILA
Dunnivag
Grunort
Overfay
Kilchalma nel
Gigay I
Lergy
Caru
CANTIRE
Kilcatan
Tresines
Campbel town
L. Kilkieran
Etar.
L. Renfil
Cock Pt
Brodic Castle
K. Michel
ARRAN
Knockcroum
Lamlash I
Kams
Rosa
Escock
Cumbrays
Lairgs
Firth of Clyd
Irwin
CUNINGHAM
Air
Ailsa
The Mul of Kantire
Sanda Pt
Avon
Killachen
CARRICK
Ardstinchar
GALLO
L. Rian
Pt. Moulin
P. Patrick
Ratlin I
Fair head
IRISH SEA
Instrahull
Green I
Lough Foyle
L. Swilly
Glenarum B
PART OF IRELAND
56
55
6
5
4
3
2

Carolina Scots

CAROLINA SCOTS

An Historical and Genealogical Study of Over 100 Years of Emigration

Douglas F. Kelly
with Caroline Switzer Kelly

1739 Publications
Dillon, S.C. • (800) 204-2506

Editorial and Sales Offices: 1739 Publications
500 East Cleveland Street, Dillon, South Carolina 29536
1 (800) 204-2506

Kelly, Douglas F., 1943-
Carolina scots : genealogical study, highland scots, scottish emigration to the Carolinas, highland scottish culture in the Carolinas / Douglas F. Kelly.
p. cm.
Includes bibliographical references and index.
ISBN 0-9662963-0-3 (cloth : alk. paper)

This book is printed on acid-free recycled paper meeting
the requirements of the American National Standard
for Permanence of Paper for Printed Library Materials.

Carolina Scots was designed and typeset by Marc Bailey of Books International in Roswell, Georgia.
Dustcover design by Wayne Clark of Radwin Creative, Charlotte, N.C.
Index by David Fisher of Columbia, S.C.
Printing and binding by Bookcrafters of Chelsea, Michigan.

Manufactured in the United States of America

Cover Picture:
The Emigrants, William McTaggart RSA

Brought up in Kintyre, McTaggart (1835-1910) retained boyhood memories of the emigrations which had begun with the Argyll Colony's departure. In the 1890s he completed a series of paintings that vividly expresses the hopes of those departing for distant shores and the empty, broken hearts of those left behind. Small boats ferry departing Highlanders to the tall ship anchored out in deep water. Families have come to watch them leave and a lone piper plays a lament among the baggage stacked on the shore.

This book is dedicated with love and appreciation to
Daniel Kelly IV
my third son, seventh generation descendant of
Daniel Kelly I
who came from Parish of Sleat, Isle of Skye,
to Moore County, North Carolina,
in 1803, at the age of 78.

*"The lines are fallen unto me in pleasant places;
yea, I have a goodly heritage."*
Psalm 16:6

Contents

Acknowledgements

Although I have been interested in the story of the Scottish Highlanders who came to North Carolina in the eighteenth century since my early childhood, I really did not think of writing this book until it was suggested by a friend in Edinburgh, Dr. Nigel Cameron, then Warden of Rutherford House, while I was on Sabbatical leave in that city during 1988. Some years earlier I had written volumes on the genealogies of the Kelly and Blue Families of Moore County, North Carolina, and in preparing those studies had become acquainted with a variety of rich genealogical resources on related families in the Cape Fear Valley of North Carolina and surrounding areas.

Having worked hard at filling out my own family trees, I felt it would be helpful to future family history researchers of this area to do three things in particular: first, to present a general historical overview of the reasons for which our Scottish ancestors left their homeland; secondly, to picture with broad strokes of the brush both the culture of early modern Highland Scotland and that of colonial North Carolina to which the Highlanders emigrated, and thirdly, to give genealogical and bibliographical resources for tracing many of the major families who settled and remained in the Cape Fear Valley of North Carolina, the Pee Dee Valley of South Carolina, and some of their descendants who migrated during the nineteenth century to the Southwest—particularly to Alabama and Mississippi.

I also came to believe that there would be many people in Scotland itself who would like to know more about what such a large number of their cousins across the Atlantic have been doing these last two centuries. When I was first living in Scotland in the late 1960s, it appeared to me (and I may well have been mistaken), that the eighteenth century emigrants to Carolina had been forgotten in their homeland, and that all that was popularly remembered was the nineteenth century clearances of the Highlanders to Canada and New Zealand. But there was no doubt in my mind that when I returned to Edinburgh to spend a year in the late 1980s, there seemed to be a fresh interest in that earlier—and indeed, larger—migration of Highland Scots to our shores in the eighteenth century. For this reason I suspect a volume such as this will be well received by many of our distant kinsmen in Scotland. Much that is told here is their story as well as our story.

It has been my feeling all during this project that while there are many who know the history of Scotland better than I, and many who know the history of North Carolina better than I, there may be few who combine such a personal, lifelong knowledge of and affection for both of these cultures through family roots and interconnections and many years' experience of living and studying in both places. Having deep roots in both places, and having actually lived in both places, I believe I can bring together many interesting aspects of the culture, history and genealogy of both lands in what I hope will be a fruitful union; one that will stimulate further historical, genealogical studies on both sides of the North Atlantic in years to come. Time will tell.

It remains for me to say profoundest and sincerest thanks to the scores of people who have in so many different ways assisted me with this project. I owe thanks to friends and relatives on both sides of the Atlantic Ocean. Since I have been working on this volume for about three years on and off, I am afraid that I will inevitably fail to mention some who have helped me one way or another during this time. Anyway, I must do the best I can.

John McPhaul of Southern Pines, N.C., has been of constant encouragement and help to me, and his wife, Jane provided the initial impetus for preparing the volume for publication. My own wife, Caroline, has done massive work on this text and has enabled me to finish the project at long last. Mrs. Helen Leary of the North Carolina Genealogical Society in Raleigh, N.C., generously assisted me in many ways, although she is not responsible for any of the weak points of this volume, nor could I necessarily claim her approbation for any of it.

The staff of the School of Scottish Studies of the University of Edinburgh have greatly enriched my understanding of the matters covered in the first half of this book, especially my former Gaelic teacher, Miss Morag MacLeod, and her colleague Mrs. Maggie MacKay. Even though they were very busy, they graciously gave of their time and expertise. The late William Watson, of the Edinburgh University Computer Services was of unfailing help. I also learned much from Mr. Ronald Black of the Department of Celtic of Edinburgh University.

Large numbers of friends have lent me valuable material on the genealogies of their own (or other) families. I will list as many of them here as I can presently call to mind (now failing with middle age): my mother, Mrs. Martha Pate Kelly, as well as Judge Henry McKinnon, Kenneth McLean, and the Rev. James B. MacLeod, all of Lumberton, North Carolina; Mrs. D.B. McFayden of Raeford, N.C.; Mrs. Lee McCaskill and Cary McLeod, both of Moore County, N.C.; Messrs. Charles McLaurin, Gordon G. McLaurin, James Atkins and Mrs. Janie P. McNeil and Mrs. Sally McR. Bennett, all of Dillon, S.C.; Harold McDiarmid and Mrs. Clarice Fairly of Jackson, Miss.; Lt. Col. Victor Clark of Dallas, Tx. and his brother, Charles F. Clark of Shubuta, Miss. I thank Attorney Osborne Lee of Lumberton, N.C. (my high school Sunday school teacher) for letting me use his office to complete some of my computer work on this project from time to time when I was at home visiting my mother. Dr. Jamie McDonald of Fayetteville, N.C., kindly provided information on his Dillon County, S.C., ancestors, while he was working on his Ph.D. in Scottish Studies at the University of Edinburgh.

I apologize to any whom I may have failed to thank, and wish to express deep gratitude to all—whether listed or not—for their kindness in helping me complete this project which belongs to all of us together.

Acknowledgements Updated–1998

Although this book was finished in 1989, it has 'lain fallow' like an unused field for nine years. This is because an institution which had hoped to publish it has been unable to do so, owing to financial pressure of some years' duration. In light of this, it has seemed best to make the material available to the public in another way, and so *1739 Publications* has been organized to do so. Partners in the project include: Mr. and Mrs. Lawrence McNeill and Mr. and Mrs. John A. McPhaul of Southern Pines, N.C.; Mr. Jerre Pearson of Auburn, Al.; Mrs. Pat Calhoun of Dillon, S.C.; and Mr. John Pitts of Forsyth, Ga.; Mr. Miles Smith, III of Salisbury, N.C.; Mr. Dean Fulghom of Atlanta, Ga.; and Dr. Michael Brown of Dillon, S.C. I am profoundly thankful to all of these friends for making it possible for this volume finally to appear.

While the text is substantially the same as it was in 1989, in the last year a few additions have been made to Part I—especially, more photographs and maps; and several additions have been made to Part II—in particular, the genealogy of more families has been included, as well as a few more photographs and maps. I wish to thank cordially all of the following people who have in various important ways assisted during the past year in the updating and enrichment of *Carolina Scots*: Mr. and Mrs. John Sam Blue and Mr. Cary L. McLeod of Moore County, N.C.; Mrs. John (Anna Henderson) Parham of Latta, S.C.; Mrs. Craig (Mary Carmichael) Stephens, Mrs. Howard (Faye McLellan) Sloan, Mrs. Ruth Norris, Mr. and Mrs. Robert L. McNiel, and Miss Martha McC. F. Kelly, all of Dillon, S.C.; Mr. Fred Plummer, Mr. and Mrs. Bill Kelly, Mrs. Gladys Harrison and Mr. Julian H. Blue, all of Raeford, N.C.; Mr. Dougald Clark and Mrs. Ric (Connie) Blue of Fayetteville, N.C.; Rev. Dr. and Mrs. Frank Gibson of Edinburgh, Scotland; Mrs. Ruby Crumpler McSwain and Mrs. Wanda Howard of Sanford, N.C. Also, Messrs. Jim Atkins, Coble Adams, "Red" and Pat Calhoun, and Mr. Elmer McCallum of Dillon helped me locate an old Gaelic cemetery in Dillon County.

I appreciate the following scholars, who read over the manuscript and commended it: Professor Thomas Burton, Dr. Norman N. Gillies, Mr. Robert A. Ivy, Rev. Canon Dougald MacLean, Dr. John Norman MacLeod, Mr. John A. McPhaul, Professor John Shelton Reed, Dr. William Storrar, and Judge H. A. McKinnon, Jr.

Douglas F. Kelly
Dillon, South Carolina
Easter, 1998

Preface

An eighteenth century English traveler in the Highlands of Scotland remarked that the people had, " . . . a pride in their family, as almost every one is a genealogist."[1] That was still much the case in the Cape Fear Valley region of Eastern North Carolina where I was reared in the nineteen forties and fifties. That section of the Eastern Seaboard was well aware of its Scottish roots and was also deeply marked by the Southern loyalty to the extended family. In neighborhood, church and school, I was surrounded by people who were proud of their Scottish Highland surnames and could easily trace their pedigree back for two hundred years.

During the summers from the time I was aged five until my last year at the University of North Carolina at Chapel Hill, I lived on the old family farm which had been granted to my father's Highland emigrant ancestors, shortly before the Revolutionary War, and had been inhabited by their descendants ever since. In that quiet, and at that time fairly remote section of Moore County, I learned not only about farm life from my father's maiden sister, Aunt Margaret Kelly, and their Aunt Maude Blue Hendren and her husband, but also about our family heritage not only in the local Carolina Sandhills but also in the far away Western Highlands and Islands of Scotland.

During those last years of the small family farm economy, there was still a great deal of neighborhood visiting with long conversations on the front porch, not to mention the talking that was done while working in the tobacco packhouse or in the cotton field. Most of the surrounding land holders of that section—and to a large degree throughout central and Southern Moore County—were related by blood or marriage, being descended from the same Scottish emigrant families, and most of them tended to be members of the various Presbyterian Churches of the area. Thus they had much in common to talk about and to bind them together. In fact, when my bride (a native of England) came to live in these parts, she noticed how very much shared experience and history these people had, and how much they seemed to know about each other and their past. She discovered that they tended not to discuss politics in general, cultural events, and contemporary ideas but rather family concerns and interests—both current and historical—as well as church, economy, and school, and in that order. Their lives were too full of wide ranging interesting family matters, past and present, for them to be worried with abstract discussions about ideas or culture in the broad sense.

Thus, as I grew up, in addition to immediate relatives, many of the people who surrounded me in the Moore County of the nineteen fifties, knew, loved and discussed the details of the lives and times of our Carolina and Highland ancestors in a way that was fascinating to me, a grammar school boy. I think of Cousins Rozella MacLeod, Neill T. Blue, Great-Uncle and Aunt Will and Mazie McLean Blue, and others too numerous to mention, who, while visiting, often sat on the east corner of the long front porch of the old Patrick Blue home in order to make the most of the shade of the tall pine trees and to catch the breeze that tended to blow on that side of the house.

They spoke of persons and events in these very fields and woods—going back to the Reconstruction, and War Between the States and indeed the American Revolution, and the first settlement of these Sandhills—as though it were yesterday. It was almost as though our remote forefathers could be called out of the next room in the old house or perhaps summoned from the family burial plots in Union and Bethesda Churchyards to tell their story. So, at the early age of twelve, I wrote my first family history, and since then have continued to learn and collect all I could on the Scottish Highland families of Moore County and of the entire Cape Fear Valley.

These genealogical and historical interests were greatly stimulated when I went to Edinburgh for doctoral studies in the late nineteen sixties and early seventies. While there, grand old Dame Flora MacLeod of MacLeod kindly befriended me, and I frequently visited my distant Kelly cousins in the Isle of Skye, who shared an appreciation of our mutual heritage as well as a strong commitment to the Christian faith.

Hand in hand with the discovery of new family connections, my understanding of Highland history was greatly expanded as I studied Gaelic under the Rev. William Matheson of the Celtic Department of Edinburgh University. Many have considered him to have the greatest genealogical knowledge of the families of Highland Scotland of any person alive today. He explained the basic events and movements that were afoot during the time our Carolina ancestors emigrated from their ancient homeland. But more than that, he put me in touch with sources, both well known and obscure, which helped to answer numerous questions that had been in my head since childhood, and gave me many fruitful leads for tracing the lines of particular forebears.

Then in later years, when I served as a minister in the Presbyterian Churches of Raeford, North Carolina, and afterwards in Dillon, South Carolina, my congregations were largely composed of the same Highland Carolina families of which I was a part. During pastoral visitation, I learned much not only about these people and their forefathers, but about my own roots, since we were frequently descended from the same emigrant heads of families. Thus an early childhood interest has been (in my view at least) providentially encouraged by the direction in which my own life and professional training and labors have flowed.

But enough of personal reminiscences. Suffice it to say that this little book is the fruit of many years of casual conversation, serious research and fairly wide reading and travel in Carolina and in Scotland. I have written it this summer in honor of the 250th anniversary of the first major settlement of Highland Scots in North Carolina: the Argyll Colony which made its home in the Upper Cape Fear Valley in 1739.

My goal is to help clarify the reasons why these people—and tens of thousands of other Highland Scots—left their homeland and settled in eighteenth century Carolina, and to assist future genealogical research and publication on the Cape Fear Scots families by including brief genealogical notices, along with indications of where further information may be gained, on as many of these families as possible.

Douglas Kelly,
Wallace House
Edinburgh, Scotland.
August 1989

Part One: From Scotland to Carolina

1

The Highlands of Scotland: Fountainhead of Emigration

In September 1739, the quiet lapping of dark waters against the thickly wooded banks of the Cape Fear river would have been disturbed by the sounds of men, women, and children talking excitedly in their native Gaelic, "Feuach, 's briagha a th'ann!"—(Look, isn't it lovely!). They had sailed in July, from Campbeltown, the main port of their home area of Argyll on the West of Scotland following the recommendation of a committee of leading citizens. These men had already made an advance trip to the Carolinas encouraged by the interest of the Governor, Gabriel Johnston, himself a Scot, who felt that the colony would be prospered by the addition of Highlanders. To attract such immigration, he offered free land grants and even possible exemption from taxation for a time.

Led by Neill Du MacNeill ("Black" Neil of Ardelay), this group of Gaelic speakers included Armstrongs, McAlesters, Clarks, Colvins, Alexanders, McKays, McLaughlins, McLachlans, McNeills, McPhersons, Stevens, Buies, Camerons, McDuffies, McCranies, Pattersons, Campbells, Stewarts, Connors, Wards, McGaws, McDougalds, McGills, Smiths, and Smylies—and as they fanned out into the surrounding sandhills during the next months, they set the pattern for future settlements, adapting their Scottish ways to the new environment.

To set the movements of our forefathers in proper context, we must begin by taking a look at the general cultural background from which they came. In so doing, we will be examining the formative influences on the Scottish settlers in the Carolinas, influences which have made a lasting mark on the Southern culture there and elsewhere.

Geography and History of the Highlands

Scotland, not including its large scattered island areas, is about the size of the state of South Carolina. It is divided into two main regions known as the Lowlands and the Highlands. The Highlands include much of the northern and western portions of Scotland, particularly above an imaginary 'Highland line' which runs along the Grampian mountains.

> It runs across the north side of the Clyde Valley, then north and east through Perthshire and Angus, and so around to the east side of Scotland close to the coast. Reaching the boundary of the counties of Sutherland and Caithness, it turns northwest to end on the northern shore near the Pentland Firth, leaving Caithness as a remote outpost of the Lowlands. In the eighteenth century the cultural and linguistic boundary approximated very closely to this geographical line. The Western Isles, or Hebrides, have always belonged to the Highlands in every respect . . .[1]

Until last century, the Highlands were isolated from the Lowlands not only by the difficulties of travel through the mountains and remote islands, but also by a difference in language. The Highlanders spoke Gaelic, a form of ancient Celtic, which is far more different from the English that was spoken in the Lowlands than is German or French. And along with the Gaelic language there was a distinct Highland, or Celtic, culture which set the region apart from the Lowlands even more than its geography.

In order to be in a better position to explore this distinctive Celtic culture and look at the changes it suffered in the seventeenth and eighteenth centuries leading to its exportation to the faraway coast of Carolina, we will begin by taking a brief look at the history of the Highlands, with reference to the rest of the British Isles, where relevant.

The Highlanders are one branch of a larger family of Celts, who belong originally to the Indo-European peoples, and who seem to have come in two large waves to pre-historic Britain—one directly into main-

The "Highland line" according to Ian Charles Cargill Graham.

1790 engraving of Duntuilm [Duntulm] Castle on the Isle of Skye, seat of the MacDonalds from the late middle ages, and abandoned around 1730. Flora McDonald is buried nearby.

land Britain and the other by way of Ireland. These people brought with them not only their language but also a peculiar structuring of society along kinship lines, which in later centuries evolved into what is known as the *clan system* of Ireland and Scotland. At one time the Celts occupied large sections of Great Britain, but by the early Middle Ages, the invasions of the Romans, and then of the Angles, Saxons, Jutes and others, had driven them back into the Northern and Western portions of Britain—to Wales, Cornwall, Ireland, the Isle of Man and Scotland.

The Highlands of Scotland, however, can trace the main development of their peculiar culture to a sixth and seventh century migration of their distant relatives from Ireland to the Southwestern Coast of Kintyre. Large numbers of Gaels or "Scots" moved into Argyllshire in the early Middle Ages. They brought with them not only a line of kings, who would become the progenitors of the Scottish Royal House, but also the form of Gaelic which would become standard in Scotland. In addition, they were accompanied by monastic Christian missionaries who helped to spread faith, language and civilization throughout the mainland of Scotland.

Eventually the MacDonald Clan became the most powerful of the clans, so that for much of the Medieval period they dominated large areas of the Highlands and Islands as well as significant parts of Northern Ireland. The MacDonalds were a counterbalance to the authority of the House of Stewart, who were, in theory, the kings of all Scotland. For several centuries, the MacDonalds essentially functioned as rulers of the Highlands, and closely connected to them were a number of other powerful clans such as the MacLeans, Camerons and others. In fact, until the sixteenth and seventeenth centuries, the Highlands, under the MacDonald hegemony as "Lords of the Isles", maintained a functional independence from the rest of Scotland. But the Highlands were not to remain isolated for long. As was so often to happen in the future, it was events further south that were to have a decisive influence in the shaping of Highland history and culture.

In 1603, the long reign of Queen Elizabeth I of England ended. But she died single and childless and the Tudor line came to an abrupt end also. Who would succeed her? In looking for a successor, eyes turned north to her cousin, James VI, Scottish monarch of the House of Stewart. Thus, when he was chosen to succeed her, the crowns of England and Scotland were united in his person and line and he moved away from Edinburgh to London. As a result, although the process would take generations, the tendency of the controlling powers of Scotland was naturally to look southwards to England, and increasingly to draw Scotland into the orbit of the economic and social system of the vastly larger and more powerful Southern neighbor.

Highland Chieftain, 1660, Sir Mungo Murray, son of Marquis of Atholl, by John Michael Wright.

From this time forward the central government would work hard to bring the independent Highlands under their sway.

Duart Castle, Mull, 1748, traditional seat of the MacLeans. These plans and engravings were made by government troops stationed there after the 1745 rebellion.

Eventually the result was that they were fused into the Lowland section, and ultimately—in a certain sense—into the whole of what would become the "United Kingdom." However, as it turned out, the actual procedure would take a long time and would be accompanied by considerable bloodshed and widespread dislocations for the Highlanders.

The English crown's most difficult assignment was to bring the High-

lands under its hegemony. There was much resistance—not surprisingly, considering the enormous differences that existed between the social structure and culture of each country. In the end, it became clear, that a political union could not be achieved without bloodshed, but at first various efforts were made to impose English ways on the Highlanders by enacting laws. The Western Islands gave the most trouble, resenting the threat to their traditional clan-based rule by a far off government. So the King decided to bring them under submission by a imposing a series of statutes:

> The chiefs of the Islands were invited to come aboard a ship off the island of Mull. They came, suspecting nothing; the ship sailed off with them, and they were all put in prison. Next year they were compelled to sign a paper, called the "Band of... Iona." This band or bond contained nine statutes for the better government of the Western Islands. By one of the statutes every gentleman in the islands was compelled to send his eldest son to school in the Lowlands, and by another every islander was forbidden to carry firearms... The following year (1610) another order was made, which did more than anything else to maintain peace in the islands. All the great chiefs were compelled to appear before the Privy Council at certain times of the year, to make sure that none of their clansmen had broken the law.[2]

Such underhanded methods inevitably strengthened resistance rather than achieving the desired union. Indeed, much of the brutal clan warfare of "the wild Highlands" must be traced to a deliberate strategy, adopted by the English, of harnessing local sympathies against the most independent and powerful clans—a policy which has been termed the *daunting of the West.*

> The daunting of the West meant, in fact, the destruction of the clan Donald, the great rivals of the Campbells. The clan Donald, through its numerous branches and allied or dependent clans, controlled the Hebrides and much of the coast of the western Highlands as the Campbells now controlled the main core of Argyll. Macdonald himself, since 1345 bearing the title 'Lord of the Isles', ruled what was virtually an independent kingdom that extended in the fifteenth century over a third of the area of Scotland. Regarding himself as the heir of the Celto-Norse kings of the isles, he kept royal state at his court . . . The destruction of this native empire was as desirable and necessary to the Scottish Crown as it was to the house of Argyll.[3]

Indeed, the Crown used the Campbells, who were rising to new power, to do this work of breaking the Macdonalds and drawing the Highlands under the sway of the Lowland government:

> The first commission of lieutenantry, to carry out the forfeiture decreed against the fourth Lord of the Isles, was given to the first Earl of Argyll in 1475. The work of destroying the Macdonald power was virtually completed by 1607. . . . Nothing survived of the confederacy of the clans which Macdonald had united under his aegis. . . . The subject chiefs and various branches of the clan Donald, once the authority of the Lordship had gone, lost all cohesion and plunged into savage feuds with one another. These were skilfully fomented by the central government and by its agent Argyll. It was indeed this use of diplomacy and stratagems rather than open violence that won the Campbells such hatred. The utter barbarity of the history of the Highlands from roughly 1475 to 1625 was largely the result of the 'daunting of the Isles' and the destruction of the Macdonald lordship.[4]

The Earls of Argyll, who thus came to control something over 3,000 square miles of territory in Argyll and parts of Inverness-shire, were noted as "king's men," but their alliance with the king was not without its problems and price. On the one hand, they recognized the very real value of integrating the Highland economy and social system into that of the more prosperous and advanced Lowlands and England. But on the other hand they were faced with a difficult decision of loyalty.

After the events of the religious revival and political upheaval known as the Second Reformation beginning in 1638, they found themselves unable to support the king in certain areas. Throughout the English Civil Wars issuing from the events of 1638, and culminating in the victory of the forces of "Puritan" Parliament over the House of Stewart in the mid sixteen forties, the House of Argyll sincerely adhered to the Reformed (or Puritan) side and thus split with the Stewart dynasty.

Without entering into the details of this struggle, we may note that after the Stewarts were restored to temporary power, the eighth Earl and Marquis of Argyll and his son, the ninth Earl, both paid for their stand against the anti-Reformed Crown with their lives. The House of Argyll ultimately won however, for their estate was returned to their heirs after the "Glorious Revolution" of 1688:

> . . . finally expelled the Stuart dynasty and established the Protestant Succession. The accession of the Hanoverian dynasty in 1714, through the timely intervention of a group of nobles of whom Argyll was one, finally sealed the triumph of the Whigs. These two events also established the

> house of Argyll in a position of unassailable power in Scotland. . . . Thus in the seventeenth century the house of Argyll had assumed a new role, that of creating and leading a new order in Church and State.[5]

John Campbell, 4th Duke of Argyll (c. 1693-1770), by the famous English painter Gainsborough in 1766. Note the pose and dress which reflect an indentification with the English aristocracy. There is not a trace of Scottishness.

The tendency to look south would be strengthened by the union of the Parliaments of Scotland and England in 1707. Over a period of time the power structure of the Highlands would more and more work to bring their region into line with social and economic practices south of the border. None would be more vigorous in this process than the Campbell lairds of Argyll.

It was at this point that the deep differences between the cultures began to cause many of those in the area seriously to consider emigration. In order to understand why the general English way of life was so alien to the Highlanders, we need to remember that they operated under a very different social structure. This structure has been variously termed the "Celtic kinship system" or the "Highland Clan System," and deeply affected the Gaelic culture as a whole.

Windows on the Past

It is hard to picture the way things were before the political and social changes affected the Highlands so radically. We are fortunate, however, that about the time that some of the distinctive characteristics of Highland life were beginning to come under severe attack from all quarters, there was arising a new breed of writer whose interest was to chronicle daily life all over the British Isles. In some cases, they were outsiders to the culture which they were describing. An example of this would be the

James Boswell, 1765, by George Willison (1741-1797)

famous *Journey to the Western Islands of Scotland*, made in the 1770's by the Englishman Johnson with his friend Boswell, a Scot. Another Englishman whose observations have become a window through which we can view Scottish life of two hundred and fifty years ago is Edmund Burt, an officer of the Royal Engi- neers, sent to Oban in the mid-eighteenth century. In his line of work as a contractor he travelled widely, and was thus able to leave for us not only written accounts of a variety of different locations and events, but also is one of the first to include engravings of daily life.

As we shall see, the Scots loved the past, and so they were not without their own chroniclers of the period. Although, naturally, they were not all writing at exactly the time of the Argyll colony, for example, very often they draw in past experiences, their own or of others, or describe features of Gaelic culture which had changed little over the years. When they do this, they can be of use to us. For example, Alexander Carmichael, made an enduring study of Gaelic Hymns and songs in the nineteenth century, and at about the same period, John Francis Campbell was traveling through the Hebrides, keeping records of his experiences.

Another fascinating resource is I.F. Grant's *Everyday Life On An Old Highland Farm 1769-1782,* as is an autobiography written by Elizabeth Grant of Rothiemurchus (1787-1885) *Memoirs Of A Highland Lady.*

Later we will find we can also draw on letters written backwards and forwards across the water, giving glimpses of life both in the old country and in the new.

We also have at our disposal illustrations of various kinds. Besides the formal portraits, there are very few engravings of interiors of houses, dress and other day to day matters. An example would be *Inside of the Cottage of MacNab a Blacksmith at Dalmally* from Faugus de Saint Fond's book, *A Journey through England, and Scotland and the Hebrides in 1784.* In addition, there is a remarkable resource for information and pictures of buildings of all kinds dating back to the time of our Carolina ancestors. The *Royal Commission on Ancient and Historic Monuments of Scotland* has compiled a complete listing of every historic structure in the country by counties.

Such illustrations are valuable not only as a record of how Scotland must have looked at the time of the emigrations, but also to offer a comparison with Carolina homes and other buildings. For example, we find

The caption reads, "Inside of the Cottage of McNab, a Blacksmith at Dalmally who Possesses some Fragments of the Poetry of Ossian."

St. Fond writes, "Macnab, after receiving us so politely in his brother's house, requested, with great importunity, that we would accompany him to his own, where we were expected; assuring us, at the same time, that such a favour would do him a great deal of honour among the inhabitants of the place. We yielded, with pleasure, to his invitation."[1]

almost exact correlations in design and size between the stone buildings, with which they had been familiar and some built out of wood when they arrived in Carolina, which demonstrates how the settlers adapted their Scottish heritage in a new environment. The books also include a very few sketches of buildings long since crumbled to the dust.

So contemporary writers and artists are available who will be our able guides through a time so interesting to many of their descendents; Carolina Scots living three thousand miles away in a land often deeply marked by that very Scottish heritage.

The Highland Clan System

Not only is it hard to picture the past in general, but for many people in modern times, with our increasingly limited experience of the extended family, it is particularly difficult to grasp the nature of the Clan System. Of course, those of us who have grown up in small town Carolina, can trace vestiges of it, in the awareness that we had as children that the large majority of the community was kin to us by blood or marriage. This engendered a sense of belonging, and a sense of security.

The local leadership, for example, did not seem remote from us; they were cousins, most likely, and we felt they would therefore listen to us and give us a chance. Similarly, at the other end of the spectrum, if part of the family had a hard time making ends meet, there could often be found a sense of responsibility among more fortunate relatives who would offer help and support. Put another way, there was an awareness that the constant daily interrelationships of the community were not merely based on business, school, or government connections, for example, but went far deeper because of the blood ties.

There is no doubt that much of this is a direct inheritance from our Scottish ancestors. The medieval Scottish family structure was based to a large degree on the economic, military and cultural interdependence of the extended family combined with certain elements of general European feudalism. However, there were such wide variations in the Celtic kinship structure of the Highlands, that it has well been said: "Precise definitions of rights and duties and of relationships generally in the Scottish clan are extremely difficult."[6]

At its simplest, one can say that it was essentially a land-based huge extended family. However, a clan was certainly more complex than a simple assembly of blood relatives:

A clan, however, was never simply a group of kinsmen dwelling together and tracing descent from a common ancestor. Besides those who bore the chief's surname and were related to him by blood ties, there were often families that had adopted the name as a means of protection in troubled times (as, for example, the MacGregors after their proscription in 1603) or out of deference to the chief or in return for a bribe. There might also be *septs*, which were smaller groups or families of a different name owing allegiance to the chief and enjoying protection and favor from him.

Among these were normally his functionaries—his harper in early times, his piper, seanachie [pronounced: *shenn`-nack-ie* and meaning story teller, historian or genealogist,] bard, henchman (who was often his foster-brother), his armour-bearer, purse-bearer, and so on. Thus the MacMhuirich family were hereditary seanachies of the Clanranald branch of the clan Donald (and earlier of the Lord of the Isles), the MacCrimmons were the pipers of the MacLeods of Dunvegan, and the MacColls were hereditary bodyguards to the Stewart chiefs of Appin. They were rewarded for their services by enjoying an unbroken succession to particular lands.

The chief of a clan might include among his followers the representatives of ancient local families too weak to stand alone in the ruthless

Edmund Burt included this illustration of a street scene in his *Letters from the North of Scotland*. Notice the piper on the extreme left.

The market Cross in Inverness—an engraving from Burt's book. Though not specifically of Argyll or the Isles, the illustrations he included give a general sense of the highland clan life which the Carolina Scots left behind.

> conditions of the sixteenth century .... Fugitives and broken clans, and their descendants, went to swell a chief's following .... Septs such as these, not related by blood to the chief, would frequently have their own chieftains and serve under these in the clan's war array.
>
> The Scottish clan in its larger sense was thus heterogeneous in composition. It was based as much on a binding lord-vassal relationship such as occurs in all feudal societies as it was on kinship.[7]

Even so, a sense of kinship was crucial to the social as well as economic life of the Highlands.

> In spite of its varied make-up and origin, the clan was remarkably homogeneous as a body of people owing loyalty and obedience to a chief, living under his authority and protection, and identifying itself with the traditions and family pride of the chief.[8]

Edmund Burt, the English army officer, discerned this Highland family pride in a famous letter he wrote in 1754:

> The Highlanders walk nimbly and upright, so that you will never see, among the meanest of them, in the most remote part, the clumsy, stooping gait of the French paysans or our own country fellows, but on the other hand a kind of stateliness in the midst of their poverty. They have a pride in their family as almost everyone is a genealogist.[9]

Basic then to the clan system was kinship, but this kinship functioned in terms of land holding and usage. Originally, people were much more important to the chief and to the system than the amount of land possessed. "Until land became commercialized in the Highlands, its function was purely to support the chief, his clan, and dependents. A chief reckoned his wealth not in sheep, cattle, or acres, but in the size of his following."[10]

Samuel Johnson's observation in 1785 was somewhat critical, though it must be remembered that it was made at the time when the land tenure based upon the clan system was beginning to collapse and follow a more English pattern:

> The chieftain lets out his land in large lots to the inferior branches of the family, all of whom must support the dignity of lairds. The renters let the land out in small parcels from year to year to the lower class of people, and to support their dignity, squeeze everything out of them they can possibly get, leaving them only a bare subsistence.[11]

Indeed, probably the most distinctive characteristic of the Highland system—and the one that would have been hardest for an English traveler like Johnson to grasp—was the fact that traditionally the land was not seen primarily in terms of its value in producing rent. Rather, it was viewed as lending basic sustenance to the people in order to strengthen the clan's military capacity.

> . . . Highland estate values before the eighteenth century were reckoned not in money but in men . . . money rents were altogether a minor matter, and not being fixed by any economic considerations, bore no necessary relation to the economic value of the land.[12]

Class Structure

There were three main levels of old Highland clan society: chief, tacksmen and tenants or commoners (and some list a fourth level of lower or subtenants). At the top of the social pyramid were the *chiefs* of the clan. The chief was "the representative of the founder of the clan,"[13] a patriarchal ruler with powers of judgeship which extended even to the right to impose death sentences. Dr. Johnson described the status of the Highland chief prior to the mid-eighteenth century: " . . . a Chieftain walked out attended by ten or twelve followers, with their arms rattling."[14] In fact, the clansmen took pride in their leader's prowess in war, his castle and equipage.

Much of the chief's actual rule over his estate, however, was delegated to the next highest level of Highland society: the *tacksmen*. Originally, the tacksmen were the younger sons or other close relatives of the chief, known in Gaelic as *daoine uaisle* (close in meaning to the English word: *gentry*). In 1813, the term tacksman was defined by a contemporary as "One who holds a lease from another, a tenant of a higher class—this term is usually used in contradistinction to Tenants in general, who are such as rent only a portion of a farm."[15] There is no doubt that they enjoyed great social prestige, and James Anderson, another contemporary, wrote (c. 1785) that:

> the class of tacksmen occupy nearly the same rank in the Hebrides as belongs to that of men of landed property in other parts of Britain. They are called Gentlemen, and appear as such; and obtain a title from the farm which they hold, nearly in the same manner as gentlemen in other parts of the country obtain from their estates.[16]

Engraving of Dunvegan Castle on the Isle of Skye, seat of the McLeods, as it was in 1790. (It was extensively renovated in the Victorian period.)

Often the tacksmen held the lease of a large property for at least three generations or eighty-one years, and in some cases in Kintyre, the same tacksman family held property continuously from 1500 to 1800.[17] Accordingly, their social prestige was raised because of their long term stability.

> Tacksmen and tenants could claim to be maintained in land by the chief and near kinsmen could expect to enjoy their farms undisturbed for a long period. The kinsmen and dependents of tacksmen and small tenants could equally expect to be maintained in land by these tenants.[18]

Furthermore although not chiefs, they had a significant military role:

> In the military organization of the clan, the tacksmen formed an essential element, since by blood, instincts, and training they were its natural lieutenants. As such they were indispensable to the chief, and they paid for their lands in full by their services.[19]
>
> They were essentially a military caste, for whom prowess and courage were the ultimate values, and war and cattle-raids a way of life. In default

> of opportunities of serving their chief at home they sought employment in the Continental armies, where they were known for their proud bearing and ferocity. They despised manual work, but dealing in cattle, being in a sense a natural extension of the cattle-raid, was regarded as an acceptable pursuit for tacksmen. The work of their farms was performed by servants and sub-tenants.[20]

Dr. Samuel Johnson saw and appreciated their feudal virtues, their generous hospitality and their important cultural leadership in what would have otherwise been a rather backward society.[21] In other words, the tacksmen did far more in society than merely collect rent from tenants. Their presence served, " . . . not only for the collection of revenue but for the reduction of hostile districts to order, for the settling of loyal colonists, for the administration of justice and policing of wide areas, and for political and strategic purposes that went a good deal beyond the simple collection of rent."[22]

Social historians have shown that the tacksmen also served their society by acting as capitalists or a sort of rural "banker", who advanced stock and materials for the yearly crop according to the custom known as "steelbow." This role, as we shall see, eventually extended to the organization of groups who wished to emigrate. For example, these were the kind of men who made up the advance party investigating the possible business opportunities in the colony of Carolina.

The third and lowest rank of Highland society was that of *tenant* or *commoner*, and as Dr. Samuel Johnson noted, there were various levels of these:

> Of tenants there are different orders, as they have greater or less stock. Land is sometimes leased to a small fellowship, who live in a cluster of huts, called a Tenant's Town, and are bound jointly and separately for the payment of rent. These, I believe, employ in the care of their cattle, and the labour of tillage, a kind of tenants yet lower; who having a hut, with grass for a certain number of cows and sheep, pay their rent by a stipulated quantity of labour.[23]

Essentially, the tenants occupied the land on a shorter term basis, often without any lease at all (though there were variations in mutual understanding on this matter), and paid their rents "partly in kind, partly in money, and partly in service."[24] "In kind" they paid with such products as butter, cheese, poultry, eggs, sheep and sometimes cloth. Their "services" could vary in length of time from as little as six or seven days a year to as many as forty-two or so days, and might include—in

addition to road work and building repair—such work as: "the cutting, stacking, and housing of peats; sowing and harvesting; carting and thatching; road making; more rarely the spinning of a certain quantity of wool or flax; and in some of the kelp islands in the Hebrides, the making of kelp."[25] They were frequently called "common tenants."

A House—an illustration from *Letters from the North of Scotland*, by Edmund Burt.

There was a special kind of land tenure, unique to the Highlands, and one which the English found hard to understand and appreciate. Hence this was one matter that was particularly marked for change as the Lairds moved toward new farming methods. Traditionally, the clan tenants

> . . . occupied a farm 'in commonty,' several of them sharing the arable land, grazings, peat, and other appurtenances of the farm, and re-allotting the arable at frequent intervals. A tenant's holding was made up of pieces of land ('rigs'), not compact and enclosed but scattered about the infield in the manner known as run-rig.[26]
>
> It was rare to find one such farm tenanted by a single tenant, and in general several tenants worked the farm in communal fashion. All took part in each operation, and the rigs of the farm were drawn by lot, each tenant receiving the produce of a number of rigs according to his share in the tenancy.

> In order to ensure that each tenant got a fair distribution of good and bad land, the rigs apportioned to any one tenant were scattered throughout the farm, and this fact probably accounts for the word Run-rig, which was the name given to the system or method. It is perhaps from the Gaelic *roinn*, a division, and *ruith*, to run, and signifies that the rigs pertaining to a tenant ran or extended over all the arable area, and were not confined to one particular part of the farm.[27]

Poetry and Music

The land-based economy and military purpose of the Highland clan does not tell us all we need to know about the life the Scots lived. One important aspect of their daily culture was, as we have seen, the speaking of Scottish Gaelic. Closely related to Irish Gaelic (though developing in its own direction during the later Middle Ages), Scottish Gaelic was a language that lent itself to a rich development of poetry and music. The history and contemporary state of that language in Scotland has recently been dealt with in two fine volumes: *Gaelic in Scotland 1698-1981: The Geographical History of a Language* by Charles W. J. Withers[28] and *Gaelic and Scotland/Alba agus a' Ghaidhlig* edited by W. Gillies.[29]

For various reasons Scottish Gaelic has tended to produce a larger oral than written literary tradition. In the first place, within the clan system, specific provision was made both for story teller/historians (seanachies) as well as bards and bagpipers. In this way, they deliberately encouraged the oral passing down of genealogies, history, folklore, poems and songs through numerous generations. Highland Scotland seems to have been like Confucian China in the sense that it produced people who committed vast amounts of material to memory in order to pass it on verbatim.

It has often been noted that one of the advantages of the Highland social structure was that it provided support for intellectuals to remain in their local area rather than congregating in one or more central locations, as is the case in post-industrial society. Those in the clan who were usually the most interested in such things were the tacksmen. As a result, since it was among this class that the Gaelic culture flourished, their emigration to Carolina and elsewhere from the eighteenth century onwards would cost the development of modern literary Gaelic a heavy price.

In the second place, in many cases, the reasons for a larger oral than written tradition were simply political. In large part because of the central government's fear of Highland disloyalty, they pursued a hostile policy towards Scottish Gaelic (as they did towards Irish Gaelic over the

Rural scene recorded in Edmund Burt's book.

water). This is why, for example, the Scriptures were not fully translated into Gaelic until well over two hundred years after the Protestant Reformation in Scotland.

In the mid-seventeenth century various ministers of the Synod of Argyll translated the Westminster Shorter Catechism into Gaelic, and during the last half of the seventeenth century they translated the Psalms into Gaelic. Then in 1767 the New Testament was translated into Gaelic under the auspices of the Society in Scotland for the Propagation of Christian Knowledge, " . . . in spite of the fears of some of its members that it might inflame Jacobitism."[30] But amazingly, they had to wait until the early nineteenth century for the whole Bible to be at last translated into Gaelic. Before that time, the Gaelic speaking ministers of the Highlands had to make their own impromptu translations of Scripture as they preached, and apparently they did so in a generally effective manner.[31]

In the third place, until the nineteenth century, the literary development of Scottish Gaelic was seriously hindered by the policy of charitable organizations such as the Society in Scotland for the Propagation of Christian Knowledge (SSPCK) of discouraging Gaelic and encouraging English in the schools which they established in the Highlands. " . . . The emphasis in these schools was on anglicising the Highlanders (which was, of course, government policy since the beginning of the seventeenth century). . . ."[32] However, after the Edinburgh Bible Society was established in 1809, they set up depots in Edinburgh and Inverness to distribute the Scriptures in Gaelic, and the next year:

> A significant step forward was taken in 1810 when the Edinburgh Society for the Support of Gaelic Schools was set up . . . . These Gaelic schools took on in a way the SSPCK schools never did. They catered for all ages and the principal text book was the Gaelic Bible. All of them were circulating schools, (i.e.they moved round the parish going to the people rather than expecting the people to travel to them).[33]

The Highlanders not only spoke their ancestral Gaelic, but, according to many contemporary reports, they also incorporated singing into the routines of daily life and often composed poetry. I.F. Grant suggests that merely looking at the rather poor agricultural existence of the Gaels fails to reveal, "how incomparably richer was the atmosphere of tradition and association that surrounded them . . . ."[34]

She speaks of the *ceilidhs*, (the word literally means: visits, and thus came to mean informal gatherings for music, stories and general enjoyment),[35] which were well described by Alexander Carmichael in the nineteenth century in his 'Introduction' to *Carmina Gadelica: Ortha Nan Gaidheal (Hymns and Chants).*

> In a crofting community the people work in unison in the field during the day, and discuss together in the house at night. This meeting is called 'ceilidh'—a word that throbs the heart of the Highlander wherever he be. The 'ceilidh' is a literary entertainment where stories and tales, poems and ballads, are rehearsed and recited, and songs are sung, conundrums are put, proverbs are quoted, and many other literary matters are related and discussed. This institution is admirably adapted to cultivate the heads and to warm the hearts of an intelligent, generous people. Let me briefly describe the 'ceilidh' as I have seen it.
>
> In a crofting townland there are several story-tellers who recite the oral literature of their predecessors. The story-tellers of the Highlands are as varied in their subjects as are literary men and women everywhere. One is a historian narrating events simply and concisely; another is a historian with a bias, colouring his narrative according to his leanings. One is an inventor, building fiction upon fact, mingling his materials, and investing the whole with the charm of novelty and the halo of romance. Another is a reciter of poems and ballads. . . . One gives the songs of the chief poets, with interesting accounts of their authors, while another, generally a woman, sings, to weird airs, beautiful old songs, some of them Arthurian . . . .
>
> The house of the story-teller is already full, and it is difficult to get inside and away from the cold wind and soft sleet without. But with that politeness native to the people, the stranger is pressed to come forward and

occupy the seat vacated for him beside the houseman. The house is roomy and clean, if homely, with its bright peat fire in the middle of the floor. There are many present—men and women, boys and girls. All the women are seated, and most of the men. Girls are crouched between the knees of fathers or brothers or friends, while boys are perched wherever—boy-like—they can climb.

The houseman is twisting twigs of heather into ropes to hold down thatch, a crofter is twining quicken roots into cords to tie cows, while another is plaiting bent grass into baskets to hold meal.

'Ith aran, sniamh muran *Is bi thu am bliadhn mar bha thu'n uraidh.'*	*Eat bread and twist bent,* *And thou this year shall be as thou wert last.*

The housewife is spinning, a daughter is carding, another daughter is teazing, while a third daughter, supposed to be working, is away in the background conversing in low whispers with the son of a neighbouring crofter. Neighbour wives and neighbour daughters are knitting, sewing, or embroidering.

The conversation is general: the local news, the weather, the price of cattle, these leading up to higher themes-the clearing of the glens (a sore subject), the war, the parliament, the effects of the sun upon the earth and the moon upon the tides.

The speaker is eagerly listened to, and is urged to tell more. But he pleads that he came to hear and not to speak, saying:

'A chiad sgial air fear an taighe *Sgial gu la air an aoidh.'*	*The first story from the host,* *Story till day from the guest.*[36]

The Highland Gaelic story-telling tradition was also charmingly described at some length by John Francis Campbell, in the mid-nineteenth century. On one occasion he was travelling on the north end of the Isle of South Uist, and visited the stone and peat cottage of seventy-nine year old Mr. McPhie who told him nine traditional stories in the following style:

He had the manner of a practiced narrator, and it is quite evident he is one; he chuckled at the interesting parts, and laid his withered finger on my knee as he gave out the terrible bits with due solemnity. A small boy in a kilt, with large round glittering eyes, was standing mute at his knee, gazing at his wrinkled face, and devouring every word. The boy's mother first boiled, and then mashed potatoes; and his father, a well grown man in tartan breeks, ate them.

Perhaps these women were singing, also, when Burt's artist captured their washday labors.

> Ducks and ducklings, a cat and a kitten, some hens and a baby, all tumbled about on the clay floor together, and expressed their delight at the savoury prospect, each in his own fashion; and three wayfarers dropped in and listened for a spell, and passed their remarks till the ford was shallow [i.e. till the tide was low enough to cross over to the next island on foot].[37]

But music was even more influential in the routines of regular work than in the relaxed ceilidhs. As Grant writes,

> . . . it was the intermingling of singing with the daily work of the people that was one of the most distinctive and charming features of old Highland life. Every task had its special tunes. Thus Burt in his 'Letters from the North of Scotland,' 1754, vol.ii, p. 87, describes the women harvesting in time to their singing; and bending, rising, and turning with the precision of a company of soldiers. Even still, in the old Scotch songs, one can trace the jerk of the loom, the swing of the scythe, the intermittent cadence of

> the old muckle wheel, and some of the other working rhythms that long-dead folk put into their music to help them through their daily toil.[38]

Later she adds:

> Mrs. Grant of Laggan speaks of the labourers dancing on the stacks to a reel tune as they piled and arranged the sheaves (p. 206). I have been told that the minister or tacksman would sometimes hire a piper or fiddler to encourage the people at their work at harvest time, and that the women, in 'waulking' [i.e. fulling—to scour and thicken by pressing] the cloth—a very toilsome process—sang all the time, and commonly said the cloth would take so many more songs to do, instead of so much more work to finish.[39]

Since the founding of the School of Scottish Studies at Edinburgh University in 1951 and earlier, song collectors have been gathering and recording these traditional melodies. Among these collectors, Morag MacLeod and others have published these traditional songs in disks,

Women at Talyskir "waulking"—an illustration from Tennant's *Tour of the Hebrides*, published in the early 1700s.

tapes, and also in scholarly periodicals such as *Tocher* of the School of Scottish Studies.[40]

Highland daily life, of course, was centered on agricultural and domestic activities. Even the homes of the upper classes, such as that of the Grant family (as described by Elizabeth Grant of Rothiemurchus, 1797-1885) were very diligent in doing work that would have been typical of the Highland home in general. Her writings are very useful to us, for though she was not exactly contemporaneous with the emigrations, her early life coincides with the later sailings. Thus her observations probably give us fairly accurate glimpses into the kind of day to day experiences the Carolina emigrants would have known since childhood. On this matter she remarks:

> At this time in the highlands we were so remote from markets we had to depend very much on our own produce for most of the necessaries of life. Our flocks and herds supplied us not only with the chief part of our food, but with fleeces to be wove into clothing, blanketing, and carpets, horn for spoons, leather to be dressed at home for various purposes, hair for the masons. Lint seed was sown to grow into sheeting, shirting, sacking, etc. My Mother even succeeded in common table linen; there was the 'dambrod' pattern . . .
>
> We brewed our own beer, made our own bread, made our own candles; nothing was brought from afar but wine, groceries, and *flour*, wheat not ripening well so high above the sea. And yet we lived in luxury, game was so plentiful, red deer, roe, hares, grouse, ptarmigan, and partridge; the river provided trout and salmon, the different lakes pike and char; the garden quite abounded in common fruits and common vegetables; cranberries and raspberries overran the country, and the poultry yard was ever well furnished.[41]

Houses of Rich and Poor

No picture of daily life and culture is complete without some account of the houses of the people. The Highlands, like every other society, had a wide variation between the dwellings of rich and poor that ran the gamut from massive castle or elegant manor house to the sod hovel of the poorest sub-tenant. It is not to our purpose to describe castles since few if any of our Carolina emigrants came from them, but we will briefly look at the homes of both prosperous tacksmen and humble tenants.

In the 1770s, Dr. Johnson made his famous tour of the Hebrides (to which we have already referred) and amongst other things, described

Erray House, Mull, as it is today. Boswell and Johnson were entertained here by Dr. John McLean in 1773, and wrote then that it was "built about 60 years ago."

two basic sorts of abode in the Isle of Skye. He wrote with his customary candor and very English perspective, and though he evidently appreciated the hospitality, his comments on the houses themselves were not always flattering!

> The habitations of men in the Hebrides may be distinguished into huts and houses. By a *house,* I mean a building with one story over another; by a *hut,* a dwelling with only one floor. The Laird, who formerly lived in a castle, now lives in a house; sometimes sufficiently neat, but seldom very spacious or splendid. The Tacksmen and ministers have commonly houses. Wherever there is a house, the stranger finds a welcome.
>
> Of the houses little can be said. They are small, and by the necessity of accumulating stores, where there are so few opportunities of purchase, the rooms are very heterogeneously filled. With want of cleanliness it were ingratitude to reproach them. The servants having been bred upon the naked earth, think every floor clean, and the quick succession of guests, perhaps not over-elegant, does not allow much time for adjusting their apartments.
>
> Huts are of many graduations; from murky dens to commodious dwellings. The wall of a common hut is always built without mortar, by a skillful adaptation of loose stones. Sometimes perhaps a double wall of stones is raised, and the intermediate space filled with earth. The air is thus completely excluded. Some walls are, I think, formed of turfs, held together by a wattle, or texture of twigs. Of the meanest huts, the first

> room is lighted by the entrance, and the second by the smoke hole. The fire is usually made in the middle. But there are huts or dwellings of only one story, inhabited by gentlemen, which have walls cemented with mortar, glass windows, and boarded floors. Of these all have chimneys, and some chimneys have grates.
>
> The house and the furniture are not always nicely suited. We were driven once, by missing a passage, to the hut of a gentleman, where after a very liberal supper, when I was conducted to my chamber, I found an elegant bed of Indian cotton, spread with fine sheets. The accommodation was flattering; I dressed myself, and felt my feet in the mire. The bed stood upon the bare earth, which a long course of rain had softened to a puddle.[42]

The common tenant most often lived in a "black house," a simple structure made out of stone and whatever other material was available.

> Varying somewhat in design from one locality to another, the black house's principal architectural feature was an enormously thick outer wall made by building two dry stone dykes, the one inside the other, and filling the space between them with earth and rubble. Seldom more than six or seven feet high, the walls were as many feet in breadth at the base but tapered slightly towards the top. On them was raised a framework of rafters, often consisting—especially in the Outer Isles where timber was almost unobtainable—of a nondescript collection of old oars, masts and pieces of driftwood. The rafters were covered with 'divots' or large turfs . . . and these were thatched with straw from the householder's corn . . .

View of a cottage in Mull by W. Watts, c. 1800.

> The traditional Highland habitation had no windows and no chimney, the smoke from the peat fire which burned day and night, winter and summer alike being left to find its way out through the thatch. Furnished with some planks and barrels, a few three legged stools, and a box bed which was often roofed over to shelter its occupants from the sooty rain-water which dripped from the thatch, the archetypal black house consisted of a single apartment. The crofter and his family lived at one end; their cattle inhabited the other . . .[43]

In addition to their humble sod houses, many Highland tenants also lived part of the year in lonely *shielings*, in remote mountain pasture lands.

> In the summer season they drive their flocks and herds many miles higher among the mountains, where they have long ranges of coarse pasture. The whole family follow the cattle; the men to guard them, and to prevent their straying; the women to milk them and to look after the butter and cheese, etc. The places in which they reside when thus employed they call shielings, and their habitations are the most miserable huts that ever were saw; (to quote Duncan Forbes about 1746).[44]

There was not always quite so much difference between the homes of the socially prominent tacksmen and those of the tenantry as one might expect. As I.F. Grant remarked concerning a prominent Sheriff, "Many people of his standing were housed very simply, for instance, Sheriff MacQueen of Corriebrough's house was partly built of turf."[45] Elsewhere she notes "the extraordinary simplicity" in which the old Highland gentlefolk lived. She quotes a description of an important and well-connected Shaw tacksman's home at Dalnavert,

> . . . the house "was a mere peat bothy, no better outside than the common huts of the same material, already falling into disuse. It was larger, for it contained three rooms, each of which had a window with four panes, not made to open, however; . . . for the kitchen fire there was as usual a stone on the floor and a hole in the roof."[46]

Yet as Grant goes on to note, many gentlefolk did live in much better houses than this, and even in the more simple turf houses, there were often good and even elegant furnishings as Dr. Johnson noted in Skye. The home of one typical, prosperous tacksman (Balnespick), included silver and sheffield plate, a mahogany table and leather chairs, "pire glasses" [i.e. pier glass] and "sewed work footstools." There was a large four-poster bed with steps and curtains, carpets, prints and family pictures.[47] There is an excellent description of a tacksman's house in the first volume on Kintyre in *Argyll, an Inventory of Ancient Monuments* by the Royal Commission on the Ancient and Historic Monuments of Scotland.

> "[Cara house was]...erected as the residence of the Tacksman of Cara, who held the island from its proprietors, the MacDonalds of Largie, [descendents of the Lords of the Isles, who have been in possession of estates in Kintyre since about the middle of the 18th century].
>
> The plan is typical of a small Laird's House of the early 18th century, a single main room being placed on each side of a central staircase on the two principal storeys. In the original arrangements, the windows of the principal front were more or less symmetrically disposed, but two of the openings on each storey have subsequently been blocked up; the entrance doorway is centrally placed.
>
> There is a closet at the rear of the staircase on the two main floors, while beneath the lower flights of the stair there is a small cellar. The attic, which is now inaccessible, appears to have been lit only by means of a window in the N[orth] gable."[48]

A kitchen was added in the early nineteenth century at the rear of the house. Until that time, a disused, tiny chapel nearby, dating from the

Cara House, 1733.

late middle ages but probably abandoned at the time of the Reformation, seems to have been used as the kitchen.

Additional valuable research on various types of Highland housing has been recently done in *Highland Vernacular Buildings* (Scottish Vernacular Buildings Working Group: Edinburgh, 1989), with a foreword by Alexander Fenton.

Social Relationships

Whether or not the houses were of equal quality seems to have made relatively little difference to the ease with which all classes of Highlanders intermingled on a regular basis. We noted earlier that the clan system tended to keep its intelligentsia at home and as we shall later see, both school and church served to a considerable degree as equalizing factors. The Englishman Burt's surprise at the Highland pride in kinship and the universal vocation of genealogist gives us a clue into the relative ease with which different social classes met one another. All were kin one way or another which did much to remove the pain of being in a lower socio-economic position. As I.F. Grant tells us:

> Although the chiefs held absolute powers over their people, both by the consent of the clan and by the law of the land, through the 'Heritable Jurisdictions,' and the much-prized 'right of Pit and Gallows,' yet class distinctions, such as were so strongly marked in eighteenth-century England, must have been almost non-existent in the Highlands, where the very word for landlord was 'ceann-cinnidh,' or 'Head of Kin,' and where every member of a clan claimed, with or without foundation, to be related to the Chief.[49]

And Mrs. Grant of Laggan (quoted by I.F. Grant) caught the Highland spirit when she said:

> People hereabouts, when they have good ancestry and manners, are so supported by the consciousness of these advantages and the credit allowed for them that they seem not the least disconcerted at the deficiency of the 'goods of fortune.' How true it was that gentle birth was the real passport to society can best be seen by the study of old family trees. Even the smaller gentlemen farmers' families not only mixed socially but intermarried with those of the greater landowners.[50]

Thus, common tenants felt part of a distinguished ancestry and held

The Marketplace in Inverary, where townspeople met to chat and exchange news. However, within a few years some would be deciding to build communities in North Carolina. This engraving by Paul Sanby was made in 1746, the year in which a "summons of removal" was served on the inhabitants soon after the 3rd Duke of Argyll began plans to establish a new town.

up their heads as they met their richer relatives in the street. One old Highlander was described this way: "By trade he was a smith; and although of the lowest order of the people, he walked about with the air and manner of a field marshal."[51] Long ago, Dalrymple's *Memoirs* described the strong 'self-image' of the rural tenants.

> The Highlanders, whom more savage nations called savage, carried in the outward expression of their manners the politeness of courts without their vices, and in their bosoms the high point of honour without its follies, 'and he goes on to describe the self-respecting respect of the country people who treated their chiefs with perfect deference, and yet argued, jested, and chatted with them with ease.'[52]

This plainness and ease of communication between the various classes in the old Highlands would, in later years, deeply mark the character of North Carolina's unpretentious middle class, small farm approach to life—as opposed to the more socially conscious neighboring colonies of Tidewater Virginia and Low Country South Carolina (colonies settled by

English rather than Scots). Furthermore, the general courtesy and friendliness of the Highlanders and Islanders of Scotland would leave deep marks on the society of their emigrant descendants in the Upper Cape Fear. What the scholar and song-collector, Alexander Carmichael noted long ago on his visits to the people of the outer (Hebridean) Isles, could also have been truly said of their cousins in distant North Carolina last century:

> They are good to the poor, kind to the stranger, and courteous to all. During all the years that I lived and travelled among them, night and day, I never met with incivility, never with rudeness, never with vulgarity, never with aught but courtesy. I never entered a house without the inmates offering me food or apologising for their want of it.[53]

School and Church

At least part of the plainness of life, general courtesy and ease of social connection in the old Highlands was related to both school and church, particularly after the sixteenth century Protestant Reformation. In those days, of course, following the centuries old tradition, it was simply assumed that it was the responsibility of the Church to provide educational opportunities. Thus it was one of the goals of the Scottish Reformers to take one third of the expropriated wealth of the Medieval Roman Catholic Church and devote it to the formation of schools for all children in every part of the nation. *The First Book of Discipline* of the Reformed Church of Scotland in 1560, specifically set forward the goal of having a school in every parish in the land. (However, it has to be said that this never happened because, before it could be enacted, the aristocracy confiscated much of the old church's funds and properties for their own purposes.)

Although this particular goal was never reached, various attempts were indeed made to educate the youth of Scotland—both peasant and privileged—in the Lowlands and the Highlands. For example, as we have seen, in 1609, Andrew Knox, Bishop of the Isles, had included in the Statutes of Iona a requirement that gentlemen and yeoman with more than sixty cattle should send an eldest son (or failing that, a daughter) to an English-speaking school in the Lowlands. But that would not have affected most people.

During the seventeenth century, we have records of other valiant efforts to set up local schools such as those for the Gaelic speaking populace in Kintyre. Representative of such efforts is the following item from the Minutes of the Synod of Argyll in October, 1650:

> Because the knowledge of the English language is so necessary for the weall of the Gospell, the scriptures not being translated in Irish [i.e. Gaelic], and seeing the country cannot have schools in every church for learning English, that therefore use be made of poor boys that can read and write English to teach the young and others that may be willing in the parish to read and understand the English in the interim till schools may be erected, and the ministers to oversee and make report of their diligence and of the fruit of it to their several presbyteries and to the next synod.[54]

Thus, over the years, these educational efforts were largely successful. By the end of the seventeenth century and particularly by the early part of the eighteenth century and largely due to the efforts of the Church, parochial schools were being opened throughout large sections of the country, including the needy Highlands.

> . . . these old parochial schools did good work, and kept the flame of learning alight in a dark age. They were attended by all the children in the parish, gentle and simple; by the sons of lairds, ministers, farmers, cottars, ploughmen, and herds alike, and a good part of our distinctive Scottish traits of character must have been formed in them. . . . These schools set many a poor boy on the first rung of the ladder of success, and their establishment, at the end of the seventeenth century, was the true beginning of democracy in Scotland. . . .[55]

Further confirmation of this "democracy" within the Scottish parochial school, is given by I.F. Grant. For instance, she quotes evidence that Sir Eneas Mackintosh, direct heir to the chiefship of Clan Mackintosh during the eighteenth century, attended the village school along with all the other local children. It is also apparent that this equality of opportunity does not seem to have restricted the quality of the education imparted in them. She goes on to quote General Stuart of Garth in his *Manners and Customs of the Highlanders,* Appendix III, as stating that the gentry and tacksmen in the Highlands were "certainly better classical scholars than men holding the same occupation and rank in society further South." Furthermore,

> He adds that he personally knew many tacksmen and innkeepers (a very gentlemanly profession according to old Highland standards) who were good Latin scholars, and that in Skye the gentry commonly talked Latin together.[56]

But far more significant than the ability of some to converse in Latin, was the new ability of vast numbers of ordinary people to read the Scriptures for themselves. They also were able to study the Westminster Shorter Catechism and then often committed it to memory—a feat which, many observers believe, has done much for the traditionally elevated character of the Scottish peasantry.[57]

General Stuart of Garth.

In other words, with education there came a fuller ability to deal with the situation immediately at hand, and an openness to the larger world beyond, but it is nevertheless true that if the local parish schools influenced the fuller development of Highland character, the Christian Church exercised far more sway not least because of its influence upon the curriculum. There was yet another very important factor, namely its antiquity and near omnipresence throughout the Highlands. Christianity had, of course, been brought to the Highlands in the early Middle Ages by monastic missionaries of the Celtic Christian Church of Ireland such as Saint Columba, but then there was a dramatic new impetus given to the spread of the faith as a result of the sixteenth century Protestant Reformation.

So strong was the movement that though many portions of the Highlands actually had no regular settled parish minister, where these were lacking dedicated lay missionary catechists (often sent out by the Scottish Society for the Propagation of Christian Knowledge) trudged through distant valleys and glens, or crossed wide bays and arms of the

Dunvegan Castle, stone in lower corridor, dated 1686. Note that Latin is used, not only for the historical record, but also for original verse, perhaps written by one of those gentry in Skye who "commonly talked Latin together".

Iohannes MacLeod Beganoduni Dominus, gentis suae philarchus, Durinesiae, Haraiae, Vaternesiae, etc. Baro: D. Florae MacDonald matrimoniali vinculo conjugatus, turrem hanc Beganodunensem proavorum habitaculum longe vetustissimum, diu penitus labefectatam, anno aerae vulgaris MDCLXXXVI instauravit.

Quem stabilire iuvat proavorum tecta vetusta
Omne scelas fugiat iustitiamque colat
Vertit in aerias turres magalia virtus
Inque casas humiles tecta superba nefas.

Translation:

John MacLeod, Lord of Dunvegan, Chief of his clan, Lord Baron Duirinish, Harris, Waternish, etc., joined in the bond of matrimony to Flora MacDonald, restored this tower, by far the most ancient part of the habitation of his ancestors for long fallen into ruin, in the year 1686.

He who his father's home would fain restore,
Must flee from vice, and love fair virtue's law,
For goodness makes the humblest cot sublime,
And even the proudest home is wrecked by crime.

sea in order to teach the local inhabitants the elements of Reformed Christianity. Some areas of the Highlands, such as the Isles of South Uist and Barra, never received the Reformation. Their chiefs and lairds remained committed to Catholicism. But the areas with which this volume is concerned (out of which all of the Carolina emigrants came) all became Reformed sooner or later following the events of the early and middle sixteenth century religious revival and controversy known as the Reformation.

Several aspects of the Reformation theology were particularly influential in Scotland. In the first place, the teaching of justification by grace through faith in Christ brought to individuals a fresh sense of a direct, personal access to the love of God, and the related teaching of the priesthood of all believers encouraged a sense of equal self-worth in the spiritual life. This sense of being level at "the foot of the cross" tended to flow over into other areas of human culture and personal relationships. Furthermore, it fit well into the ancient common kinship sensitivity of the Highland clan and went far towards engendering the sense of dignity

Former Manse, Kilchoan, erected for the parish of Ardmurchan in 1790, and doubled in size by an extension on the back in 1829. The size of this house, considering some of the other structures, is evidence of the status in the community of the minister.

Parish Church, Southend. "This church was erected in 1773-74 to replace an earlier one in the same vicinity. The designer was James Stirling, 'mason and house builder,' and the cost of the building was about £330. Although subject to a considerable number of later alterations the structure still retains much of its original character."[2]

and equality that has characterized the Scottish "peasant" at home and abroad ever since.

In the second place, the Calvinist form of Reformation that prevailed there engendered strong trust in the Sovereignty of God and put steel into the will of the masses, imparting the necessity of courage in hardship as well as a sense of the nearness and importance of eternal realities in all the checkered events of one's life. It also gave a great respect and desire for higher education which would open significant doors for the descendants of these people in the future.

Thirdly, not unrelated to these theological and psychological underpinnings was the even-handed (if not 'levelling') work of the thousands of local kirk sessions, composed of ministers and lay elders, who took responsibility for thousands of souls in their jurisdictions. In order to encourage righteous living, they were at times prepared to discipline not only tenants and fishermen but also lairds and earls. The moral, social, and political consequences of this attitude can scarcely be calculated. In fact, this is why King James VI of Scotland, after he had become James I of England, was so hostile to the Reformed Presbyterian system. He once said that "monarchy and presbytery agree as well as God and the devil," and that "no gentleman can be a Presbyterian!"

Out of the Scottish Reformation also came the peculiarly Highland development of Gaelic Psalm singing, so strange to English ears and yet a hauntingly beautiful and soul-moving form of half-singing, half-chanting, in which the united voices of the congregation is not unlike the sounds that come from the drones of bagpipes. A *precentor* sings a line and then repeats it along with the congregation in slow fashion. But the most unusual and remarkable feature is that when the people sing the line themselves, they have so much time between notes that they can add in numerous "grace notes," resulting in all kinds of different variations being sung at the same time. The School of Scottish Studies in

Parish Church, Clachan, 1760—very like some in the Carolinas in design.

Old Lowland Church, 1706, Campbeltown—a port from which many of the Carolina Scots sailed.

Edinburgh has made recordings of a number of these Gaelic Psalms.[58]

This form of music, which was such a part of the spiritual culture of the Highlanders, seems to have been a combination of ancient Celtic modes of harmonization (possibly influenced by traditional responses from the ancient Eastern Orthodox Church once taught by long-forgotten missionaries) with Lowland English tunes and Hebraic thoughts. Musicologists also believe that the Gaelic Psalmody as it was brought to the Southern colonies of America passed into the black religious culture through the slaves of the transplanted Highlanders and helped produce the beautiful spirituals of Afro-American Christianity.[59]

There is a final aspect of the Reformation which has deeply marked the Highland life to this day. As the teachings of Calvinism continued to permeate the area, the people generally tended to become strong observers of the Sabbath day and faithful church attenders when and where services were available. There were exceptions to this rule in various parts of the Highlands, and it is safe to say that nineteenth century Scotland was more Sabbatarian than eighteenth century Scotland, but there is no doubt that the day was special.

Elizabeth Grant's recollections of scenes from her own childhood give us a picture of church attendance in the Highlands which would have been typical of hundreds of other villages towards the end of the eighteenth and the beginning of the nineteenth centuries:

> The Kirk was very near our house, on a height in the field below the Drum, prettily sheltered by planting, and commanding from the gate a fine view of the valley of the Spey. The Bell tolled from time to time, and as the hour of the service approached the crowd began to pour in from either side, the white caps and the red plaids gleaming through the birch woods on the bank between the kirk field and the Drum, through which the path lay. Our farm people moved up from the low grounds to join them, and such of the house servants as understood the gaelick. The rest followed us an hour or more afterwards to the English portion of the Ceremony.[60]

She then describes the clothing of the people and the smells in the church.

> Few save our own people sat around; old gray haired rough visaged men that had known my grandfather and great grandfather, black, red, and fairer hair, belonging to such as were in the prime of life, younger men, lads, boys—all in the tartan. The plaid as a wrap, the plaid as a drapery, with kilt to match on some, blue trews on others, blue jackets on all, that was the style of the male part of the assemblage.
>
> The women were plaided too, an outside shawl was seen on none, though the wives wore a large handkerchief underneath the plaid, and looked picturesquely matronly in their very high white caps. A bonnet was not to be seen among them, no young highland girl ever covered her head; the girls wore their own hair neatly braided in the front, plaited up in Grecian fashion behind . . . .
>
> They had a custom in the spring of washing their beautiful hair with a decoction of the young buds of the birch trees, a cleanly habit at any rate. Whether it improved or hurt the hair I really do not know, but it most agreeably scented the kirk,

Highland Dress, by Edmund Burt's illustrator.

> which at other times was wont to be overpowered by the combined odours of snuff and peetreak, for the men snuffed up an immensity during the delivery of the English sermon; they fed their noses with quills fastened by strings to the lids of their mulls, spooning up the snuff in quantities and without waste, none ever dropping by the way.[61]

But such tranquil Highland scenes, and more significantly, the old structures of Highland society were destined to come under severe attack as the repercussions of events south of the border in England began more and more to be felt throughout Highland society.

17th century statue of a Skye woman
in the Dunvegan Castle courtyard.

Notes

1. Ian Charles Cargill Graham, *Colonists From Scotland: Emigration to North America 1707-1783* (Cornell University Press: Ithaca, N.Y., 1956), 1, 2.

2. P. Hume Brown, *Scotland: A Short History* (Oliver and Boyd: Edinburgh, 1908, 1961), 226, 227.

3. Creegan, "The House of Argyll and the Highlands," 156.

4. Ibid.

5. Ibid., 158.

6. E.R. Cregeen, "The House of Argyll and the Highlands" in *Scottish Studies,* 163 ff.

7. Ibid., 163, 164.

8. Ibid., 164.

9. Ibid., 162.

10. Ibid., 161.

11. Margaret Adam "The Highland Emigration of 1770" in *The Scottish Historical Review,* Vol. XVI, 1919, 288.

12. Ibid., 286.

13. Cregeen, op. cit., 162.

14. Samuel Johnson, *A Journey to the Western Islands of Scotland,* 1775, 67.

15. Quoted by Margaret I. Adam, op. cit., 285.

16. Ibid.

17. Andrew McKerral, *Kintyre in the Seventeenth Century,* (Oliver and Boyd: Edinburgh, 1948), 134, 135.

18. Creegan, op. cit., 163.

19. Margaret I. Adam, op. cit., 286.

20. Creegan, op. cit., 161.

21. Johnson, op. cit., 63-66.

22. E.R. Cregeen, "The Tacksmen and Their Successors," in *Scottish Studies,* 99.

23. Johnson, op. cit., 66.

24. Cregeen, "The House of Argyll and the Highlands," p. 162.

25. Margaret I. Adam, "Eighteenth Century Landlords and the Poverty Problem," in *The Scottish Historical Review,* Vol. XIX, No. 73, October, 1921, 13.

26. Ibid.

27. McKerral op. cit., 139.

28. John Donald Publishers, Ltd.: Edinburgh, 1984.

29. Edinburgh University Press, 1989.

30. Fergus MacDonald. "The Bible Societies in Scotland" in *The Bible in Scottish Life and Literature,* ed. David F. Wright (St. Andrew Press: Edinburgh, 1988), 28.

31. Dr. Donald Meek wrote an excellent article on this subject covering far more details than I can here, "The Gaelic Bible" in *The Bible in Scottish Life and Literature,* 9-23.

32. Fergus MacDonald, art. cit., 28.

33. Fergus MacDonald, ibid.

34. I.F. Grant, *Everyday Life On An Old Highland Farm 1769-1782* (Shepheard-Walwyn: London, 1924, 1981), 4.

35. Ibid.

36. Alexander Carmichael, *Carmina Gadelica: Ortha Nan Gaidheal (Hymns and Chants)*, Vol. I (Oliver and Boyd: Edinburgh, 1928 reprint), xxii, xxiii.

37. John Francis Campbell, *Popular Tales of the West Highlands*, Vol. I (Wildwood House, 1983, first published 1860), xxii, xxiii.

38. Ibid., 6.

39. Ibid., 118, 119.

40. For instance, *Scottish Tradition 3: Waulking Songs From Barra:* School of Scottish Studies: University of Edinburgh. *Tocher: Tales, Songs, Tradition* is published by the School of Scottish Studies of the University of Edinburgh.

41. Elizabeth Grant of Rothiemurchus, *Memoirs Of A Highland Lady*, edited with an introduction by Andrew Tod (Canongate Classics, 1898, 1988), 235, 236

42. Johnson, op. cit., 75, 76.

43. James Hunter, *The Making of a Community*, (John Donald Publishers, Edinburgh, 1976), 111, 112.

44. Margaret I. Adam, "The Causes of the Highland Emigrations of 1783-1803" in *The Scottish Historical Review*, Vol. XVII, No. 66, January, 1920, 82.

45. I.F. Grant, op. cit., viii.

46. Ibid., 90.

47. Ibid., p. 91.

48. *Argyll, an Inventory of the Ancient Monuments*, Vol. I, Kintyre, The Royal Commission on the Ancient and Historical Monuments of Scotland, Edinburgh, 1971, p. 189.

49. I.F. Grant, op. cit., 91.

50. Ibid., 125.

51. Ibid., 97.

52. Ibid., 125.

53. Alexander Carmichael, op. cit., xxi.

54. McKerral, op. cit., 155.

55. Ibid., 159.

56. I.F. Grant, op. cit., 95.

57. See for instance the article by the Oxford University historian, James A. Froude, "The Influence of the Reformation on the Scottish Character" in *Short Studies on Great Subjects*, I, 171-174.

58. *Scottish Tradition 6: Gaelic Psalms from Lewis*, School of Scottish Studies: University of Edinburgh.

59. See Jock Purves, *Fair Sunshine* (Banner of Truth Trust: Edinburgh, 1968).

60. Elizabeth Grant, op. cit., 248.

61. Ibid., 250, 251.

Notes to illustrations

1. Faugus de Saint Fond, *A Journey through England and Scotland and the Hebrides* in 1784, p. 290.

2. *Argyll, an Inventory of the Ancient Monuments*, Vol. I, Kintyre, The Royal Commission on the Ancient and Historical Monuments of Scotland, Edinburgh, 1971, p. 189.

3. Ibid., p.153.

2

Winds of Change

Driving across the Highlands today, a traveler encounters little except the occasional group of sheep grazing among the windswept heather. From time to time, however, he may see the barren signs of a long-gone community. Only the ruins of scattered crofts or the crumbling skeleton of a church, surrounded by leaning moss-covered tombstones, bear testimony to the kind of rich and busy life described in Elizabeth Grant's autobiography. From the early eighteenth century onwards, strong winds of change began to blow across the political and economic realm of Britain, which by and by would alter the culture of the Highlands forever, and set in motion an enormous exodus—often to the shores of North Carolina. So before we trace the lives of the emigrants in their new land, we must glance at the total picture of what was happening throughout the entirety of the Highlands in this period of development and dislocation.

We will begin by looking at changes which particularly affected the tacksmen. This is important, because, as we shall see, they were in many ways the initial leaders of the emigration movement, just as they were leaders (under their Chiefs) in Highland society as a whole. Furthermore, they were undoubtedly the driving force behind the very first Highland exodus to the Carolinas: the Argyll Colony.

Changes in Estate Management and Farming Practices

We have already seen how the Earls of Argyll had increasingly aligned themselves with the English leadership. They had also extended their holdings over massive areas of Argyll, so that any changes would have widespread affects. Such agricultural changes which began in Argyll would later extend to the entirety of the Highlands and lead to the emigrations of scores of thousands of people in the next hundred years.

Historians have rightly described the old farming system among the clans as backward and inefficient in comparison to that of the Lowlands and of England (though it had its positive points, as we shall see). But we must remember that the main goal of the older clan system had not

Alexander, 1st Lord MacDonald (c. 1745-1795) and his brother, Sir James MacDonald (1742-1766) by Jeremiah Davison: the sons of traditional highland chieftains learn to play the role of "southern socialites."

been efficiency of agricultural production of rents so much as maintenance of large numbers of clansmen to form potential armies.

As we have seen, the old agricultural system on the chief's wide estates consisted of leasing sections of lands to their closer relatives, the tacksmen, who then subdivided the arable portions to tenants. The strips into which the land was divided were known as *rigs* and the numerous tenants farmed the land by means of a kind of communal system which came to be known as *run-rig*. Over the years, however, this system proved rather inefficient, because since no tenant could be assured of controlling any particular portion of the land for more than one year at a time, he would not have the incentive to fertilize and build up the soil, and hence it would become depleted. There was also an absence of rotation, so that " . . . returns were poor, that of oats being often no more than two or three-fold of the seed."[1]

This relative inefficiency seems to have presented no serious concerns to the landlords of the Highland estates as long as they saw themselves primarily as patriarchal chief of a potentially military clan. But as they looked southwards, their viewpoint quite naturally changed in accordance with much that was happening in those more advanced parts politically and socially. In a word, we might say that the Highland chiefs changed from clan patriarchs to southern, (i.e. English,) landlords:

> the higher ranks of Highland society were well accustomed to moving in two cultural universes: that of the Gaelic Highlands on the one hand and that of southern Britain and the rest of western Europe on the other. . . . While away from his clan, moreover, the typical chief—conscious since childhood of his immensely aristocratic status in the Highland society whence he came—felt obliged to emulate, or even surpass, the life style of the courtiers and nobles with whom he mingled. And it was at this point that the eighteenth century chief's two roles came into irreconcilable conflict with one another. As a southern socialite he needed more and more money. As a tribal patriarch he could do very little to raise it.[2]
>
> Through the seventeenth and into the eighteenth century the family of Argyll carried a load of inherited debt which was at once a symptom and a cause of their claimant financial needs . . . . The second Duke succeeded to a family tradition grown already somewhat alien from their Highland background and to a family deeply in debt. His distant upbringing and education had given him the tastes of a great aristocrat, the revenues of his Scottish estates assigned to creditors, including the whole of the tack-duties of Mull, Morven and Tiree, it could have been predicted that heavier demands would soon be made on his tacksmen. Growing power and fortune increased rather than diminished the Duke's expenses—houses

When everything had to be done by hand, the more hands, the better. "Women Washing," another illustration from Burt's book.

> and improvements, new estates in England and Scotland, and all the cost of maintaining the style required of a grandee in that opulent age.[3]

In other words with the daunting of the West, chiefs no longer needed military reserves, but rather cash. They once had welcomed large crowds of tenants on their estates when they were militarily useful, but now these very crowds made it harder to run the kind of efficient operation which could raise much needed cash.

We can think of a modern parallel: their change of perspective is not unlike the change in views which fostered the widespread acceptance of birth control in the twentieth century Western world. As the old saw states, children used to be "numbered in terms of hands, but now they are numbered in terms of mouths." That is, large families were once desired to maintain a rural economy, but that has changed in the expensive urban setting. Something like this "fewer people and more money" attitude was taking place in early seventeenth century northwestern Scotland.

The Tacksman: Caught in the Middle

Why should this change in economy and attitude of the ruling powers have such profound ramifications for the brand new colony of North

Carolina? To state it simply: the class of Western Highlander which made up the bulk of the earlier emigrants was the one whose position was most threatened by the winds of change, the tacksmen. Since it was the tacksmen who gathered the rents for the landlords, and since—as middlemen—they reaped a certain percentage of the profits received from the general tenants, it was they who came under pressure first of all to increase the revenues of the chiefs.

Two things began to happen about the same time. First, the chiefs (and their top estate managers or "factors") raised the tacksmen's rent, and of course the tacksmen passed on their new burden to their tenants. Secondly, as early as 1710 there were moves afoot on parts of the Argyll estates, to get rid of the position of tacksman.[4]

Engraving of John, 2nd Duke of Argyll

Island House, Tiree, built in 1748 by Archibald Campbell, 3rd Duke of Argyll as a residence for his factor. Note the substantial size of the house and the formal design—evidence both of the importance of the factor to the Duke, and the success in collecting rents directly, bypassing the traditional tacksmen.

A silent revolution was thus in progress throughout the 2nd Duke's time [i.e. 1703-1743], and was transforming land-tenure and the social system well before 1737, but until the tacksmen were denounced by officials of the Duke's estate, there were few indications that the system as such was to be abolished. Characteristically, the Duke appears to have decided on a total change as a result of developments in the 1730s which convinced him that the tacksmen were of no further use to him and that the sub-tenants could offer higher rents.[5]

An important agent of the Duke, Archibald Campbell of Stonefield, had come round to this new way of thinking and a letter to his employer on 5 September 1732 gives us evidence of how attitudes were changing. He suggested entirely changing the tenurial system by granting leases for land directly to the tenants, thus bypassing the traditional tacksmen. The result would be to remove the tenants "from their dependence on the tacksmen and transfer their loyalties to the Duke."[6] And of course, by removing the middlemen, the Duke would receive more rent.

In our modern industrial economy, this seems reasonable enough, but in the Highland context of the early eighteenth century this was—to

many—a shocking abrogation of the time-honored kinship system; an undercutting of the values of the extended family. Certainly there were many who argued that the tacksmen deserved no better. The Second Duke of Argyll and the government agent, Duncan Forbes of Culloden, who worked with him to undercut the tacksman system in the 1730s, even maintained that the problems which the poorer tenants were having because of higher rents were the fault of their tacksmen overlords, not of the Duke himself.

This assessment was followed by the social historian whom we have quoted, Margaret I. Adam, who wrote very critically of the tacksmen as bad farmers and harsh masters.[7] But more recently, E.R. Cregeen has written with much more sympathetic understanding of the problems and contributions of the tacksmen in their day.[8] He shows that for all the criticism of Forbes of Culloden and the Duke of Argyll against the tacksmen for oppressing their tenants with high rents, these very critics continued to raise the rents of the tenants after the tacksmen were being moved out of the way.[9]

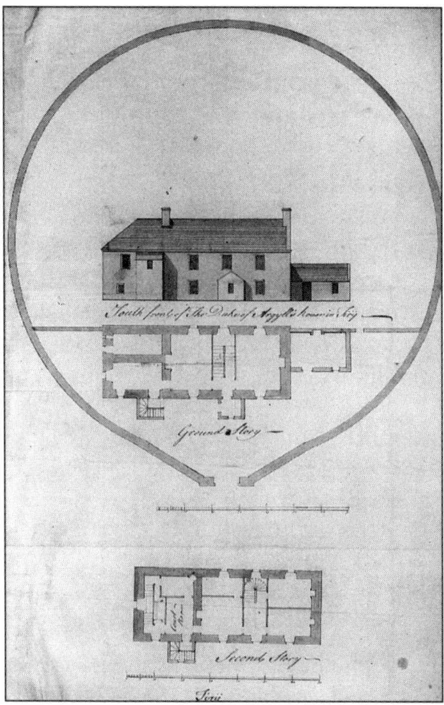

Plans for the Island House, Tiree, 1748.

In Cregeen's words, "The tacksmen were thus made the scapegoats for all the evils of the times and the way was prepared for an intensification of the very measures which had helped to impoverish the Duke's insular tenants."[10] The Duke's own agent, Archibald Campbell of Stonefield, confirmed this matter in later years, when he wrote concerning the true causes of the economic difficulties in the Island of Tiree in 1748:

> It was with intention to reform the country as much as the nature of the thing would admit of that the late Duke dismissed the tacksmen, imagining that they squeezed the undertennants by exacting high rents, but very unluckily my Lord President followed the same plan, by augmenting the rents beyond what the tacksmen ever exacted, a rent that the country was less capable to yield during the factory than in the tacksmen's time because they occupied several of the farms with their own stock and when any of the lands could not be sett, they possessed it themselves.[11]

Though some tacksmen were undoubtedly greedy and harsh to their tenants, there were many who were prepared to leave their homes entirely rather than agree to raise the rents on the tenants who looked to them with respect and trust. We shall later see that the tacksmen took many of their tenants with them when they did emigrate—an entirely voluntary arrangement, which would not have been likely if the negative assessments of the tacksmen were true.

As Duane Meyer wrote in response to Margaret I. Adam's unsympathetic portrayal of this class:

> This picture of cruelty and oppression appears overdrawn. Some tenants, because of the kind treatment they had received, exhibited great attachment to their tacksman. But, even if it be granted that the tacksmen were tyrants, it is not likely that tenants would voluntarily sell their property and follow their oppressors to America only to suffer further tyranny there.[12]

Although assessments of the tacksmen vary, as we have seen, all agree as to the process by which their economic position became untenable. Margaret Adam explains it:

> Under the new system leases are granted, but granted on rents which represent, or are intended to represent, the economic value of the land. These leases are granted to a much wider class, and so far diminish the profit and the prestige of those who had formerly held tacks. Again, the practice of subsetting was abolished, or the services which might be exacted from subtenants limited. Some of the subtenants were promoted at once to the

Killbride Farmhouse and Date Panel. This small tacksman's house near the Barbreck River, was built or remodelled in 1746, and extended in the early 19th century. The date panel bears a reversed monogram, probably for Alexander Campbell of Killbride, (d. c. 1772), the younger brother of Angus Campbell of Asknish.

dignity of leaseholders. Finally, the whole relations of landlord and tacksmen were put on a simple business footing, thereby extinguishing the tacksman's partial sense of ownership, and the half-traditional tie of kinship. The tacksmen, in fact, ceased to form a special and privileged class. Their status was lowered as that of the under tenants was raised.[13]

The Significance of the Loss of the Tacksmen

We are not to think that this process of dispossessing the tacksmen happened overnight or even in one generation. It took, in fact, many decades. As Adam says: "The decay or the destruction of the tacksman system did not proceed rapidly. It was not even complete by the end of the eighteenth century."[14] One of the reasons for the delay was, for instance, the need of the House of Argyll for military strength during the Jacobite rebellion of the 1740s, which caused them to reverse for a time their anti-tacksman policy.[15]

What were the social and economic effects of these changes? While it is no doubt correct to point out that the ending of the tacksmen system was part of the overall, long term rationalization and improvement of the Scottish agricultural economy (which is particularly true from the viewpoint of the elite landowning classes), it may well be the case that almost as much was lost as was generally gained by their removal. There were in fact several negative societal consequences of the demise of the eighteenth century tacksman:

> Local depopulation frequently resulted from the grazing activities of the new tacksmen . . . . Between the new tacksmen and the small tenantry there was not the close attachment that had bound together the *daoine uaisle* and their dependents, even where the original families remained. The divergence of interest became clear in times of war. For the first time military recruitment became difficult in the Highlands.[16]

Limecraigs House, Campbeltown, early 18th century. "The layout is typical of that adopted of a small laird's house of the early 18th century, and the building evidently dates from this period. It is known to have been occupied as a dower-house by Elizabeth Tollemache, widow of the 1st Duke of Argyll, who died there in 1735."[1]

Noting that the Duke claimed to be the benefactor of the lower tenants in removing the old class of tacksmen, the question can be raised: "What were the actual results of the competitive system on this tenantry in the long run?"[17] Taking into consideration such the factors as the arrival of the sheep-masters and various clan feuds, the resulting increase in the demand for land naturally resulted in higher rents, which in turn meant there were many ruined tenants who lost their leases on the Argyll estate through insolvency in the 1740s.[18] The consequences of the process can be summarized as follows:

> There is a general and extreme instability in the occupancy of the farms, steadily rising rents, and a rapid turnover of tenants. In 1779, for example, the rent of farms in five Kintyre parishes stood at about 250 per cent of the level of rents in 1720. In this period of half a century the surnames of the tenants, in all but seven of the fifty-five farms which were examined, changed.[19]

It is more difficult to assess what may have been the cultural impact of the loss of the tacksmen to Gaeldom, but Dr. Johnson felt that it would be serious:

> As the mind must govern the hands, so in every society the man of intelligence must direct the man of labour. If the Tacksman be taken away, the Hebrides must in their present state be given up to grossness and ignorance; the tenant for want of instruction, will be unskillful, and for want of admonition will be negligent. The Laird in these wide estates, which often consist of islands remote from one another, cannot extend his personal influence to all his tenants; and the steward having no dignity annexed to his character, can have little authority among men taught to pay reverence only to birth, and who regard the Tacksmen as their hereditary superior . . . .[20]

It would be interesting to be able to discern the effects of the departure of the tacksmen upon the development of eighteenth and nineteenth century Gaelic poetry, music and literature, but in the nature of the case, like all "ifs" in history, it is impossible to know. What we do know however is that the dispossession of tacksmen, which started in the Argyll estates spread to all of the Highlands, thus changing the structures of society and opening the doors of emigration:

> The commercialization of the agricultural structure in response to chieftains' financial necessitousness—an undertaking in which the Campbells were eventually joined by every other leading family in the region—is the great fact of eighteenth century Highland history. From it all else follows.[21]

While the emigrants hoped for a better life in America, many at home involved in shipping became prosperous. Springfield House Campbeltown, said to have been constructed by Captain Thomas Lacey, R.N., the master of a revenue-cutter, is one of a series of marine villas overlooking the harbour and built by local sea captains about the second decade of the nineteenth century.

And, of course, what followed for the ancestors of modern Carolina was the fateful decision to leave all they had known for the wooded riverbanks and sandhills that awaited them three thousand miles away.

General Causes of Widespread Highland Emigration

The tacksmen, though significant, were by no means the only segment of the population who suffered from changes due to the gradual unification of England and Scotland, and who decided as a result to emigrate. Modern social historians and others have pinpointed many other factors which eventually affected the Highlands as a whole, and which caused the more general, massive emigration that soon followed on the heels of the Argyll colony.

The first of these factors was the commercialization of agricultural property values. In other words, rather than being seen merely as the means of supporting the clan, land values began to be assessed by the modern economic assumption that "land should produce a revenue . . . like any other capital asset and that it should therefore be allocated, not

as a token of kinship, as a reward for allegiance or as a means of maintaining a following, but in response to the operation of competitive bidding."[22]

Sheep

Directly related to this commercialization of property was the introduction of large-scale sheep farming into the Highlands in the latter third of the eighteenth century. To summarize this complex matter briefly, we may note that landowners found that their estates would produce far more income by replacing their many tenants, and their relatively unproductive small fields, with few tenants and many sheep, which required wide pastures. James Loch, manager of the Sutherland family estate, wrote that " . . . the demand for the raw material of wool by the English manufacturers enabled the Highland proprietor to let his lands for quadruple the amount they ever produced to him."[23]

By the 1770s, a considerable amount of land in the Southern Highlands was being given over to sheep pastures. In *Records of Emigrants from England and Scotland to North Carolina 1774-1775*, 136 persons on

Miles of empty hillside, dotted with sheep at pasture, surround the ruins of Castle Sween on the shores of Loch Sween in Knapdale.

board the ship Jupiter bound for Wilmington, North Carolina, mostly from Appin in Argyll as well as Glenorchy and Lismore, mention sheep as a major reason for their emigration:

> Reasons assigned by the Persons named . . . for their Emigrating . . . : such of them as were farmers were obliged to quit their lands either on account of the advanced rent or to make room for shepherds. Those in particular from Apine say that out of one hundred mark land that formerly was occupied by tenants who made their rents by rearing cattle and raising grain, thirty-three mark land of it is now turned into sheep walks and they seem to think in a few years more, two thirds of that country, at least will be in the same state so of course the greatest part of the inhabitants will be obliged to leave it.[24]

This process of converting arable land into sheep walks would increase in massive proportions in the next century so that literally thousands of people would then be displaced. But for the present, an important factor held back their removal. For several decades the numerous tenants were not forcibly removed from the estates (although, as we shall see, numbers of them chose to remove themselves), because their presence was useful to the landlord in a new way: work in the kelp industry, a seaweed extract that was used in making soap and glass. Concerning the rise of the kelp industry:

> . . . in the 1740s it spread to the western isles and by the mid-1760s was firmly established in all the Hebrides and on parts of the north-western coast of the mainland . . . . By the 1790s . . . the average price was in the region of ten pounds a ton, and even that figure [thirty years before it had been worth only two pounds a ton—ed.] was transiently doubled in the 1800's. Production was accordingly stepped up.[25]

Forced Removals

Thus as long as the price of kelp held up, that is until the 1820s, the landlords tended not to evict tenants, but rather simply move them around within the borders of their estates. They generally turned over the best land in the interior of the estate to cattle (and later to sheep) and removed the tenants from the former 'run-rig' areas to the poorer land. "In Skye, therefore, the mass of the people were to be settled on the coast and the interior holdings handed over to large farmers."[26] Hence, the laird would have a dependent population available for work in the kelp industry, who were no longer encumbering his profitable cattle, and after the 1770s increasingly sheep, land.

The 2nd Lord MacDonald, by Sir Alexander Wentworth, 1803.

This was undoubtedly profitable for the lairds, but exceedingly distressing for their tenants. It was particularly hard because of the innate conservatism of this Highland populace:

> To persuade a peasantry to abandon an age-old method of cultivation is seldom easy; and the task of establishing the crofting system was no exception—not least because of a wide-spread and justifiable suspicion that the proposed change would not be for the better. A Harris crofter was subsequently to recall that he had 'seen a woman weeping at being separated from her neighbours by the division of crofts'; and in parts of Skye the abolition of runrig was said to be widely lamented even eighty years after its occurrence.[27]

Resentment at being moved around within the estate in this way caused massive emigration. Eventually, "by April 1803 about two thirds of the tenants of Strath and Sleat, two of the parishes on Lord Mac-

Coat of Arms of the 19th Chief and his wife Flora Macdonald of Sleat, over the entrance to Dunvegan Castle, the seat of the McLeods on the Isle of Skye.

Donald's Skye estate, had made or had begun to make preparations to emigrate to America; and some parts of the property, it appeared, would be completely evacuated."[28]

We will return to the events of 1803 in Skye later. But in the meantime we merely note that after the price of kelp fell in the 1820s, the landlords no longer needed their tenants for work in an unprofitable industry, and by this time sheep were rapidly replacing small farming. Thus the owners decided to clear the people from their lands forcibly in what has been known ever since as the Highland clearances.

It is not our purpose to discuss the clearances in any detail here, important as the event is to an understanding of much modern history, since relatively few of the emigrants to North Carolina came for that reason. The actual number was probably no more than a few hundred, and these were part of the later immigrations in the 1820s and '30s. Generally, however, the victims of the early and mid-nineteenth century clearances tended to emigrate to Canada, Australia and New Zealand. Highland emigration to Carolina had reduced its flow to a mere trickle by this time. For this reason then we must return our attention to the broader causes of the vast emigration from the Highlands to Carolina in the last two thirds of the eighteenth century.

Depression in Cattle Prices

Several factors came into play just at the time that the first Argyll Colony left for the Cape Fear Valley of North Carolina (1739). As we have seen, the changes in the tenurial system resulting in the insecurity of tacks, or leases, was rapidly removing tacksmen. But during the 1730s and '40s, as well as the internal shifting of populations within estates because of the kelp industry, there had been something of a depression in cattle

prices. Now cattle prices were very important, because, "Cattle were, after all, the lynch-pin of the Highland economy. There was usually little else to pay the rents . . . and a sharp fall in price or a severe winter that swept off large numbers of cattle could be disastrous to tenants—and lairds."[29]

For example, the record books of Archibald Campbell of Knockbuy (1693-1790) systematically include a listing of cattle prices from 1728-1786. These accounts " . . . show that cattle prices, though generally rising throughout the century, did so in a succession of waves with marked crests and troughs, and that the deepest trough did in fact occur between 1730 and 1740, and extended over most of the years. . . . "[30] The main problem in the mid 1730s was the low market prices, while the main trouble in the mid 1740s was disease and consequent death of the cattle, especially in Kintyre and Mull.[31]

Thus it is easy to see how these economic depressions added impetus to the emigration process that already had been set in motion by the dismantling of the tacksman system. It is these factors in particular which explain why the Argyll Colony took the long journey to Carolina in 1739.

Population Growth and Unemployment

As the mid-seventeenth century wore on, many other elements were coming together that would turn a small stream of emigration into a rampaging river before the century ended. One of the strongest elements entering into this potent movement was a rapid increase of population in the Highlands.

According to Sinclair's Analysis of the Statistical Account, 1825, and MacDonald's *Agricultural Report of the Hebrides,* 1811, there had, for instance—even with all the losses of numbers through emigration—been an increase in Argyllshire from 63,291 people in c. 1755 to 76,101 in c. 1795. The Hebrides showed even greater growth—from 49,485 in 1750 to 91,049 in 1808/9.[32] An Appendix to *The Statistical Account of Scotland, Vol. XX, The Western Isles,* shows the following remarkable increase in the Gaelic-speaking Western Islands: from 50,699 in 1755 to 77,098 in 1801.[33]

The major reasons for this increase are not unknown and have been clearly summarized as follows:

> Most eighteenth century writers were agreed that the rapid increase of population in the Highlands was a comparatively new phenomenon, not dating back much before the opening of their own century. The time of its appearance is not difficult to explain; the removal or partial disappear-

A 1790 sketch of the intended development of Tobermory, Mull. The 5th Duke of Argyll was part of a committee to establish a new settlement by the British Fisheries Society. Among the designers were the London architect, Robert Mylne, and the famous engineers, Thomas Telford and Hugh and John Stevenson.

Here is a pencil drawing of Tobermory twenty-five years later showing the finished jetty and the buildings laid out in the plans above. The expansion of the settlement not only served to accomodate the growing population, but was designed to draw the Highlands into the commercial orbit of the rest of Britain.

> ance, of such checks to population as private war and the small-pox scourge did so much; the introduction of the potato, and the natural fecundity of the Highlander did the rest.[34]

Furthermore: " . . . because potatoes with a little fish and milk are a healthy, if excessively monotonous diet, more children . . . survived."[35] Kale, also introduced to the Highlands in the mid-eighteenth century, was another element in this generally wholesome diet. Other observers have noted that the building of new Highland roads which were intended to facilitate the movement of English troops in case of rebellion also served commercial purposes, so that "the failure of a crop in one section because of drought or frost could now be remedied with food products transported from more distant areas."[36]

What this population increase meant in an economically deprived region is not difficult to comprehend. The situation in the Isle of Jura was typical:

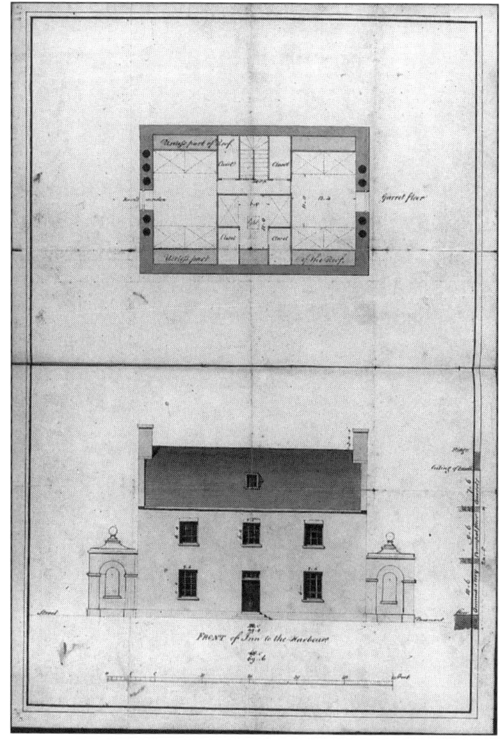

Plans for the new inn at Tobermory in 1790, drawn by architect Robert Mylne.

Jura was overrun by small tenants; a restricted amount of arable land was kept in constant tillage to its detriment; and the available pasture (plus the entire ground in the parish which was given over to the tenants' animals once the harvest was in) was not able to afford proper support for the large numbers of cattle and horses.[37]

Unemployment was therefore a grim reality all through the Highlands:

The new farming methods had increased the productivity of agriculture . . . but did not provide employment for the enlarged population. Sir John Sinclair estimated that by using new methods most Highland farms could be operated with only one-third of the servants formerly employed. Under the old agricultural system, plowing had required five men and five horses; with the English plow, one man and one horse did the same amount of work. When grazing areas were enclosed, herders were no longer needed.[38]

These related problems of low wages, high rents and unemployment are frequently mentioned as the main reasons for which Highlanders were emigrating to North Carolina in the records that remain from 1774-75. Contemporary records bear testimony to the pain of the widespread unemployment at that time in the Highlands:

John McBeath Aged 37, by a trade a farmer and shoe maker, married, hath 5 children from 13 years to 9 months old. Resided last in Mault in the Parish of Kildonnan in the County of Sutherland, upon the Estate of Sutherland. Intends to go to Wilmington in North Carolina; left his own country because crops failed, he lost his cattle, the rent of his possession was raised, and bread had been long dear; he could get no employment at home whereby he could support himself and family, being unable to buy bread at the prices the factors on the Estate of Sutherland and neighboring estates exacted from him . . . .[39]

Willm Monro, Aged thirty four, married, emigrates with his wife, a servant maid, and a servant boy, by trade a shoemaker, resided last at Borgymore in the Parish of Tongue, and County of Sutherland. Left his own country as his employment was little and he had no hopes of bettering his circumstances in it, which he their estates but rather expects to do in America.[40]

Aeneas Mackay, aged twenty, single, resided last with his father in the Parish of Tongue and county of Sutherland; hath been taught to read, write and cypher, and goes to Carolina in hopes of being employed either as a teacher or as a clerk; he has several relations and acquaintances there already, who inform him he may get from 60 to 70 pounds a year

in this way, which is much better than he had any reason to expect at home.[41]

Culloden and the End of the Clan System

We must consider one further factor which at least indirectly influenced Scottish emigration to Carolina: the Jacobite Rebellion of 1745. Without entering into the details of this event, we may briefly note that the Stewart line to the united throne of England and Scotland ran out in 1714 with the death of Queen Anne, who had no surviving children. She was succeeded by George I of the German House of Hanover.

In reaction, the son of the deposed (Roman Catholic) monarch, James VII of Scotland and II of England, who came to be known as James, "the Old Pretender" (i.e. claimant to the Throne), attempted to set himself up as king of Scotland. The rebellion he led in 1715, in defiance of the authority of the House of Hanover was put down without too much difficulty. But his Highland sympathizers, who were known as *Jacobites*, (from the Latin for James: Jacobus) were unwilling to capitulate. So some thirty years later in 1745, they decided to try to overthrow

Culloden House, 1746, where "Bonnie Prince Charlie" spent his last night before the battle.

Prince Charles Edward Stewart 1720-1788 by Antonia David (b. 1698).

Flora MacDonald, 1747, by Richard Wilson.

the House of Hanover again, this time with rather more seriously organized support among many of the Highland clans. Interestingly for modern Carolinians, so many of whom are descended from emigrants from Argyll, the most powerful clan alliance of all at that time, the Campbells of Argyll, were loyal to the Protestant succession of Hanover.

Rather than discuss the details of the conflict, we may merely state that the Jacobites, and their leader, Prince Charles Edward Stuart, "the Young Pretender," or "Bonnie Prince Charlie," were decisively crushed at the Battle of Culloden Moor near Inverness in 1746. And, of course he was the one who was befriended and smuggled to Skye by the famous Flora MacDonald, a later emigrant to North Carolina. This final routing of the rebellious Jacobites assured the Protestant succession of the House of Hanover on the united throne, but more significantly for the Scots, it hastened the end to the archaic clan system in the Highlands, which as we have seen, was already in process of decay:

> The significance of Culloden was not that it was a catastrophic defeat for Highland arms. There had been such defeats before and at the time most Highland Jacobites considered Culloden to be little more than a singularly unfortunate prelude to a future renewal of hostilities. What distinguished Culloden from previous reverses, however, was the fact that it was merely an overture to a massive assault on the social and political institutions of clanship. In 1746 and in the years that followed clansmen—Jacobite and non-Jacobite—were disarmed finally and completely, the wearing of the Highland dress was prohibited, and the chiefs' judicial powers over their clans were abolished—developments that were accompanied by a determined attempt to modernize the Highland economy and to integrate the region and its people into a civilization from which they had hitherto kept aloof.[42]

We might say that the failure of the Jacobite uprising indirectly influenced emigration to North Carolina. As the Celtic kinship system weakened, the evolution of Highland chiefs into English-type Landlords with a concern for social position and influence, moved on apace. We have already seen how the position of the tacksman, especially in the south of the Highlands, was being squeezed out with the new system of land tenure. But his position was also affected by the changing ambitions of the chiefs because the need for his services was undercut. Furthermore, the combination of these two factors caused even more dislocation for the vast tenant classes.

Hence the failure of "the '45" did not by any means start the process of disintegration, but it certainly strengthened and in a sense institutionalized it. In fact, following their victory, the powerful forces of the British central government continued to be deployed to assure the end of the dangers of sectionalism, which, as they saw it, the old clan system encouraged.

It has often been thought that Culloden was the main reason that many Highlanders left for Carolina. However, it is important to remember that Highland emigration to Carolina was already in full swing by the late 1730s, well before the battle. In other words, in itself, it was not

"The Prince's Bed" in Culloden House, an 1874 engraving.

George II, (1727-1760). Portrait by John Shackleton, 1755.

often a deciding factor, but rather merely reinforced the process of social and economic changes which were causing such major upheavals.

Although most earlier historians of North Carolina had asserted a direct relationship between Culloden and Carolina emigration, it was not until 1957 that Duane Meyer showed that such is not the case. Through a careful study of original sources, he effectively demonstrated that the failure of the Jacobite Rebellion was not a major factor at all in the great emigration to Carolina of the eighteenth century.[43]

He points out that the rebel soldiers who were exiled to the colonies did not come to Carolina, and that the land grants of North Carolina to Highland settlers indicate the following:

> . . . the statistics for 1746-51 show that no such large numbers of grants were made . . . of the 1746 total of five land grants to people with Scottish Highlander names, three of the individuals had received land grants before 1745 and were not new settlers. Of the 1749 total of six, two had received grants before 1745. Thus, the rate of land-grant issuance to Highlanders during the years 1746-51 was at a relatively stable and low level. There is no evidence here to indicate a migration of any size into the upper Cape Fear in that period.[44]

Also, as Meyer mentions, "Governor Gabriel Johnston denied in 1749 that any Jacobites lived in the colony."[45] For example, the Gaelic poet John McRae, who lived and wrote in his Moore Country, North Carolina home during the Revolutionary period, made it clear that for his part, his decision to leave the Highlands had nothing to do with sympathy for the fallen house of Stewart or hostility towards the reigning House of Hanover. Indeed, his later works, demonstrate great loyalty to King George III of Hanover.[46] Thus, though there were undoubtedly Jacobite sympathies and displeasure at the continuing union of Scotland and England among a number of Highlanders, the real reasons that impelled them to North Carolina were economic in nature, not primarily political.

The Attraction of Carolina

There was one final and most important factor which more and more induced the Highlanders to leave their homes for the unknown and far away shores of Carolina, namely—letters. As the exodus gained momentum, encouraging letters from North Carolina arrived in Scotland with glowing reports of the economy and opportunities for advancement in a place that was being thickly settled by other Gaelic speaking people.

A widely published "open letter" was written anonymously in 1773 by someone from the Isle of Islay, who called himself "Scotus Americanus." It was a thirty-two page booklet published in Glasgow and frequently republished, entitled: *Information Concerning the Province of North Carolina, Addressed to Emigrants from the Highlands and Western Isles of Scotland, by an Impartial Hand.* After attacking the landlords for their personal luxury and oppression of tenants, he largely expands on the desirable qualities of life in North Carolina for Highland Scots. Before describing the new land of hope, he seeks to strengthen his trustworthiness by referring to the many letters that the emigrants themselves were writing home:

> To show that they have made a happy exchange, and no people can be in more easy circumstances or better satisfied with their present condition, I might appeal to numberless letters from those very settlers, to their friends and acquaintances in the Highlands, which may be easily seen, and might, if necessary, be produced. In these letters, we find parents inviting over children that were left behind, children their parents, husbands their wives and families, and brothers their sisters, all describing their state there, as far preferable to what they ever knew before in every respect; and earnestly wishing their relations and connections of every tender tie would go and partake of the same happiness, and no longer remain under home oppression.[47]

John McBeath from Mault in Sutherland, whom we have already quoted, confirms Scotus Americanus in the second part of his statement to the authorities concerning his reasons for emigration to Carolina:

> . . . he was encouraged to emigrate by the accounts received from his own and his wife's friends already in America, assuring him that he would procure comfortable subsistence in that country for his wife and children, and that the price of labour was very high.[48]

Weaver's House near Bowmore in Islay in 1772—earliest known detailed illustration of a small traditional dwelling in this area. The bulk of the highland population lived in houses such as this one. Many dwellings survived until the early part of the twentieth century.

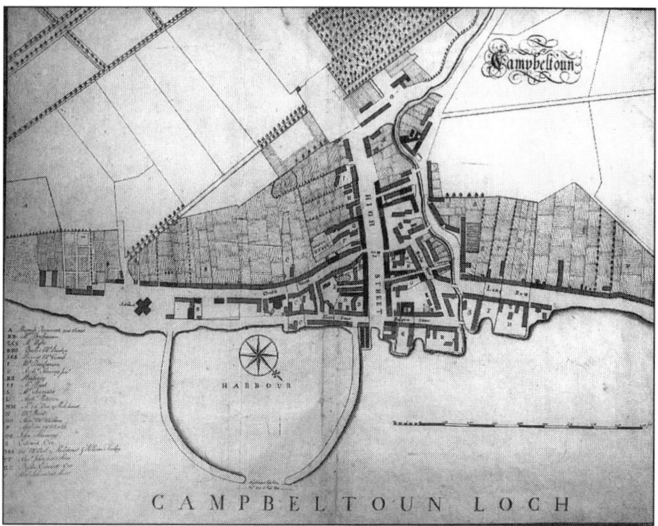

This map of Campbeltown, dated 1763, represents the way some of the emigrating Carolina Scots would have remembered it.

Large numbers of these original letters from Carolina to Highland Scotland (and their answers) still exist in the cupboards and libraries of many Carolina families, and a number of them have been published in recent years.[49] These letters cover the period from the 1730s to the 1840s, though those dated after about 1810 tend to deal much less with the specific topic of emigration than those prior to that date.

Perhaps the unsympathetic comments of the minister of the Parish of Jura and Colonsay in Argyll (in the 1792/3 *Statistical Account of Scotland*) concerning the feelings of his people about emigration are as good a summary as any of why most Highlanders left their ancient home for a foreign shore:

> The inhabitants do not feel that strong desire of bettering their circumstances, that would stimulate them to exertion and enterprise. Instead of trying the effects of industry at home, they foster the notion of getting at once into a state of ease and opulence, with their relations beyond the Atlantic.[50]

Or, to summarize the whole nexus of reasons for the great Highland emigration to North Carolina in the eighteenth century more poetically, John MacRae, North Carolina's first poet, who wrote all of his compositions in Gaelic, expressed the feelings of multitudes who took the trip in the following two poems. The first ('Thanig Leitir Iain Baitan') was written after he received a letter from the Revd. John Bethune, who had emigrated to Anson County, North Carolina in 1773. MacRae then penned this lyric:

There came a letter from John Bethune,
Which has given joy to one who has not seen it.
A few of my country people about to depart to a land of plenty,
Where we can find every kind of the most delightful hunting.
We shall find deer, buck and doe.
With permission to take as many as we wish.
We shall get the woodcock and the woodhen,
Teals, ducks and wild geese.
We shall get salmon and white fish.
And grey fish if it would please us better.
Better far than stay under landlords who won't suffer a tenantry with them.
Who would take, instead of a good man, gold were it from the claw of a lobster.
Who would take, instead of a brave man, a sulky sneak provided he was rich.
Let us depart,
And may the blessing of God be with us.
Let us go and charter a ship.
Let us depart, all of us,
For small is my esteem for a man of no courage.
I would raise a chorus of delight;
We should be delighted on seeing it.[51]

Although as the time came for departure from Kintail, his wife and others tried to dissuade him from leaving, MacRae strengthened his resolve to go with these poetic lines:

Now that we have met over a stoup and drinking shell,
Let us drink in anticipation of seeing the quarters we are to use.
Women, take courage for the voyage, and stop your mourning.
I don't think I can be induced to return to herding cattle.
Women, restrain your anxiety, now that you have gone under sails;
I don't think I can be bent backward to this country of destitution.
Everything is being tightened.

The raising has embittered us.
Trawling with great nets and salting our fish.
Many a hard day was I making dykes and walls,
My cattle dying while I paid rent with difficulty.
Many an unfortunate day have I borne expenses on your account,
And when the matter fell into ruin I sighed over them.
Small is my esteem for the landlord
Who sent us far over the ocean,
For the sake of a little wretched rent, which he did not long enjoy,
I feel inclined to go.[52]

But the truth is that he, and tens of thousands of other fellow eighteenth century Gaels, left their ancestral surroundings because of economic oppression at home and bright hopes of advancement abroad.

Historic marker on Hwy 22, near Carthage, in Moore County, N.C.

Notes

1. Duane Meyer, *The Highland Scots of North Carolina 1732-1776* (Chapel Hill: The University of North Carolina Press, 1961), 141.
2. James Hunter, *The Making of a Community*, (John Donald Publishers, Edinburgh, 1976), 7.
3. Creegan, "The House of Argyll and the Highlands," 105.
4. Creegan, "The Tacksman and their Successors," 106.
5. Ibid., 107.
6. Ibid.
7. Margaret I. Adam, "The Highland Emigration of 1770," 286, 287.
8. Especially in "The Tacksmen and their Successors".
9. Ibid., 120, 121.
10. Ibid., 121.
11. Ibid., 129.
12. Meyer, op. cit. 58.
13. Margaret I. Adam, "The Highland Emigration of 1770," 290.
14. Ibid.
15. Cregeen, "The Tacksmen and their Successors," 126.
16. Cregeen, "The House of Argyll and the Highlands," 172.
17. Ibid.
18. Ibid., 173.
19. Ibid.
20. Johnson, op. cit., 66.
21. Hunter, op. cit., 9.
22. Cregeen, "The Tacksmen and their Successors," 118.
23. quoted in Hunter, op. cit., 15.
24. *Records of Emigrants from England and Scotland to North Carolina 1774-75,* Edited by A.R. Newsome (Division of Archives and History: North Carolina Department of Cultural Resources, Raleigh, 1976, reprint of 1934), 28.
25. Hunter, op. cit., 16.
26. Ibid., 19.
27. Ibid., 20.
28. Ibid., 21.
29. Cregeen, "The Tacksmen and their Successors," 114.
30. Ibid.
31. Ibid., 127.
32. Adam, "The Causes of the Highland Emigrations of 1783-1803," 86.
33. *The Statistical Account of Scotland; Vol. XX The Western Isles,* General Editors, Donald J. Withrington and Ian R. Grant, 1983, xxxix.
34. Adam, "The Causes, etc. . . .," 87.
35. Hunter, op. cit., 31.
36. Duane Meyer, op. cit., 45.
37. *The Statistical Account of Scotland, etc. . . .* 'Introduction' by Donald J. Withrington, xxii.
38. Meyer, op. cit., 51, 52.

39. *Records of Emigrants from England and Scotland to North Carolina, etc.*, 19.
40. Ibid., 22.
41. Ibid., 23, 24.
42. Hunter, op. cit., 11.
43. Meyer, op. cit., especially chapter II, 'The Exile Theory.'
44. Ibid., 28.
45. Ibid., 29.
46. Ibid., 75-78.
47. Scotus Americanus, *Information concerning the Province of North Carolina Addressed to Emigrants from the Highlands and Western Isles of Scotland* (Glasgow: James Knox, 1773), 12.
48. *Records of Emigrants from England etc.* . . . 19.
49. See for instance Malcolm Fowler, *Valley of the Scots* (Published by Wynona Fowler, 1986), [in Raleigh, North Carolina], 21, 36, 39-40, 42, 72; and Douglas F. Kelly, *The Scottish Blue Family From Carolina to Texas* (Dillon, South Carolina, 1982), 20, 31-36; and some of these letters appear from time to time in various issues of the periodical *Argyll Colony Plus,* Scott Buie, editor, 6716 Meadow Haven, Fort Worth, Texas 76132.
50. *The Statistical Account of Scotland, etc.* . . . 283.
51. Malcolm Fowler, op. cit., 73.
52. Ibid., 74, 75.

Note to illustration

1. *Argyll, an Inventory of the Ancient Monuments,* Vol. I, Kintyre, The Royal Commission on the Ancient and Historical Monuments of Scotland, Edinburgh, 1971, p. 190

Note to ship motif

1853 engraving of the Hercules at Campbeltown. Formerly a Ship of the Line in the Royal Navy, this vessel was used to transport emigrants from the Highlands to Australia. This picture is used as a motif in the text on the assumption that it was similar to many which carried Highlanders to the Carolinas and because it carried hundreds of their cousins to a new life in the southern hemisphere.

3

North Carolina, New Home of the Highland Scots

The Earl of Selkirk, writing at the time of the departure of so many of his compatriots, seems to have been correct when he judged that North Carolina was the largest Highland settlement on the American continent.[1] We must glance only briefly at the history of this temperate Atlantic Coast territory (originally lying between the 31st and 36th degrees of latitude north) which became the lasting home of so many transplanted Gaels.

Early Colonization

North Carolina was England's only colony during the Elizabethan Age.[2] The French had discovered it and the Spanish had unsuccessfully attempted to establish a settlement, but it was the English who would eventually take and settle it. In 1584, explorers sent by Sir Walter Raleigh reached the area of North Carolina now known as Roanoke Island, and so a year later, he sent a colony to settle there.

Sir Walter Raleigh by J. Thurston.

For various reasons, including the Spanish Armada, the English were not able to return with supplies for many years. When they finally did return in 1590, the colony had totally vanished, and was given up for dead. Thus it has since been known as "The Lost Colony." There are historians who believe, however, that they did not die at all. There seems to be some evidence which suggests that they may have joined with the ancestors of the Lumbee Indians, who for several centuries have inhabited what is now Robeson County, North Carolina.[3]

At any rate, partly because of its lack of good harbors and partly for political reasons, the colony of North Carolina (named by King Charles I, Carolana, for himself in 1629) developed very slowly, trailing far behind its neighbors to the North and South, Virginia and South Carolina. In 1663, when King Charles granted the colony of North Carolina to several creditors who assisted in his restoration to the Throne, "the eight lords proprietors," we are told that North Carolina had something more than 500 persons living in it.[4]

A royal charter was granted in that year of 1663, allowing a provincial assembly and granting religious tolerance (even though the Church of England was the established church in Carolina). By the early eighteenth century, North Carolina was finally experiencing more substantial immigration and economic expansion, thus requiring more attention than the Lords proprietors had given to it. "The colony had not been properly managed by the proprietors for many years . . . . In the interests of good government, intercolonial harmony, and imperial affairs, the Board of Trade recommended that all corporate and proprietary colonies be acquired by the Crown."[5] Seven of the eight proprietors sold their rights to the Crown. Only Earl Granville retained his possession, which comprised one eighth of the colony in the northern part, above "the Granville line." This territory reverted to North Carolina at the Revolution in 1776.

By 1730, people from Wales began settling along the west bank of the Northeastern prong of the Cape Fear River, in what would become known as the Welsh Tract. From this time forward, North Carolina experienced tremendous population growth—from about 36,000 in 1729 to some 300,000 in 1776. "Most of this extraordinary growth in numbers was the result of a steady influx of immigrants from other colonies and from Europe, filling the Cape Fear Valley and spilling over into the back-country."[6] A good part of this remarkable growth consisted of perhaps as many as 50,000 Highland Scots, who came in various waves pouring into the colony from 1739 to the time of the Revolution in 1776.

The legend by "H. Moll Geographer," reads: "The English Claim the Property of Carolina from Lat. 29 &c Degrees as part of Cabot's Discoveries who set out from Bristol in 1498, at the Charge of King Henry ye 7th but they did not take possession of that Country till King Charles the II's time in 1663 who Granted a Patent to divers persons to plant all the Territories within the North Lat of 36 Deg & so west in a direct line to the South Sea." Notice that the grant runs from Virginia as far as Florida, which still belonged to Spain. Notice also serious inaccuracies of scale. The map was drawn in 1740.

The Argyll Colony

Why did this particular colony receive the largest concentration of Gaels anywhere in the world outside of the Highlands? A major reason must be the effective governorship of Gabriel Johnston, a Lowland Scot and graduate of St. Andrews University, who served as Governor of North Carolina from 1734 to 1752. He felt it would be good for the future of the Cape Fear Valley for it to be settled by large numbers of Protestant Highland Scots, so he began writing enthusiastic letters to friends in Scotland,

Apparently there is no extant portrait of Governor Johnston, but the University of North Carolina Library possesses several of his books (largely commentaries on the Holy Scriptures) in which are found copies of his coat of arms, like this one, used as book marks.

A century later, a Captain Angus McDiarmid joined fellow highlanders from Islay but died in 1856 aged only 24. His grave, in Longstreet Church cemetery, is marked by one of the few surviving Gaelic tombstones of the Highland settlement. The Gaelic inscription is taken from James 4:14: "For what is your life? It is a vapour, that apeareth for a little time, and then vanisheth away."

inviting them to come to a land where there were two crops each year, free land grants and possible exemption from taxation for a time.

It is true that three Highland names are mentioned in the Land Grant Records of North Carolina before the time of Governor Johnston. Hugh Campbell, William Forbes and James Innes had land grants in what is now Cumberland County in 1733, but it is most likely that, "... this was a purely speculative venture and it is doubtful if either of them ever set foot in Cumberland."[7]

What is certain, though, is that Governor Johnston's letters reached the ears of Argyll tacksmen such as Duncan Campbell of Kilduskland, Neill, Hector and Archibald McNeill from along the west coast, Coll McAlester and sons Hector and Alexander of Islay, Alexander Clark and others, whom we will meet later. These prosperous men, who of course were concerned at the undercutting of the tacksmen's position on the Duke of Argyll's estate as well as the depression in cattle prices in the mid 1730's, were thus prepared to take a serious look at good opportunities elsewhere. They took Governor Johnston's letters about North Carolina seriously enough to organize a committee to visit the Cape Fear Valley in 1736.

It is probable that this committee had had its attention turned towards North America by Captain Hector MacNeal, a merchant shipmaster, who sailed for many years to places as far away from one another as Boston and Africa, and elsewhere.[8] He had written his brother Neill (one of the Argyll committee) in early 1736, encouraging the bringing of a colony to New England. But the Argyll committee decided on North Carolina, probably because of Governor Johnston.

The Committee liked what they saw in Carolina, returned to Argyll

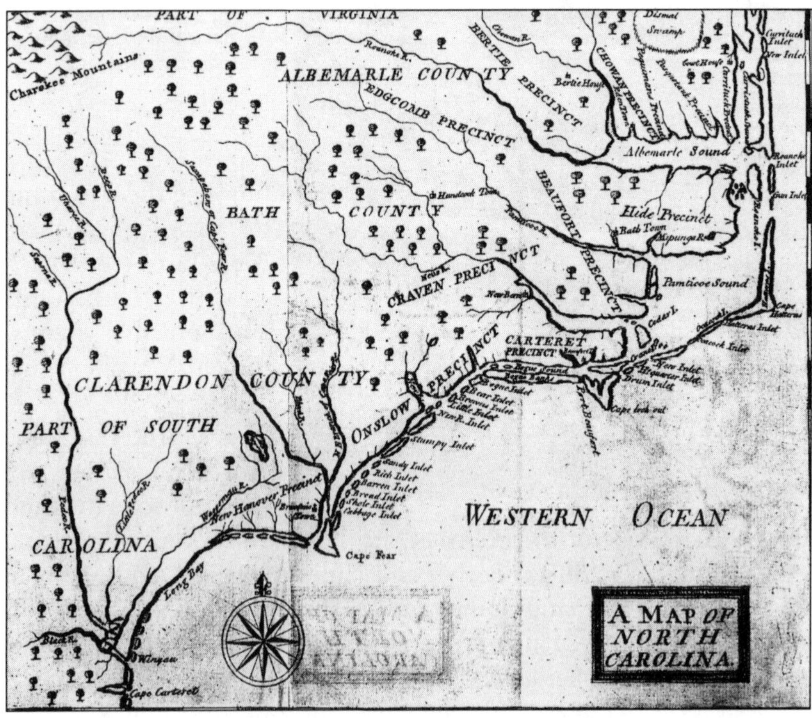

According to this 1737 map, a landscape of virgin forest would have confronted the Argyll committee visiting a year before the map was drawn. Only four settlements apparently were considered worthy of note: New Bern, Beaufort, Brunswick Town and Bath Town—all four along the coast—and only three counties along with several precincts. Very few rivers are recorded, though North and South Carolina are identified as being separate. Of interest to sea captains such as Hector MacNeal, however, is the detailed identification of numerous inlets along the capes. The map as a whole is still rather inaccurate.

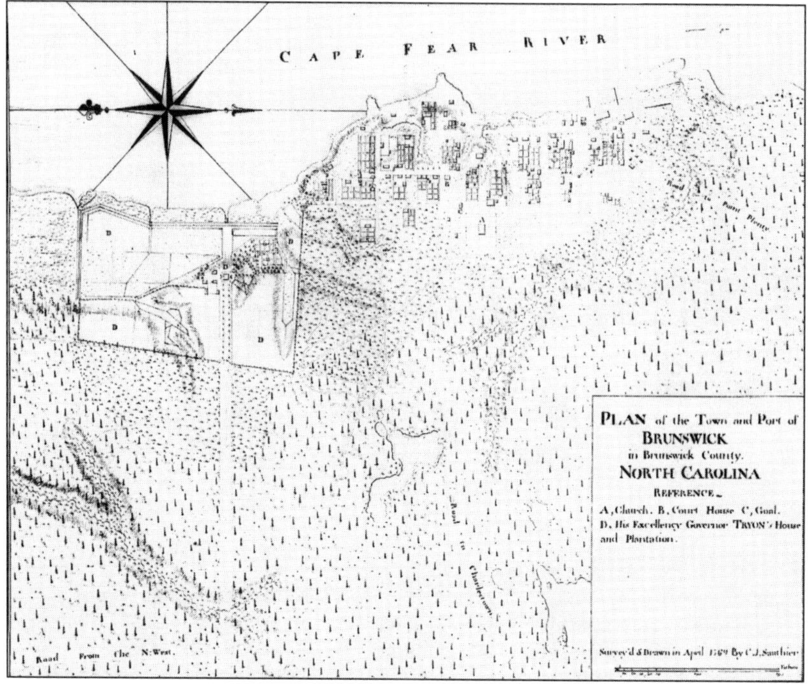

The plan of "The Town and Port of Brunswick" drawn thirty years later, shows a settlement dwarfed by endless pines. Governor Tryon's house and plantation are shown to the west of the town, in which are marked a church, court house and goal [*sic*].

and by 1739 brought a substantial colony of friends and relatives with them back to the Cape Fear. Some 350 emigrants sailed from Campbeltown in July of 1739 on "The Thistle," guided by Neill Du MacNeill ("Black" Neil of Ardelay), and landed in September, most likely in the port of Brunswick.

The Argyll Colony traveled up the Cape Fear Valley some ninety miles upstream from the port of entry to what would become the heartland of transplanted Highlanders in Carolina. This section was then known as Bladen County, but in 1754 was set off as Cumberland. It was centered on what is now Fayetteville, but was then two small, adjacent trading towns, Campbeltown and Cross Creek. As we shall later see, the Argyll colonists fanned out in the territory north of these towns, where they took substantial land grants. We must return to the fortunes of this colony later, but here we note precisely why they came this far upriver to settle and then why so many Highlanders soon followed them there.

Barbeque was founded by Highlanders in 1758, who erected a one room log structure, twenty-seven feet square, in 1765. The first building apparently looked something like this modern artist's rendition. The famous Flora MacDonald worshipped here for some months during 1774, while staying with her half-sister, Annabella, who lived at nearby Mount Pleasant (now Cameron Hill). Other buildings succeeded the log structure.

Some writers have suggested that the Scots preferred the sandy hills of the upper Cape Fear Valley to the rich bottom lands of the lower Cape Fear, and while entirely possible, that explanation seems unlikely to the present writer because these tacksmen would have known that the land downriver was much richer and would produce far more with less effort. The explanation is simpler: English colonists had already taken up the richer bottom lands along the lower Cape Fear, and thus the Scots went to the area where grants were available upstream. Also it has been noted that the Scots generally settled south of the Granville line, in the area of North Carolina which was controlled by the Crown with a more efficient and generous legal system.

The Argyll Colony was by any measure a success. They were given substantial grants of land by 1740, relief from taxation for ten years, a financial grant from the Colonial government, and several of them (including Duncan Campbell, Daniel McNeill, Dugald McNeill) were immediately appointed Justices of the Peace for Bladen County.[9] Word of their good reception was not long in reaching Argyll and other places in the Highlands as well. It is possible that another group came in 1740 from Argyll, and it is certain that the door was now open through which untold thousands of Gaels would come for nearly a century.

Highland Scots, like most people, enjoyed living among their own kind, and naturally preferred to go where there would be other Highlanders. " . . . emigrants from the same district in the Highlands sought the same part in America . . . . In general it is rare to find the Highland emigrants departing from the orthodox routes opened up by their former neighbours."[10] Not only is it true that Highlanders poured into the Upper Cape Fear Valley together, but also specific localities of Scotland are heavily represented in particular localities in North Carolina.

For instance, Barbeque Presbyterian Church, in what is now Harnett County, was at one time made up of many people with Jura connections. The early congregation of Bethesda Presbyterian Church, near Aberdeen in present day Moore County, had strong Kintyre and Knapdale connections. Union Presbyterian congregation in mid Moore County had a large element of Skye people, while some localities around Maxton, North Carolina and also the Carolina Church section near Dillon, South Carolina had strong Kintail connections. Of course, from the beginning there was mixing in all of these places, so that one cannot too literally trace the precise origin of entire communities in the Upper Cape Fear, beyond noting a preponderant original element in several of them.

We must now look briefly at the geography, economy and culture of the area into which the Highland Scots came.

Sandhills, Rivers and Pines

North Carolina is composed of three geographical areas: the Appalachian Mountains in the West, the rolling, hilly Piedmont in the Middle, and the large, flat Coastal Plain in the East, which runs inland from the Atlantic Ocean over 100 miles. In the upper part of the Coastal Plain are found the gently rising "Sandhills," consisting of hills and ridges with fairly poor sandy loam on the hills and richer soil in the bottoms between the hills.

Most of the area is covered with pine trees, which proved to be one of the greatest resources of the incoming Scots. It was filled with an abundance of game for hunting: deer, turkey, quail, rabbit, as well as plenty of fish for catching in the cold streams. Though less rich in agricultural productivity than the lower part of the state, it had the advantage of

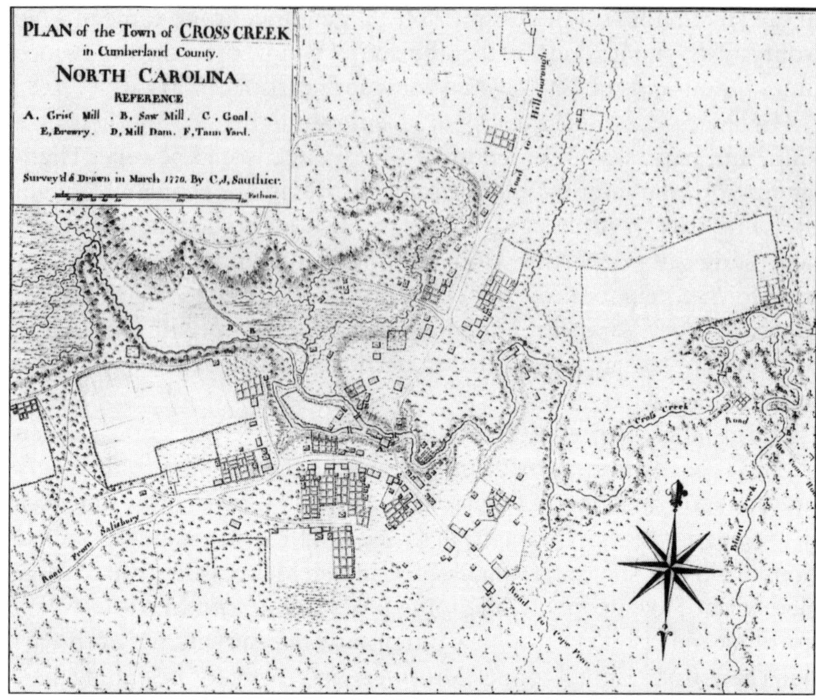

By 1770, the development of the timber industry had caused the settlement of Cross Creek to spread along the creek itself and out into the pine forest. This map shows the mill dam (D) just below the legend, providing power for no less than five saw mills, all marked with the letter B. Immediately downstream from the dam there is also a grist mill (A), not far from the brewery and the goal (*sic*). A tann yard is nestled near the center of the settlement in a meandering loop of the creek.

being less plagued by malaria and other fevers more prevalent in the lower Cape Fear.

It was into this Sandhills area, for the most part, that the Highland emigrants first came and continued to come for generations. Here they could continue the familiar practice of farming as they had done at home. As Angus W. McLean says:

> Almost universally the Scotch immigrants engaged in agriculture and sought to improve their surrounds. The products were corn (zea-maize), rye, peas, sweet potatoes, flax and cotton, the latter two being raised solely for domestic use. Some engaged in raising horses, cattle and sheep.[11]

Tobacco was also raised, but was not an important feature of the Sandhills economy in the eighteenth or early nineteenth century.

These Scots set up blacksmith forges, built tanneries and grist mills on the streams (which they dammed up to increase the flow of water), and numbers of saw mills for timber. Timber was of supreme importance for the Carolina Scots:

> When the Highlanders came into the Cape Fear country, they were confronted by one of the most magnificent forests that the world has ever known—the long leaf pine, tall, straight, free from limbs, large in size, a king among timber trees, one that developed a succession of industries that placed the colony on a basis of its own in an industrial way. For years North Carolina was known to the world by its production of naval stores, turpentine, resin, tar, and charcoal, yields of the pine forests, an abundance that supplied the shipping of the seas and the chemicals for many industries. The newcomers reveled in the vast profligacy of lumber, the like of which they had never seen. Pine, oak, juniper, cypress, gum, hickory, cedar; timber for their houses, for barns and sheds, for fuel without the slightest limit as to amount; timber for furniture, for vehicles and

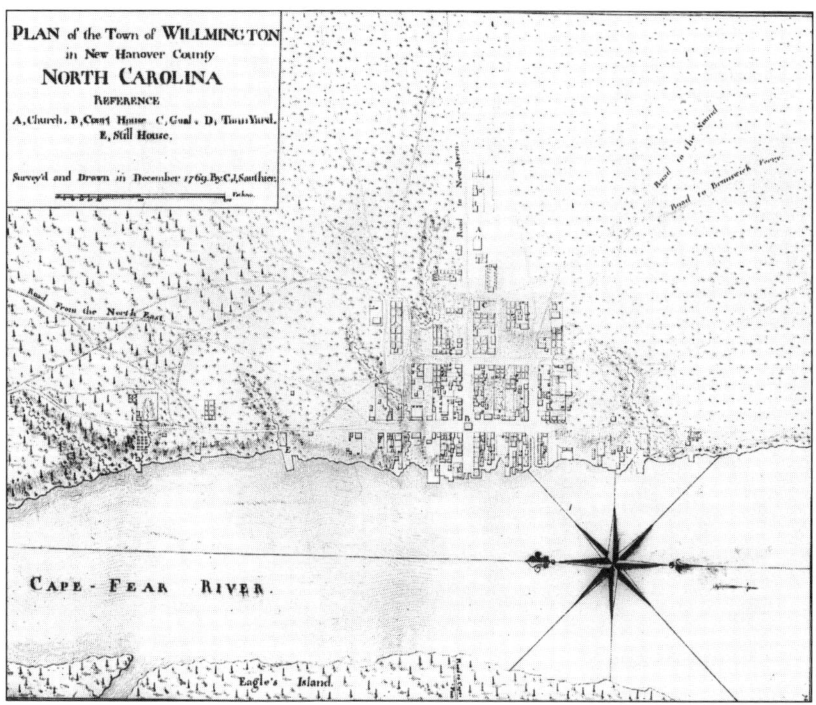

Neatly laid out around the courthouse on the banks of the wide Cape Fear down which the log rafts were floated to market, Wilmington in 1769 boasted a tann yard, "still house", church and the ubiquitous "goal".

farm-use, for water-craft . . . And with all the rest, a big river to float the product down to the ports and to the sea.[12]

The pine tree could be used for a livelihood in so many ways, and the river was essential as a route to market:

> In clearing the land the early settlers would burn the pines for tar. The boxed pines furnished turpentine, which was distilled and sold in Fayetteville and Wilmington. There was always a ready market in those places for naval stores. When the trees were drained of their productivity, they were cut, assembled into rafts and floated down the Cape Fear to Wilmington. An average raft would sell for upwards of 500 dollars in that town. At first rafters would walk back from Wilmington or pole a loaded flat boat up the river. In 1818 though, steamers appeared on the Cape Fear and the rafters would ride back to Fayetteville on these.[13]

A vivid verbal portrait was drawn of this process on the eve of the War Between the States by Dr. Daniel McNeill Parker of Halifax, Nova Scotia, who was visiting his cousins in the upper Cape Fear:

> I arrived at McNeill's Ferry Tuesday afternoon [April 9, 1861] and after an early breakfast next morning the Colonel [A.S. McNeill] took me in his

Possibly the only remaining slave cabin in Moore County, North Carolina, stands on the homeplace of Scottish emigrant "River Daniel" Blue, near the Eureka community. It was constructed between 1810 and 1815.

In much better condition than the old slave cabin although built at least 15 years earlier in 1795, this structure on the "River Daniel" Blue farm, first served as a "holding house" (for food stores), and later as a kitchen. The family slaves slept in this (warmer) house during the winter months.

carriage across the Cape Fear River to see his only sister, Mrs. Dr. Turner [Caroline McNeill]. The crossing was rather exciting as the river was much swollen by the recent rain, but the colored ferrymen, who are his slaves, managed the broad barge admirably, and we at length landed safely on the other side. The horses stood as quietly in the barge as if they were in their stables, while the men labored against the rapid currents, making as much noise as they possibly could. In fact it is the hardest thing in the world for them to do any kind of work in silence. . . .

The drive to McNeill's Ferry is through a pine forest of great beauty and value. It is the species of pine which yields all the turpentine or resin for which this State is famous, and I made myself familiar with the whole process of obtaining and manufacturing these articles of commerce, from the tapping of the tree until the product is landed in Wilmington for exportation. On McNeill's property the timber alone is worth a number of fortunes. Magnificent pines, oak, ash and all kinds of trees used here are there in abundance, and on that part of his plantation where his corn mill is situated, he has a fine sawmill in active operation, preparing timber for the

> Wilmington market. This he sends down the Cape Fear River in immense rafts, with a party of slaves who have been long engaged in the business and are thorough raftsmen. The distance to Wilmington is about 150 miles. It is an interesting sight to see these long rafts floating rapidly down stream with a cheerful fire of pine knots placed on a little heap of earth in the center. The men with their tents, and cheerful, happy faces, are singing as they pass along, making one almost envious of their happy vocation.[14]

Lifestyles

Over the years, the general economic condition of the Highland emigrants in their new homeland tended to be what we would call today, 'solid middle class,' much like the rest of the Colony of North Carolina. While some Scots became very wealthy in land and slaves and other business interests and while a few were poor, what Malcolm Fowler says about the settlers of Harnett County is probably true of most of the Carolina Scots: they were "hundred acre boys."[15] And what Governor Angus W. McLean said concerning the Carolina Scots communities shortly after 1900, was largely true a hundred years before that time, and is still relevant: "There are none very rich or very poor—it is not a place where 'wealth accumulates and men decay,' but it is a place where a just estimate is placed on human values."[16]

Of course there were exceptions to this observation. There were, as we shall see, some massive land owners among the transplanted Scots, such as Jennie Bahn Smith McNeill, some of the descendants of Duncan Blue and hundreds of others. Yet even among those Highland offspring who were more wealthy, the mentality usually stayed unpretentious and the life-style unostentatious, a generally typical feature of the State.

The early—and later—Scots of Carolina usually built fairly simple, though (particularly in later years) comfortable houses. In the Highlands the building material had generally consisted of sod, straw and stone, whereas in Carolina, the building material was wood. Most emigrants started off with a log cabin:

> The earliest houses were one or two room buildings with a loft, which was generally reached by a ladder or a narrow stairway. Sometimes a lean-to on the back beside a porch would provide a little additional room. A stick or brick chimney supplied heat for comfort in winter and for cooking year-round. Glass windows were rare for a long time, and if a log cabin had windows, there were solid shutters on wooden or leather hinges to

The "River Daniel" Blue House near the Eureka community of Moore County was constructed about 1795 by the Wadsworth family, and purchased by Argyll emigrant "River Daniel" Blue in 1804. It has seen various renovations over the years, and is still inhabited by his descendants, John Sam and Louise Blue. It is an official North Carolina historical monument.

close them. As prosperity followed settlement, houses grew. Rooms and hallways were added, and not infrequently the kitchen and dining room were removed to another building that was set a short distance away.[17]

Some of these hewn log cabins were incorporated into larger, more elegant and commodious homes after the increase of saw mills and planed boards in the late eighteenth and early nineteenth centuries, as is the case with the old 'River Daniel' Blue home near Eureka in Moore County,[18] and some still stand, as does the large two-storey log cabin first inhabited by the emigrant Daniel Kelly family on the John McLean farm in central Moore County. Many of the early log houses still exist in rural areas as packhouses and barns.

As the Highland Carolinians became more prosperous, they tended to construct better houses—usually of sawed, planed wood. Often they used heart of pine, almost impossible to rot (because its central turpentine substance is as hard as a rock), but quick to burn. Some of these structures, though relatively simple, were elegantly shaped and very roomy. Such improved dwellings of Highland descendents are, for in-

According to the 1778 census role of the MacDonald Estate in the Isle of Skye, this stone house in Capisdol (Parish of Sleat), overlooking the sound of Sleat was inhabited by the Daniel Kelly family.

The widowed Daniel Kelly at age seventy-eight with nine of his ten children and other relatives emigrated to Moore County in 1803. Like most immigrants they used local materials in 1806 for this storey and a half log building, covered with planks. It is still in use as a barn, a few miles north of Union Presbyterian Church in Moore County on the old John McLean place, now the property of Mrs. Florence Hardy.

Barely forty years after the family's arrival, John Bethune Kelly, who had emigrated with his father from the Isle of Skye in 1803, could be found living among the pines in this fine example of "up-country" Federal architecture—a far cry from the windswept stone cottage of his childhood in Skye. Now known as "The Sheriff Alexander Kelly House," after a nephew who purchased it soon after his uncle built it in 1842, it lies a few miles west of Carthage, still inhabited by the Kelly family (Mrs. Kate Kelly Kelly). Embedded in the mantle of the drawing room is an original painting by the architect of the house when it was built.

stance, the Alexander Kelly house north of Carthage built in 1842,[19] the Lauchlin Bethune house, near McCain, North Carolina, the Malcolm Blue house near Bethesda Church, Aberdeen, N.C.,[20] the Mag Blue House in Scotland County, N.C.,[21] and many others built by the first third of the nineteenth century.

Two attractive examples of the finer two-storey late eighteenth and very early nineteenth century Cape Fear Scots architecture are found in present Hoke County: the Mill Prong House, (see p. 97), which belonged to the Gilchrist family (and is now being carefully restored) and the "Red House Archie," which was bought by "Buffalo Daniel" Patterson in 1811 and passed to Archibald McMillan in 1837.[22]

The Malcolm Blue house was built in the 1830s by Malcolm Blue, prominent landowner and descendant of Highland emigrant Duncan Blue. It is near Old Bethesda Church outside Aberdeen and has been restored as a historical monument. Some of Sherman's troops stayed in this house on their way to Atlanta in 1865.

By the middle of the nineteenth century, there were some very grand residences of the popular Southern Greek Revival style such as that of Caroline McNeill and husband, Dr. Henry Marshall Turner of Buie's Creek.[23] Nevertheless, large Southern mansions, whether earlier Georgian or later Greek Revival, were nothing like so numerous among the plain Scots of the Sandhills as they were elsewhere in the South, as in South Carolina and Virginia.

Markets and Fairs

In this rural economy, the scattered farm families of the emigrant Scots usually had to go a considerable distance to markets in order to sell their raw products and buy essential supplies. In the Upper Cape Fear, the town of Fayetteville was one of the main markets, located as it was on the main river route to Wilmington and Europe. The families who lived in Moore County, some fifty or more miles from Fayetteville, had to spend two days and a night traveling through the woods to make the journey, according to letters now in the possession of the Malcolm M. Blue family of present Aberdeen.[24] The market trips of the Archibald

Ferguson family (he was b. 1841, d. 1906) who lived a few miles northwest of Aberdeen have been described as follows:

> When the children were growing up, the family would make two trips a year to Fayetteville, one in the spring and one in the fall. It would take three days for the trip, one to go, one to camp outside the city limits overnight, and one to return home. At that time in Richmond and Moore Counties one could drive all through the woods in a buggy, dodging only streams. Game was abundant and many wild hogs were available in the woods.
>
> On the trips to Fayetteville this wild hog meat was the main thing they had to sell. It brought ten cents a pound when dressed. On these two trips they had to buy salt, pepper, herbs, sugar, coffee, matches (matches cost 10 cents for 24—one box of matches would last for six months). Clothes were all homemade but a hat bought in Fayetteville for a man or boy cost 25 cents.[25]

The Mill Prong House was built c. 1795 by Scottish emigrant John Gilchrist (1740-1802) in the Federal style. He served in the North Carolina legislature in the 1790s and was a large landholder. His son, John Gilchrist, Jr., sold the house to Col. Archibald McEachern in 1834, who ran a large plantation for many years. Col. McEachern remodeled the house in the Greek Revival style in the late 1830s. This fine and well-preserved house was restored in 1993 and has been placed on the National Register of Historic Places.

This large cooking pot was brought from Scotland by the "River Daniel" Blue family in 1804 to their new home in Moore County. It was made in Falkirk, Scotland by the Carron Iron Works which remained in production until after World War II.

Typical of what would have been bought by the up-country Scots in Fayetteville are the items listed in a financial receipt of Daniel Blue II (son of emigrant "River Daniel"), who lived near present Eureka in central Moore County. This receipt is dated Jan. 8, 1857, and is signed by J. W. Williams Co., of Fayetteville:

Coffee	$13.00
Nails	$15.75
l block salt	$1.25
Sugar	$27.41[26]

Sometimes however the goods were brought to the hinterlands in the form of fairs. One of the more famous fairs was the "Scotch Fair" at Laurel Hill, N.C.:

> One of the interesting events of early days was the Scotch fair, which was held each spring and fall, one-fourth mile south of Laurel Hill church. The first fair was held in 1783 and continued until 1873. The fair was begun when there was no railroad in the world and no steamboat.
>
> Goods from foreign points were brought into the interior of the country to the head of navigation on the rivers in small boats. The nearest inland port was Cheraw in South Carolina on the Pee Dee river, and the other river port was Fayetteville, N.C. on the Cape Fear River. It was chartered by the State of North Carolina to run as long as the water in Jordan's creek runs. Covered wagons came from mountains with apples and other produce.
>
> There tanners with their leathers, hatters with their hats, tailors and shoemakers, those who had wool to sell, the gingerbread women with

their cakes came to sell. Horse racing was a major diversion, there were booths for betting, booths for sale of wine, whiskey, cakes and other food. There was not a kerosene lamp in the county when the fair was abolished in 1873. The only light was from lightwood fires built on elevated scaffolds on which soil was placed to keep it from burning. In 1873, Rev. A.N. Ferguson circulated a petition to the General Assembly and had the fair abolished.[27]

Significance of the Church

Merely to look at the houses and lands of the Carolina Scots will not reveal some of the most important realities in their lives and culture. One of the most significant influences upon the transplanted Highlanders and their posterity, was the Christian Church.

In various recent studies the story has been told of how the Argyll Colony petitioned the Presbytery of Inverary and Synod of Argyll for a Presbyterian minister to come to North Carolina. A petition was presented in 1739, 1741, and 1748, all without success.[28] However, eventually the Rev. Hugh McAden came down from Philadelphia and

Longstreet Church was also founded by Highland emigrants in 1758. They erected this Federal-style building around 1847. The congregation had to abandon their church in 1923 because the entire territory for miles around was taken over by the United States Government as part of the Fort Bragg Army Reservation. Annual reunions are held each June by the numerous descendants of this congregation.

Old Bluff Presyterian Church was founded in 1758, and first met in a log building. This beautiful frame structure was completed in 1858 and is now used only once a year for homecomings and occasional funerals.

preached among the Sandhill Scots in 1756. Among other places, he preached at the homes of John Smith, David Smith and Alexander McKay. Then in 1758, McAden's friend, the Rev. James Campbell came down to the Scottish territory of Carolina as minister.

From his ministrations to the scattered Argyll Colony people (which by that time had been joined by many other families from elsewhere in the Highlands), came the three mother churches of the Carolina Scots: Old Bluff and Longstreet (both in present day Cumberland County) and Barbeque (in present day Harnett County). The history of these important churches has been well documented by the Rev. James McKenzie, once minister of Barbeque, and now of Robbins, N.C.[29] We will later give the genealogies of several leaders of the Argyll Colony who were the original ruling elders in these churches, such as Hector MacNeill ('Bluff Hector') and Alexander MacAllister at Bluff and Gilbert Clark at Barbeque. Highlanders Malcolm Smith, Archibald MacKay and Archibald Ray were the first elders at Longstreet (now on the Fort Bragg U.S. Army Reservation).

In this volume we cannot enter into the interesting history of these three original Carolina Scots Churches nor into that of their elder daughters such as Union in mid Moore County, founded in 1797, and at one time the largest Presbyterian congregation in all of North Carolina, full of Highlanders—particularly Skye people. Nor can we look at Bethesda near Aberdeen, founded about 1788 by Highland Scots, particularly of Knapdale and Kintyre provenance. Indeed there are many other largely Scottish churches which could be mentioned, such as Bethel near Raeford, N.C., Antioch near Red Springs, Ashpole near Rowland, N.C., Carolina near Dillon, South Carolina, Centre and Smyrna near Maxton, N.C., and at least a score more.

So although we cannot discuss all the historical details of these individual churches and communities, in order to form an impression of what they meant to the emigrants and their children we must take a summary glance at some of the activities that were central to the religious

Ashpole Presbyterian Church was founded by Scottish emigrants in 1796. It is situated in lower Robeson County, near the South Carolina line, just west of the present town of Rowland, and is the mother church of Old Pee Dee Church near Dillon, South Carolina, as well as other daughter churches in both Carolinas. The present building was constructed shortly before the beginning of the War Between the States, in about 1860. Like most of the other 19th century Carolina Scots churches modelled on churches in Scotland, it has galleries around the sides of the sanctuary, originally used by family slaves.

Founded by Scottish emigrants in 1797, Union Presbyterian Church in Moore County, (a few miles east of Carthage and some miles west of Vass) has been a mother church to several other churches in Moore and Lee Counties, as well as its namesake near Lafayette, MS. This photograph of the sanctuary built fifty years after the great revival appeared in *The History of Union Presbyterian Church* which the Rev. John K. Roberts prepared for the 30th anniversary Homecoming Celebration in August of 1910. It is still in regular use by the Union congregation.

practice of these churches and their people. Among these people (in common with other evangelical Christians of the time), there was regular Biblical preaching and prayer meetings; the Sabbath Day was very strictly and yet joyfully observed; the children were taught to memorize the Westminster Shorter Catechism, and church sessions (composed of the minister and the lay elders) watched over the lives of their people very carefully and took discipline very seriously, as a study of any of the session minutes of these old churches before 1900 will demonstrate.

In the late eighteenth and early nineteenth centuries, the people of the transplanted Highland churches experienced great revival movements, interestingly just at the same time as similar movements were breaking out in their old homeland of the Hebrides. In America these religious revivals were part of the larger movement that swept up and down the

Union Church as it is today: stained glass windows were added in the mid-twentieth century, and the front porch was added in the 1970s. Union has galleries on three sides of its sanctuary, much like churches in Highland Scotland.

Atlantic Seaboard, generally called "the Second Great Awakening," occurring intermittently from the 1780s to the 1830s.

Just one description of a revival as it took place in one of the Carolina Highland churches will be sufficient to give us some insight into how these people felt about spiritual matters. The 1833 revival at Union Presbyterian Church in Moore County has been described by J.K. Roberts from contemporary accounts. (There had also been a large revival in the same church a generation before, in 1801):

> The greatest revival in the history of the church was held during his pastorate. It is known as the great revival of 1833. It continued in unabated zeal for two years and was attended with considerable physical exertion and noise. At first, Mr. McCallum endeavored to suppress the noise, but becoming convinced that the manifestations were the work of the Spirit of God, he threw himself into the meetings. This revival extended into the congregations of Cypress, Buffalo, Euphronia, Bensalem, Mineral Springs and Bethesda. It is estimated that over five hundred people joined these churches as a result of this season of grace, while more than three hundred joined Union Church.

In a letter to his father, Mr. Archibald McCallum, dated Sept. 18th, 1833, Mr. McCallum speaks of the revival in these words: 'I preach three or four times every week besides attending inquiry meetings and doing much necessary riding . . . Our meetings are crowded day and night, and many profess to have passed from death unto life . . . We hardly have a meeting at which there are no additions, and some of the subjects are of the most wicked and profligate characters in the county. There came a few days ago one who was the ring leader in every vice and his conviction seemed to have been signally marked from the beginning.'[30]

Enthusiastic movements can lead to excesses and are never lacking in critics, and thus it was with these revivals among the Carolina Scots. As The Historical Sketch of Antioch Presbyterian Church says:

The revivals of the 1800s caused a crisis. [Rev.] Colin Lindsay denounced the revivals and many members followed this handsome and eloquent man to nearby Bethel [Presbyterian Church near Raeford, N.C.]. Gillespie welcomed the revivals and those like-minded followed him to Center church.[31]

Of equal, or perhaps even greater long-term importance in the spiritual life of the Sandhill Scots Churches were the regular sacramental seasons, which before 1900, were usually every six months. Whereas revivals were by their nature sporadic, the sacrament of the Lord's Supper was celebrated consistently through the years, and had considerable social as well as strictly religious significance in the Sandhills, as it did in West Scotland. Dr. Daniel McGilvary, son of Moore County Isle of Skye emigrants and first missionary to Thailand, described in his biography what these sacramental occasions were like in the 1830s and '40s (at Buffalo Presbyterian Church near Sanford, N.C.):

The great event of the year was the camp-meeting at the Fall Communion. It served as an epoch from which the events of the year before and after it were dated. For weeks before it came, all work on the farm was arranged with reference to 'Buffalo Sacrament'—pronounced with long a in the first syllable. It was accounted nothing for people to come fifteen, twenty, or even forty miles to the meetings. Every pew-holder had a tent, and kept open house. No stranger went away hungry. Neighboring ministers were invited to assist the pastor.

Services began on Friday, and closed on Monday, unless some special interest suggested the wisdom of protracting them further. The regular order was: A special prayer meeting, breakfast, a prayer meeting at nine, a sermon at ten, an intermission, and then another sermon. The sermons were not accounted of much worth if they were not an hour long. The pulpit was the tall old-fashioned box-pulpit with a sounding-board above. For want of room in the church, the two sermons on Sunday were preached from a stand in the open air.

At the close of the second sermon, the ruling elders, stationed in various parts of the congregation, distributed to the communicants the "tokens," which admitted them to the sacramental table. Then, in solemn procession, the company marched up the rising ground to the church, singing as they went:

'Children of the Heavenly King,
As ye journey, sweetly sing.'

Sandy Grove Presbyterian Church was founded by second and third generation descendants of the Scottish emigrants to the Upper Cape Fear. Located in Cumberland County on the present Fort Bragg Reservation, it is equidistant from Longstreet, Bethel and Bethesda Churches, from which it drew its original members. The organizational meeting, on December 25, 1852, was chaired by John Calvin Currie. This building was completed two years later, in the summer of 1854. It, like Longstreet, was closed in 1928, owing to its inclusion in the Fort Bragg territory. Annual reunions were held until the beginning of World War II, and then resumed in October of 1997.

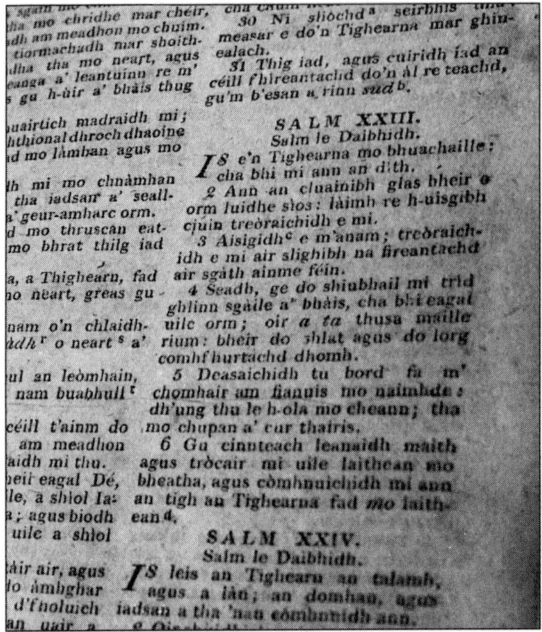

30 Ni sliochd[a] seirbhis
measar e do'n Tighearna mar ghin-
ealach.
31 Thig iad, agus cuiridh iad an
céill fhìreantachd do'n àl re teachd,
gu'm b'esan a rinn *sud*[b].

SALM XXIII.
Salm le Daibhidh.

IS e'n Tighearna mo bhuachaille;
cha bhi mi ann an dìth.
2 Ann an cluainibh glas bheir e
orm luidhe sìos: làimh re h-uisgibh
ciùin treòraichidh e mi.
3 Aisigidh[c] e m'anam; treòraichidh e mi air slighibh na fìreantachd
air sgàth ainme féin.
4 Seadh, ge do shiubhail mi trid
ghlinn sgàile a' bhàis, cha bhi eagal
uile orm; oir *a ta* thusa maille
rium: bheir do shlat agus do lorg
comhfhurtachd dhomh.
5 Deasaichidh tu bord fa m'
chomhair am fianuis mo naimhde:
dh'ung thu le h-ola mo cheann; tha
mo chupan a' cur thairis.
6 Gu cinnteach leanaidh maith
agus tròcair mi uile laithean mo
bheatha, agus còmhnuichidh mi ann
an tigh an Tighearna fad *mo* laithean[d].

SALM XXIV.
Salm le Daibhidh.

IS leis an Tighearn an talamh,
agus a làn; an domhan, agus
iadsan a tha 'nan còmhnuidh ann.

Psalm 23 in the John McLeod Gaelic Bible.

It was a beautiful sight, and we boys used to climb the hill in advance to see it. When the audience was seated, there was a brief introductory exercise. Then a hymn was sung, while a group of communicants filled the places about the communion table. There was an address by one of the ministers, during the progress of which the bread and wine were passed to the group at the table. Then there was singing again, while the first group retired, and a second group took its place.

The same ceremony was repeated for them, and again for others, until all communicants present had participated. The communion service must have occupied nearly two hours. One thing I remember well—when the children's dinner-time came (which was after all the rest had dined), the sun was low in the heavens, and there was still a night service before us. Notwithstanding some inward rebellion, it seemed all right then. But the same thing nowadays would drive all the young people out of the church.[32]

At first nearly all of the preaching in these Carolina Scots churches was in Gaelic, but within a few years English services were introduced, and so until the mid-nineteenth century in many of them there was first a Gaelic and then an English sermon, or vice versa on each preaching day. In some of the churches, such as Barbeque, Gaelic preaching still seems to have occurred intermittently until about the time of the first World War.

Use of Gaelic

Having seen its use in the churches, a central institution in the community, we must now consider the place of the Gaelic language as a whole in the Sandhills of North Carolina, a subject that has been generally

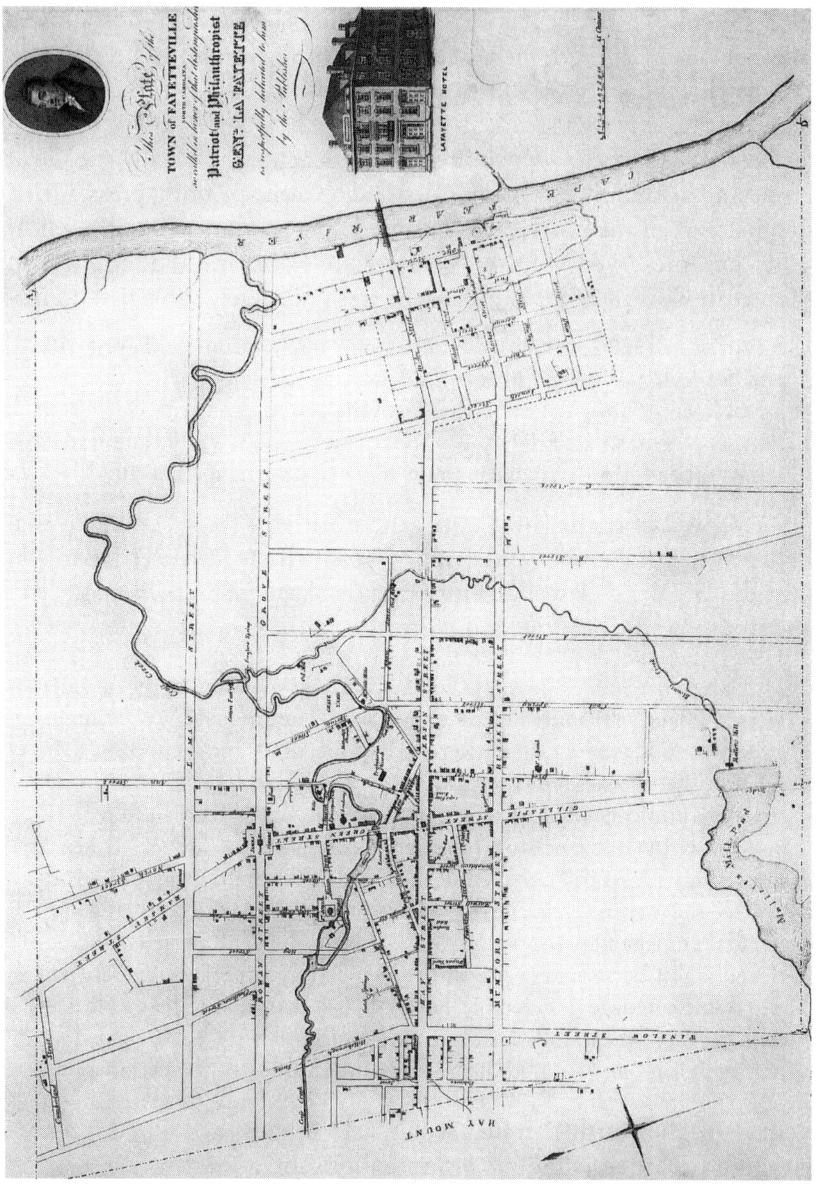

Fayetteville in 1825 has clearly progressed as a cultural and administrative centre from its humble beginnings as a scattered settlement and saw mills along the banks of Cross Creek. The legend announces: "This Plate of the TOWN of FAYETTEVILLE, North Carolina, so called in honor of the distinguished Patriot and Philanthropist GENL. LA FAYETTE is respectfully dedicated to him by the Publisher."

neglected until recently. It is a proven fact that Gaelic was almost universally spoken all through the Upper Cape Fear section from the arrival of the Argyll Colony in 1739 until about the time of the War Between the States in the early 1860s.

Most Scots families were bilingual, but Gaelic was usually spoken at home and at church. Fayetteville boasted a Gaelic printing press during the first part of the nineteenth century, and a number of their publications are preserved in the Presbyterian Historical Foundation in Montreat, North Carolina. But Gaelic was not merely spoken at home:

> A tourist in 1828 commented that so many of the people in Fayetteville and 'for four and twenty miles round' understood only Gaelic, 'that they are obliged to have a clerk in the Post Office who can speak Gaelic.' An innkeeper who spoke English also spoke Gaelic ' . . . tolerable and understands it perfectly, having been in the habit of hearing it all his life.'[33]

As for its uses in the Law Courts, there is even a record of an old trial in the courts of Cumberland County, in which the lawyers tried to win over the Highland-descended jury by a display of their own mastery of and praise for the beauties and precisions of the Gaelic tongue:

> Mr. Banks, the State Solicitor, in conducting a case, finding all the jurymen were Highlanders, addressed them in Gaelic. The language was unintelligible to the Judge, but the jury were visibly delighted, and it appeared to be positive that the solicitor would win the case. It so happened that the defendant's attorney, Mr. Leach, was even a better Gaelic scholar, though no one present was aware of it. In order to conciliate the Judge, Mr Leach began his address in English, and then said as the State Solicitor had addressed the jury in Gaelic, he begged permission to use the same language.
>
> He then began by upbraiding Mr. Banks for his faulty Gaelic, and declared that if he should ever hear his own children speaking that ancient and noble language so execrably, he would take the tawse to them. He then took the case up carefully, made an eloquent speech in Gaelic, carried the jury with him, and secured the triumphant acquittal of the prisoner.[34]

In 1776, the North Carolina Provincial Congress had found it necessary to translate certain of its proclamations into Gaelic.[35]

It is difficult to say exactly when Gaelic finally waned in North Carolina. With regard to the churches, most had dropped Gaelic services by the 1870s or so, and all of them had dropped Gaelic before 1920. A.W. McLean states that the last Gaelic sermon was preached at Galatia Presbyterian Church (in Cumberland County) in 1860[36], and that the last

Gaelic sermon at Barbeque Presbyterian Church was preached by the rather controversial minister, John Campbell Sinclair (a native of the Isle of Tiree).[37] Sinclair left Barbeque in 1865 and died in Wheeling, West Virginia in 1878.

An original diary by John S. Murphy of the Kentyre section of (present) Dillon County gives us some information on the usage of Gaelic in the early 1870s in the Pee Dee area. J.S. Murphy lived from 1824 to 1896, and kept his diary from 1856 to 1898. His diary was bought from a descendant by Mary Carmichael Stephens (Mrs. Craig Stephens) of Dillon in 1990. An entry concerning old Pee Dee Academy (which once stood by the Pee Dee River near Stanton's Bridge, not far from present Kentyre Church) states: "Pee Dee Academy tore down and moved December 1870, preachin in it by Dunlop, Sunday 5th of March, a Scotch Speech[i.e., Gaelic], Saturday 4th 1871 by Dunlop" [*sic*]. In other words, the Gaelic

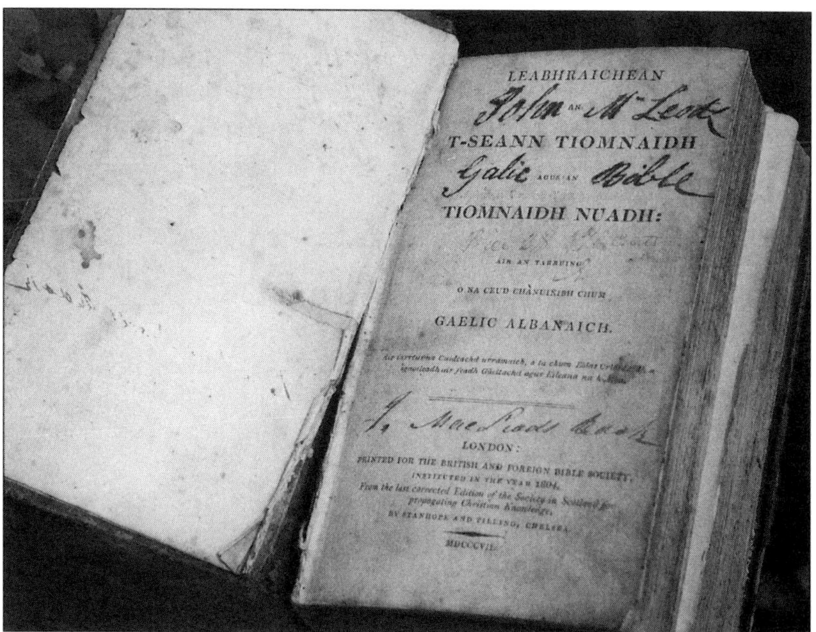

"Squire" John McLeod of Moore County, whose father emigrated from the Isle of Skye to Cumberland County, North Carolina in about 1777, purchased this Gaelic Bible sometime after 1807, when the family had been in America for over a generation. It must have been considered a real treasure since the Gaelic Old Testament was not even printed until 1801, even though the New Testament had been available since 1767. It is still in the McLeod family, and belongs to Cary L. McLeod of Eureka in Moore County.

address was given on Saturday and the English sermon on Sunday. Thus, bilingual services seem to have been typical as late as the 1870s in (present) Dillon County.

The Rev. James MacKenzie learned that occasional, though not regular, Gaelic services were held at Barbeque (and also at the black daughter church of Barbeque, the African Methodist Episcopal Church) until shortly after the beginning of the twentieth century. Thus we may say that while the old practice of two regular services on Sabbath, one in English and one in Gaelic, does seem to have stopped in the mid 1860s in the upper Cape Fear; nevertheless, Gaelic services did continue to be held occasionally in some of the churches until the early twentieth century. The Rev. James Stedman Black, who was pastor of Barbeque, Flat Branch and other local Presbyterian congregations in the early 1900s, still preached from time to time in Gaelic.

From family tradition and from what I have been able to learn from a number of other Carolina Scots families with whom I have discussed this question, it seems that Gaelic lasted as a fully spoken living language for about three generations in most families. In general, then, those families that came later naturally preserved their native tongue longer. Then for

Barbeque Church as it is today. It contains the remodeled building that was erected in 1896.

approximately two or three more generations (at least in some families such as the writer's own), many Gaelic phrases, proverbs and songs continued to be passed down, although the ability to converse fluently in it was definitely lost.

For instance, the writer's great-grandmother, Mary McCrummen Blue of Moore County spoke enough Gaelic phrases and proverbs to pass many of them down to her daughters. The last one of these daughters who knew any Gaelic was Ethel Blue Britt of Southern Pines, N.C., who died in 1975. Also John A. McLeod of the Eureka Community in Moore County, could sing some Gaelic songs, but did not remember what they meant. He died in his nineties in 1947. A.W. McLean stated in 1919 that "So far as can be ascertained there are at this time only two persons in this section who speak the Gaelic language, both belonging to the Longstreet congregation."[38]

A few members of the McFadyen family in Hoke County, where I ministered in the late 1960s, still remembered some Gaelic phrases (and they originally came from the Longstreet Congregation), and the Rev. James McKenzie in 1970 said the same was true about a handful of his members in Barbeque Presbyterian Church in Harnett County. Other than these, as far as I can tell, none of the Sandhills Scots families have preserved any significant knowledge of Gaelic past these dates (of 1947 and 1975), and most of them lost all of it long before.

The reason Gaelic was lost after approximately a century and a half of settlement is not hard to find. In fact, it is a wonder that it lasted as long as it did. Simply stated, the Gaelic-speaking parents obviously did not see the value in teaching (or having their children taught) Gaelic. What some older members of the McFadyen family told me in Raeford, N.C., in the late 1960's is the same as what Marshall McLeod wrote about his aunt, Beulah Geneva McLeod of Jackson Springs, N.C. (b. 1894, d. 1965). During her childhood in the very early twentieth century, "When the 'old folks' wanted to keep a secret from the children, they would converse in Gaelic."[39]

Undoubtedly there were, particularly in the earlier years, exceptions to this rule (of non-teaching of Gaelic in the home), such as the Currie family of upper Robeson and present Hoke Counties, N.C. The historian of this family, the Rev. W. A. McLeod, Jr., wrote in the 1930s that the widowed mother of Angus Currie, who emigrated with her son to North Carolina from the Isle of Colonsay in 1791, and lived for many years afterwards, taught her grandchildren (all of whom were born in North Carolina) to speak Gaelic.[40] One of these grandchildren, John C.

View of Longstreet Church from the cemetery surrounded by a rock wall or "dry dyke." The property is maintained by the U.S. Army.

Currie (b. 1803 in North Carolina, d. 1888 in N.C.) is remembered as having been a good Gaelic scholar. W.A. McLeod reports these memories of John C. Curries's son:

> His only living child in the year 1938, Angus D. Currie, Mount Vernon, Georgia, said he well remembered when his father would get down an old Gaelic hymnbook and sing long and earnestly—if not to English ears, musically! He would often repeat some Gaelic quotation and, after translating it for his family remark: 'That is the most beautiful language in the world.' His children were never able to appreciate his enthusiasm for the old language. In it, his mother and grandmother had sung him to sleep, but his children had no such sweet associations with it. To them, it had become a mere jargon.[41]

From my very limited knowledge of the curriculum of the various churches, community and "dame" schools of the Sandhills, several of them taught Greek and Latin in addition to English, but apparently not one of them taught Gaelic grammar as a subject. This seems to have been the case with Donaldson Academy in Fayetteville, Solemn Grove at the Head of Rockfish in Moore County and old Floral College in upper Robeson County,[42] as well as with Shoe Heel Academy near Mont Pelier in

Old Bethesda Church, site of Solemn Grove Academy, was founded at least by 1788 by Scots emigrants, near what is now Aberdeen in Moore County. This building was completed about 1860, just before the War Between the States. It is surrounded by a very large cemetery where many original emigrants are buried. The congregation left this building early in the 20th century, and now worships in Aberdeen. An annual homecoming has been held each September in the old building since the 1930s.

present Scotland County (then, Richmond County, N.C.).[43] It is certainly the case with the "dame school" run by the elderly maiden McCrummen sisters near what is now West End, North Carolina, in the last third of the nineteenth century. The McCrummens were fluent Gaelic speakers and writers, and yet only taught English and Latin to their nieces and nephews and other young scholars. Thus as the ability to read and write the language died, the ability to speak it also expired about two generations later.

In addition, the Scots of North Carolina did not have anyone like the Rev. McLean Sinclair in Nova Scotia, who diligently gathered what was being written in Gaelic in that colony so that it could be preserved and published. It was not that no native-born Carolinians could write Gaelic. Some of them wrote poetry as well as prose in Gaelic, like Archibald Blue McMillan, born in Moore County of Argyll emigrants in 1798, emigrated to Louisiana by 1830, and died in 1883.[44] This man's descendents in Texas possess several Gaelic poems which he wrote in the first third of the nineteenth century, but which were never published.

Had publication of Gaelic writing by local persons been encouraged as in Nova Scotia, the fortunes of Gaelic in Carolina might have been different, as they would have been if it had been taught in even a few of the dame or "Old Field" schools. The Gaelic printing press in Fayetteville generally seems to have published material from outside the region, although it did publish some local efforts such as the sermons of the Rev. Dugald Crawford.

Education

Having looked at the Carolina Scots economy, church and language, a word must be said about another extremely important institution in their culture: education. The respect of Scots, Highland and Lowland for education is proverbial. The emigrants saw to it that their children were well educated in terms of their generation. From the start there were dame schools in the homes of the Sandhills Scots, where not only the basics of reading, writing and arithmetic were imparted, but also history, Latin and Catechism. Some of the early ministers of the region either taught in or else encouraged and helped organize local schools.

By the end of the eighteenth and beginning of the nineteenth century, local leaders among the Scots of Carolina were organizing Academies. Malcolm Fowler has called the Highland emigrant, "Little" John Graham, the "Johnny Appleseed" of education in the Cape Fear Valley.[45]

This roving schoolmaster built schools in various parts of what was then upper Cumberland County.

He built the first school in what is now Harnett County, near Erwin; then some forty or so miles away he established a school on the Head of Rockfish (near present day Aberdeen, N.C.) in 1787. It is probable that it was this school that eventually turned into a well known academy, which prepared people for both University and Seminary (Theological College): Solemn Grove Academy, later staffed by some of the Gaelic-speaking pastors of nearby Bethesda Church. Solemn Grove was officially chartered by the Legislature of North Carolina in 1804.

Little John Graham later moved on to the Longstreet Church section on what is now the Fort Bragg Reservation in Cumberland County and opened a school. After that he moved to Gibson's Store on Lower Little River and founded yet another school. Other schools were founded in this area over the next generation, such as the one opened by Findlay Chisholm around 1825 near Cameron's Hill.

An important Academy for the Scots in early nineteenth century Fayetteville (and surrounding districts) was the Donaldson Academy. It prepared many for the University of North Carolina, Davidson College and elsewhere, as well as training those who did not go beyond it. Interesting letters have been preserved in the Alexander Kelly family near Carthage, N.C. from Angus Robertson Kelly I, who was a student at Donaldson in the early 1830s to his brother, Alexander Kelly. In the Academy's later years, one of its most famous teachers was Major Jesse R. McLean, mentioned by D.S. McAllister.[46]

To the Southeast of Fayetteville, another important and representative institution was set up by the education-minded Scots of Robeson County, Floral College for women. It was incorporated by Dr. Angus D. MacLean and John Gilchrist and flourished for many years in the early and mid-nineteenth century. Two of its well-known early teachers were Peter Shaw and his wife Rebecca Kelly Shaw, both natives of Moore County and of Highland emigrant families. There is considerable information about Floral College in Angus W. McLean's *Highland Scots in North Carolina.*

Less famous than Floral Academy, and shorter lived, was its older neighbor, Shoe Heel Academy, near Mont Pelier in what was then Richmond (now Scotland) County. It was taught by two Presbyterian ministers, the Reverends Lindsay and Matthew McNair. Neil Blue, who moved to Alabama in the 1830s discussed this school in his *Genealogy*

The Shaw House, which features two finely carved pine mantles, was built in 1839 by another member of the family, Charles C. Shaw, at the junction of two pre-Revolutionary roads running through Moore County: Pee Dee and Morganton. The later town of Southern Pines grew up around it, and the builder's son became mayor in 1887. The house was acquired by the Moore County Historical Society from descendants of the Shaw family in 1946.

of the Blue Family, and noted that it taught the classical languages as well as the standard English subjects.[47] Some well known public officials of North Carolina studied at Shoe Heel with Neil Blue in the first decade of the nineteenth century: William Graham, North Carolina State Treasurer and his brother, John Graham, father of Chancelor N.S. Graham. This Academy was superseded by Spring Hill Academy at a newly founded Baptist Church sometime after 1808.[48]

Significant as these Academies became in the nineteenth century, most of the work in the eighteenth century was done by parents, ministers and traveling school-masters such as Little John Graham and (for a few years) the well known citizen, Col. James McQueen, who taught school in the 1790s in Anson County before establishing his home near Maxton in Robeson County,[49] and by a host of others whose names have been long forgotten.

A typical parent-organized school is described by Dr. Daniel McGilvary in the 1830s in Moore County:

> Scottish folk always carry the school with the kirk. Free schools were unknown; but after the crops were 'laid by,' we always had a subscription school, in which my father, with his large family, had a leading interest. The teacher 'boarded around' with the pupils. Our regular night-task was three questions and answers in the Shorter Catechism—no small task for boys of ten or twelve years.[50]

The descendants of the Highland Scots went in large numbers to the University of North Carolina (opened in the 1790s), Davidson College (opened in the late 1830s) and other colleges and universities further away. The majority, of course, in a farm-based economy did not attend university or college before the twentieth century (though a large percentage did from the late eighteenth). The general literary and grammatical standard of the Highland Carolina communities, however, was a high one with much reading and discussion of politics, history and religion.

An illustration of this literary interest among the transplanted Scots is found in the earliest lending library of North Carolina, which was among these people. J. McN. Johnson of Aberdeen once described it:

> The first private circulating library owned and operated in North Carolina was instituted by Archibald Ray Black, Martin Black and Dr. Kenneth Black. Each member of the group would buy a book for exchange until a small library was soon accumulated. Archibald Ray Black, a graduate of the University of North Carolina was an educator during the period of the classical schools. He taught in Haywood, N.C. and was assisted by his sister, Kate Black, who was principal of the Female College as it was called. He also taught at Carthage. . . . Several books from the first circulating library are in the possession of Miss Bessie Black (now deceased)—and now her sister, Mrs. Angus Cromartie.[51]

The Arts and General Culture

Though there was always an interest in reading among the Sandhills Scots, they do not seem to have turned out a great deal of writing or, for that matter, musical compositions—at least not of a famous nature. We have already met the first poet of North Carolina John MacRae, who emigrated to what is now Moore County shortly before the Revolution. He was one of those Highlanders who chose the losing Tory side at Moore's Creek Battle in 1776, and sadly became embittered through that experience. Since all of the poems he wrote in Carolina were in Gaelic, ironically North Carolina's first poetry was produced in a language which it has now forgotten. After MacRae's death (date and place in Carolina unknown), his poems were taken back to his home in Kintail. They have been published in Canada[52] and some of them are discussed in Malcolm Fowler's last book.[53]

Other emigrants and their descendants wrote poetry in English (and a little in Gaelic, as we have seen with Archibald Blue McMillan), but presumably not of the quality of John MacRae's—at least not much of it seems to have been widely published. Many sermons (in both Gaelic and English) and a number of political or patriotic speeches have been preserved from fairly early years among these Scots, but there is not much of note as far as the wider literary world is concerned.

Certainly, however, these people were very expert at both orally memorizing long generations of family history and descent and also at writing it down. In this sense, there remains a wealth of historical culture among the Sandhill Scots, which along with numerous late eighteenth and early nineteenth century letters to family and friends (both in Gaelic and English), is a heritage still waiting to be collected and published.

As far as their musical culture is concerned, we have already discussed the prevalence of Highland Gaelic Psalmody among them until the later nineteenth century. But as far as what was sung in the English services, these communities would have been like the rest of the popular Evangelical South in the hymns and songs that they sang and played. We are not sure how long they continued to teach bagpiping. We do know that Malcolm McCrummen of upper Moore County and many others were pipers. For example, Malcolm Fowler discusses the life and piping of the blind piper, Archie Buie, who played in the Cape Fear Valley from the 1760s to his death in 1805.[54]

While I am not at all certain of this, I would hazard a guess that the great revivals of the early nineteenth century may have indirectly contributed to the ending of the piping tradition, in that piping was often connected to dancing, and dancing was frowned upon in the revival tradition. Archie Buie was not a churchman, though whether or not this was the tendency among pipers, I do not know. At any rate, in the later eighteenth century, dancing seems to have been fairly widely accepted in the upper Cape Fear Valley. Peter McLaughlin, ancestor of thousands of Carolina Scots (including the writer) was listed as a "dancing master" in Fayetteville at that time. But later, attitudes changed, and one assumes that the pipes tended to go the way of the dance.

In sum, while the culture of the Sandhills Scots could scarcely be compared with that of some parts of New England—for example, in the production of such things as books, music and painting—yet in its quiet, unobtrusive way, it tended to produce thoughtful, well-read men and women of solid character (and these people educated their women early on—as with Floral College). An interesting and probably fairly typical profile of what these emigrant descendants were like is given (albeit in a flowery, Victorian style) in a Memorial Volume for the famous Carolina educator of the late nineteenth century, Charles Duncan McIver. What is said of him is typical of thousands who have lived in the Sandhills from the eighteenth to twentieth centuries:

> The region around what is now the town of Sanford was peopled by settlers whose ancestors came from the Highlands of Scotland. Evander McIver, when eight years old, bade farewell to . . . (the) Isle of Skye, and with his father made his new home in the pleasant sandhills of North Carolina. In his son, Matthew Henry, the father of Charles D. McIver, were exemplified the many sterling traits that history shows to be characteristic of the Highland Scotch.
>
> Among these traits may be mentioned earnest piety, devotion to liberty, respect for law and order, and love for education. A successful farmer, a respected elder in the Presbyterian Church, a useful and influential citizen, he was an admirable type of that class upon which in greatest measure rests the stability of state and society. . . . Loyal and true, [were] these Scotch ancestors, decided in their convictions on questions of church and state, yet tolerant and charitable. . . . It is worth something to be born in a community of which such men are citizens.
>
> . . . Amid the thrifty and orderly influences of this Christian home and community, in attendance upon the excellent private schools of the neighborhood, and in the daily performance of all the various labors that fall to the healthy farmer. . . . Here were laid the foundations of that vigorous health . . . and here were implanted that love for man and nature, and that intelligent and sympathetic appreciation of the needs of our rural commonwealth. . . .[55]

It would of course be unrealistic to think all of these folk were of the standard of Duncan McIver or Daniel McGilvary. We have descriptions of some who led a very different mode of life, such as "Red" Neill McNeill and Archie Buie. There is no doubt that these men would have been representative of many others who leaned in a more libertarian direction.[56] One has only to read the Session Minutes of the Scots Churches such as Bethesda, Barbeque, Bensalem, Union, Philadelphus (near Red Springs, N.C.) to see the large numbers of cases who were disciplined for typical human failings such as public drunkenness, illegitimacy, cursing, fighting, etc. In general, however, there seems to have been relatively little stealing or murder among these people, and all told, it is likely that their educational standard was higher than anywhere else in rural Eastern North Carolina.

From earliest days they were heavily represented in the State Legislature and later can be found listed among the Governors and other leadership posts in education, government and church, almost certainly out of all proportion to their relative numbers. While there have never lacked scoundrels and sloths among them, the generality have tended to be usually quiet and self-effacing builders and achievers, most often in small ways but sometimes more significantly, as any study of their genealogy will demonstrate.

Carolina Scots and the American War for Independence

Before we go to the genealogy of the Highland Scots in the Cape Fear Valley, we must address one final historical subject, which was to have much influence on their genealogy and the direction of their culture in the future: their part in the American War for Independence.

It is not necessary to record the details of the events of the American Revolution as it engulfed the Highland emigrants of the Upper Cape Fear Valley. This story has been accurately and interestingly related by such different writers as Duane Meyer and Malcolm Fowler.[57] Here we will merely summarize the main points relating to the loyalty that the majority of the Cape Fear Scots showed toward Britain.

Generally speaking, the Scots who came with the early immigrations, tended to join the Whig or American side. This was particularly true of the Argyll Colony people at Barbeque Church, such as the Clarks. Yet the Smiths, who were also among the earliest settlers, further down on the Cape Fear, were Tories. Nonetheless, it is generally true to say that those Highlanders who came later, especially after the mid 1760s, sided with the British. Fowler pointed out that in what is now Harnett County, the Scots on the east side of the Cape Fear tended to be for the Revolution, and those on the west side against it.[58]

Several factors predisposed the majority of Sandhills Scots to resist the Revolution. The later arrivals had taken an oath of loyalty to the House of Hanover in order to be able to emigrate and take up land in Carolina and these Presbyterians did not take oaths slightly. All of the Highlanders, whether early or late-comers to the Cape Fear knew of the effective victory of the English in 1746. It was hard for them to imagine that it would not happen again. Many of them feared government reprisals either on themselves in Carolina or on their relatives still in Scotland if they joined an open rebellion. Furthermore, in this Upper Cape Fear area many who first declared for the Revolution were part of a rougher element of people, looked down upon by the Scots as something like lawless gypsies, "the Buckskins," alleged to be from a penal colony in Virginia. The law-abiding Scots were not keen to identify with such people! Finally, some of the later leadership of the tacksman class, such as the famous Flora MacDonald's husband, Allan, were still commissioned officers of the British Army, although not on active duty. It would have taken extremely strong incentives to have given up such a position.

Among those who did take the Tory side, many of the Scots were moderate—such as the family of Duncan Blue, near Lakeview in Moore County—and wanted to avoid controversy as much as possible without compromising what they felt to be their duty. Some however, such as

"A New and Accurate MAP of NORTH CAROLINA in North America" made in 1779 during the Revolution could have facilitated the movement of troops, especially those not native to the state.

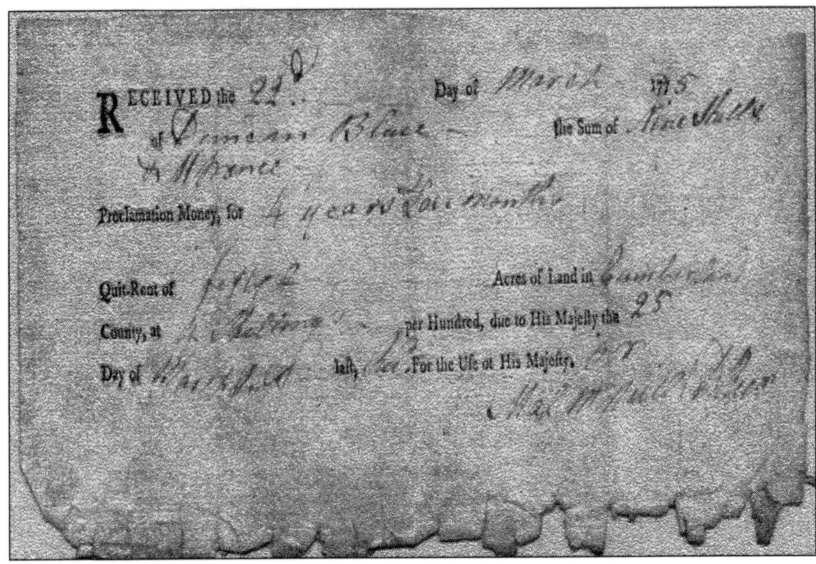

RECEIVED the [illegible] Day of March 1775
of Duncan Blue the Sum of [illegible]
Proclamation Money, for 4 years four months
Quit-Rent of [illegible] Acres of Land in Cumberland
County, at [illegible] per Hundred, due to His Majesty the 25
Day of March last, [illegible] For the Use of His Majesty.
[illegible]

A tax receipt registers taxes "due to His Majesty" in 1775 by Argyll emigrant to Cumberland County (now Moore County), Duncan Blue.

Alexander McKay, were fervently pro-British, feeling that the Tory cause was utterly right. After they lost, a large number of the latter, including Alexander McKay, emigrated to the Bahama Islands, and far more went to Nova Scotia. Indeed, some historians estimate that as many as half or more of the Sandhill Scots left for these parts after 1781.

There were two phases of the War in the Upper Cape Fear. The Highlanders were first recruited for the British cause by the last royal governor of the colony, the Scot, Josiah Martin. His strategy was to work through the tacksmen in order to assemble a fighting force, for since they had been the natural leaders of the people back home, they were still looked up to in the colony. Among those he enlisted were Allan MacDonald (Flora's husband), Bard John MacRae, Surgeon Murdoch MacLeod, Colonel Donald MacLeod, Captain Scalpay John Campbell and many other Highlanders, all under the command of General MacDonald.

It was hoped to use the North Carolina loyalist Scots to cut off the American troops in the Northern Colonies from those in the Southern Colonies. This effort decisively failed at the Battle of Moore's Creek when the American Patriots numbering about a thousand under Colonel James Moore, surprisingly and easily defeated the Scots Loyalists who numbered around 1,500. Because of this drastic defeat, the Sandhills Scots were not very active in the War for some time to come. " . . . the rank and file remained quietly at home for four long years until Cornwallis invaded North Carolina in the early days of 1781. Under pressure again to show their loyalty to King George, a goodly number of Highlanders took up arms again. Hence the fire, blood and terror in the Cape Fear Country in 1781."[59]

When they did go back into action, however, they were once again unsuccessful. About 600 Highland troops led by Archibald McDougald, Duncan Ray, Leather-Eye Hector McNeill and James Elrod (leading some of the troops of the Tory fighter, Fanning, from the Piedmont) were beaten in the waters of Big Raft Swamp near McPhaul's Mill by some 1,400 Patriots under General Rutherford. This event in 1781 effectively ended Highland Tory resistance to the Revolution.[60]

The period between these two phases of the Revolution was probably the most difficult and bloody in all the history of the Upper Cape Fear. The area was seriously divided internally, in some cases one plantation was Tory and the next was Whig. Thus the horrors of the worst kind of war—civil war—was experienced here for several long years. Atrocities were committed on both sides. For example, a Tory raid when they looted the area around Cross Creek, was followed by the Whig Massacre of Piney Bottom (on what is now the Fort Bragg Reservation) in which, in revenge for earlier Tory attacks on them in the area, they killed several innocent Tory citizens, including a boy, Alexander McLeod.[61] On another occasion, Old Kenneth Black who lived near the present Southern Pines in Moore County was murdered by the Whigs for having given shelter to Flora McDonald after her husband had been captured and imprisoned following the Battle of Moore's Creek.

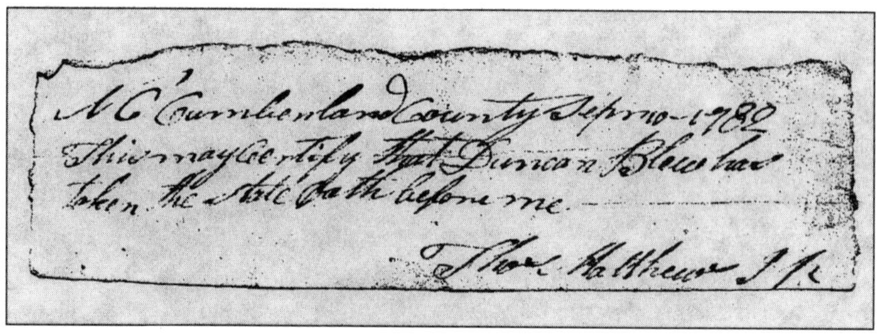

N C Cumberland County Sepr 10 – 178[illegible]
This may Certify that Duncan Blew has
taken the State Oath before me.

Thos Matthews J P

Duncan Blue swore this oath of loyalty to North Carolina, taken one year after the Americans won the War for Independence in 1782.

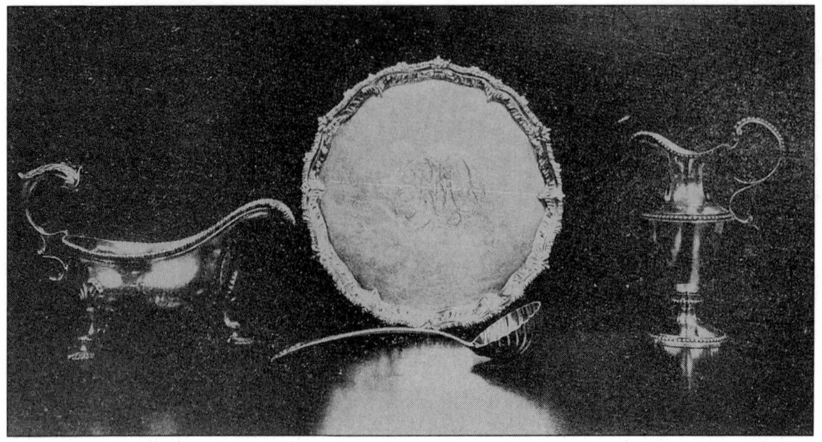

Some remnants of Flora MacDonald's silver which was on display at the Jamestown Exhibit in 1907, and is discussed in John A. Oates' *The Story of Fayetteville* (p. 64-B).

Thus both sides experienced many losses, until eventually the War ended in victory for the Patriot Americans. Then the question had to be faced as to how to treat those who had opposed the Revolution—which happened to include most of the population of the Upper Cape Fear. During the conflict the property taxes of those who were suspected (or known to be) disloyal to the American cause had been increased in Cumberland county, as a penalty for their loyalty to the Crown. Then in April of 1777, the Provincial Congress passed a law calling for the banishment of Loyalists who would not swear allegiance to the revolutionary government, and many Scots left at that time.[62] Even after the War was over, various other acts were passed in North Carolina, all generally tending to rather heavy punishment of the Tory leadership (such as confiscation of land or banishment.) The ordinary rank and file did not escape retribution altogether, but usually their punishment was lighter.

Fortunately for the Loyalist Highlanders of the Cape Fear, statesmen were not totally lacking among the victorious Whigs, who wished to help peaceable Tories. The Patriot, William Martin of upper Moore County, whose father, John, had been a leader among the Tories, was instrumental in seeing that legislation was passed in the North Carolina House to protect the rights of the defeated:

William Martin (b. c. 1768, d. Apr. 24, 1819) became a wealthy landowner in Moore County, and a lawyer. He served in the North Carolina House of Commons, 1788-1793. He was Clerk of Superior Court, 1808-1810. He was Moore County's representative to the First and Second (1788 and 1789) State Convention for ratification of the new U.S. Constitution. He did much to protect the loyalists who had remained after the war, and their civil liberties.[63]

In accordance with "The Acts of Oblivion and Forgiveness," former loyalists who would swear an oath of allegiance to the new State of North Carolina could retain their property and be considered citizens in good standing. A member of the Sinclair family has the original slip of paper on which Duncan Blue of Lakeview, N.C., emigrant from North Knapdale in 1769, and ancestor of thousands, took this oath in 1782 before Thomas Matthews, Justice of the Peace.[64]

While many Highlanders left the state (no one knows the exact percentage, but it may have been as many as half of them or more), those tens of thousands who remained joined with their former foes to rebuild their lives and the economy of the Cape Fear Valley. The families which they engendered intermarried with one another—and for generations Carolina Scots tended to marry other, neighboring Scots—and produced a numerous progeny. A hundred years later, some of these, because of their helpfulness in restoring the state government after another sad war and reconstruction period in the 1870s, became widely known as "the God-blessed Macs."

With this general picture in our minds of their daily activities and concerns, we are now ready to turn to the histories of a number of these families of the old emigrant Highlanders, whose lives have been intertwined with the history of North Carolina to this day.

Notes

1. Duane Meyer, *The Highland Scots of North Carolina 1732-1776* (Chapel Hill: The University of North Carolina Press, 1961), 68.
2. Hugh T. Lefler and William S. Powell, *Colonial North Carolina: A History* (Charles Scribners' Sons: New York, 1973), 1.
3. See Dial and Eliades, *The Only Land I Know.*
4. Lefler and Powell, op. cit., 32.
5. Ibid., 88.
6. Ibid., 89.
7. Malcolm Fowler, *Valley of the Scots* (Published by Wynona Fowler, 1986), [in

Raleigh, North Carolina], 20.

8. A.I.B. Stewart, art. cit., 7.

9. Angus W. McLean, *Highland Scots in North Carolina,* Vol. I (1919), 48 (quoting *North Carolina Colonial Records,* Vol. IV, 447).

10. Margaret I. Adam, "The Causes of the Highland Emigrations of 1783-1803," 75.

11. Angus W. McLean, op. cit., 84, 85.

12. Bion H. Butler, *Old Bethesda* (Grosset & Dunlap: New York, 1933), 160-162.

13. Malcolm Fowler, *They Passed This Way: A Personal Narrative of Harnett county History* (1955), 23.

14. Taken from Daniel McNeill Parker, *His Ancestry and A Memoir of His Life,* compiled by William F. Parker, printed by Wm. Briggs: Toronto, 1910, as reproduced in an article by Everette McNeill Kivette, "The Unusual Family Heritage of Julia and Esther McNeill of the Saint Pauls Review," in *Argyll Colony Plus,* Vol. 3, No. 4, Fall, 1988, 136, 137.

15. Fowler, op. cit., 22.

16. Angus W. McLean, op. cit., 680.

17. Lefler and Powell, op. cit., 184.

18. See Douglas F. Kelly, *Scottish Blue Family,* 232, 238.

19. Ibid., 142, 485.

20. Emma and Thomas Richardson, *History of Aberdeen* (The Malcolm Blue Historical Society: Aberdeen, N.C., 1976), 21, 166.

21. Douglas F. Kelly, op. cit., 187a.

22. An article by Lenora Thompson discussed this house in *Fayetteville Observer,* March 26, 1961, 1D-2D.

23. *Argyll Colony Plus,* Fall, 1988, Vol. 3, No. 4, 136.

24. Emma G. B. Richardson and Thomas C. Richardson, *History of Aberdeen* (The Malcolm Blue Historical Society: Aberdeen, N.C., 1976), 31.

25. Murdoch Ferguson and Descendants (n.a., n.d.), 10.

26. Among the papers of John Sam Blue of Eureka community in Moore County, and listed in Douglas F. Kelly, *Scottish Blue Family,* 30.

27. Roderick L. Carmichael, *The Scottish Highlander Carmichaels of the Carolinas* (privately published in 1935, republished by The R.L. Bryan Company: Columbia, S.C., 1978), 32.

28. *Argyll Colony Plus,* April and October 1986, Issues Nos. 1 and 2, 30a, 56; and Malcolm Fowler, Valley of the Scots, chapter 5.

29. James McKenzie, *Colorful Heritage.*

30. John K. Roberts, *History of Union Presbyterian Church* (Kelly Printing Co.: Carthage, N.C., 1910), 10.

31. *Historical Sketch of Antioch Presbyterian Church,* Red Springs, North Carolina 1833-1983, 5.

32. Daniel McGilvary, *A Half Century Among the Siamese and the Lao, An Autobiography* (New York: Fleming H. Revell Company), 12-14.

33. Lefler and Powell, op. cit., 93.

34. A.W. McLean, op. cit., 449.

35. J.P. MacLean, op. cit., 143.

36. A.W. McLean, op. cit., 96.

37. Ibid., 491.

38. Ibid., 445.

39. Kenneth A. McLeod, Jr., *Descendants of John MacLeod and Wife Nancy Campbell MacLeod* (The John Alexander McLeod Association: 1979, revised), 60.

40. W.A. McLeod, Jr., *The Curries and Their Kin* (unpublished, written in the 1930s in Cuero, Texas), 4.

41. Ibid., 21.

42. The curriculum of Solemn Grove Academy is briefly discussed in Isabel C. Patterson's *Builders of Freedom and Their Descendants,* 17.

43. Neil Blue, who was educated at Shoe Heel Academy before 1808, discussed briefly its curriculum (which, he said included English and the Classical languages, but makes no mention of Gaelic) in *Genealogy of the Blue Family,* embracing a *Sketch of Neil Blue,* Matthew P. Blue, ed. (privately printed at Montgomery, Alabama, 1886), 13.

44. Douglas F. Kelly, *Scottish Blue Family,* 851-855.

45. See Malcolm Fowler, *They Passed This Way,* chapter 13.

46. D.S. McAllister, *Genealogical Record of the Descendants of Col. Alexander McAllister of Cumberland County, N.C.,* Also of Mary and Isabella McAllister (Richmond, Va.: Whittet & Shepperson, 1900), 107.

47. Matthew P. Blue, ed., op. cit., 13.

48. Ibid.

49. Annabella Bunting MacElyea, *The MacQueens of Queensdale* (Charlotte, N.C., 1916), 16.

50. McGilvary, op. cit., 21.

51. James McNeill Johnson, *History of the Black Family of Moore County, N.C.,* 15.

52. Margaret MacDonell, *The Emigrant Experience: Songs of Highland Emigrants in North America.*

53. Malcolm Fowler, *Valley of the Scots,* chapter 9.

54. Ibid., chapter 10.

55. W.C. Smith, et al., *Charles Duncan McIver Memorial Volume* (Greensboro, N.C.: Jos. J. Stone & Company, 1906), 258-260.

56. Fowler, *Valley of the Scots,* chapter 10.

57. See Meyer, op. cit., chapter 7, and Fowler, *They Passed This Way,* chapter 5, and Valley of the Scots, chapter 7.

58. Fowler, *They Passed This Way,* 24.

59. Fowler, *Valley of the Scots,* 55.

60. Ibid., 70.

61. Rozella McLeod, *Neill McLeod Family of North Carolina* (1981), 12, 13.

62. Meyer, op. cit., 160.

63. From a typed, unpublished History of John Martin Black and Nancy Ray by Flora Ann Black Moran of Burlington, North Carolina, 2.

64. Douglas F. Kelly, *Scottish Blue Family,* 263. Meyer, op. cit.

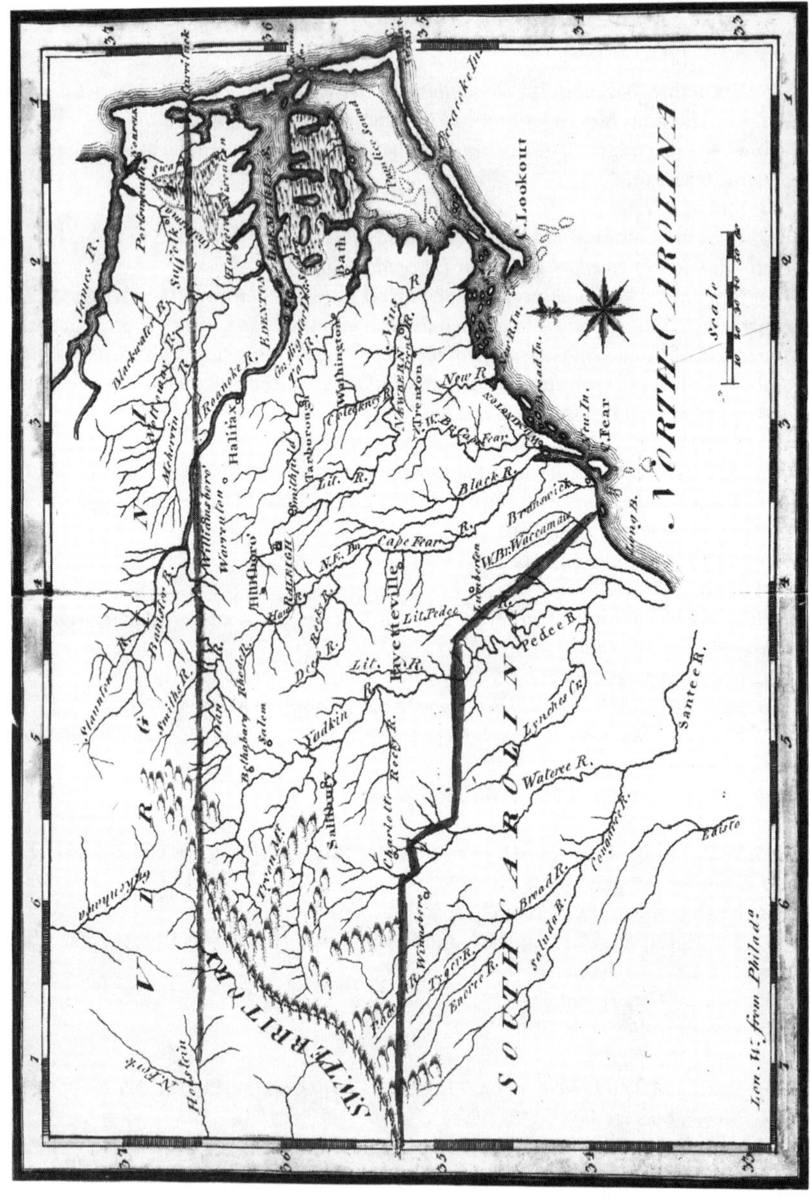

In this detailed and well-proportioned map of 1795 the focus is no longer on the coast. Physical features are accurately noted throughout the state and there are now numerous cities large enough to receive mention. Raleigh is firmly marked as the capital.

Appendix to Chapter 3

The Status of Gaelic in North Carolina, Historic and Contemporary

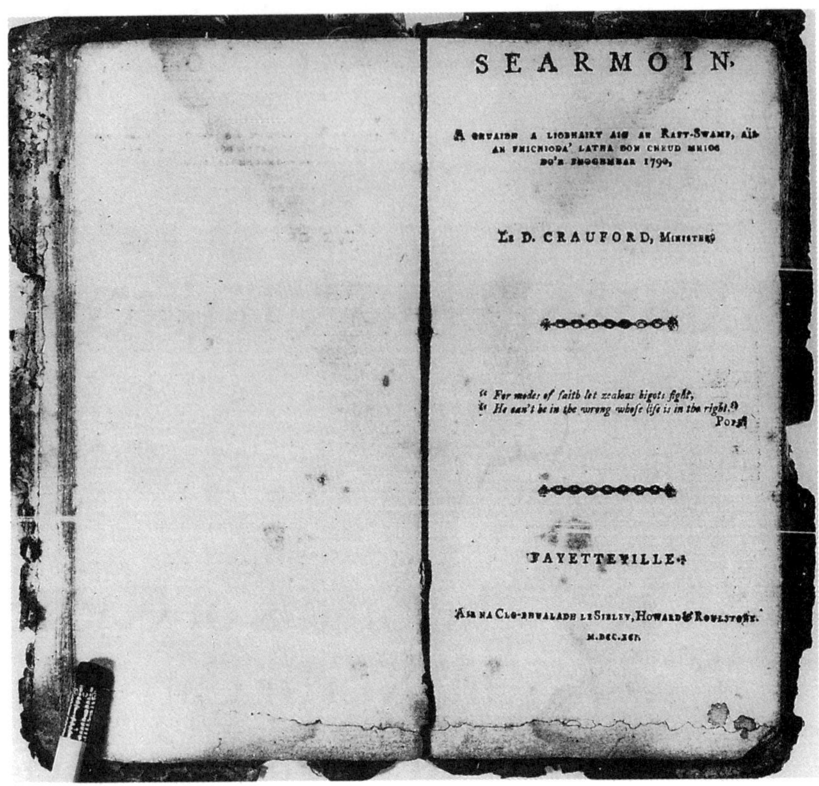

SEARMOIN,

A CRUAIDH A LIOBHAIRT AIG AN RAFT-SWAMP, AIR AN FHICHIODA' LATHA DON CHEUD MHIOS DO'N FHOGHMHAR 1790,

LE D. CRAUFORD, MINISTEIR

"*For modes of faith let zealous bigots fight,*
"*He can't be in the wrong whose life is in the right.*"
POPE

FAYETTEVILLE:

AIR NA CLO-BHUALADH LE SIBLEY, HOWARD & ROULSTONE.
M.DCC.XCI.

Title page of the Gaelic sermons of the Rev. Dugald Crawford. Preached in various Presbyterian Churches of the upper Cape Fear Valley, they were published at Fayetteville, North Carolina in 1791. Crawford was born in the Isle of Arran in 1752, educated at the University of Glasgow, licensed by the Presbytery of Dunoon in 1781, and came soon afterwards to minister to the Scots in North Carolina. He returned to Scotland, continued his ministry there, and died in 1821.

Two main articles are appended here (in the mother tongue); one on the early predominance of Gaelic in the Cape Fear Valley, and the second on the declining remnants of it.

I. The Historic Status of Gaelic in North Carolina

This article by the late Professor Urban T. Holmes, Jr., of the University of North Carolina at Chapel Hill appeared in 1953 in a small Celtic publication in Canada:

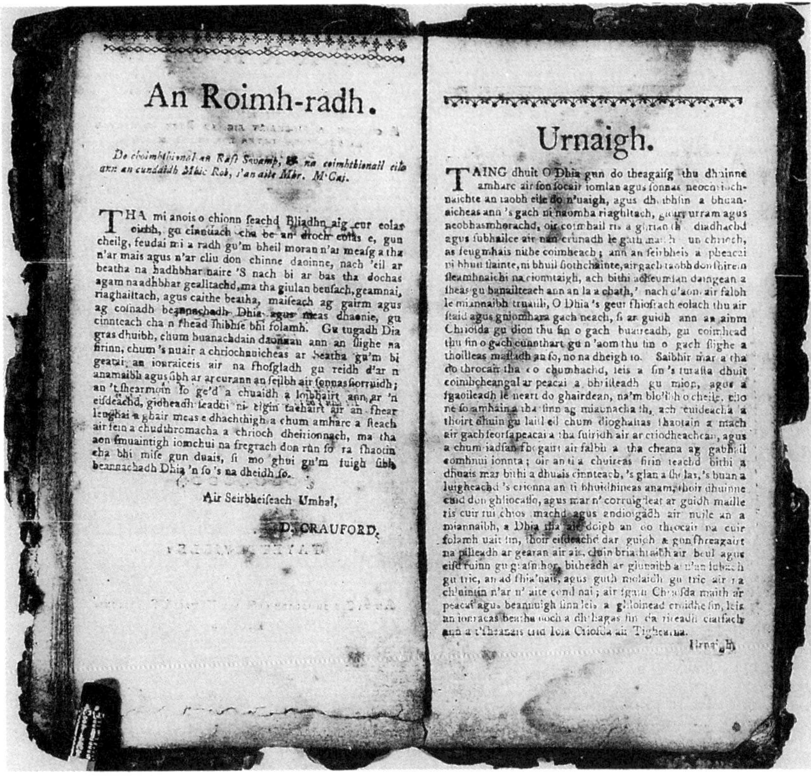

An Roimh-radh.

Do choimhthional an Raft Swamp, & na coimhthionail eile ann an cundaidh Mhic Rob, s'an aite Mhr. M'Cai.

THA mi anois o chionn seachd Bliadhn aig cur eolas oirbh, gu cinnuach cha be an droch eolas e, gun cheilg, feudai mi a radh gu'm bheil moran n'ar measg a tha n'ar mais agus n'ar cliu don chinne daoinne, nach 'eil ar beatha na hadhbhar naire 'S nach bi ar bas tha dochas agam na adhbhar gealltachd, ma tha giulan beusach, geamnai, riaghailtach, agus caithe beatha, maiseach ag gairm agus ag coinadh beannachadh Dhia agus meas dhaonie, gu cinnteach cha n fhead sibhse bhi folamh. Gu tugadh Dia gras dhuibh, chum buanachdain daonnan ann an slighe na firinn, chum 's nuair a chriochnuicheas ar beatha gu'm bi geatai an ionraiceis air na fhosgladh gu reidh d'ar n anamaibh agus sibh ar ar curann an seilbh air sonnas siorruidh; an 't shearmoin so ge'd a chuaidh a loibhairt ann ar 'n eisdeachd, gidheadh feadui ni eigin tachairt air an fhear leughai a ghair meas e dhachthigh a chum amharc a steach air fein a chudthromacha a chrioch dheirionnach, ma tha aon smuaintigh iomchui na fregrach don run so ra shaotin cha bhi mise gun duais, si mo ghui gu'm suigh sibh beannachadh Dhia 'n so 's na dheidh so.

Air Seirbheiseach Umhal,

D. CRAUFORD.

Urnaigh.

TAING dhuit O Dhia gun do theagaisg thu dhuinne amharc air son socair iomlan agus sonnas neochriochnaichte an taobh eile do n'uaigh, agus dhuibhsin a bhuanaicheas ann 's gach ni naomha riaghltach, gloir, urram agus neobhasmhorachd, oir coimhail ris a ghrian [illegible] diadhachd agus subhailce air nan crunadh le gath [illegible] un chrioch, as feugmhais nithe coimheach; ann an seirbheis a pheacai ni bhuil slainte, ni bhuil siothchainte, air gach taobh don shirein sleamhnaichi na ciomtaigh, ach bithi adheumlan daingean a sheas gu banailteach ann an la a chath, ' nach d'aon air falbh le miannaibh truaill, O Dhia 's geur fhiosrach eolach thu air staid agus gniomhara gach neach, si ar guidh ann an ainm Chriosda gu dion thu sinn o gach buaireadh, gu coimhead thu sinn o gach cunnthart gu n 'aom thu sinn o gach slighe a thoilleas masladh an so, no na dheigh so. Saibhir mar a tha do throcair tha do chumhachd, leis a sin 's turasta dhuit coimhcheangal ar peacai a bhrilleadh gu mion, agus a sgaoileadh le neart do ghairdean, na'm blo'idh o cheile, [illegible] ne so amhain a tha sinn ag miaunacha [illegible], ach cuideacha a thoirt dhuin gu laidh eil chum dioghaltas shaotain a mach air gach seorsa peacai a tha suiridh air ar criodheachean, agus a chum iadsan fhogairt air falbh a tha cheana ag gabhail comhnui ionnta; oir an ti a chuireas sinn teachd bithi a dhuais mar bithi a dhuais cinnteach, 's glan a [illegible], 's buan a luigheachd 's crionna an ti bhuidhineas anam, thoir dhuinne cuid don ghliocas so, agus mar n' corruig leat ar guidh maille ris cuir rui chios machd agus andiolgadh air nuile an a miannaibh, a Dhia tha [illegible] dcigh an do throcair na cuir folamh uait sin, thoir eisdeachd dar guidh a gun fhreagairt na pilleadh ar gearan air ais, cluin briathraibh air beul agus eisd ruinn gu grasmhor, bitheadh ar glunaibh a n'an lubadh gu tric, an ad fhia'nais, agus guth molaidh gu tric air na chluintin n'ar n' aite comhnai; air sgath Chriosda maith ar peacai agus beannuigh sinn leis a ghloinead croidhe sin, leis an ionracas beatha noch a dh' hagas sinn da rireadh ciatfach ann a t'fheasais tria Iosa Criosda air Tighearna.

Urnaigh.

On the left is the foreword (An Roimh-radh) to his Cape Fear Valley, N.C., Gaelic Sermons. On the right is an opening prayer (Urnaigh).

AN LUCHD-GAIDHLIG ANN AN CAROLINA-MU-THUATH

"Eadar 1715 agus 1775 thainig àireamh mhór de Gaidheil na h-Albann gu Carolina-mu-thuath. Thatar ag radh gu'n robh mu thimchioll na bliadhna 1775 corr agus fichead míle air cur an aghaidh air Inbhir-Cape Fear: firionnaich 's boirionnaich 's leanabain. Thubhairt an *Gentleman's Magazine* de'n Òg-mhios, 1775, gu'n robh ceithir luing móra ann a' dol a dh'fhagail Glaschu agus Grianaig, agus móran cuideachd de'n luchd-Gaidhlig (seachd ciad anam) air bord ag a shireach an dùthaich America, a dh-aindeoin gach cnap-starra a dh'faodadh a bhi anns an t-slíghe. Sin, ma tha, tòiseach Cogaidh na Ceannairce! Cheana an 1771 bha air seòladh a mach cóig ciad fear-imrich, agus an 1770 bha míle agus da chiad fear diubh ann. Chaidh iad bho taobh an iar, bho'n tuath, bho na h-Innse Gall, bho measg na Gaidhealtachd, ach troimh nan trí fichead bliadhna bha cuid na's mó de na daoine a'tighinn bho Earra-Ghaidheal, agus Ile airson dol air bord.

"An uair a ruigeadh na luing móra air taobh nall a' Chuain-Siar b'eudar dhaibh a thionndadh deasail, seachad Cape Hatteras, thun Smith Island, agus 's an àite sin a chur mu'n cuairt a dh'ionnsuigh a' chladach leathan na Cape Fear. B' urrainn dhaibh a shiubhal troimh braighe na h-aibhne ciad gu leth míle gus an eudomhain an t-sruth far an do chuir MacLaurin air chois Baile nan Caimbeul no Campbeltown anns a' bhliadhna 1730. Gu luath an déidh sin thogadh suas air laimh baile eile ris an do chanadh Cross Creek air ainneachadh, ach an déidh na Ceannairce thugadh 'Fayetteville' mar ainm air a' bhaile so. Tha cunntas na seann eachdraidhe a' foillseachadh gu'n robh míle tigh gu leth ann an Fayetteville roimh 1775. Bha a' Ghaidhlig air gach fear diubh 's na cnocan gainmheineach an Cumberland County, an Richmond, an Robeson, agus uaithe sin tar a' chrioch a stigh Carolina-dheasail. An 1756 bha Hugh MacAden a' deanamh searmoin an t-soisgeil ann an Cross Creek agus dh'fhaigh esan na fir-éisdeachd gun eòlas air Beurla Shasuinn. Bha eadhon na tràillean dubha 'nam fior Gaidheil gu am brogan agus bha spiorad na Gaidhealtachd air an teangannan. Ochon a righ, thig crìoch air gach ni, co dhiu 's math no dona e, agus mar sin thainig crìoch na cainnte ann an Carolina. Bha ath-neartachadh ann a chaidh bho Charolina-deasail an 1797, ach bha an t-àiteachas ùr cus lag. Faodar a thugsinn gu'n robh anns an naoitheamh linn deug a' Ghaidhlig a' gabhail bàis. An 1868 thainig David McRae gu America airson leabhar a sgriobhadh. Bha e a' fantainn ann an Fayetteville far an robh e a' fiorsrachadh air Cor nan Gaidheal an déidh a' Chogaidh. Mholainn dhuibh leughadh an leabhair aig am bheil an t-ainm *Americans at Home.* Anns an eaglais Galatia (Harnett County) [acutally, Cumberland County -ed.] bha a' searmon-achadh an comhnuidh an Gaidhlig an t-Urramach Colin McIver, agus 'na dhéidh lean Mhgr. J. Sinclair. Bha an t-Urramach Evander McNair cuideachd a' deanamh shearmonan 's an eaglais Cypress. Chithear clò-bhualadh cóig leabhraichan Mhaois an Gaidhlig anns a' Charolina Room de'n Oilthigh North Carolina, agus aig ceann an leabhair sgriobhar an t'ainm Colin McIver, agus ri taobh tha na litreachan J. S. comhla ris an t-àm, ainmichte mar June 30, 1852. Tha sin làn seadh. Sin a d'fhuaradh air a' chlàr-ainme a' Bhiobaill so fo an tiodal:

Clodh Bhuailte 'an Dun-Eidin Le Uilliam Smellie; Air iarrtas na Cuideachd urramaich, a ta cum eolas Criosdaidh a sgaoileadh air feadh Gaeltachd agus eileana na h-Alba.

"Tha a' fuireach ann an Fayetteville fear-lagha gasda còir, Mhgr. John Oates, a tha glé churamach air na cùisean so. Tha esan air sgriobhadh na h-eachdraidhe na's fhearr air na Gaidheil an Carolina. Tha e a' toirt dhuinn cunntais air piobaire àraid leis an ainm Urquhard aig am b'àithne dhà 'nuair a bha Mhgr. Oates 'na bhalachan. Bha am bodach a' seachranadh 'na aonar troimh Cumberland County agus ag labhairt na Ghaidhlig. Anns a' bhliadhna 1921 chaochail am fear deireannach aig an robh a' chainnt. B'e so J. Hector Smith a bha a' comhnuidh an Moore County, faisg aig Southern Pines. An diugh tha a' Ghaidhealtachd air dol as ar sealladh ann an Carolina-mu-thuath. Chan 'eil 's an dùthaich uachdarach na aibhne Cape Fear ach na ainmean de dhà fhicheadh clann 's a cóig, mur 'eil seinn ciùil na h-Albann am Beurla no dannsa. Tha mi fhéin a' smaoineachadh gu'm bheil leithid de thaladh anns na h-òranan 'gus nach faodar an diochuimhneachadh. Bha an luchd Fayetteville an 1939 a' cumail féille airson tighinn nan Gaidheal a chuimhneachadh. Bha Mhgr. Oates 'na fhear cathrach agus bha an 'Highland Call,' sgriobhte le Paul Green, air a chur air an ionad-cluiche ann an Fayetteville ré cheud-mhios a' gheamhraidh. Tha mise glé phròiseil airson mo mhnàtighe a' coimhlionadh na pearsa Flora Nic Domhnuill. Bha ath-dheanamh a' chluich 's an t-samhradh de 1940 agus a nis tha mi dìreach a' cluinntinn gu'm bheil miann le Mhgr. Oates air cur suas a' chluich cheudna an 1954. Air do Paul Green sgriobhadh a' chluich thoir esan a stigh móran òran agus dannsan a tha uile glé fhreagarrach. Bha grunnan nan caileag bho colaisd Flora McDonald an Red Springs (N. C.) aig an robh tlachd de nithean Gàidhealach a' dannsadh aig an fhéill. Bha gu leòir 'nam measg de Ghaileil agus Ghoill air cur suas an fhéile-bhig. Mo thruaighe, cha'n robh ann ach aon chùis a bha 'na ghann - cha robh Ghaidhlig a' togail a cinn. Tha sinne 'n dòchas nach bi fada gus am faicear sealladh air leughad agus air sgriobhadh am Fayetteville na cainnte a tha cho sean ri linn Oisein."

II. The Declining Remnants of Gaelic in Contemporary North Carolina

This article appeared in the weekly Gaelic column of Mr. Ronnie Black of the Celtic Department, Edinburgh University, in *The Scotsman* on Saturday, February 13, 1988. It consisted of an interview of Douglas Kelly of North Carolina by Mr. Black on the subject of how much Gaelic still remains in the Cape Fear Valley today. It was translated into English and appeared in *Argyll Colony Plus* in 1989 (Vol. 4, No. 3).

NA GAIDHEIL A CHAIDH AN DIOCHUIMHN?

Chan eil fhios aig móran gu bheil a' Ghàidhlig beò an Carolina, gėd 'sann air éiginn. Sheinn Seumas MacDhòmhnaill á Carolina (fear a mhuinntir an Eilean Sgitheanaich) aig mòd Shruighlea an-uiridh, 's tha e nis an Dun Éideann a' cur faobhar air a chuid Ghàidhlig 'san Oilthigh. Leanadh e anns a' bhliadhna ùir le sgoilear is diadhaire suaicheanta, an t-Ollamh Dubhghlas Ceallach á Oilthigh Mississippi.

'Sann bho Ethel Nic Ille Ghuirm (1896 - 1975), piuthar a sheanmhar air taobh athar, a fhuair Dubhghlas a chuid Ghàidhlig. Cha robh a bheag dhith idir aig athair fhéin, ach 'na òige chuirte Dubhghlas a h-uile samhradh bho an dachaigh an Wilmington [actually, Lumberton, ed.] gu an luchd-dàimh Guirmeach aig an robh planndachadh cotain is tombaca an Siorrachd Moore, a bha Gaidhealach gu cùl a-nuas gu àm an Dàrna Cogaidh Mhóir.

Bha eachdraidh na Gàidhlig an Gleann Cheap Fìr coltach ri eachdraidh na cànain an gleann sam bith air Gaidhealtachd na h-Alba. Bhiodh seirbhis Ghàidhlig a h-uile feasgar Sàbaid gu 1880 no mar sin. Thogadh a' chlann i aig glùn am mathar gu mu 1900. Co-dhiùbh bha i riamh air a teagasg 'sna sgoiltean, chan fhios do Dhubhghlas. Eadar mu 1930 is 1960 cha robh searmonachadh 'sa chànain idir ann. Ach an uairsin thàinig tomhas de dh'athbheothachadh. Phòsadh ministear le Gàidhlig á Ceap Breatainn, Seumas MacCoinnich, ri coithional Barbecue (anns an robh Fionnghal a' Phrionnsa uaireigin) agus a-nis tha seirbhis Ghàidhlig uair 'sa bhliadhna aig cléir Fayetteville.

Dh'fhaighnich mi do Dhubhghlas am b'urrainn dha an darìreabh làmh a chur an cridhe 's innse dhomh gu bheil a Ghàidhlig beò an Carolina. "Tha an dùthchas aig grunnan sheann daoine fhathast. Cha chanainn gu bheil i marbh." Agus 's cinnteach gun tuig esan a' chànain glé mhath, ged tha e car meirgeach 'ga bruidhinn an-dràsda. Nuair dh'iarr mi air beagan de Ghàidhlig piuthar a sheanmhar innse dhomh, chuimhnich e air "Bi sàmhach!" agus "Meal is caith e!" agus "Deoch an dorais" agus an t-òran "Dean cadalan sàmhach" - agus rudan mar "seasam" an àite "seasamh", mar tha aig cuid a mhuinntir taobh deas Earra-ghaidheal cho fad 's as fiosrach dhomh.

'Sann an 1769 a chuir a shinnsrean, Dòmhnall Mac Ille Ghuirm agus a bean Maighread, cùl ri eilean Dhiùra 's Cnapadal mu thuath. Fhuair iad tabhartas fearainn bho'n Rìgh Deorsa III. Thàinig Fionnghal a' Phrionnsa uaireigin a thadhal orra. Tha an t-aon fhearann aig na Guirmich an-diugh, agus fhuair Dubhghlas fhéin agus a bhean Shasannach, Caroline, pàirt dheth mar thiodhlac posaidh.

Ach ma bha cainnt àraidh sam bith a fhuair buaidh an Gleann Cheap Fir, b'e siud a' Ghàidhlig Sgitheanach. 'Se Sgitheanaich a bh' anns na Ceallaich fhéin. Rugadh Dòmhnall Mór Ceallach an Sléibhte an 1725, phòs e Ceit Pheutan nuair nach robh i ach 14 's bha teaghlach aca. Chaochail Ceit 's thiodhlaiceadh i an Sléibhte. Nuair chuir Dòmhnall Mór agaidh air Carolina an 1803 bha e 78; thug e leis ochdnar de theaghlach, seachdnar dhuibh le céile pòsda, agus dh'fhàg e aon mhac pòsda aig an taigh. 'Se bhuil a bh'ann gun do dh'fhàg e sliochd 'san dà dhùthaich nach do chaill aithne riamh air cach-a-chéile.

Mar leughas sibh seo bidh Dubhghlas 'san Eilean a' tadhal aon uair eile air a dhlùth luchd-dàimh, Clann a' Phearsain Taigh-Òsda Dhùn Ruingeil an Caol Acainn, Criosaidh Cheallach an Druim Feàrna, agus Lachlainn MacFhionghain's a phuithar Peigi an Heasta. Còmhla ris bidh Gaidheal eile a mhuinntir Charolina, Carey MacLeòid, aig am bheil iomadh sgeul math r'a innse, oir chunnaic a sheanair an Cogadh Sìobhalta, agus a shìnseanair Àramach Aimeireaga.

Chan eil na deagh sgeòil a dhith air Dubhghlas fhéin. "Bha barrachd thràillean aig na Ceallaich na aig duine sam bith eile an Siorrachd Moore. Luchd-togail a' chotain. Chaill sin trì cheud dhuibh an déidh a' Chogaidh Shìobhalta. Bha Gàidhlig aca. Nuair fhuair iad an saorsa chuir iad suas eaglais Methodist dhaibh fhéin le aodhaire dubh. Ach dh'iarr iad air ministear geal tighinn a shearmonachadh dhaibh 'sa Ghaidhlig uair 'sa mhìos is lean fad iomadh bliadhna.

Tha Dubhghlas fhéin 'na mhinistear an Eaglais Chléireach Aimeireaga. Tha cóignear chloinne aca, 's iad a' giùlan a shloinntireachd 'nan ainmean: Dubhghlas Floyd (13), Martha NicCruimein Fhriseal (11), Aonghas Robasdan (9), Dòmhnall (7) agus Pàdraig Guirmeach Mac a' Mhaoilein Caimbeul (5). Tha an dithist as òige a' frithealadh bunsgoil Chaitligeach feadh nan sia miosan aca an Dun Eideann, ged 'sann aig seirbhisean na h-Eaglais Shaoir a gheibhear an teaghlach air an t-Sàbaid. Tha Dubhghlas ag obair air mìneachaidhean Laidinn Chalvin is Nocs air an t-Seann Tiomnadh 's air ceistean lagha mu bhuntanas eaglais is stàite. Bidh e an Steòrnabhagh 'sa Chéitein a' gabhail pàirt an deasbadan diadhaidh "Seachdain Taigh Rutherford."

'Sann eadar 1740 agus 1810 a bha na h-eilthirich Ghaidhealach a' deanamh air Carolina. " 'Se luchd-tac a bh' ann an cuid dhiubh, 's bha iad gu math dheth. Bha mo shìn-seanmhair, Màiri Nic Cruimein, naoi bliadhna dh'aois nuair thàinig saighdearan tuathach Sherman an rathad a losgadh Atlanta an 1865. Bha seirbhis-dhìnnearach ghràbhalta airgid aig na Cruimeinich a thug iad leotha ás an Eilean. Na fhuair na saighdearan 'san taigh dhith, ghabh iad dha le làmhaighean 's shad iad dha'n teine e. Bha cuid air a leigeil leis an tobar air sreing, ach bha iad eòlach air a chleas sin 's fhuair iad e. Ach bha trì pìosan a bha Màiri bheag air an tiodhlacadh. Fhuair mise iad sin an t-Samhain sa chaidh nuair shiubhail piuthar m' athar. Dà ladar airgid agus gobhal, 's *McCrummen* gràbhalta orra air fad."

III. A Gaelic Blessing Brought from Scotland to Carolina

Mr. Ronald Black of the Department of Celtic, University of Edinburgh, gave me a copy of an emigrant blessing (or amulet), which was worn by Dugald McFarland from the Highlands of Scotland to North Carolina around the year 1750. The custom of obtaining a verbal (and written) blessing or protective charm, often folded and sewn inside of one's clothing appears to have been followed by some Highlanders who were going into dangerous situations, such as emigration and war. Although this custom is obviously pre-Reformational (for it involves the invocation of saints such as Columba or the Archangel Michael), and has remnants of paganism (mentioning "fairy paths"), it is said to have endured even in some Protestant parts of the Hebridean Islands at least until World War I.

From the rather difficult original manuscript (which is not clear enough to photocopy in this book), Ronald Black has offered the following:

A. *Tentative transliteration*

1. In the name of the Father, Son and Holy Ghost.
2. Na Naodha. Ùba seo air a h-uile mìr
3. a thubhairt Calum Cille, is rinn e
4. naodha dubh-mhìorbhala móra a
5. chuir brìgh anns na facail seo air
6. an t-saoghal bheag agus air an t-saoghál mhór 's
7. air a' Chruinne Ché: 's nach bogaich
8. naodha beanna is ar naodha
9. gleanna naocha conaire seanga
10. sìthe th' aig sìth, a-null
11. ud thall, gu' n tog Crìosd dhiotsa, I. D. [Iesu Domine]
12. gach olc 's gach tinneas 's gach
13. farmad, is bu leat Dia 's Calum Cille.

B. *Tentative translation*

1. In the name of the Father, Son and Holy Ghost.
2. "The Nines." This is a charm for every part
3. that Calum Cille [Saint Columba] uttered, and he performed
4. nine great arcane miracles that
5. put substance in these words on
6. the little world and on the big world and
7. on the Universe: and won't
8. nine mountains and our nine
9. glens shift nine slender fairy paths
10. that are at peace, to over
11. yonder, until Christ lifts off you, I. D. [Iesu Domine - i.e. O Lord Jesus]
12. every evil and every sickness and every
13. jealousy, and may God and Calum Cille be with you.

One wonders how many of our emigrant ancestors may have worn some similar charm to give them comfort as they left home for the distant and unknown wilderness of North Carolina. Such a practice does not seem compatible with traditional Calvinism. However, some historians of Highland religion indicate that the tenets of Reformational preaching and teaching were rather late in penetrating at a deep level many parts of the Highlands and Islands. In some cases it was not until the evangelical revivals between the 1740s and 1859 that the rank and file of the population, especially in remote areas, really understood the basic teachings of Scottish Calvinism.

Part Two: Genealogy of Representative Carolina Scots Families

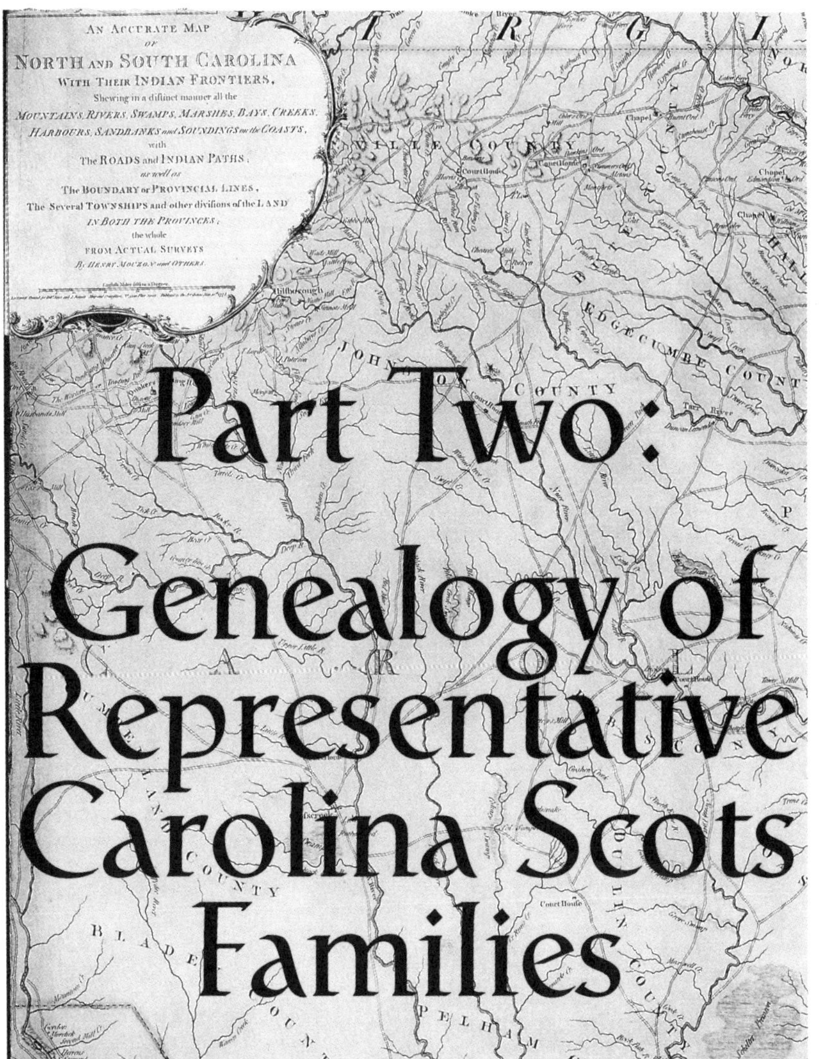

4

Some 1739 Argyll Colony Families & Other Early Settlers in Mid-Cumberland & Harnett Counties

THREE HUNDRED AND FIFTY MEN, women and children came on the first wave of the Argyll Colony 250 years ago and it is possible, though not yet established, that another significant number joined them as soon as 1740. Over the next century, a torrent of Scots flooded the area, so that today there are more people of Highland descent in the Carolinas than remain in the Highlands of Scotland herself. In fact, given the vast numbers who came, it would take thousands of pages in a multi-volume series to begin to cover them!

Carolina Genealogical Tradition, its Scope and Limits

Thus first, let me state that not all of the Highlander families who remained in Carolina are included in this genealogical section. For one thing, not only were the numbers so vast, but among some families, considerable information has been lost over the generations owing to wars, fires, moves or lack of interest. What I have done here is to concentrate on those families either known to me one way or another, or in many cases, not personally known, but who had genealogical information readily available.

Undoubtedly many, many important families are not included, and that is simply because of the author's problem in not having the historical material available at this time. I wish to make it very clear that there has been absolutely no "hidden agenda" of choosing families which somehow may be deemed to be of more significance (or for that matter, of less significance) than any others. People are listed in this genealogy who were rich, poor, and somewhere in the middle (as is the case with the majority). Some were highly educated, some were not; a few were famous, most were not. I have done my best to be fair, careful and impartial in presenting this information, and trust that it will be charitably received as such.

Secondly, if sufficient interest should be shown in this volume, perhaps there could be another edition at a later time. If that be the case, then the author will be delighted to include any and all other families who can present their historical material. At best, this book is only a first stage. Whether it goes beyond it will depend on the response of the public, and perhaps most of all on the present day Scots of Carolina.

Methodology

Thirdly, let me mention the method I have followed in presenting these representative genealogical notices. It of course would be impossible to attempt to trace *all* the descendants of the original settlers in a book such as this. What I have tried to do is to list the first two or three (or possibly four, in some cases) generations, and give references which will help the genealogical researcher find more information (insofar as such resources are known to me). Thus I hope the book will be helpful to many people in this regard, if in no other.

Fourthly, a concern for strict historical integrity requires me to underline the point that much of the genealogical section of this volume is presented in the form of folk history. That is, I have not attempted to document, from state, church or Bible records, every name, date and relationship in these chapters, which would of course need to be done in order to put this material in the class of an officially accredited genealogical record. Therefore, I cannot and do not claim to have provided acceptable documentary proof for every fact in the genealogical section. A fair question must immediately be raised: what then is the value of this mass of genealogical material? The answer is simple: the validity of what I repeat here depends directly on the validity of the sources from which I have compiled my information. I have tried to document with the greatest care exactly where my information comes from, so that those who wish to research a particular family will know where to go in order to assess the material I have used, as well as to get ideas for other potential sources. But how would I assess the genealogical material from which I have drawn these chapters?

I have been working with this sort of material for over twenty five years, and it is my opinion that most of what I have used is well grounded historically and genealogically, although I do not doubt that there will inevitably be mistakes here and there. Certainly, I have not included any single fact which I knew to be wrong, and matters which I knew to be questionable are appropriately marked. Sources such as Purcell's *Lumber River Scots,* Admiral Patterson's *Highland Scots Pattersons of North Carolina,* Kenneth Kelly's *McIver Family of North Carolina,* General Carmichael's *The Scottish Highlander Carmichaels of the Carolinas,* Rozella McLeod's *McLeods of Tuckahoe & Horses Creek,* and many other similar volumes are either well documented themselves, or have been generally confirmed in their accuracy by those who have used them over the decades. Probably the least accurate as to detail is the history of the Moore County Camerons (and I have been able to correct much of it by cross reference to McLeods, McIvers, Blues and others), but even it is generally reliable in giving us a useful outline and structure for the main heads of the Cameron families over several generations.

We must remember that in the Cape Fear Valley we are dealing with people of Highland background, who were part of a centuries' long oral culture. That is to say, vast amounts of Highland Gaelic poetry, stories, music, and particularly history and genealogy had been traditionally committed to memory and passed down orally from generation to generation, not unlike the remarkable oral tradition of Confucian China. In my viewpoint, material that comes from an oral rather than from a written tradition is much less reliable and frequently wrong, but not totally unworthy of consideration. Obviously, the oral tradition is much more open to exaggeration and historical abuse than is the written, and therefore it must be treated with much greater reserve. Above all, integrity requires that an oral fact must be stated to be such so that written documentation is never claimed for it, unless of course further research does confirm it.

In sum, I feel that great care and reserve, but not total scepticism is called for when dealing with Highland and Carolina Scots oral-based genealogies. Families who have lived on the same land for generations—at least in the pre-television age—generally could be relied upon to know a fair amount about their ancestry and connections. A good illustration of this would be the *Genealogical Record of the Descendants of Col. Alexander McAllister* by Rev. D.S. McAllister, who got much of his information from an elderly aunt.

It is obvious that further research in Cumberland County records would be necessary to establish each name, date and relationship alleged by McAllister, but my point is that it would be a great loss not to present such genealogies to a wider public. Otherwise, many valuable clues for the family history researcher would be unavailable, and much of our valued cultural tradition—even though it must properly be termed "folk history"—would be lost. I think there is no problem with presenting such material *as long as the nature of the material is made clear.* The serious genealogical researcher will then be able to make use of much of it, as he or she does further research in written sources. This material could be one step along the way in establishing an accredited family history based on generally acceptable genealogical procedures.

Possibly the most important part of the book for the genealogical researcher will be the index. If names and sections seem confusing in these genealogical chapters, the index should help you locate those in whom you are interested, presuming they are included. Even if they are not, material on related families may well help you know where to look next. That has certainly been the intention of the author in this work which of necessity must be all too limited.

Format

I have formatted these genealogies in a straightforward, common sense way so that the three or four generations covered would be clearly and easily discernible. I have basically followed J.E. Purcell's approach in his *Lumber River Scots* (which he seems to have taken from W.A. McLeod's *History of the Currie Family*) of putting the first generation of descendants from the emigrant parents in capital letters after a Roman numeral, the next generation in lower case letters following the letters of the alphabet, and the next generation in lower case following the normal Arabic numerals.

One of the greatest values of this approach is that every one of the literally hundreds of different family groups has been formatted alike, so that with relative ease one can survey the various Carolina Scots generations up and down the Cape Fear and Pee Dee Valleys in a uniform manner. The material from which these generations were compiled presented them in a multitude of different ways, so that listing them all here in the same format prevents considerable frustration and loss of time, if not confusion, for the reader.

Order

The order in which I list the families is largely determined by the geographical locality in which they settled (or at least in which they have lived for most of their time in the state). But instead of starting downriver, let us say in the Brown Marsh section and in lower Bladen County, I have chosen to begin in the middle, that is, in mid-Cumberland County, where most of the Argyll Colony first settled in 1739/40, since this volume was written in commemoration of their 250th anniversary of settlement.

We will first cover much of central and upper Cumberland County (and what is now Harnett), then go up and over to Moore County, and back downstream to the eastern section of Cumberland (and present Hoke), Robeson, Scotland, and Richmond Counties, and then further down to lower Bladen, and finally across the state line to the Pee Dee section of South Carolina, significant sections of which, are culturally an extension of the Cape Fear Valley. A few will be mentioned in surrounding territories, and in quite a few cases there will be frequent overlapping between counties and sections. While there will be exceptions, this is still the general rule of order.

The Argyll Colony 1739

We will begin, as we have stated, with a list of passengers travelling in the Argyll Colony. Of the numbers who landed in late September, 1739, these are the fifty-two names which are considered verified.

1. Thomas Armstrong
2. Alexander Clark
3. John Clark
4. Archibald Clark
5. Alexander Colvin
6. Alexander McAlester
7. Coll McAlester
8. Hector McAlester
9. James McAlester
10. John McAlester
11. Alexander McKay
12. Hugh McLaughlin
13. James McLachlan
14. John McPherson
15. Archibald Buie
16. Duncan Buie
17. Daniel Buie
18. Hugh McCranie
19. Murdoch McCranie
20. Duncan Campbell
21. Archibald Campbell
22. Edward Connor
23. Neill McNeill
24. Nector McNeill
25. Archibald McNeill
26. Lachlan McNeill
27. Hector McNeill(Carver)
28. Neill McNeill (Long)
29. Nathaniel Smylie
30. Matthew Smylie
31. James Campbell
32. Malcolm McNeill
33. Torquil McNeill
34. Will Stevens
35. Daniel McNeill
36. John Cameron
37. Daniel McDuffie
38. Gilbert Patterson
39. Black Neill McNeill
40. Dugal Stewart
41. Patrick Stewart
42. Malcolm Clark
43. Miles Ward
44. Samuel McGaw
45. Daniel McDougald
46. Archibald McGill
47. Neill McGill
48. John Smith
49. Neill McNeill (Little)
50. Arch'd Buie (Gum Swamp)
51. Dugald McNeill
52. Hugh Ward

McNeill Families

A number of McNeill families are discussed in this and other chapters of *Carolina Scots.* It is important to note here that the Carolina McNeills are all branches of the Southern or Gigha McNeills. When I was first living as a student in Scotland in the late 1960s, occasionally I would comment to someone interested in Highland genealogy that I was descended from the McNeills (among others). Nearly always they said: "That means they were Roman Catholics." When I replied, "No, they were Presbyterians," I was usually met with smiles of tolerant incredulity, preceding the rejoinder: "But the McNeills are from Bara, an island that never accepted the Reformation."

I later discovered that the solution is as follows: according to Dr. George F. Black's *The Surnames of Scotland: Their Origin, Meaning, and History* (The New York Public Library), "There are two clans of this name: (1) of Barra, and (2) of Gigha (550). The Barra McNeills rejected the Protestant Reformation and the Gigha (Southern) McNeills accepted it."

Neill Du McNeill Family

Among the several interrelated McNeill families on the ship, the man most often considered to be the leader of the Argyll Colony was Neill "Du" (*Dubh*, Gaelic for black or swarthy) McNeill of Ardelay. He was perhaps the wealthiest of the group and of a distinguished ancestry, for his father, Hector, controlled the valuable lands of Ardelay in Gigha.[1] Hector McNeill's wife was Elizabeth McTavish (daughter of Donald McTavish of Dunardry). Neill Du married Grissella Campbell, a lady of wealth and daughter of Captain Archibald Campbell of Auchendarroch.[2] The article by Sheriff A.I.B. Stewart in *Argyll Colony Plus* (6.1), which has already been mentioned, should be consulted for important background information on this family.

Although Neill Dubh McNeill is often said to be the prime leader of the Argyll Colony (and was stated to be such in Sheriff A.I.B. Stewart's first article in *Argyll Colony Plus* (Vol. I, No. 1), in accordance with other evidence present by George Stevenson of the North Carolina Department of Archives, Sheriff Stewart later concluded:

> Although there is no written evidence substantiating the claim, I agree with the suggestion made by Mr. George Stevenson . . . that Duncan Campbell of Kilduskland is the likeliest to have been the leader of the expedition. Everything known points to him as a man of substance and of probity . . . Unlike Dugald[McNeill] who seemed to be concerned only with his own position, he behaved as a leader anxious for the welfare of the other emigrants when on February 27, 1739, he appeared with his nephew by marriage, Duncan McTavish Yr. of Dunardry before the Presbytery of Inverary and presented a Petition from the intended Argyll Colony with a call to the Rev. Robert Fullerton, minister of Kilmichael, Glassary.[3]

Neill Dubh did not, after their arrival in North Carolina in 1739, move with the rest of the Argyll Colony to live upriver in (what is now)

Cumberland County (then, Bladen County), but remained instead downstream in Brunswick, where he operated a tavern or inn. This may serve to indicate that Duncan Campbell, rather than he, was the leader of the group. Neill Dubh died by 1749.

Neill Du and Grissella had:

I. "BLUFF" HECTOR
II. NEGALENA
III. FLORA
IV. DUNCAN (The "Traditional Genealogy" of Hugh McLean inserts Duncan, though some other references do not mention him.)[4]

I. "BLUFF HECTOR MCNEILL," who had large lands above the Cape Fear near Old Bluff Presbyterian Church, was one of its elders and the first sheriff of Cumberland County (founded in 1754 out of Bladen). He married Mary McAllister (daughter of Coll McAllister of Balinakill). "Bluff" Hector died before his wife, and she married secondly Duncan McLean and had more children. Hector and Mary had:[5]

A. John
B. Jane
C. Margaret (Peggy), died without issue
D. Mary (Polly), died without issue
E. Betsy
F. Flora
G. Draughon (E., F., and G. are listed by Hugh McLean but not by D.S. McAllister)[6]

A. John McNeill m. Ann (Nancy) McKeithan. They had:
1. Mary m. Hector Stewart. They had: Robert, John McN., Thomas D., Mary Jane, Ann Eliza (d. age 9).
2. Hector m. (?). Left two daughters in Florida or Texas
3. Henrietta m. Peter McKellar in 1812.

B. Jane McNeill m. Duncan Buie. They had:
1. Marian m. John Armstrong. They had: Henry Clay, Melinda, John Thomas.
2. Neill d. single.
3. Malcolm m. (?)

E. Betsy m. Malcolm McKay
F. Flora m. Duncan Ochiltree

II. NEGALENA MCNEILL, b. in North Carolina in 1740, m. Robert Stewart (son of Dugald and Margaret Thompson Stewart of the Argyll Colony). They had:

A. Elizabeth b. 1768
B. Grissella b. 1771
C. Hector b. 1773
D. Dugald
E. Robert

I have information only concerning:

B. Grissella Stewart m. Neil McNeill (son of Archibald and Jennie Bahn Smith McNeill). They had:
   1. Caroline McNeill b. 1808, d. 1898, m. Dr. Henry Marshall Turner d. 1907.[7]
   2. Col. Archibald Stewart McNeill b. 1805, d. 1876, m. first Sarah Willis Howze and had: Mildred b. 1837, d. 1911 and Anna Hayes b. 1844, d. 1899. He m. secondly Mary Virginia Herndon (Covington).

E. Hector Stewart m. Mary Shaw. Their son:
   1. Neil S. Stewart m. Hannah Armstrong.

III. FLORA MCNEILL m. Col. Alexander McAllister (son of Coll McAllister and Janet McNeill). Their descendants are traced under the McAllister family.

IV. DUNCAN MCNEILL (his order of birth among the other children is uncertain) m. Lovedy (dau. of Rev. James Campbell). Duncan is buried in the cemetary of Old Bluff Presbyterian Church in Cumberland County, N.C. His tombstone states that he was "the son of Neill McNeill of Kintyre, Scotland the pioneer and friend of the Scottish emigration to the Cape Fear Region." Duncan and Lovedy Campbell McNeill had:

A. James
B. Grissella
C. Duncan
D. Isabella

A. James McNeill m. Catherine McAllister (dau. of Alexander McAllister). They had:
   1. David
   2. Lovedy Jane
   3. Randall
   4. Alexander
   5. Flora
   6. John Hector
   7. Grissella

B. Grissella McNeill m. Thomas Gilmore. They had several daughters.

C. Duncan McNeill died single

D. Isabella McNeill m. the widowed husband of her late sister, Grissella. They had:
   1. Mary m. Neill McDougal

Alexander McAllister Family

A second Argyll Colony family was that of Col. Alexander McAllister, who came in 1739 and stayed in Brunswick, helping with Neill Du McNeill's tavern until about 1743, when he took land near where Bluff Church is now located. He became an elder there when it was founded in 1758. Some of his letters to Scotland are quoted in Malcolm Fowler's *Valley of the Scots*[8] He was twice married (some have said three times).[9]

A valuable resource on this family (and other relations such as the McNeills) is found in *McAllister Family Papers Cumberland County, North Carolina 1747-1935* (North Carolina Archives file PC 1738. 1-2 : papers on file in the North Carolina Archives, 109 E. Jones Street, Raleigh, N.C. 27601-2807, finding aid completed by George Stevenson and William C. Fields on 6 July 1990). It contains 231 items (one of them a volume having another 20 items mounted or laid in), given by Mrs. Alexander Pope McAllister, September 22, 1984. It is described as follows:

> This collection of papers is comprised of the family correspondence and related papers of a Cumberland County family who came to North Carolina from Scotland in the 'Argyll Colony' of 1739. This group of gentlemen-adventurers with servitors and tenants included among the former class, Coll McAlester of Balinakill (a property in Kintyre, Argyllshire), his wife Janet McNeill of the family of Lossit in Kintyre, and five of their six children: Hector, Alexander, Mary, Grissella, and Isabella (their daughter Ann remaining in Scotland). The parents dying in 1741, an aunt apparently helped with the younger daughters while Hector worked as head of the family to produce a marketable crop. In 1744 Hector returned to Scotland (presumably on pressing family business) leaving his brother Alexander to conduct the family's North Carolina affairs. Having been implicated in the 1745 uprising in support of Prince Charles Edward Stuart, Hector appears to have been forbidden under a governmental writ of *ne exeat regno* to leave Scotland. During this time, Hector married Mary Fullarton of the family of Corse and commenced a family. Consequently, he remained in the Island of Arran in the Inner Hebrides and never returned to North Carolina, despite constantly expressing an intention to do so right up to the opening of the American Revolution.
>
> Alexander, in the interim, married and commenced his family, marrying as his first wife Flora McNeill of the family of Ardelay in the Island of Gigha (known in North Carolina as the McNeills of The Bluff), his sister Mary McAlester marrying Alexander's brother-in-law, Hector McNeill of The Bluff. Their youngest sister Isabella married Ferquhard Campbell of

Cumberland County, while their sister Grissella remained unmarried. Upon the death of his first wife, Alexander married Jean Colvin of the New Hanover County family residing at Colvin Hall.

Understandably, the family's standing as county gentry determined Alexander McAlester's position not only among the Scottish community but in the county at large. He was named in every commission of the peace for Cumberland County from December 1757 through December 1762, and it is probable that he presided in his community as a single justice of the peace during this period. For reasons no longer clear, however, he sat with his fellow magistrates in the Court of Pleas and Quarter Sessions during the duration of his 1761/62 commission only, and even then it appears that he sat without having properly qualified by taking the necessary oaths. During the last year he was in the commission of the peace, Alexander McAlester was concurrently promoted in his military rank from captain to lieutenant colonel. Upon the death of Colonel Thomas Armstrong, McAlester was raised to a full colonelcy in February 1766.

Colonel McAlester represented Cumberland County in the General Assembly in 1762 and again in the session of 1773/4, and in the Provincial Congress of 1775. Though Colonel McAlester's son Neill was an officer in the American Army upon outbreak of the American Revolution, when the colonel's relations, Ferquhard Campbell and Thomas Rutherford, were implicated in the Highland uprising that culminated in the Battle of Moore's Creek (February 1776), Colonel McAlester resigned his military commission in May 1776 and abstained from attending the 1776 session of the Provincial Congress to which his county had returned him.

After the peace, Colonel McAlester was a member of the 1788 state convention to ratify the United States Constitution (his reference in Letter #60, however, is to the federal, not the state, convention), and he served as a senator in each of the four General Assemblies held from 1787 through 1790.

Long active in Presbyterian circles, as his letters will show, Colonel McAlester was an elder of the congregation meeting first at Roger's Meeting House, then from 1787 at a new meeting house built at The Bluff (see Letter #60). His son Alexander continued the tradition and served both as elder and as stated clerk of the session for the meeting at Bluff Church [see map on next page]. It was this son who continued the Scottish correspondence, and through him the family papers ultimately descended to the colonel's great-great grandson, Alexander Pope McAllister, whose widow gave them to the North Carolina State Archives on September 22, 1984.

Tables showing the descent of the papers as well as relationships of the principal family members mentioned in the letters will be found in Appendix I.

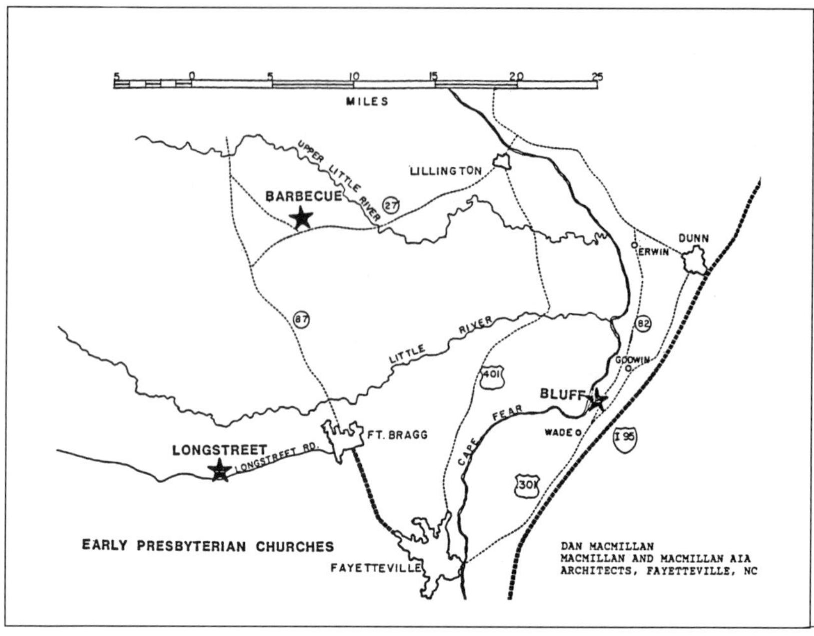

Bluff, Barbeque and Longstreet were the first three Presbyterian churches founded by the early Carolina Scots in the upper Cape Fear Valley, (1758). Only Barbeque is still in regular use, though the old buildings are still preserved for occasional services at Bluff and Longstreet.

Family Correspondence, [1747]-1935. The most important of the family letters are those dating from [1747] to 1809. Those seventy letters include those exchanged between the brothers Hector (in Scotland) and Alexander (in North Carolina) and have as their common theme Hector's efforts to retrieve his business affairs concerning his North Carolina plantation called New Troy as well as an indebtedness owing to him from the estate of their mother's brother, Dugald McNeill of Lossit, who died in the colony in 1741. The brothers' letters contain, as well, substantive information concerning emigration from Scotland to North Carolina. Almost all of Alexander's other correspondence with kinsmen and friends in Scotland prior to 1776 have emigration as their central subject. Following the interruption in the correspondence caused by the American Revolution, the brothers resumed their letter writing. After Hector's death in 1790, his daughter Mary (Mrs. Shannon) continued until 1809 a correspondence first with her uncle Alexander then with her cousin Alexander in the hope of securing at least some part of her father's share in the North Carolina property. A fairly full abstract, sometimes amounting to a paraphrase, of the first seventy letters in the collection will be found in Appendix II.

The remainder of the family correspondence is altogether of family interest. The six letters dating from 1839 to 1857 are those of McLean kinsmen, the third Alexander McAllister having married Janet McNeill McLean. The correspondence dating from 1868 to 1916 (with one letter from 1926) is that of his son, John Alexander McAllister whose interest in the family was spurred by the publication of the Rev. D.S. McAllister's *Geneological Record of the Descendents of Col. Alexander McAllister* (Richmond, Va.: Whittet & Shepperson, printers, 1900). John Alexander McAllister's son, Alexander Pope McAllister, inherited his father's interest in family history, and by 1929 he had prepared typescripts of a number of the earlier letters and had reopened a correspondence with Scottish cousins as well as others that he thought might help him in his research; his correpsondence ranges in date from 1929 to 1935 and is altogether genealogical in nature. Reference to the letters of A.P. McAllister will greatly assist the researcher in identifying many of the persons named in the eighteenth century family correspondence.

Family Papers. These materials include some papers of family interest only, but other papers of a much wider import. The folder of Cumberland County land papers includes deeds, patents for land, and some plats of survey. The five folders of records concerning Bluff Presbyterian Church, Wade, N.C., include records of baptisms, rough copies of session records, pay of ministers, building fund, and reports to the synod and general assembly; additionally there are some historical notes on the church and a brief historical pamphlet concerning the Lumberton Presyterian Church. A folder of Civil War material includes Lt. John A. McAllister's January 8, 1865 request for a 20-day leave from the 24th Regiment, N.C. Troops, at Petersburg, Va., and a typescript of Captain James S. Evans' history of Company F, 24th Regiment ('The Cumberland Plough Boys'). This is followed by an account by Elizabeth Ann Harllee McRae (Mrs. Alexander McRae of "Argyle") of a night attack on her house by a gang that included Henry Berry Lowrey ('The Raid of the Yankees and Robbers') in March 1865. The folder of "literary compositions" includes school essays and debate notes as well as an undated draft of a letter addressed to the editor of *The Methodist Christian Sentinel.* Included in these miscellaneous family papers is a folder containing three veterinary formulae—one for a febrifuge powder, one for curing a fistula in a horse, and one for curing the sleepy staggers in a horse. The four folders of genealogical notes relate to the McAllister, McNeill, Richardson, and Whitfield/Bryan families, and are followed by a folder containing a typescript copy of Jean Colvin's 1761 Covenant with God. The folder marked 'Estates' contains an undated contemporary copy of the will of Alexander Colvin of Colvin Hall, 1774. A bound ledger commenced in 1928 as an intended scrapbook to be entitled 'Some Sketches of Scotch History' includes newspaper clippings and materials relating to the McAllister family (Stevenson and Fields, *McAllister Family Papers,* 1-3).

According to McAllister Family Papers (Appendix I), Alexander McAlester was the son of Coll McAlester of Balinakill (1688-1740), who died in North Carolina, and was married to Janet McNeill, daughter of Hector McNeill of Lossit. Coll was the son of Ronald McAlester of Balinakill (and was in Dunskeig before 1717). Coll McAlester and Janet McNeill had six children: Ann McAlester (died without issue in Scotland); Hector McAlester (1716-1790), returned to Scotland and married Mary Fullarton of the family of Corse. They had Charles, Mary (who married Neill Shannon, Laird of Lepenstrath, and wrote letters to her Carolina cousins, which are in the *McAllister family papers),* Grace (who married Captain James McAlester) and others. In addition, Coll and Janet McAlester had: Alexander McAlester (dealt with below); Mary McAlester, who married Hector McNeill of The Bluff (Ardelay); Grissella, who died without issue in North Carolina, and Isabella McAlester, who married Ferquhard Campbell of Cumberland County, N.C.[10]

According to the Reverend D.S. McAllister, Alexander McAllister first married Flora McNeill (dau. of Neill Du McNeill of Ardelay). They had:

- I. COLL
- II. GRISELLA
- III. JANET
- IV. NEILL d. single in 1779

I. COLL MCALLISTER m. Janet Buie. They had:

- A. Archibald b. 1776, d. young
- B. Alexander b. 1779
- C. Flora b. 1782
- D. Mary b. 1785
- E. Neill (II) b. 1788, d. without d. issue
- F. Janet b. 1792, d. without issue
- G. Coll (II) b. (?), d. without issue

B. Alexander McAllister m. in 1809 Ann Wright. They had:

1. Coll d. without issue
2. Louise d. without issue
3. James m. Frances Shepherd in 1840
4. Mary m. James Mitchell. Childless.
5. Archibald Buie d. without issue
6. Betsy Jane d. without issue
7. John m. Thetis Adams
8. Janet Ann m. Dr. Leroy DeWitt McMannon

C. Flora McAllister m. Daniel McLean (son of John and Katie Buie McLean of the Isle of Jura). They had:

1. Janet m. first John Murchison and secondly John McNeill
2. John m. Luenza Leach. He was sheriff of Johnson County, N.C.
3. Alexander Duncan m. Catherine McLean
4. Ann m. Archibald Graham of Fayetteville (his second wife)
5. Archibald m. Ellen Weisigler; went to Texas
6. Hector m. Catherine McDougald (dau. of Rev. Alan McDougald)
7. Mary Margaret m. Nat. E. Jones and moved West
8. Flora Catherine m. John Greene
9. Effie Isabella m. Neill Shaw
10. Sarah Jane m. Alan Cameron

D. Mary McAllister m. Col. Duncan McLean in 1802.[11] They had:

1. Coll m. Annie Atkins
2. John Alexander d. single in New York in 1826
3. Archibald Neill m. Elizabeth Ingraham of Fayetteville, N.C.
4. Mary Jane m. William Sexton
5. Hugh (twin) b. 1810, d. 1899, single
6. Hector (twin) b. 1810, d. 1902, single

II. GRISSELLA MCALLISTER m. (Blind) John McKethan. They had:

A. John Jr.
B. Flora
C. Janet
D. Christian

A. John McKethan, Jr. m. first Miss McDougald, secondly Marian Carruth. By his first wife:

1. Flora
2. Alexander

By his second wife:

3. Grissella
4. Cyrus
5. Robert
6. Darius
7. Daniel
8. John W.

B. Flora McKethan m. first Neill Galbraith, secondly Daniel Kyle. By her first husband:

1. Grissella Galbraith
2. Angus Galbraith

By her second husband:

3. Robert Kyle
4. John Kyle

C. Janet McKethan m. Angus Phillips. They had:

1. Flora d. single
2. James, M.D., d. single
3. Stephen d. single
4. Eliza (or Lizzie)
5. Grissella
6. John W.

They moved to Georgia before 1850.

D. Christian McKethan m. Neill McLeran. They had:
1. Alfred Augustus McKethan
2. Margaret
3. Grissella

III. JANET MCALLISTER m. Malcolm McNeill (son of Archibald and Jennie Bahn Smith McNeill). They had:

A. Coll
B. John
C. Janet
D. Flora
E. Isabella

A. Coll McNeill m. Effie Buie. They had:
1. Malcolm Jr.
2. Janet
3. Neill
4. Ann
5. Archibald

B. "Red" John McNeill m. first Louvisa Robeson, secondly Mrs. Janet Murchison. By his first wife:
1. Sarah
2. Flora
3. "Priest" John
4. Janet
5. Ann
6. Isaac
7. David

By his second wife:
8. Janet Ann
9. Martin

C. Janet McNeill m. John Atkins, who d. age 93. They had:
1. Ann
2. Janet
3. James
4. John Lewis
5. Flora Isabella
6. Katherine

D. Flora McNeill m. Neill McKay in 1805. They lived in Summerville, N.C.[12] They had:
1. Archibald Alexander
2. Janet Isabella
3. Malcolm
4. Murdock Murphy
5. Ann Gilchrist
6. Neill
7. John W.
8. Flora
9. Sarah Jane Kate
10. Mary Elizabeth

E. Isabella McNeill m. first James Atkins and secondly Rev. James Purefoy. By her first husband:
1. Sophia
2. Annie Jane
3. Isabella
4. Benjamin Franklin

Alexander McAllister married secondly on July 14, 1763 Jean Colvin, who was born on the ship during the voyage from Scotland to North Carolina on Sept. 20, 1740. They had:

V. MARGARET b. 1764
VI. ALEXANDER b. 1766, d. 1823
VII. HECTOR b. 1768, d. 1810
VIII. FLORA b. 1769, d. 1807
IX. MARY b. 1772, m. Joel Williams, d. without issue
X. RONALD b. 1774, d. 1794 without issue
XI. CHARLES, twin to Ronald, d. 1840
XII. JOHN b. 1776, d. single on the Isle of St. Kitts
XIII. CATHERINE b. 1778
XIV. ANGUS b. 1780, died in childhood
XV. ISABELLA b. 1782

V. MARGARET MCALLISTER m. Col. Ben Rogers of Marlboro County, S.C. (his first wife). They had:

A. Jane
B. Elizabeth
C. Flora
D. Sarah
E. Mary
F. Catherine
G. William

VI. ALEXANDER MCALLISTER m. in 1799 Rachel Smith. They had:

A. Ronald died young
B. Charity
C. Mary Jane
D. Alexander
E. David
F. Hector
G. Rachel
H. Flora
I. Margaret
J. Edith I.

VII. COL. HECTOR MCALLISTER, Sheriff of Cumberland County, m. first Margaret Armstrong, secondly Isabella McDuffie. By his first wife:

A. Alexander
B. John
C. Annie J. died young
D. Thomas died without issue

By his second wife:

E. Duncan J.
F. Flora
G. Loveday

VIII. FLORA MCALLISTER m. Col. John Colvin in 1792. They had:

A. Alexander
B. John
C. Charles
D. James, M.D.
E. Mary J.
F. Henry De Rosset
G. William
H. Timothy

Only Alexander and William married and had children.

Col. John Colvin m. secondly Elizabeth Jones and thirdly Catherine Rutledge.

XI. CHARLES MCALLISTER m. first Elizabeth Thames and secondly her cousin, also named Elizabeth Thames. By his first wife he had ten children, all of whom died in infancy. By his second wife:

A. Cornelius d. in infancy
B. Alexander C.
C. Mary Jane m. John T. Council

XIII. CATHERINE MCALLISTER m. James McNeill (son of Duncan, son of Neill). They had:

A. David, elder in Bluff Church, Chairman of Cumberland County Court
B. Alexander d. single
C. Loveday J.
D. Ronald
E. John
F. James d. in infancy
G. Flora Eliza
H. Charles d. single

XV. ISABELLA MCALLISTER m. William Smith. They had:

A. Flora Ann
B. William Jr.
C. Jane

William Smith m. secondly Sarah Bertram Robeson and had one daughter, Sarah Bertram Smith.

John Smith Family

A third large Argyll Colony family of the "Old Bluff" section of Cumberland was that of John Smith (I).[13] He was born c. 1700 in Knapdale, Argyll and died before 17 March 1749 in Cumberland County, N.C. He m. c. 1717 in Scotland Margaret Gilchrist, b. c. 1702/04, d. in N.C. c. 1739. She is said to have died on the way up the river from Brunswick to upper Cape Fear. They had two children who were both born in Scotland and accompanied their parents to North Carolina in 1739:

I. MALCOLM (I)
II. JENNET ("Jennie Bahn")

I. MALCOLM SMITH (1) b. c. 1718/22 in Knapdale, d. 20 Dec. 1778, Cumberland County, N.C. He m. c. 1745 Mrs. Sarah Peterson McKissick. Malcolm was an elder of Longstreet Presbyterian Church. Their children:

A. Margaret b. 1746
B. John II b. 1748
C. Sarah b. 1750
d. 1763, (twin)
D. Patrick b. 1750 (twin)
E. Ann (Nancy) b. 1752
F. Malcolm b. 1754
G. Archibald b. 1756
H. Duncan b. 1758
I. Neill b. 1761
J. Daniel b. 1764

A. Margaret Smith m. Neill Ray (no information)

B. John Smith (II) d. 1784, m. c. 1769 Flora Clark b. 1745, d. 1796. They had:
1. Malcolm
2. David
3. Nancy (Ann)
4. Margaret
5. John

D. Patrick Smith d. before 11 May 1816 in Robeson County, N.C., m. Ann Clark c. 1795 of Barbeque Church community (in present Harnett County). They had:
1. Malcolm
2. John
3. Margaret
4. Rev. Archibald
5. David
6. Flora
7. Ann m. Neill Brown of Philadelphus Church, near Red Springs, N.C.[14]
8. Daniel

Many of the offspring of these people emigrated to Alabama, Mississippi, Louisiana and Texas.

F. Malcolm Smith (Jr.) d. 1795 in Richmond County, N.C., m. c. 1779 in Cumberland County, N.C., Sarah Moran Smith, b. 1754 in Glasgow, Scotland and d. 1839 in Alabama. They had:
1. John Smith b. 1780
2. Sarah d. 1841 in Alabama
3. Malcolm III d. 1811, single
4. Dr. Neill Smith II d. in Alabama
5. Mary (Polly) Smith m. Moses McClure in Alabama
6. Archibald
7. Margaret m. ___ Smylie
8. Catherine m. ___McAlpine
9. Duncan Crawford m. Ann Smith (dau. of Daniel and Ann McKay Smith). They went to Alabama.
10. Ann m. Thomas M. Brumby in Alabama

G. Archibald Smith m. Catherine Brown of Robeson County

(dau. of Hugh Sr. and Mary Buie Brown). They had at least:

1. Neill b. 1777
2. Rev. Daniel b. 1779, d. 1825 in Robeson County, m. Elizabeth Brown (dau. of Neill and Ann Smith Brown)
3. Hugh Smith b. 1779, d. after 1825
4. John b. 1782 (may have died before 1825?)

I. Neill Smith, d. before 1805 in Cumberland County, m. c. 1780 Mary E. McNeill (dau. of John McNeill). He served in N.C. House of Commons 1793-99. They had (order of birth uncertain):

1. Jennet b. c. 1793/4, m. in 1817 in Moore County, John Graham (son of Archibald)
2. Mary m. before 1819 James Alfred Yarboro
3. b. 1805/06, m. Daniel Graham, moved to Alabama
4. Malcolm b. 1795 in Moore County, d. 1857 near Prattville, Ala., m. Mary Baxter Graham of Cumberland County, b. 1800 (dau. of Archibald)

J. Daniel Smith d. 1841 in Cumberland County, m. 1785 Ann McKay (dau. of Alexander and Margaret McNeill McKay). All of their sons and three of the daughters moved to Alabama. They had:

1. Archibald McKay Smith b. 1786, d. 1843, m. Jeanette Gordon
2. Margaret b. 1788, m. Daniel McLean, d. in Alabama in 1827.
3. Sarah b. 1790, m. 1819 Neill McKeithan, Jr. b. 1793, d. 1830. He is buried at Longstreet Church and she at Cypress Church.
4. Mary b. 1791, m. Duncan McMillan Blue in 1816, d. after 1860 in Moore County, N.C.[15]
5. Alexander McKay b. 1793, d. in Alabama 1871, m. first Catherine McMillan (dau. of John B. McMillan and Mary McKeithen).
6. Anne b. 1795, m. in 1816 in Cumberland County, Duncan Crawford Smith (son of Malcolm Smith Jr. and Sarah Moran Smith). They went to Alabama.
7. Jannet b. 1797 in Cumberland County, d. 1867 in North Carolina, m. 1821 Archibald McMillan Blue. Both are buried at Bethesda Church near Aberdeen.[16]
8. Catherine b. 1799, d. 1801 in Cumberland County.

9. Lovedy b. 1800, d. 1857 in Cumberland County.
10. Daniel b. 1803, d. 1840, m. first Margaret McNeill, secondly Flora Ann Graham (dau. of John P.). They went to Alabama.
11. Neill McKay b. 1805, d. in Alabama, m. Ann Stover
12. Lauchlin McKay b. 1807, d. in Louisiana, m. Jane Graham (dau. of John P.).
13. Eliza b. 1809 in Cumberland County, d. 1891 in Cumberland, m. Neill McK. Blue. Both are buried at Sandy Grove Presbyterian Church (on the Fort Bragg Reservation in Cumberland County).[17]
14. Christian Catherine Blue b. 1816 in Cumberland County, d. 1866 in Cumberland, m. in 1846 John Alexander McKeithan. Both are buried at Sandy Grove Church.

II. JENNET ("JENNIE BAHN") SMITH b. in Scotland c. 1728/29 and d. in Cumberland County 1791. She m. Archibald McNeill, who d. 1801 in Cumberland County. He is thought by some to have been the son of "Daniel McNeill Taynish" of Bladen County, second son of the Chief of "Southern Clan McNeill" of Argyll. Jennie Bahn was noted as a remarkable woman. She helped to amass large portions of land, perhaps some 20,000 acres, and is said to have driven cattle to Philadelphia, where tradition has it that she met Benjamin Franklin.

Her family (except for one son) were all of Tory sympathies during the Revolution, when, on one occasion, she bravely drove horses away from the presence of army officers into the swamps to keep them from being confiscated. Her exploits have been described by several writers[18] and the playwright, Paul Green (a descendent of her husband), wrote a play about her, entitled "The Highland Call."

Jennet Smith and Archibald McNeill had (order of birth not certain):

A. Malcolm
B. John
C. Captain Daniel
D. Hector
E. Archibald
F. Lauchlin
G. Neil
H. Margaret
I. Mary

A. Malcolm McNeill d. 1798, m. 1771 Janet McAllister. Their offspring are traced under the McAllister section of this volume.

B. "Cunning" John McNeill (called "cunning" because he managed to escape punishment for his involvement in the Tory side in the Piney Bottom affair, discussed earlier, on p. 123).

He m. Agnes Shaw. Their only son died in a gun accident.

C. Captain Daniel McNeill b. 1752, d. 1818, m. Mary Nutting (dau. of John and Mary Walton Nutting). They had (at least):
   1. Sophia Margaret m. first Stephen Terhume and secondly William Parker
   2. Mary Janet m. Frances Parker. They had:
      a. Dr. Daniel McNeill Parker and others.[19]

D. Captain Hector McNeill ('One-Eyed' Hector) m. Susan Barksdale. They had (at least):
   1. Daniel McNeill b. 1788, d. 1835, m. Rachael Murchison (dau. of Kenneth Murchison, Sr.). They had:
      a. Dr. William McNeill m. Julia Turner

E. Archibald McNeill was single

F. Lauchlin McNeill was single

G. Neil McNeill m. Grissella Stewart (traced under the line of Neill Du McNeill in this volume).

H. Margaret McNeill b. 1758, d. 1829, m. John McNeill of "Skerobline," a farm in Kintyre, Argyll, b. 1754, d. 1810. They had (at least):
   1. Mary b. 1798, m. Dr. John McKay, b. 1796, d. 1843, parents of:
      a. Dr. John A. McKay m. Christianna Foy

I. Mary d. at fifteen

"Taynish Daniel" McNeill Family

Let us now look briefly at the family of "Taynish Daniel" McNeill. Although they were mainly located in lower Bladen County rather than Cumberland, I include them here since they were among the leaders of the first Argyll Colony and were closely connected to the families listed immediately above. My information on them comes from the brief, but fine notice of Everette McNeill Kivette. Sheriff A.I.B. Stewart's article (*Argyll Colony Plus* 6.2) should be consulted concerning the background of the Taynish McNeills.

Archibald [McNeill, husband of Jennie Bahn Smith] was one of the many children of Daniel "Taynish" McNeill of Bladen County by his two wives. Daniel was the second son of yet another Neil McNeill. This Neil was the last chief of the name to hold the old family property of Taynish (on the western coast of the Argyllshire mainland). Daniel's father, Neil of Taynish, married Elizabeth Campbell, daughter of Alexander Campbell, "Commissar of the Isles," an Auchenbreck Campbell, and then after she died, married Margaret Campbell, eldest daughter of George Campbell of Airds, a sept of the House of Cawdor.

Daniel McNeill held land also on Gigha Island (Ardminish Farm on its eastern shore facing Kintyre), but emigrated in 1739 with Neil of Ardelay and established himself near Brown Marsh Church in Bladen County where it is said he managed his plantation "Tweedside." From one of his marriages, probably his second, came eventually James McNeill Whistler through a daughter Elizabeth who married a McNeill (William) and had a son, Doctor Daniel McNeill. To Doctor McNeill was born a daughter, Anna Matilda McNeill (1804-1881), who married George Washington Whistler and became "Whistler's Mother."

Elizabeth, the grandmother of Anna was daughter of "Daniel Taynish's" second wife, Margaret McTavish, daughter of Archibald, also a Chief of McTavish. Archibald McNeill, who married Jennie Bahn Smith, was very probably the son of Daniel's first wife, whose name unfortunately has not come down to us. This Archibald was brother to Col. Hector McNeill who was of considerable notoriety in North Carolina during the American Revolutionary War, being the British officer who captured Hillsboro with David Fanning in September 1781.

William Frederick Parker in his research into McNeill genealogy at the end of the 19th century in North Carolina makes a clear reference to a Bladen County connection between Archibald McNeill of Cumberland, Jennie's husband, and Col. Hector and his sister, Izabella McNeill McAlester Slingsby (widow of Colonel John Slingsby of Bladen), who was and is known to be a great-aunt of Anna McNeill Whistler. (See Parker's *Daniel McNeill Parker, M.D., His Ancestry and A Memoir of His Life,* 1910, Canada, pp.48-60, the will of Dr. Arch. McNeill, Dorchester, S.C. 1771, and *Fasti Ecclesiae Scoticanae,* Vol. IV, p. 54; there see "William Mouat.")[20]

Appendix I of McAllister Family Papers also lists as children of Daniel McNeill of Taynish and Margaret McTavish:

Margaret McNeill, who m. the Reverend Mr. Mowat in Gigha and Jean McNeill, who m. John DuBois of Wilmington, N.C.

Daniel McNeill Family

There is another McNeill family traditionally said to be related to the founder of the Argyll Colony, Neill Du McNeill. This family of Moore County, N.C. (near Union Presbyterian Church) is descended from

Archibald McNeill of Argyll, who is claimed to have been a half-brother of Neill Du (although I have not seen documentation of this). Archibald lived on Gigha. His son, Daniel, came to North Carolina—according to tradition in 1758, supposedly with the last colony his half-uncle (if this relationship be true) brought over. When he arrived he first settled in Cumberland County on James Creek (now in Hoke County) but later moved to Moore County. He m. Sarah McKay (dau. of Archibald and Ann McKay), and they are both buried at Union Presbyterian Church. They had:

I. ARCHIBALD
II. "BIG" NEILL
III. "LITTLE" JOHN
IV. MALCOLM
V. ALEXANDER
VI. DANIEL
VII. ANNE

I have information at present only on II., 'Big' Neill.[21]

II. 'BIG' NEILL MCNEILL b. 1777, d. 1844, m. Mary Moore Matthews, b. 1782, d. 1866. He lived first in Cumberland County at Pike's Pond, then moved to Moore County, near Union Church. They had:

A. John or "Squire Jack"
B. Daniel
C. Sarah McKay
D. Mary Ann
E. Elizabeth Jane
F. Christian Margaret
G. Eliza Jane (Betsy)
H. Neill McKay ("Coy")
I. Thomas Jefferson

My information on this family is limited to A., John.[22]

A. John McNeill b. 1806 near Herd's Creek, N.C., m. Martha Eliza Oats b. 1811, d. 1883/4. They had:

1. Malcolm Alexander
2. Dr. John Norman
3. Sarah Jane
4. Mary Catherine
5. Martha Nicey
6. Neill James
7. Isabella McKay
8. James Alfred
9. Henry Thomas
10. Neill Daniel

Another Daniel McNeill Family

We have already looked at two Daniel McNeill families, who may have some relationship between them (although it is not actually documented). But this third Daniel McNeill family came from Scotland much later than the other two, and there is no known tradition of any close kinship with the previous McNeills. My information on this family largely comes from Rozella McLeod's *McLeod's of Tuckahoe & Horses Creek*.[23]

According to the research of Rozella McLeod, the McNeill Family Bible states that Daniel McNeill was b. 1778 in Scotland.[24] He had emigrated to North Carolina sometime before his marriage c. 1802 to Margaret McLeod (dau. of Daniel and Martha McKinnon McLeod) b. 1785 in North Carolina (according to the 1850 census). We do not know the names of his parents, nor whether they emigrated with him. Daniel and his wife lived in the vicinity of Bethesda Presbyterian Church near present Aberdeen, N.C. They had nine children:

I. ALEXANDER MCNEILL b. 1804
II. JOHN MCNEILL b. 1806
III. MARY MCNEILL b. 1807, d. 1898
IV. ANNA MCNEILL b. 1809
V. DANIEL MCNEILL b. 1811
VI. NEAL MCNEILL b. 1813
VII. MALCOLM NCNEILL b. 1815
VIII. ANGUS MCNEILL b. 1817
IX. CATHERINE MCNEILL b. 1819, d. 1879

Rozella McLeod traces only:

VII. MALCOLM MCNEILL m. 1846 Flora Ann Isabel Buchan b. 1822, d. 1891. Malcolm d. 1892. Both are buried at Bethesda Presbyterian Church.[25] They had:

A. Sarah E.
B. Daniel Alexander
C. Malcolm Baxter
D. Martha M.
E. Infant
F. John Archibald
G. Duncan James McQueen
H. William Angus
I. Flora Isabel

A. Sarah E. McNeill b. 1848, d. 1913, single.

B. Daniel Alexander McNeill b. 1850, d. 1911, m. 1876 Margaret Blue Ray b. 1850, d. 1930. Both b. and d. in Moore County, N.C., and buried at Bethesda Church. They had eight children.[26]

C. Malcolm Baxter McNeill b. 1851 in Moore County, N.C., d. 1923 in Robeson County, N.C., m. first in 1883 Mary Martitia Hodgin b. 1864, d. 1892. They are both buried at Antioch Presbyterian Church between Red Springs and Raeford, N.C. He m. secondly Sarah Margaret McKeithen b. 1857, d. 1942 in Vass, N.C., buried at Cypress Presbyterian Church. By his first wife he had four children but none by his second wife.[27]

D. Martha M. McNeill b. 1852, d. 1876, was single.
E. Infant b. and d. May 20, 1854.
F. John Archibald McNeill b. 1855, d. 1922, m. 1876 Sarah Jane Ray, b. 1848, d. 1914. Both were born and died. in Moore County, where, as Rozella McLeod states: "An unusual circumstance of the funerals of John A. and Sarah Jane McNeill was the fact that double funeral services were held for both. A double funeral service was held at Bethesda for Sarah Jane McNeill and Margaret Elizabeth Kelly, the sister-in-law of Sarah Jane's daughter Annie Kelly, who both died September 8, 1914. A double funeral service was also held at Bethesda Church for John A. McNeill and his grandson, William Edgar McDonald, who were killed by a train at Aberdeen when their car stalled on the track on July 1, 1922." John A. and Sarah Jane had four daughters.[28]
G. Duncan James McQueen McNeill b. 1857 in Moore County, d. 1922 in Scotland County, N.C., m. first Mrs. Georgia A. Davis Conner, b. 1864, d. 1912. Both buried at Smyrna Presbyterian Church. They had no children but raised two boys, Ollie and Henry McNeill, even though they never legally adopted them. Both are now dead.[29] He m. secondly in 1917 Mary Pearl Heustess, b. 1895, d. 1964, buried in Hillside Cemetery, Laurinburg, N.C. They had three children.[30]
H. William Angus McNeill b. 1858 in Moore County, d. 1919 in Moore, m. 1895 Mary Ann Ray b. 1871, d. 1934 in Moore County. Both are buried at Bethesda Church. They had seven children.[31]
I. Flora Isabel McNeill b. 1860, was single.

McNeills of the Bridge

A different McNeill family which came considerably later than the others, but intermarried with them was that of Neill McNeill who settled at Rockfish Creek in Cumberland County. Evelyn Smith includes very little on this family,[32] but there is a helpful article by Judith B. Thomson in *Argyll Colony Plus* which gives fuller information, which we draw upon here.[33]

Neill McNeill b. 1771 at Ardlussa, Isle of Jura, Scotland, d. 1858 in Cumberland County, N.C. (son of Hector McNeill and Margaret

Darroch) landed in Wilmington, N.C., 1792.[34] He left a brother Malcolm in Scotland, and another brother, Laughlin, drowned at sea on the way to America. He first lived at the Bluff on the upper Cape Fear River in Cumberland, where he worked for Farquhard Campbell. In 1799 he m. Sarah Graham, known as "Prettie Sallie" (according to *McNeills of the Bridge* by Mrs. G.T. Bullock). He was captain of a river boat on the Cape Fear and later bought a farm in lower Cumberland County south of Big Rockfish Creek on Chicken Road. He was also a charter elder of Big Rockfish Presbyterian Church. His wife d. 1867, age 88.[35] They had ten children (three of whom were named Margaret, after his mother):[36]

I. MARGARET b. 1801, d. 1803
II. ALEXANDER b. 1804, d. 1843, m. Mary Holmes
III. JANNET b. 1806, d. 1879, m. John McDonald
IV. HECTOR b. 1808, d. 1900, m. Mary McNeill. He was sheriff of Cumberland County and lived at his wife's home, once called "The Bridge" and later changed to "Ardlussa" (in 1898). It no longer stands.
V. CHRISTIAN MCNEILL b. 1810, d. 1889, m. Archibald Buie McFadyen
VI. FLORAH MCNEILL b. 1812, m. James McFadyen
VII. MARGARET MCNEILL b. 1815, d. 1815
VIII. MARGARET MCNEILL b. 1817, d. 1900, m. Roderick McRae
IX. LAUCHLIN MCNEILL b. 1819, d. 1828, drowned in Rockfish Creek
X. NEILL GRAHAM MCNEILL b. 1821, d. 1863, single

Further Research on the McNeill Families

Much work remains to be done on the various large McNeill families of the upper Cape Fear. It seems appropriate to mention here the continuing research of Elvalee Swift, 6101 West Suburban Drive, Miami, Florida 33156, who according to *Argyll Colony Plus* is compiling much material on the Carolina McNeills, and welcomes correspondence on this subject.[37]

Another helpful source of information for the McNeill researcher is found in the letters which passed between Dr. A. C. Bethune of Raeford,

N.C., and his cousin the Rev. W. A. McLeod of Cuero, Texas in the 1930's and '40s. This and other correspondence relative to the Cape Fear Scots has been "organized, typed and indexed for Lt. Col. Victor E. Clark, 14262 Southern Pines Drive, Dallas, Texas 75234 by Ruby G. Campbell, Ph.D. of Baton Rouge, Louisiana" (1987). It is entitled: *CORRESPONDENCE and DOCUMENTS pertaining to the BETHUNE, KEAHEY, MCLEOD, MCFARLAND, PATTERSON and other Related Scottish Highlander Families of North Carolina.* Particularly concerning the McNeills, one should consult the following letters (as numbered in the volume by Dr. Campbell): 5.11, 5.23, 5.39, 5.51, all of section 9.00 and all of section 29.00.

Alexander McKay Family

A fourth original "Argyll Colony" family was that of Archibald McKay of near Longstreet Church in Cumberland County. He was the son of Alexander McKay (I), who came in the 1739 group with Neill Du McNeill. This large family has been carefully traced by Mrs. Barbara McKay Thomas and Mrs. Bettie McKay Fraine in a work already quoted.[38] Mrs. Evelyn Smith also gives information on this family, although some of it does not always agree with the former (which is much more thoroughly researched).[39]

Archibald McKay b. 1720 in Kintyre, Argyll, d. 1797 in North Carolina. He m. first Ann Gilchrist, and secondly Katherine Mullin. Alexander McKay (I), the father of Archibald, came to North Carolina in 1739, and his son, Archibald and grandson, Alexander (II) are said by Evelyn Smith to have joined their father in Cumberland County in 1752. Mrs. Fraine's and Thomas's book says that Archibald (b. 1720) is their first documented ancestor in America, so they obviously feel that documentation is lacking for the father-son relationship between Alexander I (who came in 1739) and Archibald who came in 1752.

According to the research of Fraine and Thomas:

> Archibald Elder was married twice (that we know) and had 16 children—eight by each of his wives. He was married first to Ann Gilchrist. We do not know to which Gilchrist family she belonged or whether her family ever came to America. Archibald's second wife was Katherine Mullin. In Gaelic, she was called "Ketrin" or "Catrin." Some records say that he had a third wife named Margaret Bethune and had in all, 18 children!
>
> We are unable to find any proof of this latter marriage. If there was a Margaret, she would have been wife number two, as Ann was dead, and in his will he names Katherine as his wife. He also named only 16 children.

However, it is very possible and probable that he did have more children. It would be very unusual if he raised to maturity all his children, due to the high infant mortality rate in those particular times. It is possible that he had other children who died young and without heirs to be mentioned in his will.[40]

Archibald McKay had by his first wife, Ann Gilchrist, eight children:

I.	JANET	V.	JOHN Sr.
II.	SARAH	VI.	ARCHIBALD Jr.
III.	ALEXANDER	VII.	MALCOLM
IV.	ISABELLA	VIII.	NEILL

I. JANET MCKAY b. c. 1744 in Scotland, m. ____ Shaw. No data.

II. SARAH MCKAY b. c. 1746 in Scotland, m. Daniel McNeill (presumably the son of Archibald McNeill). This line is traced in this volume under the Archibald/Daniel McNeill section.

III. ALEXANDER MCKAY II b. 1738, Scotland, d. Aug.1793 in Grand Exuma Island, Bahamas, British West Indies. He m. Margaret McNeill (dau. of Lauchlin and Margaret Johnstone McNeill) who d. July 1819 and is buried at Juniper Creek, N.C. Alexander II was a Captain in the British Army during the American Revolution and Angus W. McLean writes of him that: "Alexander McKay was such an uncompromising loyalist that he refused to live under the American government after the close of the Wars and together with his family moved to the Bahama Islands . . ."[41] They had:

- A. Ann Nancy McKay b. 1768, d. 1844 in North Carolina, m. Col. Daniel Smith. They had (at least):
  - 1. Catherine b. 1799, d. 1801
  - 2. Lovedy b. 1801, d. 1858
- B. Daniel McKay b. 1770, d. 1793
- C. Archibald McKay b. 1772, d. 1804/07, Bahamas. His wife Ann and baby are buried next to him there.
- D. Lauchlin McKay b. 1774, d. 1832 in Leaf, LA.
- E. Alexander McKay III b. 1778, d. 1787

IV. ISABELLA MCKAY b. c.1750 and d. before 1797. She is said to have married a Dr. Thomas McDonald Reid, a surgeon and doctor of physics, who lived on the Yadkin Road near Archibald McKay. They had one son:

- A. David Reid b. 1768 in North Carolina, d. 1838 in Madison

County, Tennessee, m. 1798/99 Mary Ramsey. They had eleven children.[42]

V. JOHN MCKAY SR. "probably the first child born in this country to the family"[43] c. 1753, d. 1821 in Cumberland County, N.C. While his three brothers, Alexander, Archibald and Malcolm were Loyalists, John was in the North Carolina Legislature. He m. c. 1771-74 Chloe Matthews and had eight children. Chloe d. 1811, and John m. secondly in 1814 Ann Brennan, widow (dau. of John Montgomery of Chatham County). They are thought to have had no children. John and Chloe had:

A. Mary McKay b. 1771, d. 1846, m. Frank Shackleford, Esq. of Charleston, S.C.
B. Alexander McKay b. 1776, d. 1839 in Hinds County, Miss., m. Feraby Williams. They lived in Clinton, MS. (a number of the family went to Mississippi in 1821). They had thirteen children.[44]
C. Ann McKay b. 1778, d. 1833, m. 1805 John McLennan b. 1785. They had seven children.[45]
D. Thomas McKay b. c. 1792, m. 1820 Catherine Johnson. He served in the War of 1812 and d. 1857 in Cumberland County, N.C. Catherine b. c. 1800, d. c.1880. They had ten children.[46]
E. James McKay b. c. 1794, d. after 1870, m. Susan A.(?) b. 1823-26, d. after 1900. They lived in Cumberland County and had eleven children.[47]
F. Archibald McKay b. c. 1795/97 in Cumberland County, d. c.1877, m. Mary Ann Munroe (Monroe) in 1833. She was b. 1807/09, d. 1894. No children.
G. Sarah McKay b. in the 1780's, d. 1834, m. David Douglas Salmon in 1805. He was b. 1778, d. 1857 of Morris County, N.J., and Statesville, N.C. They had one daughter.[48]
H. George McKay said to have m. Rebecca Kirkpatrick and worked in the lumber business with his father.

VI. ARCHIBALD MCKAY JR. b. c. 1758 in Cumberland County, joined Cornwallis's army in 1781 as Captain of Militia. After the war he went to Nova Scotia, then to London, finally returning to Cumberland County in 1790 and m. Mary Gilchrist (dau. of John Gilchrist Sr. and Effie McMillan). He died in 1799 with great land holdings. They had one son: Hector.[49]

VII. MALCOLM MCKAY b. c.1762, d. 1846, m. Elizabeth Campbell

(dau. of Sir Farquard Campbell, one of the 1739 Argyll Colony). They had no children. He was known to be a scholar, and was another one of the family who was a Loyalist in the Revolution.

VIII. NEILL MCKAY b. 1766, d. 1830, m. 1805 Flora McNeill (dau. of Malcolm McNeill and Janet McAllister). This line has already been traced under the Col. Alexander McAllister section.[50]

Archibald McKay m. secondly Katherine Mullin d. 1808. They had eight children:

IX.	JOHN Jr.	XIII.	FARQUARD
X.	THOMAS F., M.D.	XIV.	ISABELLA
XI.	MARGARET	XV.	CHRISTIAN
XII.	ELIZABETH	XVI.	MARY

IX. JOHN MCKAY JR. b. c. 1776, Cumberland County, N.C., d. 1829 in Hinds County, MS. He married 1807 in Cumberland County Izilla Williams b. c. 1788, d. 1838 in Clinton, MS. They had three children, all b. in Cumberland County, N.C. About 1828 they all moved to Clinton, MS.

A. Catherine Belle McKay b. 1812, d. 1867 in Denmark, Tenn., m. first 1836 Henry Green in Hinds County, Miss., and secondly Thomas Reid (grandson of Archibald [Elder] McKay and Ann Gilchrist). They had two children, and he already had eight by two previous marriages.[51]

B. Pheraby W. McKay b. c. 1814-15 in Cumberland County, N.C., m. James D. Goff in Hinds County, MS. 1834. They moved to Memphis, Tenn. in 1844, and had five children.[52]

C. Henry Thomas McKay b. c. 1819, Cumberland County, N.C., d. 1864 in Prairie County, Arkansas, m. his second cousin, Fanny McKay 1854 in Memphis, TN. They had children.[53]

X. THOMAS F. MCKAY, M.D. b. 1778 in Cumberland County, N.C. and d. 1828 in Jefferson County, MS. They had:

A. Laminda (Lucinda?) Hinds McKay b. c. 1810 in Cumberland County, m. Thomas Woolridge 1835 in Hinds County, MS. Two children.

B. Mary Elizabeth McKay b. c. 1812, m. Nelson Kavenaugh 1836 in Hinds County, MS. They had at least one son.

XI. MARGARET MCKAY b. 1782, Charleston, S.C., d. 1811, m. Angus

Gilchrist b. 1773, d. 1834. She is buried at Longstreet Church, Cumberland County, N.C. Angus Gilchrist married secondly Mrs. Elizabeth McNeill Graham and had three children by her. He had five children by his first wife:

A. Catherine Gilchrist b. 1800, d. 1801

B. Effie Gilchrist b. 1801 Cumberland County, d. 1883 in Harrison County, Texas, m. Dushee Shaw c. 1822. They had ten children.[54]

C. Mary Gilchrist b. 1803, d. 1849, m. first 1827 Duncan McNeill b. 1800, d. 1832. They had one son. She m. secondly Malcolm McBryde, her second cousin. They had four children.[55]

D. Archibald McKay Gilchrist b. 1805 in Richmond County (now Scotland County), N.C., d. 1854. He graduated from the University of North Carolina and practiced law in Lowndes County, Alabama. He m. Margaret Davidson Mushat. They had seven children.[56]

XII. ELIZABETH MCKAY b. c. 1785, no information.

XIII. FARQUARD MCKAY b. 1787, d. 1814, buried at Longstreet Church, m. in 1814 Isabella Strong. He died within three months of marriage.

XIV. ISABELLA MCKAY b. 1790 in Cumberland County, and d. 1862 in Phillips County, Arkansas, m. Richard Davidson 1823 in Jefferson County, MS., a widower with four children. She had no children, but reared his.

XV. CHRISTIAN MCKAY b. c. 1792 in Cumberland County. She is said to have m. John McNeill in 1816. No information.

XVI. MARY MCKAY b. 1794, Cumberland County, m. Peter Strong, a silversmith and jeweler from Switzerland. They had two known children.[57]

Nearly all of the families we have covered up to this point were strong Tories during the Revolution (as were the majority of the upper Cape Fear Scots). But other descendants of the original Argyll Colony were on the American side, especially those in the Barbeque Church section of (present) Harnett County. We must glance at a few of these (and my information here is regrettably lacking).[58]

Clark Family

Alexander Clark of Jura came to North Carolina to settle in 1739, having been one of those who had come on the original Argyll search committee in 1736 with Neill Du McNeill, Alexander McAllister and other tacksmen. He died in 1762 in Cumberland County. His father was Gilbert Clark of Jura, b. c. 1690 and his uncle was Kenneth Clark. Alexander m. Flora McLean in Jura. Lt. Col. Victor Clark (USAF, Ret.) has carefully researched this family (and others) for many years. His *Genealogy of Clarks From the Isle of Jura, Scotland and Allied Families* (privately printed by Lt. Col. Clark: P.O. Box 397, Rochester, MN 55903-0397) is based on the family Bibles of Gilbert Clark and son David, as well as that of Hugh Clark, plus wills in Cumberland County, N.C., and other legal, family and church documents (including the Rev. Henry W. Foote's *Sketches of North Carolina*). He has also done considerable research in Scotland. Here I abstract only the most basic information concerning the Clark genealogy. All names, dates and relationships are fully documented by Lt. Col. Clark.

Alexander Clark and Flora (or Florah) McLean had four sons and four daughters (the daughters' names are unknown at present):

I. GILBERT
II. JOHN
III. DANIEL
IV. ARCHIBALD b. Isle of Jura, d. 1765 in Cumberland County, single

I. GILBERT CLARK b. 1723, Jura, d. Oct. 8, 1798, Cumberland County, North Carolina, m. Ann Alexander, who d. Cumberland County, Aug. 10, 1805. Ann Alexander was the step-daughter of John Dobbins.[59] Gilbert was an elder in Barbeque Presbyterian Church, Justice of the Peace and Captain of Militia. Gilbert and Ann had:

A. David b. 1756 in North Carolina, d. 1835 in North Carolina
B. Mary b. 1751, d. after 1798, single
C. Daniel b. 1753, d. before 1798, single
D. Flora
E. Ann
F. Margaret
G. Alexander
H. Archibald
I. Gilbert

A. David Clark b. Sept. 10, 1756, d. Apr. 7, 1835, m. his cousin, Nancy McLean (dau. of "Sober John" McLean and Effie McCrainie of Cumberland County), b. Aug. 6, 1770, d. July 8, 1858.[60] Laverne Raisch provided an article on David Clark in *Argyll Colony Plus* (8.1). According to *Genealogy of Clarks*. . . , David Clark and Nancy McLean had:

l. Margaret Clark b. Apr. 21, 1790, d. Mar. 10, 1869
2. John Clark b. May 12, 1792, d. 1811
3. Flora (Florah) Clark b. Apr. 23, 1794, d. 1872, m. Kirk Brantley and moved to Tennessee. They had:
    - a. Mary Brantley
    - b. Ann Brantley
    - c. Catherine Brantley
4. Effie Clark b. July 6, 1796, d. June 24, 1872
5. Gilbert Clark b. Feb. 12, 1798, d. Sept. 24, 1851 in Columbus, GA., m. Nancy . . . He was a schoolmaster in Columbus, Georgia. They had:

a. John	e. Neill
b. Catherine	f. Elizabeth
c. David	g. Mary
d. Sarah	h. Gilbert

6. Daniel Clark b. Apr. 29, 1801, Cumberland County, N.C.
7. Ann Alexander Clark b. Mar. 15, 1804, d. Sept. 15, 1884, m. Malcolm Buie and moved to Mississippi.
8. Catherine Clark b. Apr. 14, 1807
9. Hugh McCrainie Clark b. Oct. 24, 1809 in Cumberland County, N.C., d. Oct. 29, 1897 in Perry County, AL., m. Feb. 14, 1839 in Bibb County, AL., Cinthia Moarning Perkerson, b. Mar. 15, 1818 in Jackson County, GA., d. Aug. 8, 1896, Perry County, AL.
    - a. David Alexander Clark b. Sept. 7, 1840, Bibb County, AL., d. July 27, 1850, Bibb County.
    - b. Joel Erwin Clark b. Sept. 7, 1842, Bibb County, d. Feb. 20, 1843 in Bibb County.
    - c. Sarah Ann Margaret Clark b. May 24, 1844, Bibb County, d. June 27, 1900, Perry County County, AL., She was single; her fiancé was killed in the War Between the States.
    - d. Mary Stuart Clark b. July 21, 1846, d. 1939, m. James David Dinkins, no children.
    - e. Cinthia Moarning Clark b. Aug. 26, 1848, Bibb County, d. May 28, 1928 in Selma, AL. She was single; her fiancé was killed in the War Between the States.

f. Martha Jane Clark b. May 12, 1850 in Bibb County, d. in Perry County, AL., Single.
g. James Crawford Clark b. June 13, 1853 in Bibb County, m. Nov. 4, 1888, Dollie Adelia DeWitt. He d. Mar. 23, 1910 in Selma, AL.[61]
h. Catherine M. Clark b. Apr. 11, 1856, d. Oct. 18, 1948, m. Gabriel Moon, Bibb County.[62]
i. Didamiah Bollin Clark b. Sept. 23, 1858 in Bibb, d. Mar. 4, 1934 in Tuscaloosa County, AL., m. William Hopson Hooper.[63]

D. Flora Clark b. 1754, d. 1796, m. 1769 John Smith II. See under Malcolm Smith I section of this book for their children.
E. Ann Clark b. 1758, m. Patrick Smith. See ibid. for their children.
F. Margaret b. 1760, may have died before 1798, as she is not listed in her father's will that year.
G. Alexander b. Feb. 25, 1762, went to Bibb County, Alabama in 1823, m. Marian McLean. They had:

1. Mary	5. Effie
2. John	6. Ann
3. Daniel	7. James
4. Margaret	

H. Archibald Clark b. 1764, m. Christian Buie in Cumberland County, N.C. They had:

1. Margaret	3. Ann
2. Jannet	4. Daniel

I. Gilbert Clark b. Apr. 2, 1767, Cumberland, m. in Cumberland County, Jennett ____.

II. JOHN CLARK b. Jura, d. Cumberland County, N.C. He m. _______. They had:[64]

A. James	E. Catherine
B. Alexander	F. Flora
C. John	G. Mary
D. Margaret	H. Euphemia

In *Argyll Colony Plus* (10.2), there is an article on "The Immigrant John Clark of Jura and His Descendents" by Louise Currie, whose material was compiled from information in Billie Louise Clark Crook's *Our Clark Family*, plus additional material from Irene Cook, Gloria Hargrave, Sue Johnson, Laverne Raisch, and Mary Sue White (123-139 of *ACP*).

III. DANIEL CLARK m. ________. They had:[65]

A. Alexander
B. Archibald
C. William

Some Clark family letters from Scotland have been published in *Argyll Colony Plus* (Vol. 3, No. 4, Fall 1988, 131, 132), in addition to more recent material listed above.

John McLean Family of Cumberland (Harnett) County

Not far from the territory settled by the Clarks of Jura, another Jura family (who intermarried with the Clarks) also settled. These were the "Sober" John McLeans. Lt. Col. Victor Clark, Jr. has compiled information on this family in *My Isle of Jura Clarks and McLeans,* based largely on information from the late Margarett Clark Floyd and "Descendants of Hugh McLean of Jura, Scotland", compiled by the late Henry Hodgin of Red Springs, N.C., as well as from the Family Bible records of David and Gilbert Clark and Reverend Henry W. Foote's *Sketches of North Carolina* and Reverend E.W. Caruthers' *Revolutionary Incidents and Sketches of Character Chiefly in the "Old North State"* (Philadelphia: Hayes & Zell, 1854), in addition to *The State Records of North Carolina,* collected and edited by Walter Clark, Vol. XVI-1782-83 (Nash Brothers: Goldsboro, N.C., 1899).

"Sober John" McLean was born in Jura in 1730 and emigrated with his father, Hugh McLean, and mother, Margaret McArthur (McLean) to Cumberland County, N.C. in 1749. The parents of emigrant Hugh McLean were John McLean and Katy Buie of Jura.

"Sober John" McLean married Effie McCranie, daughter of Hugh McCranie, Sr. and Catherine Buie. Effie died Mar. 10, 1810, and John died Oct. 17, 1793 in Cumberland County. Governor Angus W. McLean's *Highland Scots in North Carolina* describes their burying place in his 1919 manuscript:

> The Mill Place Cemetary is located on the Sheriff Brown place, later the estate of the late Colonel Kenneth Murchison, about three miles southwest of Lillington [in Harnett County, N.C.—originally Cumberland County, ed.], and a quarter of a mile to the rear of the old Murchison residence . . . There are a number of MacLeans buried here, most of them from the immediate community, some from neighboring settlements" (McLean then lists the tombstone inscriptions of Hugh, John and others), (p. 671).

John McLean was known as "Sober John" because of the leadership he gave on the Tory side during the Revolutionary War. He remained sober while his other compatriots became inebriated, and thus could be entrusted with difficult tasks (such as handling prisoners of war). He acquitted himself well in such duties, especially on the 13th of September, 1781, when he was in charge of taking the captured Whig Governor of North Carolina, Burke, and his council and several Whig military officers under guard to Wilmington to be turned over to the British. According to both Caruthers (47-55 and 203) and to Clark's *State Records*, Vol. XVI (40-42, 591), "Sober John" treated the captured Governor and other officials so well, that after the War, they asked the North Carolina legislature to pardon him for having been on the Tory side, which was granted.

According to Victor Clark, "Indications are that toward the end of the hostilities 'Sober John' became disenchanted with the Tories, became neutral and left his family on Upper Little River and took his negroes down to the swamps on the Cape Fear, nearly opposite Bluff Church, where he rented land from his Whig friend, John Smith, and under his protection lived safely . . ."[66]

"Sober John" McLean and Effie McCranie had:

I. MARION MCLEAN b. 1785 in Cumberland County, N.C., m. Alexander Clark. This family moved to Bibb County, AL. in 1823. They had four children:

A. Mary Clark
B. John Clark
C. Daniel Clark
D. Margaret Clark

II. DANIEL MCLEAN m. Flora McAllister and had:

A. Effie McLean
B. Ann McLean
C. James McLean

III. JOHN MCLEAN m. Catherine Ochiltree

IV. DUNCAN MCLEAN b. 1777 in Cumberland County, N.C., d. Jan. 5, 1824 in Bibb County, Ala., m. Mary McAllister.

V. HUGH MCLEAN m. Betty Ochiltree.

VI. CATHERINE MCLEAN m. Parson Allen McDougald. They are buried in Mill Place Cemetary in present Harnett County, N.C. Rev. Allen McDougald is described by Gov. Angus McLean as "one of the pioneer religious leaders of the Scotch, and the sixth pastor of Bluff and Barbeque Churches. His grave is unmarked save by two small stones that bear no inscription" (op.cit., 671).

VII. NEIL MCLEAN m. Margaret Murphy.

VIII. NANCY MCLEAN b. Aug. 6, 1770 Cumberland County, d. July 8, 1857, m. her cousin, David Clark, b. Sept. 10, 1756, d. Apr. 7, 1835. Their children are traced in the Clark Family under I. GILBERT CLARK (father of David), immediately preceding this section.

IX. MARGARET MCLEAN

Darroch Family of Harnett County, N.C.

Another Isle of Jura family which lived in the Clark and McLean territory is that of the Darrochs. The Darrochs, however, arrived nearly one hundred years later than their neighboring Clarks and McLeans. The Darrochs also joined Barbeque Presbyterian Church in Harnett County, and some of them also later belonged to Cypress Presbyterian Church in Moore County, N.C.

My information on this well known family is at present very limited, and lists only the first two generations. According to the late Rev. Donald Budge (*Jura, an Island of Argyll: Its History, People and Story*—as quoted in *Argyll Colony Plus* Vol. 10, No. 2 (154):

> Darroch is an early Jura surname. To begin with it was "Mac ill riabhaich," and was later anglicized to Darroch. The connection is not simple, and the following are the explanations which are given locally and elsewhere. At the time when the people were altering their names, and it was wiser not to have a MacDonald name, a Jura Mac il'riach was walking home, aided by his stout oak walking-stick, when he suddenly stopped and said, *'is darach mo bhat agus is Darach mi fheil'* (Oak, is my stick, and from now on Darach shall be my name). The other explanation is in connection with the Gaelic meaning of the old form 'Mac il'riach', the son of the gray or grizzled lad, it having been in some cases 'Mac il'an dath riabhach', son of the gray or grizzled colour, and so becoming 'Dath riabhach' or Darrach. It would be amusing if, after these far-fetched explanations, it turned out to be simply that of 'Durach' meaning 'man of Jura or Dura', and becoming Darroch by the simple and not at all unlikely changing of a vowel and the adding of an extra 'r'.

Some information on the Harnett County, N.C., Darroch genealogy is given in "Findings of the Darroch History on my Trip to Scotland" by Dennis W. Cameron (transcribed by Louise Curry) in *Argyll Colony Plus* Vol. II, No. 1 (58-60). Dennis Cameron in addition to his research in the Isle of Jura and the Registry House in Edinburgh, also made use of a

paper prepared around 1975 by Dennis W. Cameron, Register of Deeds, Surry County, N.C. According to his material:

Alexander Darroch and wife, Janet Shaw, immigranted to North Carolina about 1849. They brought their children with them:

- I. ANGUS DARROCH b. Oct., 1829 and buried at Cypress Church, Moore County, N.C.
- II. MARY DARROCH
- III. JANET DARROCH
- IV. NANCY DARROCH
- V. DANIEL (or DONALD) DARROCH

Dennis Cameron states that "Session book 32 of Cypress Presbyterian Church [shows that] . . . Alexander Darroch and Joannett were received into Cypress Church on Certificate from the parish of Jura and Colonsay, Scotland on Sept. 24, 1848. This convinces me that Janet Shaw was born and baptized on the island of Colonsay which lies to the northwest of Jura, just above Islay."

Other Darroch families also came to this Upper Cape Fear area of North Carolina. In the article quoted above, reference is made by Dennis Cameron to a letter from the late Miss Katie Darroch (written on Aug. 4, 1975) stating that "Alexander Darroch Senior and his wife Mary Campbell left Jura on August 18, 1847, on board *Rappahenock,* and arrived in North Carolina Sept. 30, 1847" (art. cit., 60).

Deerfield March 25) 1819

Dear Uncle I again take the opportunity
of writing to you to inform you that we are well at
this time hoping that this may find you and yours in the
same Condition your letter dated January 1818 came
to hand the [illegible] Day after you entered it in
the post office which gave us satisfaction in hearing
from you [illegible] nothing [illegible] gives us greater
[illegible] than to hear once in while from our friends
[illegible] on the world [illegible]
[illegible] being well [illegible]
state of health Brother Allan and wife are well
uncle Malcom is well and enjoys is health [illegible]
years past [illegible] than formerly Cousin Daniel and
family are well he hath three Children two
boys and one girl Malcom Alexander and Catherine
Cousin Alexander was married about one year ago
and he hath a boy nearly three months old named
Archibald uncle Dugald and family are well
except mary she had a very sick turn last summer
and do not enjoy her health very well since
I suppose that you have heard that Duncan Smith
Departed this life he Died the [illegible] of march
a year ago the rest of your old acquaintance are
well at this time except one of Malcom Camp
bell Daughters she had a turn of sickness three
years ago and lost the use of one of her legs and are
[illegible] to walk without Crutches [illegible]
ten years old P S uncle Dugald is
Doing [illegible] well he has one hundred acres of
land and [illegible] nearly paid — market for cattle
and horses [illegible] wonderfull high among us this
year grain is plenty in this quarter wheat is
from 10 to 12 shillings per bushel rye from
6 to 7 shillings Corn 7 shillings per bushel
barly from 6 to 8 shillings — last summer was
very warm here and in some [illegible]
the [illegible] of this state had [illegible]
the whole [illegible]

This letter was written by an Argyll emigrant to Deerfield, New York, Duncan Blue, to his uncle, "River" Daniel Blue, who also had emigrated from Argyll in 1804. "River" Daniel lived in Moore County, N.C. More detail about this family is found on pages 232 and following.

Notes

1. For his ancestry, see A.I.B. Stewart, art. cit. in *Argyll Colony Plus,* Issue Number 1, April 1986 and also Everett McNeill Kivette, *The McNeill's Ferry Chronicle and Campbell University* (Yancey Graphics: Burnsville, N.C., 1983), 40, 41. Sheriff A.I.B. Stewart's original article was considerably enlarged and enriched in *Argyll Colony Plus* (Vol. 6, No. 1).

2. For her ancestry, see Kivette, op. cit., 41.

3. A.I.B. Stewart, "Highland Emigration to America With Particular Reference to North Carolina" in *Argyll Colony Plus,* Vol. 6, No. 1, 15.

4. See *Argyll Colony Plus,* Issue Number 1, April 1986, 43ff.

5. Taken from Rev. D.S. McAllister, *Genealogical Record of the Descendants of Col. Alexander McAllister of Cumberland County, N.C. Also of Mary and Isabella McAllister* (Richmond, Va.: Whittet & Shepperson, 1900), 165-167.

6. See *Argyll Colony Plus,* Issue Number 1, April 1986, 43ff.

7. For an article on this family see article mentioned by Kivette in footnote 1 above.

8. pp. 33ff.

9. See D.S. McAllister, op. cit., 23 and Hugh McLean in art. cit. in footnote 3.

10. William C. Fields, III of Fayetteville, N.C. wrote a biographical sketch of Farquhard Campbell (his ancestor) in John A. Oates, *The Story of Fayetteville and the Upper Cape Fear* (3rd ed., 1981, 821-23), and Ruby G. Campbell attempted to trace more of his background in "Unsolved Mystery: The Origins of Farquhard Campbell (Ca. 1721-1808) in *Argyll Colony Plus* (Vol. 10, No. 3, 178-181).

11. See ibid.

12. More information on them can be found in *Archibald McKay 1720-1797: Scotland to Cumberland County, N.C.* by Mrs. Barbara McKay Thomas of Texas and Mrs. Bettie McKay Fraine of Oklahoma (published 1979).

13. Part of this family is traced in *Charn Cuimhne To Our Scots of North Carolina* by Evelyn Futch Smith (1969), 16ff.

14. This line is traced by Evelyn Smith, op. cit., 23ff.

15. Their line is traced in Douglas F. Kelly *Scottish Blue Family,* 373ff.

16. Their line is traced in ibid., 286ff.

17. Their line is traced in ibid., 740ff.

18. See Malcolm Fowler, *They Passed This Way,* 36ff.; Sion Harrington III, "Jennie Bhan McNeill: Legend of the Upper Cape Fear" in *Argyll Colony Plus,* Vol. 3, No. 2, Spring 1988, 44-50; and Everett McNeill Kivette, "The Unusual Heritage of Julia and Esther McNeill of the St. Paul's Review" in ibid., Vol. 3, No. 4, Fall 1988, 134-141.

19. See art. cit. in footnote 3.

20. Kivette, *The McNeill's Ferry Chronicle and Campbell University,* 40.

21. More information on the others could be traced in the volume listed in footnote 10.

22. See Evelyn Smith, op. cit., 214, 215.

23. Privately printed in Aberdeen, North Carolina, 1981, 26-50.

24. Ibid., 26.

25. Ibid.

26. Traced in ibid., 27-29.

27. Traced in ibid., 29-33.

28. Traced in ibid., 35-42.

29. Ibid., 42.
30. Traced in ibid., 42-45.
31. Traced in ibid., 45-50.
32. Evelyn Smith, op. cit., 218.
33. Vol. 2, No. 3, 105-108.
34. Thomson, art. cit., 106.
35. Ibid.
36. All of these names and dates come from ibid.
37. See Vol. 3, No. 4, 147.
38. See footnote 10.
39. Mostly from Evelyn Smith, op. cit., 285, 286.
40. See footnote 10, op. cit., 4.
41. Angus W. McLean, op. cit., 669.
42. See Fraine and Thomas, op. cit., 14-21.
43. Ibid., 21.
44. Line traced in ibid., 22-24.
45. Line traced in ibid. 24.
46. Line traced in ibid. 25-27.
47. See ibid. 27.
48. Ibid. 28.
49. Traced in ibid. 29-34 and in Purcell, *Lumber River Scots and their Descendants* (1942).
50. For much fuller detail also see Fraine and Thomas, op. cit., 35-72.
51. Traced in ibid., 76.
52. Traced in ibid., 77.
53. Traced in ibid. 43-58.
54. Traced in ibid. 78-81 and (in different order) in Purcell, op. cit. 492ff.
55. All five children traced in Fraine and Thomas, op. cit., 81, 82.
56. Traced in ibid. 82, 83.
57. Mentioned in ibid., 85.
58. Much of my information is taken from the dedicated work of Lt. Col. Victor E. Clark, Jr., of Dallas, Texas, who pioneered the *Argyll Colony Plus* periodical in 1986 and compiled *The Highland Scots Clarks From the Isle of Jura, Scotland* (1983).
59. Victor Clark, *The Genealogy of the Clarks . . .*, 35.
60. The 'Sober John' McLean Family is dealt with in the next section of this chapter.
61. Their descendents are traced in Family Group 7 of Victor Clark, *Genealogy . . .*
62. Their descendents are traced in Family Group 10 of Victor Clark, *Genealogy . . .*
63. Their descendents are traced in Family Group 11 of Victor Clark, *Genealogy . . .*
64. According to Family Group 3 of Clark, op. cit.
65. Ibid.
66. Victor Clark, *My Isle of Jura Clarks and McLeans* (no pagination).

5

The Buie Family: Carolina then Westward

Now let us move into upper Cumberland County, part of which became Harnett County, home of another "Whig" family with Argyll Colony origins. We refer to the prolific Buie connection who lived near Barbeque Church in (present) Harnett County and intermarried with McAllisters, Clarks, McNeills, McMillans, Shaws and others. The heads of this family were officers in Barbeque Church and were much involved in the life and politics of the area.

Until quite recently, it has been difficult to obtain firm and extensive genealogical information on this important family. The reasons are not hard to find. As late as 1979, Admiral Patterson wrote: "Now this family, once so numerous and prominent, has gone from Harnett County and so far as I know, none remains there."[1] In fact, so many of them migrated to the Southwest in the early nineteenth century, that few representatives of the Buie tradition remained in the upper Cumberland area to pass on the information.

The tombstone of a Janet Buie stands out among others in the ancient cemetery on a hill in Jura near the Columban site of Keils. Many Buies are buried here as well as Clarks, perhaps related to Buies and Clarks who emigrated from the Isle of Jura to the Cape Fear valley of North Carolina during the eighteenth century.

There was another problem, as Dr. Scott Buie has written: "Many county records were destroyed thus hampering research in these areas. The Bladen County courthouse burned in 1800 and 1893 and therefore most records of Buies in North Carolina from 1739 to 1754 were lost. Also, the Moore County courthouse burned in 1889 and very few records of Buies living in Moore from 1784 to 1889 survived . . ."[2]

However, all who are interested in Buie family research were massively assisted in 1983 by the appearance of Drs. T.R. Buie and Scott Buie's *The Family Buie: Scotland to North Carolina.* It is a model of careful genealogical research and sound historical writing, and deals clearly and realistically with a massive amount of material, which would otherwise be daunting, if not confusing. Since this volume (of 448 pages, including index) is widely available, all I shall do here is to mention the major family groups of Carolina Scots Buies, which are covered in the work, and give specific references so that the researcher can pursue these lines in it.

T.R. and Scott Buie write concerning the Scottish origin of the Carolina Buies:

> The first confirmed Buies arrived in North Carolina in September 1739, but others probably immigrated to the colony in 1745 and 1767 and perhaps other dates also. Furthermore, there were instances when Buies left North Carolina, so their presence in certain records do not necessarily mean they remained in North Carolina until their death . . . All of the researchers of early North Carolina history and the compilers believe that practically all of the early Buies who came to North Carolina originated from the Island of Jura in Scotland. . . .[3]

The Buie compilers first give a preliminary list of 24 Buie heads of families in early North Carolina, and where possible, suggest relationships between many of them. They properly note, however, that " . . . the very early Buie families of North Carolina are quite complicated, with various interconnections extending back to Scottish ties on Jura."[4]

Secondly, T.R. and Scott Buie present the genealogy of 40 family groups of Buies, of whom 23 have definite Cape Fear Valley, N.C., Scots roots. It is appropriate to list these 23 Buie family groups here briefly, and to refer the interested reader to the original volume for details.

Duncan Buie Family of Moore County, North Carolina

Duncan Buie b. c. 1760 in North Carolina, lived in Moore County, and had several sons and probably some daughters.[5] He moved to Catahoula Parish in Louisiana in 1812, and died there Aug. 21, 1836. He m. Susanna ______, b. in N.C., d. June 22, 1832 in Catahoula. Their known sons were:

I. NEILL BUIE b. c. 1785, Moore County, d. 1852, Franklin Parish, LA., m. 1816, Elizabeth Jones b. 1798 in S.C., d. Sept. 4, 1857, Ft. Necessity, LA. Their six children are traced in Buie.[6]

II. DANIEL BUIE b. c. 1792, Moore County, d. 1880, Moore County, m. Laney Dixon of Franklin County, N.C. Their ten children are traced in Buie.[7]

III. GILBERT BUIE b. 1792, Moore County, d. c. 1866, Upshur County, Texas, m. 1822, Alicia Humble b. 1802 in Amite County, MS., d. c. 1863, Upshur County, TX. Their three children (b. in Catahoula Parish, LA.) are traced in Buie.[8]

IV. MALCOLM BUIE b. c. 1794, Moore County, d. Mar. 19, 1844, Franklin Parish, LA., m. c. 1825, Mary ______. No living descendants have been located.

Archibald and Sarah "Sally" McFetter Buie of Bladen County, North Carolina

Archibald Buie b. c. 1750 presumably in Bladen County, m. c. 1775, Sarah "Sally" McFetter, who d. shortly after giving birth to their only son: I. ARCHIBALD BUIE JR. b. c. 1775, N.C., d. after 1850 in Bladen County, N.C., m. 1796, Ephamie Campbell b. c. 1775 in N.C., d. after 1850 in Bladen. They were members of Brown Marsh Presbyterian Church on the Cape Fear in Bladen. Their twelve children are traced in Buie.[9]

Malcom Buie and Ann McCraine Buie of Cumberland and Robeson Counties, North Carolina

Malcolm Buie was born on Jura c. 1735, and came to the Upper Cape Fear region with his brothers, Archibald, John and Neill, where he married Ann McCraine (or McRainey), daughter of Hugh McCraine and Catherine Buie McCraine c. 1760. Malcolm lived first in Cumberland, then in what is now Robeson County, near Richland Swamp, where he d. in Feb. 1781, and is buried in the family cemetery there. His three brothers remained single. Malcolm and Ann Buie had five children:

I. NEILL BUIE b. c. 1765 in Cumberland County, d. Aug. 10, 1837, Robeson County, N.C., m. Ann Monroe: no children.

II. DANIEL BUIE b.c. 1770 in Cumberland County, d. 1823 in Robeson, m. Flora McPherson b. 1775 in Cumberland, dau. of Daniel McPherson and Sarah McNeill, d. Nov. 10, 1859 in Robeson. Their ten children are traced in Buie.[10]

III. ARCHIBALD BUIE b. N.C.; no information

IV. JOHN BUIE b. N.C.; no information

V. ANNABEL "NEPSEY" BUIE b. c. 1775 in Bladen (now Robeson) County, N.C., d. Nov. 10, 1851 near Junction City, Union County, AR., m. Finlah McCorvey b. Scotland, d. c. 1837 in Robeson County, N.C. They lived in Robeson County, and after the death of her husband, she moved with several relatives and friends to Union Church, Mississippi, and finally to Arkansas. Their four children are traced in Buie.[11]

Archibald and Ann Buie of Cumberland County, North Carolina

Archibald Buie b. c. 1740-45 in Bladen (now Cumberland) County, d. c. 1784 in Cumberland, m. Ann ______, d. before 1784 in Cumberland, leaving three small children, including a son John, known as "John the shoemaker," who moved from North Carolina to Union Church, Mississippi. Offspring of Archibald and Ann:

I. JOHN BUIE (THE SHOEMAKER) b. 1775, Cumberland County, N.C., d. Oct. 22, 1845 in Franklin County, MS. He moved to Union Church, MS. c. 1810, and later to Franklin County. He m. twice, and by his first wife (name unknown) had one son. He m. secondly, Mary Ford in 1817 at Union Church; no known issue. The family of his son, Archibald B. Buie are traced in Buie.[12]

Gilbert Buie of North Carolina and Union Church, Mississippi

Gilbert Buie, son of Gilbert and Jennett—Buie, b. June 17, 1773 in North Carolina (in Barbeque district of Cumberland, according to the Buie compilers, though others have placed it in Robeson).[13] Around 1809 he moved to Jefferson County, Mississippi, and he and his wife Catherine were charter members of Union Church in 1817. He d. Feb. 24, 1848, and is buried in the Short Cemetery in Jefferson County, MS. He m. first, c. 1799 in N.C., Nancy ______, d. c. 1810. They had three children:

I. JENNETT BUIE b. Apr. 9, 1800 in Moore County, N.C., d. Jefferson County, MS., m. May 6, 1820, Daniel Patterson. Their two children are listed in Buie.[14]

II. DANIEL BUIE b. Dec. 29, 1803 in Moore County, N.C., said to have d. young.

III. MALCOLM b. c. 1805 in Moore County, N.C., said to have d. young. Gilbert Buie m. secondly Catherine "Catie" Cameron (?), b. N.C., d. MS. After Gilbert's death she is said to have m. a Batey and then a Jennings; no children by these marriages. Gilbert and Catherine had:

IV. SUSANNA BUIE b. 1812, Jefferson County, Miss.; d. young.

V. ANN BUIE b. Feb. 6, 1814, Jefferson County, m. Mar. 21, 1835, John H. Cunningham in MS. They moved to Louisiana, where one of their sons became Attorney General.

VI. JOHN ALEXANDER BUIE b. 1816, Jefferson County, MS.

VII. SARAH ADELINE BUIE b. Dec. 27, 1817, Jefferson County, MS.

VIII. MARY JANE BUIE baptized May 23, 1818, Jefferson County, m. Apr. 29, 1843, Aaron Burwell Short in Jefferson County, MS. Their three children are listed in Buie.[15]

IX. GILBERT BUIE JR. b. Jan. 24, 1824, Jefferson County, MS.

X. EMILY CATHERINE BUIE b. Oct. 4, 1825, Jefferson County, MS. d. Sept. 9, 1907, Jefferson County, m. first on Aug. 3, 1848, John M. McDonald, who d. 1857, by whom she had six children, who are listed in Buie.[16] Secondly, she m. Levi Clines by whom she had two children, who are listed in Buie.[17]

XI. JOSEPH PAISLEY BUIE b. Nov. 26, 1827, Jefferson County, MS. d. Aug. 1881 in MS., m. Feb. 21, 1870, Sarah Elizabeth Millsaps in MS., who d. May 4, 1901, and is buried in Brookhaven Cemetery in Lincoln County, MS. Their five children are traced in Buie.[18]

Neill Buie and Dorothy Mercer Buie of North Carolina and Union Church, Mississipi

Neill Buie, son of Gilbert Buie and Jennett ______ Buie, b. Mar., 1764 in North Carolina, near Barbeque Creek in Cumberland County, according to the Buie compilers,[19] the brother of Gilbert Buie, whose family has just been dealt with. He m. Dorothy Mercer in Robeson County, N.C. c. 1792, and in 1805 moved from Robeson County to Georgia. In 1810 he moved to Union Church, Mississippi, where he and Dorothy were charter members of the Presbyterian Church in 1817. This family later lived in Franklin County, where many of them are buried in the Wright's Cemetery. Neil and Dorothy had:

I. JOHN BUIE b. May l3, 1793, Moore County, N.C., d. c. 1846 in MS.; lived in Yazoo County, MS. The Buie compilers discuss the information concerning the name of his wives and three children.[20]

II. GILBERT M. BUIE b. Feb. 19, 1795, Moore County, d. Nov. 20, 1873, Union Church, MS., m. first on Apr. 20, 1824, Lovedy Caroline Brown, b. Apr. 8, 1810 in Jefferson County, MS., dau. of Archibald and Mary Brown Brown (dau. of Hugh Brown and Mary Buie Brown—who are also covered in this volume), d. Nov. 20, 1873, Union Church, MS. Their nine children are traced in Buie.[21]

Gilbert may have m. secondly, Mary Perry: no children.

III. DANIEL BUIE b. July 15, 1797, Moore County, N.C., d. Sept. 17, 1862, MS., buried in Franklin County, MS. He m. Mary Lemons b. Jan., 1810, N.C., d. Sept. 12, 1871, MS. Their seven children are traced in Buie.[22]

IV. WILLIAM BUIE b. Oct. 18, 1799, Moore County, N.C., d. Sept. 9, 1823, Franklin County, MS.; was single.

V. NEIL BUIE JR. b. Oct. 4, 1801, Robeson County, N.C., d. Oct. 8, 1861, Copiah County, MS., m. Nancy Smith, b. c. 1802, Georgia. Their seven children are traced in Buie.[23]

VI. HENRY BUIE b. May 26, 1804, Robeson County, N.C., d. MS. He lived in Yazoo County, MS.; no issue.

VII. DAVID BUIE b. Feb. 7, 1807, Georgia, d. Oct. 19, 1871, MS. He lived in Copiah County, MS., and m. Jane McLaurin b. May 28, 1840 near Waynesboro, MS., d. Feb. 23, 1906, MS. Their five children are traced in Buie.[24]

VIII. MILTON BUIE b. Mar. 4, 1809, Georgia, d. Aug. 20, 1880, Oxford, MS., m. Apr. 18, 1855, Bettie Jane Hume of Claiborne County, MS. Their two children are listed in Buie.[25]

IX. ANN BUIE b. Jan. 14, 1812, Jefferson County, MS., m. Felix Ryan, lived in Copiah County, MS., then moved to Angelina County, Texas. Had descendants; no information.

X. JOSEPH BUIE b. Jan. 11, 1815, Jefferson County, MS., d. Apr. 9, 1840, MS.; was single.

XI. ELIZABETH BUIE b. Sept. 1, 1818, Jefferson County, MS. Information on her four marriages, though not on her descendants, is in Buie.[26]

William Buie and Margaret McIver Buie of Moore County, North Carolina

The Buie compilers think that this William Buie, who lived near Buffalo Creek in what was then Moore County, was the son of Archibald Buie and Catherine Shaw for reasons discussed in their genealogy of Archibald.[27] William Buie, was an elder in Buffalo Presbyterian Church in upper Moore County (now Lee) in 1804. He m. (as his second wife) Margaret McIver, dau. of Roderick and Nancy ______ McIver. The name and offspring of William Buie's first are unknown. The offspring of

William and his second wife, Margaret McIver Buie, have already been alluded to in this volume under the McIver Family, Roderick McIver section, as traced by Kenneth L. Kelly. They are also traced in Buie.[28]

Neal (Neil) and Sarah Buie of Cumberland County, Pennsylvania

This couple is known to have come from Cumberland County, PA. to Moore County, N.C., in 1797. It is generally believed among their descendents (though at this stage without any documentary proof) that they were originally from North Carolina, and went to Pennsylvania during the American Revolution. What is certain, however, is that Neal (Neil) and Sarah ______ Buie's son, John Buie, m. Mary Cox in Philadelphia, PA. on Dec. 28, 1797. She was b. c. 1771 in Philadelphia, dau. of Andrew and Hannah Cleany Cox of Kingsess, PA., according to papers in possession of the descendants of the late William McC. Blue and wife, Mazie McLean Blue of Eagle Springs, N.C. This family moved from Philadelphia to North Carolina by ship in 1797, and settled on Mill Creek in western Moore County in 1798.

Neal (Neil) and Sarah ______ Buie had two children:

I. JOHN BUIE b. c. 1773, d. 1802, while on a trip to Georgetown, S.C., buried in Moore County in the old Buie Cemetery near Mill Creek (in the Eagle Springs vicinity), m. Mary Cox, d. 1845 in Moore County, buried in Buie Cemetery. Their two sons are traced in Buie[29] and John's son, John C., is also mentioned under the Martin family in this volume, and many of his descendants are traced under the Patrick A. Blue section of Douglas Kelly's *Scottish Blue Family.*

II. SARAH BUIE m. Lochlin Currie, Moore County, N.C. Their one son is listed in Buie.[30]

John Buie and Archibald The Piper of Cumberland County, North Carolina

Archibald Buie the Piper first appears in North Carolina records in 1755, according to the Buie compilers, when he bought 91 acres of land on the northeast side of the northwest branch of the Cape Fear River in Cumberland County.[31] Later tax records show him to have lived in the Barbeque district of then Cumberland County. Piper Archie d. 1806, and left his property to the children of his brother, John. According to the

Buie compilers, "Piper Archie never married, but John's sons Malcolm, Archibald and John moved to Tattnall County, Georgia. Apparently Malcolm and John moved first about 1800 followed by Archibald around 1808."[32] The parents of Piper Archie and John are unknown. John Buie, brother of Piper Archie (who is described in Malcolm Fowler's posthumous *Valley of the Scots*) b. probably Scotland, d. Cumberland County, N.C., wife unknown, had:

I. MALCOLM BUIE b. c. 1770, Cumberland County, N.C. d. c. 1829, Decatur County, Georgia, m. Margaret ______. Their six children are traced in Buie.[33]

II. ARCHIBALD BUIE b. c. 1775, Cumberland County, N.C., d. 1852, Gadsden County, Fla., lived in Tattnall County, GA., c. 1800-1825. He m. Mary McArthur, b. Apr. 12, 1775, Cumberland County, N.C., dau. of Daniel and Jennette McArthur. Their four children are traced in Buie.[34]

III. JOHN BUIE b. c. 1775, Cumberland County, N.C.; documentation in Georgia records is uncertain, according to the Buie compilers.[35]

IV. MARY "POLLY" BUIE b. c. 1780, Cumberland County, N.C., m. John McArthur on July 7, 1800, according to marriage bond in Robeson County, N.C., where they lived.

John Buie and Flora McDuffie Buie of Upper Little River, Cumberland County, North Carolina

This family is traced by the Buie compilers[36] and also by Admiral Patterson, whose sketch we follow here (though it should be supplemented in later generations by the Buie compilers' information):

John Buie d. 1823, m. Flora McDuffie d. c. 1820. " . . . John Buie was a man of prominence and a leader in his community. In his first will we find that he lived on the south side of Upper Little River, adjoining Archibald Clark's estate and according to his father's will it was the family plantation."[37]

John and Flora had (not necessarily in this order):

I. SARAH d. c. 1837 single
II. DUNCAN BUIE d. c. 1837 probably single
III. MALCOLM BUIE
IV. MARY BUIE

V. MARGARET BUIE
VI. JOHN BUIE, Jr.
VII. ARCHIBALD BUIE, marital status uncertain
VIII. NEILL BUIE d. 1840, marital status unknown
IX. CATHERINE BUIE, marital status uncertain
X. DANIEL BUIE, marital status unknown

III. MALCOLM BUIE m. first Annabella Cameron in 1820 and Anna Clark in 1828. Malcolm later moved to Tennessee. According to John Buie's will, three sons of Malcolm are mentioned:

A. Daniel
B. Archibald
C. William

IV. MARY BUIE d. c. 1820, m. Duncan Patterson b. 1782, d. 1864. They had six children who are listed under the line of Duncan Patterson later in this work.

V. MARGARET BUIE m. 1813 John Patterson. They lived on Upper Little River in (present) Harnett County. Many of their descendants live in the Sanford-Broadway section of North Carolina, according to Admiral Patterson.[38] They had:

A. Archibald Patterson
B. Daniel Patterson
C. Evin Dubb Mhaula Buie Patterson
D. Mary Patterson
E. John Buie Patterson

VI. JOHN BUIE, JR. m. Sarah ______. They moved to Robinson County, Tennessee. No further information.

As Admiral Patterson writes: "Now this family, once so numerous and prominent, has gone from Harnett County and so far as I know, none remains there."[39]

Daniel Buie of Moore County, North Carolina

Daniel Buie, b. c. 1735 in Scotland, d. 1795, Moore County, N.C., bought 100 acres on Buie's Creek from Gilbert Buie and 160 acres on Cape Fear River from John McDaniel in 1756. His wife's name is unknown, and the Buie compilers list his children in the order in which they appeared in his 1795 will:

I. GILBERT BUIE b. before 1775, Cumberland County, N.C., d. probably Maury County, TN. Suggested information on his family is found in Buie.[40]

II. ALEXANDER BUIE b. c. 1770, Cumberland County, N.C., d. May 1818, Moore County, N.C. He lived on northeast side of Upper Little River, and m. Margaret (McLean?) b. c. 1778, N.C., d. after 1850. Their six children are listed in Buie.[41]

III. ANGUS BUIE b. c. 1775, Cumberland County, N.C., was single, may have moved to Louisiana (?)

IV. DANIEL BUIE b. Cumberland County, N.C., d. Probably Moore County, N.C.

V. WILLIAM BUIE b. c. 1778, Cumberland County, d. 1833, Lawrence County, Tenn., m. Nancy______ in c. 1798, N.C., b. c. 1777 in N.C., d. c. 1850-60, Lawrence County, TN. Shortly before 1820, William and his brother Gilbert moved to Maury County, Tenn. William later moved to Lawrence County, c. 1825. William's six children are traced in Buie.[42]

VI. REBEKAH BUIE b. Cumberland County, N.C.; not married at the time of her father's death.

VII. MARY BUIE b. Cumberland County, N.C. m. ______ Mclean. See Buie for possible identification of her tombstone.[43]

VIII. MARGARET BUIE b. Cumberland County, N.C., apparently not married in 1795.

IX. EFFY BUIE b. Cumberland County, N.C., apparently not married in 1795.

Mary Buie and Hugh Brown of Cumberland and Robeson Counties, North Carolina

This family is traced in Buie[44] and is dealt with in this volume in the Robeson County section, under Vol.III of Mrs. Mable S. Lovin: *Descendants and Collateral Lines of Mary Buie and Hugh Brown.*

John Buie, Sr. of North Carolina and Union Church, Mississippi

This John Buie Sr. was b. Jan. 26, 1751, probably in Bladen County, N.C. (now Harnett County), d. Aug. 27, 1831, Union Church, MS. He m. Elizabeth ______ c. 1772, who d. c. 1795 in Robeson County, N.C. Some of his children moved to Union Church, MS., in 1809, and John Sr. followed them in 1820. His children:

I. SARAH ELIZABETH BUIE b. Mar. 5, 1777, Cumberland County, N.C., d. May 12, 1820, Jefferson County, MS., m. Archibald Smith Sr., b. N.C., d. MS. Some of their children are listed, and one is traced by the Buie compilers.[45]

II. MALCOLM BUIE b. Oct. 15, 1777, Cumberland County, N.C., d. May 7, 1848, Jefferson County, MS., m. Anable "Nepsy" McMillan d. Oct. 30, 1825, Jefferson County, MS.; no issue.

III. MARGARET BUIE b. c. 1779, Cumberland County, N.C., d. Sept. 20, 1824, Union Church, MS., m. Daniel Baker, M.D. d. 1837, Union Church, MS. The Buie compilers have traced one of their sons.[46]

IV. JENNET BUIE b. Apr. 15, 1781, Cumberland County, N.C., d. Aug. 29, 1840, Jefferson County, MS.; was single.

V. NEILL BUIE b. Feb. 16, 1783, Cumberland County, N.C., d. May 31, 1859, Union Church, MS., m. according to the Robeson County marriage bond on Feb. 11, 1809, Catherine Brown, dau. of William Brown and Mary Campbell. They moved to Mississippi in 1809. Their children are traced in Buie.[47]

VI. CATHERINE BUIE b. June 10, 1784, Robeson County, N.C., d. Sept. 21, 1875, Jefferson County, MS.; was single.

VII. JOHN BUIE JR. b. Apr. 12, 1786, Robeson County, N.C., d. Sept. 4, 1860, Jefferson County, MS.; was single.

VIII. REBECCA BUIE b. May 13, 1788, Robeson County, N.C., d. Oct. 17, 1821, Jefferson County, MS.; was single.

IX. DUNCAN BUIE b. c. 1790, Robeson County, N.C., d. Aug. 27, 1813, Jefferson County, MS.; was single.

X. ANABEL BUIE b. Mar. 9, 1792, Robeson County, N.C., d. Mar. 6, 1851, Jefferson County, MS.; was single.

Duncan Buie of Scotland and Raiford's Creek, Cumberland County, North Carolina

Duncan Buie was born in Scotland, undoubtedly on the island of Jura in 1724. He came to North Carolina in 1739 and first lived on the Upper Cape Fear River near Buies Creek and acquired land in 1750. About 1755 he moved to the Barbeque Creek area and was named an elder at Barbeque Church in 1765. He was known for his piety and knowledge of

church doctrine. During the Revolution, perhaps for political reasons, Duncan left Barbeque and settled near the mouth of Raiford's Creek opposite Bluff Church on the Cape Fear. Duncan Buie died on October 10, 1819 at the home of his son, John Buie, in Cumberland County.[48]

His wife's name was Sarah ______. Their six children:

I. DUNCAN BUIE JR. b. c. 1748, Bladen County, N.C. (now Harnett); no record of marriage.

II. JOHN BUIE b. c. 1750, Bladen County, N.C. (now Harnett), d. 1825, Cumberland County, N.C., m. Mary MacPherson b. c. 1760, N.C., d. 1846, Cumberland County, N.C. Their seven children are listed and one is traced by the Buie compilers.[49]

III. CATHERINE BUIE b. May 30, 1752, Bladen County, N.C. (now Harnett), d. Oct. 5, 1839, Maury County, TN., m. Malcolm Gilchrist c. 1770 in Cumberland County, N.C. He was b. Feb. 8, 1744 in Kintyre, Scotland, d. Apr. 12, 1821, Maury County, TN., to which his family had moved in 1809. His children are traced in Purcell's *Lumber River Scots,* 747-781 and in Buie.[50]

IV. NANCY BUIE b. c. 1755, Cumberland County, N.C. (now Harnett), m. Malcolm Clark, Cumberland County, son of Malcolm and Nancy McCraine Clark, d. 1794, Cumberland County. They lived on the east side of the Cape Fear River near Buies Creek and attended Bluff Church. Their nine children are listed in Buie.[51]

V. REBECCA BUIE b. c. 1757, Cumberland County, N.C. (now Harnett), m. Daniel Shaw. Their five children are listed in Buie, who also gives further references to their descendants in Purcell's *Lumber River Scots* (492-495) and Fraine's *Archibald McKay* (78-81).[52]

VI. DANIEL BUIE b. c. 1760, Cumberland County, N.C. (now Harnett), d. c. 1805, m. Mary Margaret McDuffie, dau. of Archibald McDuffie of Cumberland County, N.C. She d. 1834 in Cumberland. They attended Bluff Church. Their six children are traced in Buie.[53]

Archibald Buie of Gum Swamp, Cumberland County, North Carolina and Catherine Shaw

Archibald Buie first acquired land on Gum Swamp in Cumberland County by land grant in 1765 and the compilers think that he was also called Archibald Buie of Cypress Swamp in the very early records. He lived within the Barbeque District of Cumberland County but also owned land in Moore County. In 1765, he was named an elder at Barbeque along with Duncan Buie . . . Gilbert Clark, and Daniel Cameron who were all noted to be pious men and devoted to their duties as elders. Archibald married Catherine Shaw also of Cumberland County. It is generally accepted that Archibald was born in Jura, Scotland and came to North Carolina as a young man.[54]

He was b. c. 1735-40, d. 1811, Cumberland County, N.C. Their children:

I. MARY BUIE b. c. 1763, Cumberland County, N.C., d. Dec. 29, 1800, Buried at Longstreet Church, m. Sept. 10, 1790 in Cumberland County, Archibald McFadyen b. 1754, Isle of Islay, Scotland, d. Apr. 4, 1830, North Carolina. Their five children are listed in Buie, as are those Archibald McFadyen had by his second wife, Nancy McNeill.[55]

II. CHRISTIAN BUIE b. Feb. 3, 1765, Cumberland County, N.C., d. Sept. 25, 1841, m. Archibald Clark b. Nov. 29, 1764, Cumberland County, son of Gilbert Clark and Ann Alexander. They may have moved to Gibson County, TN. Their seven children are listed by Buie.[56] See also the Clark family in this volume.

III. MARIANN BUIE b. Cumberland County, N.C., m. Daniel McFarland; no information.

IV. DANIEL BUIE b. Cumberland County, N.C.

V. WILLIAM BUIE b. Cumberland County, N.C. The Buie compilers suggest that this may be the William who m. Margaret McIver of Moore County.

VI. ARCHIBALD BUIE (Rev.), b. c. 1774, Cumberland County, N.C., d. Feb. 12, 1857 in present Dillon County, S.C. Licensed by Orange Presbytery in North Carolina in 1811, he served churches first in the Cape Fear Valley of N.C. and then in the Pee Dee Valley of S.C. He m. Feb. 1812 Catherine Brown of Robeson County, N.C. Their children are traced in Buie.[57]

Hugh Robert Buie and Deliah (Baker) Buie of Cumberland County, North Carolina

Hugh Robert Buie and Deliah Baker were married in Cumberland County, North Carolina in 1845. Hugh Robert Buie enlisted in Co. F, N.C. Vol. for the

Mexican War and family tradition has it that he was killed in action when his son, Hugh Robert Buie Jr. was six months old . . . According to census records, Hugh Robert Buie, Jr. and family were living at Stewarts Creek, Harnett County in 1880 and Pearce's Mill, Cumberland County in 1900. The descendants of Hugh Jr. are listed in Buie.[58]

Daniel Buie and John Buie of North Carolina and Union Church, Mississippi

Daniel and John Buie moved from North Carolina to Union Church, Mississippi and were listed as charter members of the Presbyterian Church there in 1817. Although not explicitly stated, they were undoubtedly brothers.

I. DANIEL BUIE b. c. 1770, N.C., d. Jan. 24, 1820, Union Church, MS., m. Margaret ______, lived in Robeson County, N.C. and then in MS. Their three children are traced in Buie.[59]

II. JOHN BUIE b. c. 1770, N.C., d. Jan. 7, 1830, Union Church, MS., m. Elizabeth ______. There is some uncertainty about their offspring, but six children are traced in Buie.[60]

Neill Buie, Sr. of Cumberland County, North Carolina

Most of the information on the early history of this family is based on an account written by Duncan Campbell Buie in 1950 shortly before his death. He stated that Neill Buie, Sr. and his wife came to North Carolina about 1735 with four children named Martha, Nancy, Daniel, and Duncan. Six months after their arrival, another son, Neill Buie, Jr., was born who was the only child to ever marry.

The compilers believe that the date 1735 is probably incorrect and rather, Neill Buie, Jr. was born about 1770. Census records, however, do verify in some degree Duncan Campbell Buie's narrative since in the 1810 Cumberland County census page 246, Daniel Buie is listed living next to Neill with two males, ages 24-45, one female, age 26-45, and one female over age 45 in Daniel's household. Neill Buie, Sr. lived in the Carver's Creek and Raiford's Creek area just north of Fayetteville in Cumberland County. He has not been connected to the other Buies living in this locality.[61]

According to old papers from Mrs. Marvin R. Graham of Fayetteville, N.C., Neill Buie Jr. was born October, 1769 in Cumberland County, N.C., and his father's name was John, (not Neill Sr.), who had come to North Carolina from the Isle of Jura in 1768.[62]

The only child of Neill Buie, Sr. to marry was:

I. NEILL BUIE, Jr. b. c. 1770, Cumberland County, d. c. 1835, Cumberland County, m. Elizabeth Zachary b. c. 1791, Orange County, N.C., d. Apr. 29, 1877, Kingsbury, N.C.; lived in Cumberland County. Their four children are traced in Buie.[63]

John Buie, Sr. of North and South Carolina and Hardin County, Tennessee

Since there is so much uncertainty about the specific descent and connections of this family, I will not attempt to trace it out here, but will refer merely to what is definitely known about its founder, according to the Buie compilers:

> According to his pension application dated March 7, 1835 in Hardin County, Tennessee, John Buie was born in Scotland in 1759 and came with his father Duncan Buie to Cumberland County, North Carolina before the Revolution. John Buie enlisted in the American army under Capt. Clark's command in 1776, served six months, and then in 1779 moved to the 96th District of South Carolina where he again enlisted in the American army. John apparently moved back to North Carolina and may be the John who lived on Beaver Creek and later Richmond County in the mid 1780's (see discussion later in this volume under John Ray Buie and Margaret McFarland Buie). John Buie first appeared in Tennessee in the 1830 Hardin County census and again was listed in the 1840 census as "John Buie, Sr."[64]

The Buie compilers discuss some of the descendants of this family and suggest other possible relationships to various Buie families.[65]

"Red" Duncan Buie and Flora Baker of Cumberland County, North Carolina

According to the Buie compilers, "'Red' Duncan Buie, so named because of his red hair, and his wife Flora lived in the 71st District of Cumberland County and attended Camp Ground Methodist Church. From existing available records, the compilers suggest that he may be the son of John Buie who died in 1825 (see earlier in this volume). Catherine (Buie) MacPherson, daughter of John, and her husband Alexander lived very near Duncan in 1850. Before John Buie's widow Mary (MacPherson) Buie died in 1846, she named her son Duncan Buie, and Alexander MacPherson as administrators."[66]

Duncan Buie ("Red") b. c. 1776, Cumberland County, d. Feb. 10, 1864, Cumberland, buried at Campground Methodist Church, m. May 9, 1809, Flora Baker b. c. 1784, d. Dec. 9, 1848, Cumberland, buried at Campground Methodist. They had eight children:

I. ANNIE BUIE b. Dec. 22, 1813, Cumberland County, N.C., d. July 11, 1903; was single.

II. FLORA BUIE b. c. 1815, d. c. 1840, N.C., m. David Taylor Nov. 4, 1830. Their three children are listed in Buie.[67]

III. JOHN BUIE b. May 24, 1816, Cumberland County, d. Jan. 29, 1897, buried at Campground Methodist Church, m. Eliza McEachern b. Oct. 1, 1820, N.C., dau. of Archibald McEachern and Effie Sellers. They had no children of their own, though they adopted Margaret McIver Baker.

IV. ARCHIBALD BUIE b. c. 1823, Cumberland County, d. 1889, Cumberland, m. first Oct. 8, 1857, Sarah Black b. c. 1826, N.C. Their six children are listed in Buie.[68] He m. secondly, Sarah McFadyen b. c. 1836, N.C., dau. of James McFadyen, d. Apr. 16, 1917, Cumberland County, N.C.

V. CATHERINE BUIE b. c. 1826, Cumberland County, N.C.

VI. NEILL BUIE b. Aug. 18, 1828, Cumberland County, N.C., d. Mar. 26, 1912, buried at Campground Methodist Church, m. Sallie Torrey McEachern b. Apr. 1, 1834, dau. of Archibald McEachern and Effie Sellers, d. Mar. 11, 1916, buried at Campground Methodist. Their four children are listed in Buie.[69]

VII. SARAH BUIE b. May 4, 1830, Cumberland County, N.C.

VIII. MARGARET BUIE b. Cumberland County, N.C.

John Ray Buie and Margaret (McFarland) Buie of Cumberland and Richmond Counties, North Carolina

John Ray Buie b. Jan. 18, 1792, Cumberland County, N.C., d. Mar. 10, 1852, Richmond County, N.C., buried Old Laurel Hill Church Cemetery in Richmond County. He was a school teacher and m. Feb. 14, 1822, Margaret McFarland b. Aug. 6, 1806, N.C., dau. of Duncan McFarland and Mary Porter, d. Aug. 29, 1839, buried at Old Laurel Hill Church. They lived near Old Hundred in present Scotland County (then Richmond). Duncan McFarland was the son of Catherine (Buie) McFarland McNair d. Aug., 17887 and grandson of Donald Buie of Jura, Scotland.

Six of the seven children of John Ray Buie and Margaret McFarland are listed in the Buie compilers, with further information on the descendants of two of them: Dr. Duncan McFarland Buie and wife Mary Jane McKay, and Sarah Margaret Buie and husband William Turner Owen.[70]

John Buie of Moore and Randolph Counties, North Carolina

The descent and wider connections of this family are as yet unclear, but the Buie compilers have definite information on part of them. "The three brothers and two sisters presented here, John, Allen, William, Mary, and Ann lived near Big Juniper Creek in what is now Lee County (then Moore). In 1844, a John Buie of Moore County deeded 230 acres on Big Juniper to his wife Catherine which upon event of her death would belong to his son William. In 1851, the heirs of William Buie, deceased, i.e. Allen Buie, John Buie, Ann Buie, and Mary Buie agreed to allow Mary to have 280 acres on Big Juniper which formerly belonged to William Buie. Therefore, the compilers believe that the parents of these siblings were John and Catherine Buie of Moore County."[71]

The Buie compilers trace the descendants of one of these siblings, John Buie of Moore and Randolph Counties, N.C.[72]

William Alexander Buie and Barbara Isabella McLean of Cumberland, Harnett and Moore Counties, North Carolina

The information on this family is also unclear, but according to the Buie compilers: "William Alexander Buie first appeared in North Carolina census records in 1850 when he was listed in the following household in the Western Division of Cumberland County: Duncan M. Buie, age 26; William J. Buie, age 24; Mary Buie, age 22; Allen C. Buie, age 21; Isabella M. Buie, age 16; William A. Buie, age 23; Duncan O'Hanlon, age 14, Mary S. O'Hanlon, age 14; Charles McCallum, age 23; and Laney Rising, age 19. In 1860, William Alexander Buie was listed with Margaret Johnson, age 50, in Moore County next to the family of Duncan D. Buie and Margaret Lee (Shaw) Buie. The descendants of William Alexander Buie believe that his mother was Elizabeth Buie, daughter of a Gilbert Buie, and his father was a man named Johnson, but for unexplained reasons, William used his mother's maiden name. Research could not confirm or dispute this relationship."[73]

The Buie compilers give some information on several of the Buies listed in this part of the 1850 census and also on some of the seven children of William Alexander Buie b. Apr. 6, 1827, N.C., d. Apr. 9, 1906, and wife Barbara Isabella McLean b. Mar. 5, 1837, d. Feb. 28, 1918. They m. on Aug. 9, 1860, and lived in Moore and Harnett Counties, N.C.[74]

McDuffie Family

A family closely related to the Harnett County Buies was the McDuffie group. Patterson writes:

> It has been possible to trace our McDuffie ancestry back to one Daniel, whose will was dated 4 July 1782. He lived on the Cape Fear River, north of the present city of Fayetteville, in what is now Harnett County. He willed property to his wife, Marian, who, according to the late Reverend W.A. McLeod, was a Lindsay; to daughter Isabella, wife of John Patterson . . . to daughter Margaret, who married a McArthur; to son Archibald and to Archibald's sons Archibald, Daniel, George and William.[75]

Hence, Daniel McDuffie and Marian Lindsay had:

I. ISABELLA
II. MARGARET
III. ARCHIBALD

I. ISABELLA MCDUFFIE m. John Patterson of Cumberland County, one of the guarantors of the salary of Rev. James Campbell (of Barbeque, Longstreet, Bluff). John was b. c. 1730 in Scotland and d. c. 1812 in Moore County, N.C. He was a founder first of Longstreet Church, then of Bethesda Church. They had nine children (according to his will in Moore County).[76]

A. Mary b. 1756, d. 1846, Moore County
B. Daniel b. c. 1756, Cumberland County, d. c. 1843
C. Barbara b. c. 1805, d. c. 1878
D. Flora
E. Duncan
F. Elizabeth b. c. 1769, d. c. 1793
G. Catherine b. c. 1770
H. Isabel b. c. 1772
I. Malcolm apparently died young

A. Mary Patterson m. first Alexander Black b. c. 1756 Scotland, d. 1820 in Moore County, N.C. She m. secondly Colin Bethune b. 1756 Scotland, d. 1820 (?) in Moore County. According to

Patterson (425) "Of the Patterson-Black union there was at least one child, the ancestor of the late sheriff Roderick McMillan of Robeson County, N.C. Of the Patterson-Bethune union there was issue-5, ancestors of the Bethunes and other prominent families of the state and the south":

1. Lauchlin Bethune b. 1785, d. 1874, Moore County, N.C., served in U.S. Congress. He married his first cousin, Annie Patterson (dau. of 'Buffalo Daniel"). They had:
   - a. Mary Bethune m. Neill McFadyen
   - b. Margaret S. Bethune m. Charles Monroe
   - c. Dr. Colin Bethune m. ______
   - d. Alexander Bethune single
   - e. William J. Bethune marital status unknown
   - f. Sarah Anne Bethune m. William Holliday
   - g. Catherine Bethune m. first Daniel Blue, secondly C.W. Shaw
   - h. Harriett Bethune m. Archibald Ray
   - i. Andrew J. Bethune m. Sarah Ann ________
   - j. Maximillan D. Bethune
   - k. Caroline Bethune m. Edward Byrd
2. John Bethune b. c. 1787, marital status unknown
3. Mary Bethune b. c. 1790, m. John McLeod. Moved to Mississippi c. 1817.
4. Sarah Bethune b. c. 1795, d. c. 1830, m. Alexander Patterson (son of "Buffalo Daniel"). They lived in Talladega County, Alabama. They had:
   - a. John Patterson
   - b. William Patterson
   - c. Eliza Patterson m. _____ Terrell and lived in Texas.

B. Daniel Patterson m. Margaret Graham b. c. 1746 Scotland, d. c. 1830 in Cumberland County, N.C. According to Admiral Patterson, "They lived on Buffalo Creek, about 5 miles west of the present town of Raeford, N.C. He was called "Buffalo Daniel" to distinguish him from other Daniels in the area. She was the daughter of John and Elizabeth (Smiley) Graham . . . He moved to Alabama, where several children had already gone."[77] They had:

1. Archibald Patterson b. c. 1784, d. c. 1820, m. Sarah (Sallie) McEachern (McEachin) b. c. 1784, d. c. 1869. They lived

on Buffalo Creek and had:
a. Elizabeth (Eliza) b. 1816, d. 1892, m. Neill Sinclair
b. Margaret b. 1818, d. 1901, m. first Hector McKinnon, secondly Neill Archie McLean

2. Isabella Patterson b. c. 1786, d. c. 1805, m. Samuel McKeahey (McKeachey?)
3. Elizabeth Patterson b. c. 1788, lived in Moore County, m. John Keahey and had:
a. William Jackson Keahey d. 1843 single
b. James B. Keahey d. young
c. Margaret Keahey m. John C. Currie, lived in Cumberland (now Hoke) County
d. Mary Keahey d. c. 1895 single
e. Archibald P. Keahey d. c. 1855, single
f. Eliza Ann Keahey m. Lauchlin McFadyen of (present) Hoke County, ancestor of the Hoke County McFadyen family.
4. Margaret Patterson m. her cousin Archibald Graham, Jr. and moved to Florida. Their children later moved to Alabama. They had:
a. Thomas Baxter Graham m. Isabella Archibald Graham
b. Elizabeth Graham m. _____ Morrison
c. Annie Graham m. William Brown
d. Isabella Graham m. first Evans, secondly Calvin Love
e. John Graham marital status unknown
f. Henry Graham m. _____ Patterson
g. Dr. George Graham m. _____
5. Mary Patterson b. c. 1795, d. c. 1825, m. Col. Roderick D. Gillis b. c. 1780, d. 1872. They lived on the west side of Rockfish Creek in Cumberland County and were members of Sandy Grove Presbyterian Church. Of their children, one was known to Admiral Patterson,[78] and one to me.[79]
a. Flora Ann Gillis b. c. 1822, d. 1862, m. Daniel Leslie, d. 1852.
b. John A. Gillis, b. 1831, d. 1896, m. Catherine Jane Blue (dau. of Neill McK. Blue) in 1868.

Some members of this family can be traced in part through *The Gillis*

Family in the South by Clayton G. Metcalf.[80] Information is also available in *Scottish Blue Family*.[81]

6. John Patterson b. c. 1798, m. ____ Love. Moved to Alabama.
7. Daniel Patterson b. c. 1800, marital status unknown. Last of the family to have moved to Alabama.
8. George McDuffie Patterson d. 1890, m. Catherine McKinnon and moved to Alabama and later Texas. They had:
   a. Fannie Patterson b. 1845, d. 1921, m. George S. Terrell b. 1840, d. 1916.
   b. Daniel Patterson
   c. Hector Patterson
   d. Malcolm Patterson
   e. Annie Patterson
   f. Effie Patterson
9. Alexander Patterson b. c. 1800 m. Sarah Bethune (dau. of Colin and Mary Patterson Bethune). She was b. c. 1795, d. c. 1830. Both moved to Alabama and died early.
10. Malcolm Patterson b. c. 1800, d. 1838, m. first Mary Murphy, secondly Jane Brown. He was the first of the family to move to Alabama. He had children by both wives, but we know only of the following by his first wife:
    a. Margaret Patterson b. 182l, Robeson County, N.C. m. Isaac Newton Buie. They moved to Alabama then Texas.
    b. Annie Patterson m. Dr. John Calvin McDiarmid and lived in Alabama.
    c. Mary Patterson b. 1834, d. 1899, m. Robert Dougald Torrey of the Robeson County, N.C. Torrey family. He was m. first to Mary McNair. More is available on this family in *Lumber River Scots* by John Edwin Purcell (238-248).
11. Annie Patterson b. c. 1805, d. c. 1878, m. Lauchlin Bethune b. 1785, d. 1874. This family is discussed by Admiral Patterson in some detail.[82]

C. Barbara Patterson b. c. 1765, d. c. 1824, m. Archibald McNeill, known as Archie "Ghar" (Proud Archie). Curries, Hodgins and others are descended from them according to Patterson.[83]

D. Flora Patterson m. John Black (brother of Alex Black).

E. Duncan Patterson m. _____ McNeill. They moved to Alabama and had:

1. Isabel d. young
2. Margaret m. Dr. William Kelly

F. Elizabeth Patterson b. c. 1769, d. c. 1793, m. Alexander Patterson, b. c. 1760, d. 1850 (son of "Raft Swamp Daniel"). They lived in Robeson County, N.C. They had:

1. Angus Patterson b. 1790, d. 1854 in Barnwell, S.C., m. Hannah Frizzell Trotti. This family's history is written by Isabel Patterson in *Builders of Freedom.*They had:

a. Francis Alexander Patterson b. 1820, d. 1821

b. Edward Lawrence Patterson b. 1822, d. 1893, m. Sarah Louise Myers

c. Hannah Patterson b. 1824 d. 1848, m. Adolphus Nott

d. Anna Elizabeth Patterson b. 1825, d. 1862, m. Gen. Lewis M. Ayer, II

e. Isabel Coroneus Patterson b. 1829, d. 1847, m. James Thomas Aldrich

f. Alex Francis Patterson b. 1831, d. 1833

g. Lucretia Haseltine Patterson b. 1834, d. 1915, m. Abner W. Atkinson

h. Angus Patterson Jr., b. c. 1836 died single

i. Marian Patterson b. c. 1838, d. 1917, m. Francis Trotti

j. Jabez Patterson b. 1840, d. 1873 single

k. Julia Patterson b. 1842, d. 1920, m. William May

G. Catherine Patterson b. c. 1770 m. John Buchan of Moore County.

H. Isabel Patterson b. c. 1772, m. Daniel Monroe (son of Malcolm and Margaret Patterson Monroe of Moore County).

I. MALCOLM PATTERSON is believed to have died young.

II. MARGARET MCDUFFIE m. _____ McArthur. No further information.

III. ARCHIBALD MCDUFFIE m. Mary _____. According to his will they had:

A. Archibald

B. James

C. William

D. Catherine

E. Mary m. ____ Matthews

F. Flora m. John Buie. This family is traced under the John Buie section.

Notes

1. Patterson, op. cit., 65.
2. T.R. Buie and Scott Buie, Compilers, *The Family Buie: Scotland to North America* (Chelle-Kirk Printing: Arlington, Texas, 1983), 35.
3. Ibid., 36.
4. Ibid, 47.
5. Ibid., 50.
6. Ibid., 51-54.
7. Ibid., 54-58.
8. Ibid., 58-80.
9. Ibid., 82-124.
10. Ibid., 126-140.
11. Ibid., 140-141.
12. Ibid., 142-152.
13. Ibid., 153.
14. Ibid.
15. Ibid., 154.
16. Ibid.
17. Ibid.
18. Ibid., 155-156.
19. Ibid., 157.
20. Ibid., 157, 158.
21. Ibid., 158-162.
22. Ibid., 162-163.
23. Ibid., 164.
24. Ibid., 164-165.
25. Ibid., 166.
26. Ibid., 157.
27. Ibid., 313, 314.
28. Ibid., 167-172.
29. Ibid., 173-189.
30. Ibid., 173.
31. Ibid., 190.
32. Ibid.
33. Ibid., 190-206.
34. Ibid., 206-207.
35. Ibid., 207-208.
36. Ibid., 209-222.
37. Patterson, op. cit., 17.
38. Ibid., 19.
39. Ibid., 17.
40. Buie compilers, op. cit., 237.
41. Ibid., 237, 238.
42. Ibid., 238-250.

43. Ibid., 238.
44. Ibid., 271-286.
45. Ibid., 287-289.
46. Ibid., 289-291.
47. Ibid., 291-301.
48. Ibid., 302.
49. Ibid., 302-304.
50. Ibid., 304-305.
51. Ibid., 305.
52. Ibid., 305-306.
53. Ibid., 306-312.
54. Ibid., 313.
55. Ibid.
56. Ibid., 313, 314.
57. Ibid., 314, 315.
58. Ibid., 328-330.
59. Ibid., 331-332.
60. Ibid., 332-336.
61. Ibid., 347.
62. Ibid., 357.
63. Ibid., 347-356.
64. Ibid., 359.
65. Ibid., 359-365.
66. Ibid., 366.
67. Ibid.
68. Ibid., 366, 367.
69. Ibid., 369, 370.
70. Ibid., 372-374.
71. Ibid., 378.
72. Ibid., 378-382.
73. Ibid., 383.
74. Ibid., 383-389.
75. Patterson, op. cit., 16.
76. The following information taken from Ibid., 424-430.
77. Ibid., 426.
78. Ibid., 428.
79. Douglas F. Kelly, *Scottish Blue Family*, 748ff.
80. Printed in Enterprise, AL., 1975, 335.
81. Douglas F. Kelly, op. cit., 748-756.
82. See Patterson, op. cit., 425-429.
83. Ibid., 429.

6

The Most Scottish County in North Carolina

Bethune Family

NOW LET US MOVE WESTWARD INTO MOORE COUNTY, which today is still one of the counties with the most Scots descendents in the whole United States. One of the early families to settle there, and shape its history was the Bethunes, originally from the Isle of Skye. This was a relatively small but highly influential family of the upper Cape Fear area, which later became Moore and Hoke Counties.

We have already met Lauchlin Bethune above (see p. 202), who married into the Patterson/McDuffie connection. In addition to Bethune material in the volumes of Alex Patterson[1] and Douglas Kelly,[2] there is also a brief article on this family in *Argyll Colony Plus.*[3]

Colin Bethune was the head of this family, and came from the Isle of Skye to present Moore County in 1771 'with others including a McQueen.'[4] He is buried in Bethesda Church Cemetery near Aberdeen. He m. Mary Patterson b. 1756, d. 1846 (dau. of John Patterson and

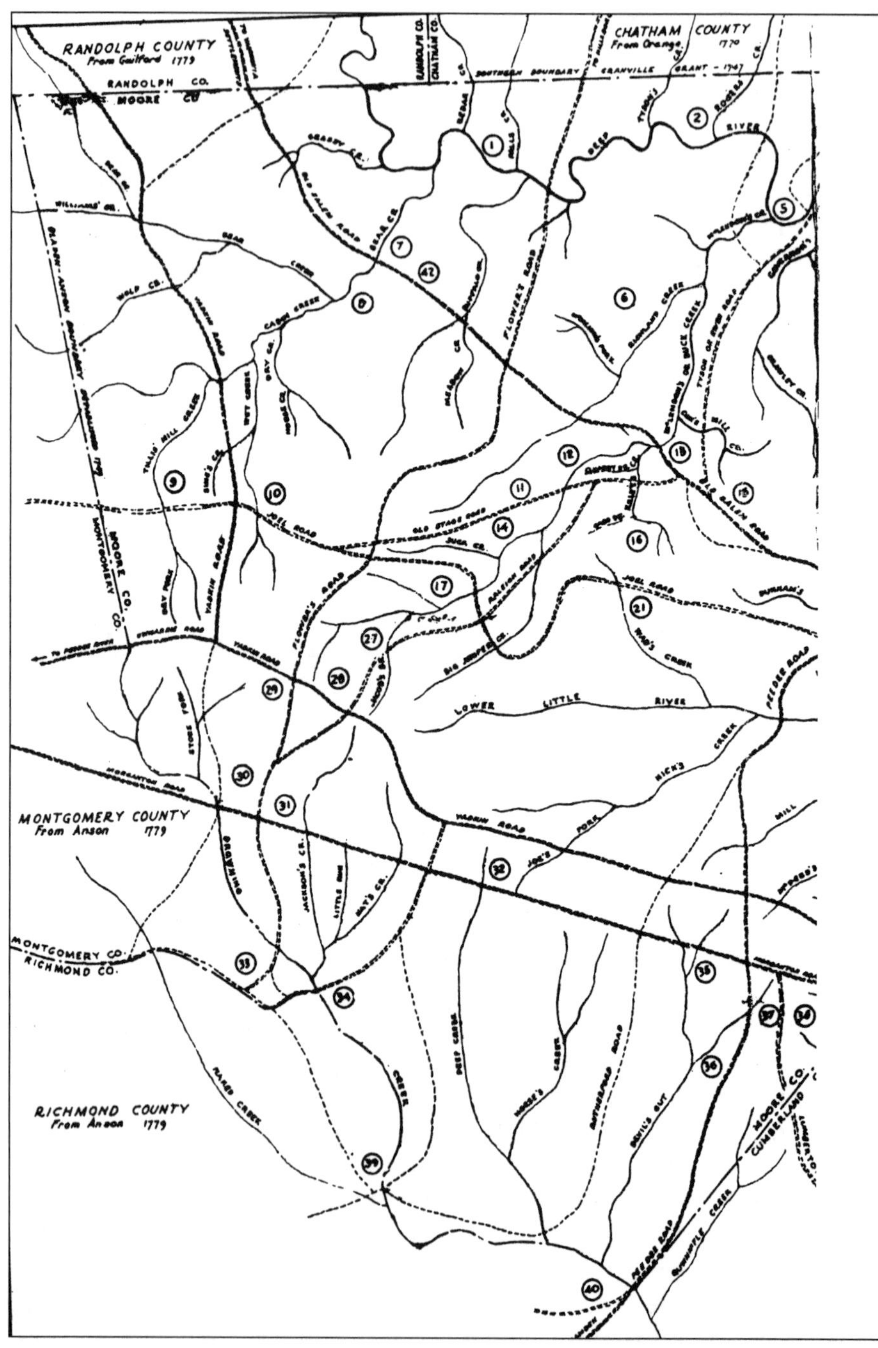
RANDOLPH COUNTY
From Guilford 1779
RANDOLPH CO.
MOORE CO.
CHATHAM COUNTY
From Orange 1770
SOUTHERN BOUNDARY GRANVILLE GRANT - 1747
DEEP RIVER
FLOWER'S ROAD
OLD SALEM ROAD
YADKIN ROAD
JOEL ROAD
OLD STAGE ROAD
RALEIGH ROAD
LOWER LITTLE RIVER
MORGANTON ROAD
MONTGOMERY COUNTY
From Anson 1779
MONTGOMERY CO.
RICHMOND CO.
RICHMOND COUNTY
From Anson 1779
PEE DEE ROAD
DEEP CREEK
DEVIL'S GUT
MOORE CO.
CUMBERLAND
MOORE CO.
MONTGOMERY CO.

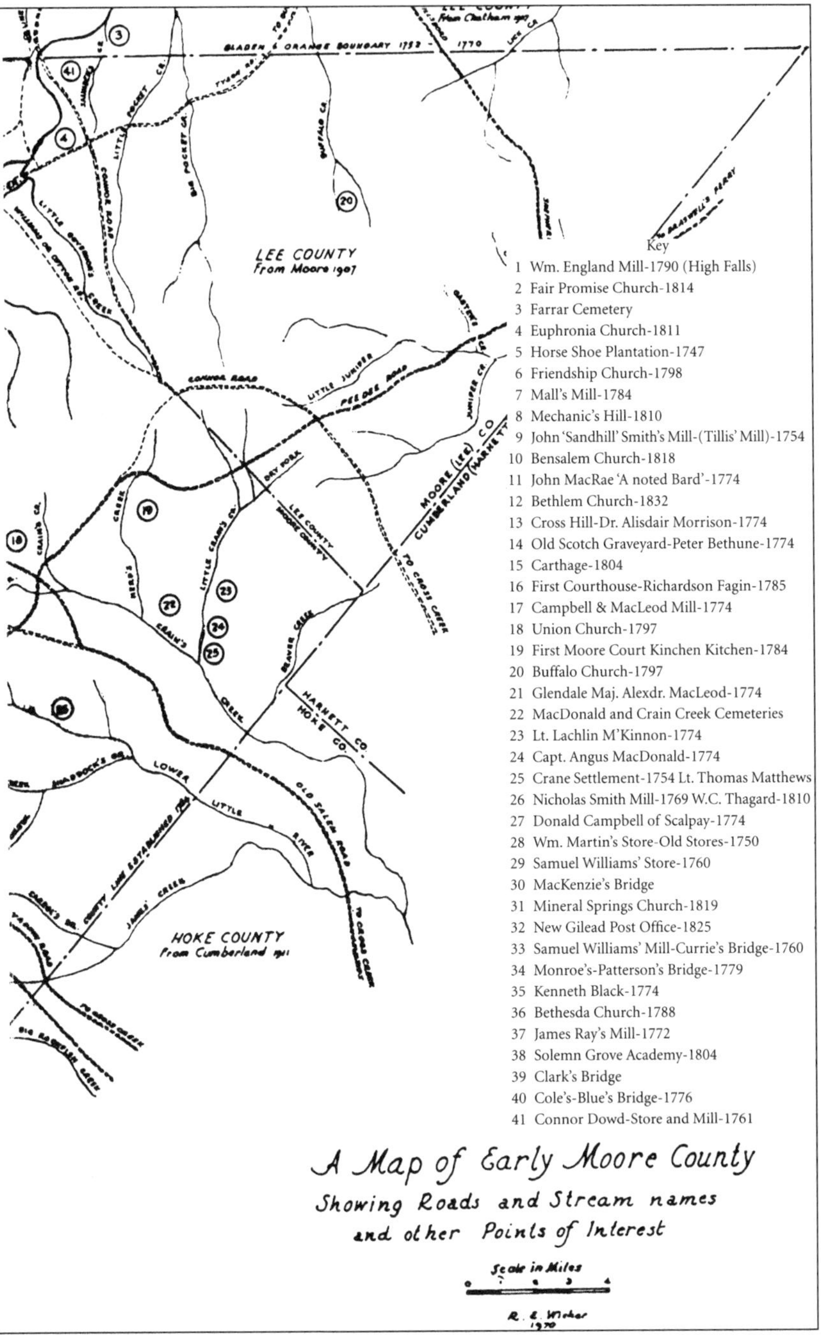

LEE COUNTY
From Moore 1907

HOKE COUNTY
From Cumberland 1911

Key

1 Wm. England Mill-1790 (High Falls)
2 Fair Promise Church-1814
3 Farrar Cemetery
4 Euphronia Church-1811
5 Horse Shoe Plantation-1747
6 Friendship Church-1798
7 Mall's Mill-1784
8 Mechanic's Hill-1810
9 John 'Sandhill' Smith's Mill-(Tillis' Mill)-1754
10 Bensalem Church-1818
11 John MacRae 'A noted Bard'-1774
12 Bethlem Church-1832
13 Cross Hill-Dr. Alisdair Morrison-1774
14 Old Scotch Graveyard-Peter Bethune-1774
15 Carthage-1804
16 First Courthouse-Richardson Fagin-1785
17 Campbell & MacLeod Mill-1774
18 Union Church-1797
19 First Moore Court Kinchen Kitchen-1784
20 Buffalo Church-1797
21 Glendale Maj. Alexdr. MacLeod-1774
22 MacDonald and Crain Creek Cemeteries
23 Lt. Lachlin M'Kinnon-1774
24 Capt. Angus MacDonald-1774
25 Crane Settlement-1754 Lt. Thomas Matthews
26 Nicholas Smith Mill-1769 W.C. Thagard-1810
27 Donald Campbell of Scalpay-1774
28 Wm. Martin's Store-Old Stores-1750
29 Samuel Williams' Store-1760
30 MacKenzie's Bridge
31 Mineral Springs Church-1819
32 New Gilead Post Office-1825
33 Samuel Williams' Mill-Currie's Bridge-1760
34 Monroe's-Patterson's Bridge-1779
35 Kenneth Black-1774
36 Bethesda Church-1788
37 James Ray's Mill-1772
38 Solemn Grove Academy-1804
39 Clark's Bridge
40 Cole's-Blue's Bridge-1776
41 Connor Dowd-Store and Mill-1761

A Map of Early Moore County
Showing Roads and Stream names
and other Points of Interest

Scale in Miles

R. E. Wicker
1970

Early places of residence of many of the Scots in Moore County are shown in this map made by R. E. Wicker

Isabella McDuffie—see pp. 201-202). Mary was first married to Alexander Black. Colin Bethune and Mary Patterson (Black) had:

I. CATHERINE BETHUNE b. c.1784, d. 1856

II. LAUCHLIN BETHUNE b. 1785, d. 1875. His children are traced under the Isabella McDuffie section above. He served in the U.S. Congress and his home is still standing, not far from McCain, N.C.

III. JOHN BETHUNE b. c. 1787

IV. MARY BETHUNE b. c. 1790, m. John McLeod, moved to Mississippi.

V. SARAH BETHUNE b. c. 1795, d. c.1830 m. Alexander Patterson.

Their children are listed under the Isabella McDuffie section above.

Further information on the Bethune family can be found in some of the letters of Dr. A.C. Bethune, George Bethune and others in *CORRESPONDENCE and DOCUMENTS Pertaining to the BETHUNE, KEAHEY, MCLEOD, MCFARLAND, PATTERSON and other Related Scottish Highlander Families of North Carolina*, section 17.00. We should also mention a new book from John McDonald Publishers in Edinburgh, Scotland, by John Bannerman, *The Beatons: A Medical Tradition in the Classical Gaelic Tradition*, which gives some historical and a little genealogical material as does the older *The Bethunes of Skye.*

Cameron Families

Another large group of families in the general "Barbeque" section of present Harnett County who reached over into Moore County was the Camerons. I have little material on these old families, but John Burton Cameron in 1968 published two booklets on the subject.

Volume One deals with the descendants of Allan Cameron and wife, Mary Stewart, and Volume Two with the descendants of Norman Cameron and wife, Rachel Bruce. Volume One of John Burton Cameron's booklet (on "The Descendants of Allen Cameron and his Wife Mary Stewart") has been transcribed by Louise Curry and reprinted in *Argyll Colony Plus* (Vol. 11, No. 2, 132-142). In addition, many of the descendants of Neill Cameron and Mary Worthy of Governor's Creek in upper Moore County are dealt with in *Scottish Blue Family* by Kelly[5]—as are other groups of Camerons, such as the descendants of John and Mary Johnson Cameron[6] which are also dealt with in the more recent publication by James Vann Comer, *Ancestors and Descendants of*

Kenneth Henderson Worthy, Sheriff of Moore County, North Carolina 1850-1856, 1860-1972 (Published by Ruby Vann Crumpler McSwain: Sanford, N.C., 1996). Several members of these families are also mentioned in *McIver Family of North Carolina* by Kenneth L. Kelly.

I have some information on the family of Neill Cameron (and his father, John Merchant Cameron) and also on the family of John W. Cameron of Argyll which was given to me by the late Howard Ulsh of Charleston, S.C., who was married to one of the Cameron descendants. In these papers are several letters discussing the genealogy of the John Merchant Cameron family, written in the early 1920s from Mrs. Arlin Dobbs Wright (Mrs. John G.) of Deport, Texas, to John W. Cameron of Cameron, North Carolina.

Among these papers, there is also a fourteen page genealogical table of both the John Merchant Cameron family and the John W. Cameron family of Argyll, which is said to have been copied from "a book loaned by Mr. John W. Cameron," from which I extracted information as follows.

John Merchant Cameron Family

John Merchant Cameron emigrated from Scotland to Moore County, N.C. about 1775. He m. in Scotland Margaret Munroe. John was both a merchant and millwright. They had ten children, some of them were born in Scotland and some in North Carolina:

I.	"GOVERNOR" NEILL	VI.	LAUGHIE
II.	HUGHIE	VII.	ALLEN
III.	DANIEL	VIII.	PHIL
IV.	ANGUS	IX.	JOHN
V.	DUNCAN	X.	JANIE

I. "GOVERNOR" NEILL CAMERON (so called because he lived on Governor's Creek near the border of present Moore and Lee Counties) b. c. 1785 in North Carolina, d. between 1860-1870 in Moore County; m. Mary "Polly" Worthy b. c. 1790, Moore County, d. between 1860-1870, Moore County (daughter of John Worthy and Elizabeth Riddle). This family is also listed in James Comer's *Ancestors and Descendants of Kenneth Henderson Worthy* (Published by Ruby Vann Crumpler McSwain: Sanford, N.C., 1996). Neill Cameron and Mary Worthy had:

A. William Pitt Cameron b. 1824, d. 1893, m. Catherine Blue (dau. of John M. Blue) b. 1834, d. 1889. Their children are traced in *Scottish Blue Family* by Kelly, 431-446.

B. John Worthy Cameron b. July 27, 1812, Moore County, m. ____ and had (at least) a daughter who married Dan Morrison, who were parents of Cameron Morrison, Governor of North Carolina. John W. Cameron is said to have been Moore County's first graduate from the Law School of the University of North Carolina (1841). A short biography about him, of which I possess a copy, is said to have been taken from "a book in possession of Mrs. Beulah Cameron."

C. Margaret Cameron (Peggie) b. c. 1815, Moore County, d. after June 29, 1860; m. first Thomas A. Tyson and had one daughter, and secondly m. Archie McFadyen and had four children.[7]

D. Nancy Cameron b. c.1837 (but James Comer says c. 1810—op. cit., 118), had a son named Ham Cameron.

II. HUGHIE CAMERON (known as "Sugarfoot") m. Kattie McDougald. They had:

A. Laughlin Cameron, single
B. John A. Cameron who went to Texas
C. Daniel Cameron m. Lethie Buie and had one child.[8]
D. Sallie Cameron m. Lillis Gibbs and had five children.[9]

III. DANIEL CAMERON, no further information

IV. ANGUS CAMERON m. Kattie Cameron and had:

A. John A. Cameron b. 1823, d. 1916, single
B. Angus Cameron (II)
C. Bella Cameron was deaf
D. Margaret m. Mak (Malcolm?) Morgan
E. Kate Cameron
F. Narciss Cameron m. Daniel Darroch
G. Suranna (Susanna?) Cameron
H. Jane Elliott Cameron

V. DUNCAN CAMERON, no further information

VI. LAUGHIE (LAUGHLIN?) CAMERON m. Ann Johnson, no children

VII. ALLEN CAMERON m. Mary Johnson and had one child:

A. Chalmers Cameron

VIII. PHIL CAMERON m. ____ Rae and had:

A. Jimie Cameron B. Margaret Cameron

IX. JOHN CAMERON m. Pollie Johnson and had:

A. Archie J.L. Cameron b. 1804, d. 1875 m.1812 Isabella McFadyen b. 1803, d. 1892. They had ten children.[10]
B. Samuel Johnson Cameron m. first Catherine Blue and secondly Effie McIver.[11]
C. Jack Cameron m. Lizzie Shaw and moved South.
D. Peggie Cameron (known as "Big Peggie") m. William Cameron and had eleven children.[12]
E. Jenie (on p. 4 of the Cameron Genealogy spelled Jeirie, but elsewhere, Jenie) m. "Red John" McD. Cameron and had seven children.[13]
F. Mary Cameron m. Peter Monroe and had six children.[14]

X. JANIE CAMERON m. Neill Johnson and had three children:
A. Sarah Johnson
B. Mary Johnson
C. Anna Bella Johnson

John W. Cameron Family of Argyll

John W. Cameron emigrated from Argyll to North Carolina c. 1775 when he was about thirteen years old and m. in North Carolina Jene Cameron. They lived near Johnsonville, N.C., and had nine children. There is some material on this family in Rozella McLeod's *McLeods of Tuckahoe & Horses Creek.*[15] John W. Cameron and Jene Cameron had:

I. DANIEL E.
II. RANDALL
III. NEILL W.
IV. ALLEN A.
V. MARY
VI. NANCY
VII. ELIZABETH
VIII. FRODEE (FODA)
IX. REBECCA

I. DANIEL E. CAMERON b. 1828, d. 1904, m. Maggie McLeod. More information is found on this line in Rozella McLeod's *McLeods of Tuckahoe & Horses Creek,* from which I take the following material. Margaret McLeod (dau. of Neill and Sarah Cameron McLeod) b. 1846, d. 1919, m. 1866. Both are buried at Cameron Hill Church Cemetery.[16] They had ten children, according to the research of Rozella McLeod:
A. Sarah Jane (Babe) Cameron b. 1867, d. 1949, m. Daniel Graham McFadyen b. 1862, d. 1927. Both are buried at Cypress Church Cemetery. They had six children.[17]
B. Mary Catherine Cameron b. 1869, m. George Stewart, no children.
C. Zebulon Vance Cameron b. 1873, d. 1939, m. Lou Hopkins b.

1889. No children. They are buried at Cameron Hill Cemetery.

D. Martha McLeod (Mattie) Cameron b. 1875, d. 1952, m. John Norman Cameron b. 1877, d. 1933. They had six children.[18]

E. Florence Cameron b. 1877, d. 1920, m. 1896 John Duncan Black Lindsay. They had six children.[19] See also the Lindsay section of this volume for this same line.

F. Neill Daniel McLeod Cameron (Mack) b. 1880, d. 1938, m. Maggie Swan b. 1887, d. 1967. They had five children.[20]

G. Louise Huske Cameron b. 1882, m. Robert Stewart, b. 1885, d. 1971. No children.

H. Ada Grizelle Cameron b. 1885, d. 1971, m. Angus Dougald Cameron b. 1880, d. 1949. They had three children.[21]

I. Lena Rebecca Cameron b. 1889, d. 1952 in Jacksonville, Florida, m. first Leroy Moore McLeod b. 1881, d. 1924, buried Morris Chapel, Swans Station. She m. secondly John Gale. She had seven children by her first husband and two by the second.[22]

II. RANDALL CAMERON m. Mary Eliza Cameron (dau. of Samuel Johnson Cameron and Catherine Blue. See the section IX. B., p. 215, above in order to trace their children).

III. NEILL W. CAMERON b. 1849, d. 1917, m. Lizzie McNeill, no children.

IV. ALLEN A. CAMERON was single.

V. MARY CAMERON was single.

VI. NANCY CAMERON was single.

VII. ELIZABETH (ISABELLA) CAMERON m. Neill H. McNeill, d. 1922. They had:

A. John W. McNeill
B. Sallie McNeil
C. Mary Jane McNeill
D. Janie McNeill

VIII. FRODEE (FODA) Cameron was single

IX. REBECCA CAMERON m. Hugh A. Cameron (son of John Cameron, who was the son of John Merchant Cameron, mentioned in the section above, p. 214).[23]

Allen Cameron Family

According to the booklet already mentioned by John Burton Cameron

(recently reprinted in *Argyll Colony Plus* 11.2), Allen Cameron was born and reared at Auchternchity (County of Fife in Scotland), where he married Mary Stewart of that place. They, with their first three children, emigrated to North Carolina in 1791, arriving at Wilmington in August. Allen Cameron died at the family home in Baker's Creek in 1800. Their children were:

I. ARCHIE CAMERON b. c. 1774 in Fife, d. 1842 in Cumberland County, N. C.

II. DOUGALD CAMERON b. c. 1784 in Fife

III. JAMES CAMERON b. c. 1786 in Fife

IV. MARGARET CAMERON (unsure of her age or order of birth) had already married a McLaughlin and remained in Scotland.

V. NANCY CAMERON b. on Baker's Creek in Bladen County, N.C., after the family settled there in 1792. Nancy married Daniel Cameron and had no children.

VI. INFANT CAMERON, who was taken from Bladen County and buried in Cameron Hill in present Harnett County.

I. ARCHIE CAMERON m. Christian McKeithen and settled near Bluff Church in Cumberland County. They had six children:

A. Jimmie Cameron b. 1812, m. Miss Maxwell and moved to Georgia. He was killed while bathing in a river by striking his head against a log. His widow never returned to N.C. and nothing more is known of this family.

B. John Allen Cameron b. 1824, m. Sallie Baker near Bluff Church and moved to Jacksonville, FL. in 1856, where he reared a large family. He was still living in 1895.

C. Hugh Dougald Cameron m. Belle Colvin and settled near the mouth of Little River (Lane Station). He reared a large family and was a historian well versed in the early traditions of the Cape Fear.

D. Christian Cameron b. 1819, d. 1864, m. Mr. Bass and moved to Georgia while still a young woman; no further information.

E. Mary Catherine Cameron b. 1828, d. 1874, m. her cousin Jimmie Cameron, son of Archie's brother, James.

F. Sarah Ann Cameron b. 1830, d. 1864, m. William Senter. The only member of this family was living a few years ago, near Humbolt, TN., according to what John Burton Cameron wrote in 1968.

II. DOUGALD CAMERON b. Jan. 5, 1784, Scotland, d. Feb. 14, 1867, m. Barbara Morris b. Nov. 1, 1793, d. May 5, 1849. He entered a tract of about 800 acres of land south of the Upper Little River. Swann Station was located on this tract when the railroad was built. They had twelve children:

A. John M. Cameron b. Sept. 19, 1814, d. Dec. 8, 1889, m. Sally Morris b. Aug. 12, 1829, d. Mar. 5, 1921, daughter of "Big Jim" Morris. Their five children are traced by J.B. Cameron.[24]

B. Alexander M. Cameron b. Aug. 13, 1818, d. Dec. 4, 1872, m. Susan Stone b. Oct. 11, 1818, d. June 3, 1889. They had nine children, traced by J. B. Cameron.[25]

C. Daniel Cameron b. Feb. 22, 1829, d. Oct. 16, 1877, m. Kate Dalrymple, and had three children, traced by J.B. Cameron.[26]

D. Allen M. Cameron b. Mar. 25, 1836, d. Apr. 4, 1909, m. Sarah C. McLean b. Aug. 31, 1834, d. May 2, 1911. They had eight children, traced by J.B. Cameron.[27]

E. Hugh Cameron b. 1825, d. Feb. 19, 1857, m. Mary Buie of Moore County, and lived on Juniper Creek near St. Andrews Church. They had two children, traced by J.B. Cameron.[28]

F. Dougald C. Cameron Jr. b. Nov. 19, 1838, d. June 30, 1863. He is buried in the "May Plot" near Swann Station on the Ora McKeithan property. No further information.

G. Barbara Cameron b. Mar. 24, 1827, m. Spence Edwards. They had one daughter (listed by J.B. Cameron).[29]

H. Nancy Cameron m. William Morris. They had two sons and several daughters.[30]

I. Jennet Cameron b. Sept. 17, 1824, d. Feb. 23, 1897, m. John P. May. He had been found an infant on the doorsteps of a Dalrymple family near Jonesboro (present Lee County, N.C., originally part of Moore County). It was never known who he was. He was raised by the Dalrymples and named John (after a member of the family) and May (because of the month in which he was found). After John May had reared his family for some years, he disappeared and was never heard of again. They had four children.[31]

J. Mary A. Cameron b. Sept. 17, 1824, d. June 9, 1893, m.

William Thomas b. June 12, 1818, d. June 20, 1885. They had five children.[32]

K. Sarah Cameron d. Oct. 26, 1889, m. Henry Gales and had children.

L. Catherine Cameron: no information.

III. JAMES CAMERON: no information.

Black Family

The Black Family had close ties with Flora and Allan McDonald for a time during the Revolutionary War. James McNeill Johnson of Aberdeen prepared a sketch for this family (which has already been mentioned), and Rassie Wicker also deals with this family.[33]

According to Rassie Wicker:

> Of this family, there were old Kenneth, Archibald, Alexander, John and perhaps Hugh. They originally obtained grants on Big Rockfish, in Cumberland. John came up into Moore, and in 1765, entered a fifty acre tract upon which the late L.E. Pender built . . . just beyond Little Creek, and adjoining Country Club of North Carolina tract. John apparently never lived in Moore. He is buried in Hoke, on Puppy Creek, below Raeford, and it is supposed, lived in that vicinity. Alexander lived on Quewhiffle Creek, Hoke County. He was shot and left for dead by Wade and Culp, in their raid in retaliation for the Massacre at Piney Bottom, but he recovered and later removed to Florida. Old Kenneth was the only one of the family known to have lived in Moore . . . [34]

I have information only on Kenneth Black. He was b. in Jura c. 1730 and m. Catherine Patterson (mentioned later under the Patterson section, p. 225). They emigrated to North Carolina some years before the Revolution and lived latterly in Moore County near the present town of Southern Pines (then non-existent). In the words of J. McN. Johnson:

"Kenneth Black was a friend of Alan McDonald of Kingsborough, husband of the illustrious Flora, and it was to Mr. Black that Flora appealed for aid when her house was burned in 1777 at Killegrey, and it was at his house that Flora's daughters were visiting when the rude soldiers ripped their silk dresses with their swords. [Again, says Johnson, see *Caruther's Notes*, but he has his dates wrong as to this incident]."[35]

Kenneth Black was murdered by the American soldiers under Col. Alston soon after the Piney Bottom Massacre of 1781. His widow lived on their land for some forty years after his death. They had:

I. ARCHIBALD
II. HUGH
III. MALCOLM
IV. EFFIE
V. MARGARET (PEGGY)

I. ARCHIBALD BLACK b. 1760, d. 1838, m. Flora Martin (dau. of John Martin). They lived on Little River in Moore County and had:

A. Kenneth
B. John
C. Martin
D. Hugh (Oulan Voir or Big Hugh)
E. Malcolm d. in infancy 1813
F. Sallie
G. Katie
H. Effie
I. Jane

A. Kenneth Black b. 1793, d. 1875, m. Mary (Polly) Blue b. 1802 Scotland, d. 1858, Moore County (dau. of "River Daniel" Blue of Eureka Community in Moore County. See p. 234). Both are buried at Union Presbyterian Church. Further information is available on this family.[36] They had:
   1. Martin lived in Wilmington, N.C. and left a widow but no children
   2. Daniel died young, no issue
   3. Archie died in war, no issue
   4. Flora single, lived at her parent's home
   5. Lidda died in childhood
   6. Kate single, lived at her parents' home
   7. Elizabeth Jane married Archibald Alexander Ray of Eureka community and had seven children.[37]

B. John Black b. c. 1795, d.c. 1870, m. Nancy Ray (dau. of Archibald Ray). They had:
   1. Archibald Ray Black taught school in Rocky Point, N.C., m. Nancy Moore of New Hanover County, N.C. and had seven children.[38]
   2. William Black b. 1835, d. 1894, Sheriff of Moore County, m. Margaret Seawell and had six children.[39]
   3. Malcolm Black single
   4. Murdock Black m. Antoinette McLean, d. at Point Caswell, N.C., had twelve children.[40]
   5. Flora Black d. c. 1900, m. Ivor Patterson, no issue.

6. Eliza Black m. Henderson Muse, no issue
7. Margaret Ann Black m. her second cousin, Daniel McKenzie
8. Effie Black m. Sam Blue.

C. Martin Black b. 1797, d. 1821 single

D. Alexander ("Sandy") Black b. 1808, d. 1832, m. Belle Currie (dau. of Lauchlin Currie) and lived on his father's old homeplace. They had:

1. Archibald single
2. Christopher m. Miss Robinson and had children
3. Lauchlin single
4. Sarah single
5. Flora single
6. Mary single

E. Hugh Black (Oulan Voir) b. 1806, d. 1882 m. Sarah McDonald (dau. of "Scotch Allan" who came to America as late as 1833). All of their children died in infancy.

F. Sallie Black single, lived with brother Hugh

G. Katie Black m. Peter Monroe and lived where the village of Manly now stands (in Moore County). They had:

1. Archie Monroe d. in Civil War
2. William Monroe d. in Civil War
3. Hugh Monroe d. in Civil War
4. Daniel Monroe single
5. Flora Martin Monroe m. Angus Ray
6. Sarah Monroe single

H. Effie Black m. Nevin (or Niven) Ray, the Surveyor. They lived near the present Whispering Pines in Moore County and are buried in the old Ray Cemetery located near Thagard's Millpond. They had several children, among them, John Ray, who m. and lived in the same place and had children.

I. Jane Black m. John R. Currie of Orange County, N.C. and had children.

II. HUGH BLACK m. Polly Johnson. They had:

A. Katie single

B. Belle m. Hugh McKenzie and had many children. Their descendants live in the Culdee section of Moore County.

III. MALCOLM BLACK b. 1775, d. 1863, m. Sallie Patterson (of the "Beaver Dam" Patterson family). They had:

A. Dr. Kenneth Black b. 1820, d. 1870 at Hickory, N.C. Practiced medicine in Fayetteville, N.C., many years, a graduate of Edinburgh University. He m. Miss Crow. They had:

1. John
2. Eddie
3. Mary
4. Fannie

B. Lauchlin Black b. 1825, d. 1863 in the Confederate Army, single.

C. Katie Black b. 1818, d. 1870, m. Kendrick Dowd and lived near the head of McLendon Creek. They had children, among them: James Dowd of Rockingham, N.C.

D. Margaret Black b. 1822, d. 1870, m. Patrick McKeithen. No information.

E. Lovedy Black b. 1833, m. first Daniel McKeithen, who lived only a few weeks after their marriage; secondly, Mr. Griggs of South Carolina by whom she had three children, and thirdly, Mr. Byrd by whom she had three: a son, James Byrd, and two daughters.[41]

F. Jane Black b. 1830, d. 187?, m. Byran Dowd (a brother of Kendrick Dowd). They lived in Moore County and had:

1. Neill Dowd
2. Byran Dowd Jr.
3. Harriet Dowd m. William Ritter
4. Annie Mariah m. Thomas Shields

IV. EFFIE BLACK b. 1765, d. 1850, m. Dougald Black and lived on Little River in Moore County. They had:

A. Peter m. Miss Brown
B. Kenneth single
C. Flora m. James Ray, gunsmith
D. Christian m. John McDonald
E. Peggy m. Needham Byrant
F. Katie m. James Caddell of Horse's Creek in lower Moore County

V. MARGARET (PEGGY) BLACK m. Angus Black of Robeson County, N.C. They lived near Philadelphus Church near Red Springs, N.C., and had:

A. Katherine
B. Sarah
C. Angus Jr.
D. Duncan
E. Calvin
F. Caroline
G. Mary A.[42]

Patterson Families

A cluster of several Patterson families was centered in southern Moore

County near present Aberdeen and to the east in Cumberland County in present Fort Bragg Reservation, spreading out into other surrounding regions. These families (the relationship between several of these Pattersons themselves is not determined) intermarried with the other large Scots connections such as Black, Buie, Blue, McNeill etc.

Rear Admiral Alex M. Patterson (whose work we have referred to many times) did remarkable research on these families in 1979 in *Highland Scots Pattersons of North Carolina and Related Families*. He covers more than twenty main family groups in the upper Cape Fear. It would be impossible and unnecessary to attempt to reproduce his work here, but I will take a glance at the heads of the main groups he has covered and indicate where these may be further traced in his volume.

The First Duncan Patterson Family

Duncan Patterson came (presumably) from Argyllshire before 1745, when he purchased land on the Cape Fear River just north of the present city of Fayetteville. Later he took other land in upper Little River, and was known as a farmer and weaver. He was also an elder in Barbeque Presbyterian Church. He d. 1793; his wife had died before him. They had:

I.	ARCHIBALD	IV.	JOHN
II.	NEILL	V.	FLORA
III.	DANIEL	VI.	MARGARET

Patterson has information on the children of Archibald who m. Mary____ and moved to Georgia.[43]

The Second Duncan Patterson Family

This Duncan was the son of John and the grandson of the first Duncan Patterson listed above. He m. 1808 Mary Buie (dau. of John and Flora Buie, listed under the Buie section, p. 192). In 1827 he m. Flora Munn, who lived near the Pattersons. By his first wife he had six, and by his second wife eight children. He was an elder in Barbeque Church and later in Mt. Pisgah Church. He d. 1864.

Duncan Patterson and Mary Buie had:

I. NEILL PATTERSON b. 1808, d. 1877, m. Margaret Ann Eliza McLean b. 1817, d. 1891.

II. RANDEL (RANDLE) PATTERSON b. c.1810, no information

III.SARAH (SALLIE) PATTERSON b. 1812, d. c.1885, m. first ____ McDougald, and secondly John Ray Jr.

IV. CATHERINE (KATE) PATTERSON b. 1813, d. c.1875, no record of first marriage, m. secondly George W. Rising b. 1810.

V. MARTHA PATTERSON b. 1814, d. c.1880, m. Daniel McDonald b. 1810, d. 1876.

VI. MARGARET PATTERSON b. c.1816, d. c.1836, single.

Duncan Patterson and Flora Munn had:

VII. FLORA ANN PATTERSON b. 1828, d. 1888, m. John Ebenezer Clark b. 1817, d. 1875.

VIII. DUNCAN ALEXANDER PATTERSON b. 1830, d. 1864, m. Annie Small b. 1836.

IX. MARY PATTERSON b. 1832, d. 1920, single.

X. SARAH ELIZABETH b. 1834, d. 1919, m. Archibald A. Bishop b. c. 1831, d. 1890.

XI. MARGARET WALKER PATTERSON b. 1836, d. 1888, m. Malcolm McNeill b. 1833, d. 1908.

XII. MALCOLM PATTERSON b. 1839, single, no information.

XIII. JOHN PATTERSON b. 1843, d. 1864, died at sea while serving in the Confederate Forces and is buried at Fort Monroe, Virginia.

XIV. DANIEL PATTERSON b. 1845, d. 1862, marital status unknown.[44]

Rear Admiral Patterson devotes the majority of his large work to tracing in particular the descendants of:

I. NEILL PATTERSON and Margaret Ann Eliza McLean who had sixteen children

VII. FLORA ANN PATTERSON and John Ebenezer Clark who had six children

VIII. DUNCAN ALEXANDER PATTERSON and Annie Small who had one child

XI. MARGARET WALKER and Malcolm McNeill who had ten children

Admiral Patterson also includes information on the family of Gilbert Patterson (Pattison) who was granted land near (present) Buie's Creek in 1740 and in 1748 moved to Orange (now Chatham) County. He was b. c. 1770 in Scotland, arrived in Carolina (presumably in the Argyll Colony in 1739).[45]

He deals with the family of the widow Catherine Patterson (husband's name unknown), who with her children arrived from Argyll in c. 1748, first in Cumberland County, then in Moore County. According to Patterson's research, her children were:

I. JOHN PATTERSON b. c.1730, d. c. 1812 in Moore County, m. Isabel McDuffie (children are traced by us under the McDuffie line, p. 201).

II.CATHERINE PATTERSON b. c. 1732, m. Kenneth Black (their children are traced under the Black section, p. 219).

III. DUNCAN PATTERSON, marital status unknown.

IV. MALCOLM PATTERSON, marital status unknown[46]

Other Patterson families which Admiral Patterson traces include the family of "Raft Swamp" Daniel Patterson b. c. 1731, Scotland, d. 1809 in Robeson County, m. Mary McMillan. They had eight children.[47]

Also mentioned is the family of Daniel Patterson who lived near the present town of Maxton, either in present Scotland County or Robeson County. He was b. c. 1793, m. Nancy Leach b. c.1799 in Scotland (dau. of Dougald and Mary McCollum Leach who came from Scotland in 1801). They had six children.[48]

The family of Daniel Patterson of Bladen County, N.C. is listed (though their relationship to the other Pattersons is unclear). This Daniel was b. in Scotland and d. 1832 in Bladen County. He m. Nancy L. ____, b. Scotland, d. 1851 in Bladen County. They had three children.[49]

Finally, Admiral Patterson traces the family of Alexander Patterson of Richmond County, N.C., many of whom lived near Maxton, N.C. Alexander was b. c. 1819 in Richmond County, N.C. (now Scotland County), possibly the son of James Patterson. Alexander m. first (name unknown) and secondly Mary, the widow of Roderick McGill. He had five children by his first wife and four by the second.[50]

Blue Families

One very large Scots family connection of Moore County, N.C., was the five major Blue families, who came from Argyll at different times, and were almost certainly related, although their relationship is not known to us at present. These families were discussed in some detail by this author in a work in 1982, *The Scottish Blue Family From Carolina to Texas.* Here we can only make general reference to the heads of the five families and indicate where further information may be found on them in the original work.

The Malcolm Blue Family

This is the first of the five Blue families to have come to Cumberland County, N.C., from Argyll. According to J. McN. Johnson, Malcolm Blue and family arrived in 1748 from Knapdale, bringing three children with them. They had five more in Cumberland County. They lived near Longstreet Presbyterian Church. Malcolm b. c. 1700, d. 1766, m. in Kintyre, Scotland, Mary Smith, b. 1710, d. 1812 aged 102. They had:

I.	DUNCAN	V.	DUGALD
II.	DANIEL	VI.	NEILL
III.	JOHN	VII.	MALCOLM
IV.	JAMES	VIII.	SARAH

I. DUNCAN BLUE b. 1741, Scotland, d. 1828, Cumberland County, N.C., m. first his cousin, Effie Blue, and secondly, in 1775, Margaret Graham. He had three children. (I am not certain, but I think all were by the second wife: at least the last two certainly were):

A. Daniel Blue d. 1845, m. Margaret Ray b. 1782, d. 1847. They lived in the Longstreet Section of Cumberland County and had at least three children.[51]

B. Neill Blue b. 1777, d. 1852, m. Elizabeth Galbraith 1803 in Cumberland County. They moved to Robertson County, TN. and then to Audrain County, MO. They had ten children, several of whom died young.

C. Flora Blue d. 1818, m. Dugald Graham and lived first in Robeson County, N.C., and then moved to Telfair County, Georgia in 1816, where she died at the birth of twin sons, John and Archibald. They also had six other children.

II. DANIEL BLUE b. 1739 in Scotland, settled in Bladen County, N.C. No information.

III. JOHN BLUE (I) b. 1745 in Scotland, d. 1781 in Fayetteville, N.C., m. Mary McKay, and served on the American side in the Revolutionary War. They had children. I have information on:

A. John Blue (II) b. 1776, d. 1831, m. Effie Gilchrist in 1813. They had ten children.[52]

IV. JAMES BLUE b. 1751, no information

V. DUGALD BLUE b. 1753, d. 1836, moved to Richmond County, N.C.

where in 1783 he m. first Mary McLaughlin, and secondly Mary McLaurin after his first wife's death in 1808. About 1819 this family moved to Montgomery, Alabama. By his first wife he had:

A. Angus	E. Neil
B. Catherine	F. Sarah
C. Daniel	G. Duncan
D. John	H. Malcolm

By his second wife:

I. John Andrew	L. Effie
J. James	K. Mary

VI. NEILL BLUE b. 1755, d. 1800 in Richmond County, N.C. m. ______, and had no children.

VII. MALCOLM BLUE b. 1758, d. 1806, m. Flora McGill, who after his death was living in Marion County, MS. in 1820 and in Monroe County, AL. in 1830. They had six daughters[53] and at least one son, John.[54]

VIII. SARAH BLUE b. 1760 in Cumberland County, N.C., d. 1822 (or 1832?) in Clark County, Alabama, m. Alexander Watson. They had:

A. John Watson	E. Duncan Watson
B. James Watson	F. Sarah Watson
C. Daniel Watson	G. Catherine Watson
D. Samuel Watson	H. Mary Watson

The "Lakeview" Blue Family

The second Blue family to come over from Argyll was that of Duncan Blue, who settled near what is now Lakeview in Moore County, N.C., c. 1768 or 1769. They were granted land in this area on Shaddock's Creek in 1770, which is still in the family. Duncan Blue was b. 1734 in the Isle of Jura and d. 1814 in Moore County. About 1763 he m. Margaret Campbell b. 1740 in North Knapdale and d. in Moore County in 1820. Both are buried in the family cemetery at Lakeview (sometimes known as the McKeithan Cemetery). They sided with the Loyalists during the Revolution, but took the oath of loyalty after the War ended. His oath is pictured on p. 123. They had:

I. JOHN CAMPBELL BLUE
II. PATRICK CAMPBELL BLUE
III. DUNCAN CAMPBELL BLUE
IV. CATHERINE BLUE

V. SARAH BLUE
VI. EFFEY BLUE

Also they had a daughter who died of typhoid as a small child during the Revolutionary War, and is buried near her parents in Lakeview.

I. JOHN CAMPBELL BLUE b. 1765 on the Isle of Jura, d. 1834 at Lakeview, N.C. He m. first (name unknown) and secondly Catherine McMillan (dau. of Archibald McMillan and Lovedy McLauchlin, dau. of Peter) in Moore County. Catherine was b. 1765, d. 1862 in Moore. They lived near Shaddock's Creek in what is now the village of Niagara in Moore County. By his first wife he had:

A. Daniel Blue who m. _____ Wadsworth (dau. of John and Flora Wadsworth). They had one son, Daniel, before elder Daniel's early death.

B. Margaret Blue b. c.1783 in North Carolina, d. after 1832, m. John McKeithen (son of Neill and Mrs. Lovedy McL. McMillan McKeithen) before 1809. They had three children.[55]

By his second wife John Campbell Blue had:

C. Archibald McMillan Blue b. 1796, d. 1877, buried at Bethesda Church, near his home. He m. first Jennet Smith (dau. of Daniel and Ann McKay Smith, already mentioned in this volume) in 1821. She was b. 1797 in Cumberland County, and d. 1867, buried at Bethesda. Secondly Archibald m. Flora Jane Ray in 1871 (dau. of Niven Ray and Effie Black). He had seven children by his first wife and none by the second.[56]

D. Duncan McMillan Blue b. 1797, d. after 1860, m. first in 1816 in Cumberland County Mary Smith b. 1791, d. before 1851 (dau. of Daniel and Ann McKay Smith). He m. secondly in 1851 in Moore County Mary Ray b. 1811. They lived on the old Kenneth Clark place on Drowning Creek. He had seven children by his first wife and two by his second.[57]

E. John McMillan Blue b. 1799 near Lakeview, d. 1863, buried at Bethesda, m. first in 1828 Elizabeth Ray (dau. of Archibald and Elizabeth McSween Ray). They lived at the old Archibald Ray homestead in what is now Eureka section of Moore County. Elizabeth d. as a result of childbirth in 1842 at age 36. Secondly John m. Margaret Cameron b. 1848 near Pinehurst, N.C. By his first wife he had eight children and two by the second.[58]

F. Mary Blue b. 1801, m. Randolph (or Randal) McDonald (son

of Allen and Polly McKenzie McDonald). They moved to Richmond County, N.C., and lived near Mark's Creek Presbyterian Church. They had nine children.[59]

G. Malcolm McMillan Blue b. 1802 at Shaddock's Creek, m. 1833 Isabella Patterson who d. 1834 at age 26. In 1843 Malcolm m. Flora Ray of the Bethesda community. Their home was near Bethesda Presbyterian Church not far from Aberdeen, and has been turned into a historical museum. Malcolm was Clerk of Session at Bethesda Church and a large landholder. He and Flora had seven children.[60]

H. Anna Blue b. 1804, d. 1893, buried Union Presbyterian Church, m. Daniel Blue II (son of emigrant "River Daniel" Blue, whose family is described on pp. 232-235) b. 1804, d. 1882. They lived on the homeplace of "River Daniel" (still standing, and pictured on p. 93) in the Eureka community of Moore County. They had eight children.[61]

I. Patrick McMillan Blue b. 1806, d. 1884, lived on his father's homeplace on Shaddock's Creek and was an elder in Union Presbyterian Church. He m. first in 1842 Sarah E. McNeill (dau. of "Little John" McNeill) b. 1816, d. 1857. They had three children. He m. secondly Mary Catherine (dau. of John McNeill and Martha Eliza Oats), widow of Neill McKeithan by whom she had one daughter. Patrick had three children by his first marriage and five by his second.[62]

J. Neill McK. Blue b. 1812 in Moore County, d. 1892 in Cumberland County, buried at Sandy Grove Presbyterian Church. They lived on his wife's land at Piney Bottom in Cumberland County, site of the Revolutionary massacre, (see p. 123.) He m. Eliza Smith who d. 1891 at age 83. They had eleven children.[63]

II. PATRICK CAMPBELL BLUE ("PETER"), son of Emigrant Duncan, b. 1768, d. 1838 (?) in Moore County, m. Phoebe Shields. They lived near Lakeview, N.C., on the Angus McNeill place. They had four children. After Patrick's death, his widow and children moved first to Tennessee and then to Texas.[64]

III. DUNCAN CAMPBELL BLUE, son of Emigrant Duncan, b. in Lakeview in 1780, d. 1851, m. Sarah Ferguson b. 1806, d. 1878 (see p. 239). They lived on the original Duncan Blue land in Lakeview and their descendants have preserved many of the old family papers. They had eleven children.[65]

IV. CATHERINE BLUE, dau. of Emigrant Duncan, b. in Lakeview 17(?) and d. 18(?), m. Morris Morrison (son of Captain Cain Morrison who came from Jura to Moore County, one of the few emigrants whom we know definitely to have been a Jacobite). They had two sons who lived not far from what is now Vass, N.C. in Moore County.[66]

V. SARAH BLUE, dau. of Emigrant Duncan, b. in Lakeview c. 1773-75, m. Archibald McMillan who emigrated with his parents to North Carolina when he was 16 years old in 1774. They had five children, all of whom moved to Alabama, Louisiana or Texas.[67] One of their sons, Archibald Blue McMillan, wrote poetry in both Gaelic and English.

VI. EFFIE BLUE, dau. of Emigrant Duncan, b. in the 1780s in Lakeview, d. in Moore County c.1857. She was first a member of Bethesda (is named in the 1812 list) and later of Union Presbyterian Church. She m. John Black (son of John Black Sr., relative of Kenneth Black, already discussed). They lived in Moore County not far from what is now Thagard's Pond (Whispering Pines). They had six children.[68]

"Guinea" Blue Family

The third family of Blues to emigrate from Argyll to Moore County, N.C., were popularly known as "the Guinea Blues", supposedly because some of them were small of stature. They were from the Isle of Jura and settled in what is now Pinebluff, N.C. There were five emigrant brothers (not necessarily in this order of birth):

I. ARCHIBALD
II. DANIEL
III. JOHN L.
IV. PETER O.
V. DUGALD

We have information only on III. John Blue and IV. Peter O. Blue.

III. JOHN BLUE is said to have had three sons and six daughters. We have information only on two of the sons: Daniel and John.

A. Daniel Blue b. 1785 in Scotland, d. in Robeson County, N.C., sometime after 1855, m. Elizabeth Smith, b. 1792 in Robeson County, d. after 1860. They had six children.[69]

B. John Blue is said to have married and to have had children, among whom were two daughters, Mary and Christian. No further information.

IV. PETER O. BLUE came from Jura to Moore County sometime before 1793 (when he purchased land from Archibald Patterson near Pine

Bluff) and died in 1828. He was an elder in Bethesda Church near Aberdeen, and a member of Pansophia Masonic Lodge. His wife's name is unknown. They had ten children:

A. Malcolm Blue b. 1785, Moore County, N.C., m. first Viney Merritt, and secondly Matilda F. Carter of Union Springs, Alabama in 1848. They had six children.[70]

B. Duncan Blue said to have m. Tiny Brabham, d. before 1828. Said to have had at least one son, Danny.

C. Catherine Blue m. Duncan McLean and member of Bethesda Church.

D. Sarah Blue, no information

E. John Blue d. 1848 near Pine Bluff, N.C. He m. Florah Sophia McNeill, b. 1796 in Moore County, d. in Bullock County, Alabama (formerly part of Pike's County). They had nine children.[71]

F. Archibald D. Blue b. 1789 in Moore County, d. 1856 in Elba, Alabama. He moved with five of his brothers to Pike County, Alabama in 1835. He m. and had six children.[72]

G. Daniel Blue b. c.1792 (97?) in Moore County, d. c.1867. His full name is said by some to have been John Daniel Blue. He moved to Alabama in 1835 with his brothers and lived first in Pike County, then in Coffee County for ten years, and finally moved to Texas. He m. Mary Louvenia Elizabeth Gilmore of Ireland. She remarried after the death of Daniel. Daniel and wife had four children.[73]

H. Isabelle Blue is listed as a member of Bethesda Church near Aberdeen in 1812; no further information.

I. Peter Blue b. 1795, d. 1862, moved to Alabama in 1835. He m. first _____, and secondly Mary "Polly" McDonald, b. 1812 in Scotland, d. 1903. By his first wife he had five children, and by his second wife, seven children.[74]

J. Hector Patrick Blue b. 1803 in Moore County, N.C., d. 1879 in Bullock County, Alabama, near Bethel Presbyterian Church. He m. 1831 (or 32) Mary McKinnon, b. 1810 in North Carolina, d. 1882 in Union Springs, Alabama. They also moved to Alabama in 1835. They had eight children.[75]

"Bridge" Blue Family

The fourth Blue family to come to Carolina became known as "the

Bridge Blues," because they settled near Blue's Bridge (giving their name to it) on Drowning Creek in lower Moore County. They came from the Isle of Jura. The head of this family was Angus Blue, b. 1733 in Scotland, and came to Carolina about 1803. He d. 1823 and is buried at Bethesda Church. He m. Flora _____, b. in Scotland 1746, d. 1827 in Moore County, buried at Bethesda. They had one son, Daniel.

I. DANIEL BLUE b. 1768 in Scotland, d. 1844 in Moore County, N.C., m. Catherine McLaurin (dau. of Hugh McLaurin). Because of his prosperity and willingness to lend money, Daniel was popularly known as "The Bank". They had nine children:

A. John Blue b. 1793, d. 1861, m. Margaret McGoogan of Lumber Bridge, N.C., b. 1801, d. 1883, buried in McGill Cemetery near Wagram, N.C. They had eight children.[76]

B. Christian Blue b. 1794, d. 1865, buried at Bethesda Church, single.

C. Flora Blue, b. 1798, d. 1889, m. Archibald McFarland, apparently had no children.

D. Daniel Blue m. Mary Graham and migrated to Mississippi. They had five children.[77]

E. Archibald Blue b. c.1805, d. between 1860 and 1870. He lived on Target Point on Drowning Creek (now in Camp McColl). He m. Mary McPherson (dau. of John). They had eleven children.[78]

F. Sara Blue m. Martin McGilvary of Moore County, N.C. They had two daughters, both born in the upper part of Robeson County, N.C. This family moved to Alabama, where Sarah and Martin McGilvary both died. The two daughters then returned to live in North Carolina before 1858.[79]

G. Mary Blue m. John McGougan and had three daughters.[80]

H. Malcolm Blue b. 1809, d. 1871 was single and lived at his parents' old home.

I. Isabella Blue m. Duncan McGougan, no further information.

"River Blue" Family

The fifth family of Blues to come from Argyllshire were known as "River Blues" because of their location in Moore County in what is now the Eureka community. Although they sailed from the Isle of Jura, rental lists show that their home was in the now derelict village of Arichonan in North Knapdale. The head of this family was "River Daniel" Blue b. 1770 in Scotland, m. Christian Lamonds in North Knapdale prior to 1790.

They emigrated to North Carolina in 1804 and bought the Wadsworth house (believed to have been built in 1795), which is still standing and still in their family (owned by John Sam Blue of Eureka, see p. 93). They had large land holdings. Daniel's numerous letters, written in the first half of the nineteenth century, give interesting insights into the beginnings of the settlement.[81] A letter he received is pictured on p. 180. He d. 1858 in Moore County and is buried at Union Church, where he was an elder. His wife was b. 1774 and d. 1865, and is buried at Bethesda. Daniel and Christian Blue had:

I. KATIE
II. CHRISTIAN
III. MARY (POLLY)
IV. DANIEL II
V. SARAH (SALLY)

I. KATIE BLUE b. 1790 in Scotland, d. 1885 in North Carolina, m. John Leach of Richmond County, N.C. They had three sons and six daughters.[82]

Ruins of one of several once substantial stone houses, which are all that are left of Arichonan, in North Knapdale, Argyllshire. The town was settled in 1686 but 'cleared' forcibly in the 1840s. It is now maintained by Historic Scotland. The family of "River" Daniel Blue emigrated from here in 1804 to Moore County, NC.

II. CHRISTIAN BLUE b. 1792 in Scotland, d. 1886 in North Carolina, m. Alexander Leach of Cabin Creek, Moore County, N.C., b. 1784, d. 1886, age 103. They had:

- A. Archibald A. Leach b. 1813, d. 1862, m. first ____ Davis (dau. of Stephen Davis), secondly ____ Hix. He had four children by his first wife and two by his second.[83]
- B. Margaret A. Leach b. 1815, d. 1875, m. Rev. David Wright, a Baptist minister, who d. at Troy, N.C. They had one son.[84]
- C. Daniel A. Leach b. 1817, m. Rebecca Leach (dau. of John Leach, Daniel's first cousin on his mother's side). They lived at Moravian Falls in Wilkes County and had several children.[85]
- D. Edwin Leach b. 1818, m. Margaret Murchison, and had six children.[86]
- E. Malcolm M. Leach b. 1821, m. Tamar Coggins. They lived near Troy, N.C., and had five children.[87]
- F. Mary Blue Leach b. 1825, m. W.B. Owen, who d. 1864. They lived at Star, N.C. and had no children.
- G. Angus B. Leach b. 1830, d. 1864 as a Confederate soldier at Petersburg, Virginia, m. Deborah Allen (dau. of John Allen), who d. 1891. They had four children.[88]
- H. Alexander A. Leach b. 1833, m. Sarah Catherine Currie (dau. of Daniel B. Currie of McClennon's Creek). They had two children.[89]
- I. Jane M. Leach b. 1839, no information.

III. MARY BLUE (POLLY) b. 1802 in Scotland, d. 1858, m. Kenneth Black, son of Kenneth Black who was killed during the Revolution. This family is traced under the Black section (p. 220).

IV. DANIEL BLUE II b. 1804, d. 1882 in Moore County. He m. Anna Blue (dau. of John Campbell Blue). Their family is traced under the John C. Blue section (pp. 229).

V. SARAH BLUE (SALLY) b. 1806, d. 1854, m. Archibald Currie, b. 1814, d. 1879. They lived at Curriesville, N.C., and had:

- A. Dr. Daniel Alexander Blue Currie b. 1845, d. 1905, m. first Margaret F. McDonald by whom he had Victoria. Secondly he m. Margaret Ann McInnis 1879, b. 1851, d. 1933. They had eight children.[90]
- B. Flora Ann Currie b. 1841, d. 1897, m. Malcolm J. Blue (son of

John McMillan Blue, son of John Campbell Blue). Their children are traced under the John Campbell Blue section (pp. 227-229).

Murdoch Ferguson Family

The Ferguson family of central Moore County was closely connected by marriage to the Blues, McLeods, McIvers, Kellys, and others. Different groups of Fergusons came from Argyll to Moore County. We will deal first with the family of Murdoch Ferguson.

Murdoch Ferguson b. not in Skye, as so many of the other Moore County immigrants, but in the Isle of Jura, in 1750; d. 1830 in Moore County, m. Mary McDonald in Scotland, who was b. 1765, d. 1825 in Moore County. They emigrated about 1802 and settled about two miles south of the present town of Cameron, in Moore County on the Carlton Matthews place. They are buried in the McDonald Cemetery between Cameron and Vass (No. 200 in the Book of Moore County Cemeteries). They had:

I. DANIEL
II. NORMAN
III. NEIL
IV. JOHN
V. MURDOCH
VI. SARAH
VII. NANCY
VIII. RACHEL[91]

I. DANIEL FERGUSON b. 1788, d. 1866, m. first Mary (Polly) McIver (dau. of "Little Daniel" and Margaret Monroe McIver). They lived on the Old Raleigh Road. He m. secondly Jeannette MacDonald. They are referred to under the Roderick McIver section of this volume (p. 250). By his first wife he had:

A. Murdock Ferguson b. 1829 m. Maggie Jordan, a Methodist minister in South Carolina. No children.
B. Daniel Monroe Ferguson b. 1830, d. 1900, m. Eliza Kelly b. 1841, d. 1910. They had seven children.[92]
C. Mary Ann Ferguson b. 1833, d. 1901, m. 1854 Malcolm Kelly (son of Peter Kelly, son of Emigrant Daniel). They had nine children (see Peter Kelly section of this book, p. 257).
D. Margaret Ferguson b. 1835 m. Alexander Chisholm. They had one daughter.[93]
E. Neill William Ferguson b. 1838, d. 1885, m. Lula Paisley; no children.
F. Elizabeth Jane Ferguson b. 1842, m. James H. Monroe. They had one daughter.[94]

G. John A. Ferguson b. 1843, single.

By his second wife he had:

H. John Archibald Ferguson, who was killed in the Confederate Army.

II. NORMAN FERGUSON b. 1789, d. 1863, m. first Catherine Campbell (dau. of John Campbell) who d. 1839 at age 33, secondly Ann Campbell (dau. of Daniel Campbell). His two wives were first cousins. By his first wife he had:[95]

A. John C. Ferguson b. 1824, d. 1896 m. first Jane Campbell, secondly the widow McIver (born Baker) by whom he had one son and five daughters (no children by first wife).

B. Murdock Ferguson b. 1826, d. 1898 m. Mary McIntyre. They had one son and three daughters.

C. Fergus Ferguson b. 1830, d. 1902 m. Catherine MacDonald who d. in Moore County before 1890 when Fergus and children, (four sons and three daughters) moved to Mississippi.[96]

D. Rev. Angus Ferguson b. 1837, d. 1906, m. first Jeanette Stewart and secondly Catherine McNeill. By his first wife he had two daughters. He was pastor of Laurel Hill Presbyterian Church for thirty years (not far from Laurinburg, North Carolina).

E. Mary Ferguson b. 1829, d. 1830.

By his second wife he had:

F. Daniel Ferguson b. 1840, d. 1869, m. Jennie Monger. They lived in Cameron, N.C., and had one daughter.

G. William Ferguson b. 1845, d. 1863

H. Norman Ferguson b. 1846, m. Annie Wooten and lived in Bladenboro, N.C. They had two sons and four daughters.

I. Catherine Ferguson m. first Captain Martin Leach, d. 1864 in the Confederate Army. They had one daughter. She m. secondly Dr. Hector Turner. They had one son and one daughter.

III. NEILL FERGUSON m. ____ MacDonald and moved to Bladen County. According to the research of Dr. Ferguson, Neill is said to have been murdered by his brother-in-law, who was afterwards hanged for the crime. Neill and wife had two sons and five daughters:[97]

A. Murdoch Ferguson
B. Daniel Ferguson
C. Flora Ferguson
D. Nancy Ferguson
E. Rachel Ferguson
F. Mary Ferguson
G. Sarah Ferguson

IV. JOHN FERGUSON b. 1793, d. 1866, m. first Mary Jane MacDonald (sister of Red Allen MacDonald). According to Dr. Ferguson's research, John Ferguson and family lived on the old Plank Road about four miles east of Carthage, where he kept a public inn during the time the Plank Road was in use. He m. secondly Christian McQueen b. 1805, d. 1855 from near Fayetteville, N.C. By his first wife (according to Dr. Ferguson) he had one son:

A. Dr. John Ferguson who lived in Chatham County

By his second wife (according to the booklet on Murdoch Ferguson, which refers to the 1840 census) he had:

B. Archibald
C. William
D. James
E. Angus
F. Peter
G. Kate
H. Sara

V. MURDOCH FERGUSON m. Mary Bethune and raised a large family in Chatham County, N.C.[98]

VI. SARAH FERGUSON b. 1804, d. 1893, was single and lived with her nephew, John C. Ferguson, son of Norman.

VII. NANCY FERGUSON b. 1802, d. 1860, m. Daniel Shaw and moved to Bladen County, N.C. They had:[99]

A. a son who died in the War Between the States
B. Mary Jane Shaw who was single

VIII. RACHEL FERGUSON b. 1800, d. 1824, m. Daniel Kelly. They had:[100]

A. Rachel Kelly m. James Gilchrist[101]

John Ferguson Family

A second Ferguson family which settled in Moore County was that of John Ferguson. Whether or how he was related to Murdoch Ferguson, we do not know at present, although according to Janet Neuville (in *MacDonald Family History*, privately printed before 1993), these two families may have emigrated together. Both had land grants joining John MacDonald on Crain's Creek. John (son of Norman MacDonald) is said to have been related to Murdoch Ferguson's wife, Mary MacDonald Ferguson (according to Neuville).

Some of my information on this family comes from an 1846 legal action concerning the settlement of property in the estate of John Ferguson (who had been dead for several years at that time) in the Court of Pleas and Quarter Sessions of Moore County, N.C.,[102] as well as from *Ferguson Descendants 1804-1993* (privately printed) by Mrs. Louise B. Barkley of Newton, N. C., who was assisted in research by Treva King Crissman, Robert Paul Ferguson, Archie Ferguson, Joyce Ferguson, Zelda King Blue and Wooten Ferguson. John Ferguson, the emigrant and wife, Maria, brought with them six children sometime between 1802 and 1804. According to Louise Barkley:

> In 1810 John Ferguson is listed as having a land grant on Herd's Creek, a tributary of Crain's Creek, slightly northeast of the main body of Crain's (or Crane's) Creek, just above the John McDonald homeplace. John and Maria are buried in the Old MacDonald Cemetery northwest of Highway # 1 between Vass and Cameron in Moore County. Maria's age at death is given as 60 (maybe 50—hard to read), therefore she would have been 30 (20?) years old when Murdoch, her first child, was born and 51 (41) when her last one, Sara, was born. John's age at death on his tombstone is given as 55 . . . (p. 2).

I. MURDOCH Ferguson, b. 1785, d. 1857, lived in Moore County and was single.

II. PETER FERGUSON b. 1787, d. 1832, married Christian Campbell and had two children:

- A. Sarah Ann (Annie) Ferguson who m. Archie McMillan of Beaver Creek
- B. John A. Ferguson, who owned land in Moore County, and moved to Texas in 1855.

III. JOHN FERGUSON m. Christian (MacDonald ?) and, according to Louise Barkley, lived on his father's land and had five sons and three daughters. Seven of these children survived to adulthood (Barkley, op. cit., 2). Mrs. Barkley traces many of the descendants of these children (op. cit., 4, 5):

- A. Catherine Ferguson b. 1827, d. 1910, single.
- B. William Ferguson b. 1832, d. 1863 while serving in the Confederate Army during the Battle of the Wilderness.
- C. Angus Ferguson b. 1831, d. 1863. He also was a Confederate soldier and died in the Elmira, N.Y. prison camp.
- D. Polly Ferguson d. in infancy
- E. Peter Ferguson b. 1835, d. 1908, single.

F. James Ferguson b. 1838, d. 1862 as a Confederate soldier. His death occured in the hospital at Petersburg, Virginia.

G. Archibald Ferguson b. 1841, d. 1906, m. Mary Ann Persons Patterson b. Dec. 22, 1845, d. 1937, who was first married to William Patterson, who died in the War Between the States. The seven children of Archibald and Mary Ann are listed in Barkley, op. cit., p. 5.

IV. MARY (POLLY) FERGUSON b. 1790, d. 1835, m. John Campbell. They had one child:

A. Sara John Campbell, who m. William Johnson, father of John A. Johnson.

V. RACHEL FERGUSON b. 1795, d. 1822, m. Jonathan Hart. Rachel is buried with her parents in the Old MacDonald Cemetery. They had:

A. James Hart B. Matilda Hart

VI. NANCY FERGUSON b. 1794, d. 1850, m. John McNeill and had:

A. Angus McNeill, who lived at Lakeview, N.C. (Moore County)
B. Catherine McNeill, m. Dan MacDonald
C. Mary E. McNeill m. Daniel Kelly
D. Sarah McNeill was single

VII. SARAH FERGUSON b. 1803, d. 1868. She was the second wife of Duncan Campbell Blue (see p. 229). Their eleven children are traced in *Scottish Blue Family* by Douglas Kelly (787-838). They were:

A. Margaret Ann Blue b. May 25, 1826, d. Mar. 5, 1916, m. Duncan Keith.

B. Katherine Jane Blue b. Sept. 25, 1828, d. Mar. 28, 1914, was single.

C. Sarah Eliza Blue b. June 7, 1830, d. 1909, m. John Arch Cameron.

D. Mary Elizabeth Blue b. Feb. 1832, d. Apr. 30, 1892, m. John Keith.

E. Martha Blue b. July 28, 1833, d. Dec. 29, 1897, m. Angus McNeill: no children.

F. John Paisley Blue b. Aug. 12, 1835, d. Jan. 16, 1855, m. Christian Ann Stewart.

G. Duncan Ferguson Blue b. 1838, d. 1862 at Winchester, Virginia, while in the 46th N. C. Regiment of the Confederate Army. He m. Catherine Ann Cameron.

H. Malcolm Patrick Newton Blue b. Sept. 22, 1840, d. Feb. 16, 1918, m. Flora Ann Cameron.
I. Telitha Blue b. Nov. 4, 1842, d. Mar. 14, 1920, m. Hiram Duncan McDonald.
J. William Daniel Blue b. Oct. 13, 1844, d. Aug. 28, 1915, m. Effie Frances McFadyen.
K. Murdock James Blue b. Apr. 5, 1846, d. Apr. 13, 1903, m. first, Mary Cameron, and secondly, Mary Ella Ferguson.

Dalrymple Family

The Dalrymples were another Highland family of upper Moore County, who lived near the McGilvarys and McIvers, (see Chapter 8). Like the McGilvarys and unlike the McIvers, they were not numerous. My information on them is taken from a privately printed work by Jo White Linn, C.G.[103]

The emigrant head of this family was John Dalrymple b. 1726 in Wigtonshire, Scotland, d. 1805 in Moore County, N.C., m. Margaret Gordon (dau. of Archibald Gordon) b. 1736 in Wigtonshire, d. c. 1795 in Moore County, N.C. This couple with their seven children (as listed in *Records of Emigrants from England and Scotland to North Carolina 1774-1775*, p. 11) landed in Wilmington, N.C. 31 May 1775 on board the "Jackie" of Glasgow. They gave as the reason for their emigration "high rents." Their children are listed in *Records of Emigrants* as:

I. MARY DALRYMPLE, age 19 (i.e. in 1775)
II. JOHN DALRYMPLE, age 17
III. ARCHIBALD DALRYMPLE, age 15
IV. JAMES DALRYMPLE, age 11
V. ANN DALRYMPLE, age 9
VI. JANET DALRYMPLE, age 7
VII. JEAN DALRYMPLE, age 5
VIII. WILLIAM DALRYMPLE, age 2

My information is limited to III, ARCHIBALD DALRYMPLE, whose family is traced in part by Jo White Linn in the work just mentioned. Archibald b. 1761 in Galloway, Scotland and d. 1836 in Moore County, N.C., was buried in the Dalrymple Cemetery in Lee County, N.C. He served the American forces as a courier during the Revolution and in the North Carolina House of Commons in 1801.[104] His wife, Mary (Gaster) Buie was the widow of Captain Daniel Buie, who d. in Wilmington, N.C., while a prisoner of war, and the daughter of Captain Henry Gaster, who moved to Cumberland County from New Hanover County, N.C., in 1756, and served with the Whig forces during the Revolution). She was b. 1761 and d. 1820. Archibald and Mary Dalrymple had:

A. Elizabeth Dalrymple b. 1785, m. Jessie Wicker of Moore County, no children

B. Margaret Dalrymple b. 1787 in Moore County near Sanford, N.C., d. 1883 in Salisbury, N.C., m. at age 25, Malcolm McNair b. c.1787, d. 1823, buried at the McAlpine Grove Cemetery near Red Springs, N.C. They were m. at St. Pauls Presbyterian Church in St. Pauls, N.C. Their children are traced by Jo White Linn.[105]

C. Mary Dalrymple b. 1790, d. 1871, m.1820 John Ban McIver Jr. b. 1782 in the Isle of Skye, d. 1838 in Moore County, buried in Scotch Ever Cemetery.[106] Their seven children are traced by Kenneth L. Kelly.[107]

D. Prudence Dalrymple d. 1817 at age 25, m. Robert McNair b. c.1790, d. before 1850. He m. secondly Betsey Patterson of Robeson County, N.C. (dau. of Alexander Patterson and his second wife Margaret McLaughlin). No children by Prudence and five sons by Betsey.[108]

McCallum Family

Finally we will mention another Scots family of Moore County, that of Duncan McCallum. They were closely related by marriage to the Keiths, (see following chapter), and both were somewhat fewer in number than the majority of families which settled in the area.

Duncan came to North Carolina shortly before the Revolution and is mentioned in *Caruthers' Sketches* as having been on Crane's Creek in 1781. (Caruthers relates how Duncan McCallum tried to prevent the death of the McLeod boy at the "Revenge of Piney Bottom," during the Revolutionary War, which was mentioned above, p. 123).

Duncan m. c.1789 Mary McKay b. 1764, d. 1859, and lived on Crane's Creek on what is now known as the Archibald McLauchlin farm near Lobelia, N.C., in Moore County. He was a member of Cypress Presbyterian Church and d. 1846.[109] Duncan and Catherine had:

I. CATHERINE III. MARY
II. ANNE IV. ARCHIBALD

I. CATHERINE MCCALLUM b. 1791, d. 1863, m. 1809 Hugh Keith (see the Keith section above).

II. ANNE MCCALLUM b. 1795, d. 1860, m.1824 James Duncan Currie.

III. MARY MCCALLUM m. ______ Thompson and had (at least) a son named:

A. Duncan Thompson (mentioned in his grandfather, Duncan McCallum's will in Cumberland County Courthouse, *Book C.P.*, file 877, p.132, written 1845).

IV. ARCHIBALD MCCALLUM b. 1803, d. 1870

Notes

1. op. cit., 424, 425.
2. Kelly, op.cit., 322-324, 622-640.
3. Vol. 2, No.3, 104, 105.
4. See art. cit., in *Argyll Colony Plus,* 105.
5. Douglas F. Kelly, *Scottish Blue Family,* 431ff.
6. Ibid., 736ff.
7. See Cameron Genealogy of John W. Cameron, 5 for their names.
8. Whose descendants are listed in ibid., 2.
9. Listed in ibid.
10. These children are traced in ibid., 5, 7, 8, 9, 10, 11.
11. His children by his first wife are traced in D. Kelly, *Scottish Blue Family,* 736-739, and those by his second wife in K.L. Kelly, *McIver Family,* 287, and also Cameron Genealogy, 6,10.
12. Listed in Cameron Genealogy of John W. Cameron, 6.
13. Traced in ibid., 7, 9.
14. Listed in ibid., 7.
15. Rozella McLeod, *McLeods of Tuckahoe & Horses Creek* (1981), 51-63.
16. Ibid., 51.
17. Traced in ibid., 51, 52.
18. Traced in ibid., 52-54.
19. Traced in ibid., 55-58.
20. Traced in ibid., 58-60.
21. Traced in ibid., 60, 61.
22. Traced in ibid., 61-63.
23. Their children are listed in Cameron Genealogy of John W. Cameron, 8.
24. See also copy in *ACP* 11. 2, 134.
25. See also *ACP* 11. 2, 134-135.
26. See ibid., 135.
27. See ibid.
28. See ibid.
29. See ibid., 133.
30. See ibid., 134 for the sons' names.
31. See ibid.
32. See ibid., 135-136.

33. Rassie Wicker, *Miscellaneous Ancient Records of Moore County,* 364-366.
34. Ibid.
35. James McNeill Johnson, op. cit., 1.
36. See Douglas F. Kelly, op. cit., 242-244 and Kenneth L. Kelly, op. cit., 93, 94.
37. See ibid. for their offspring.
38. See Johnson, op. cit., 10 for offspring.
39. Ibid. for offspring.
40. Ibid., 17 for offspring.
41. Ibid., 4.
42. For more on this family see *History of Alexander Black* by Rev. William Black in Presbyterian Historical Foundation, Montreat, N.C.
43. Patterson, op. cit., 24, 25.
44. Further information on the children is found in Patterson, op. cit., 30, 31.
45. See Patterson, op. cit., 423,424.
46. See Patterson, op. cit., 424-430.
47. Ibid., 431-439.
48. Ibid., 439.
49. Ibid., 440-442.
50. Ibid., 442-446.
51. Part of these are traced in Kelly, *Scottish Blue Family,* 90-96.
52. Traced in Purcell, op. cit., 700-735, as well as Kelly, op. cit., 52-89.
53. Kelly, op. cit., 50.
54. Ibid., 98.
55. Traced in ibid., 282-286.
56. Traced in ibid., 290-372.
57. Traced in ibid., 373-384.
58. Traced in ibid., 385-526.
59. Traced in ibid., 523-619.
60. Traced in ibid., 622-640.
61. Traced in ibid., 641-726.
62. Traced in ibid., 726-739.
63. Traced in ibid., 744-783.
64. Listed in ibid., 784-786.
65. Traced in ibid., 792-838.
66. Traced in ibid., 839-845.
67. Traced in ibid., 846-877.
68. Traced in ibid., 879-896.
69. Traced in ibid., 148-161.
70. Traced in ibid., 110-111, 898.
71. Traced in ibid., 112-118.
72. See ibid., 118, 119.
73. Traced in ibid., 123-129.
74. Traced in ibid., 130-136.
75. Traced in ibid., 137-144.
76. Traced in ibid., 171-191.
77. Traced in ibid., 192-193.
78. Traced in ibid., 194-227.

79. Their offspring traced in ibid., 227-230.

80. See ibid., 231.

81. Some are quoted in ibid., 234-254.

82. For limited information see ibid., 239.

83. Ibid., 240.

84. Ibid.

85. Traced in ibid.

86. Ibid., 241.

87. Ibid.

88. Ibid.

89. Ibid., 241, 242.

90. Traced in ibid., 244-248.

91. This information comes from the papers of the late Mrs. Rozella McLeod (Mrs. C.L.) of Eureka community and is composed of two sources: one said to have been compiled c. 1912 by Dr. Ferguson, then of Southern Pines, N.C., later of Virginia, and the other written in the 1960's by Louise Barkley and Robert Ferguson (of Southern Pines, N.C.), and printed privately as a booklet: "Murdoch Ferguson and Descendants."

92. See Kenneth L. Kelly, op. cit., 215-220.

93. See ibid., 227.

94. Ibid.

95. Part of my information on these children comes from handwritten papers of the late Mrs. Rozella McLeod (Mrs. Cary L.) of Eureka in Moore County, N.C. In these papers there are further details on the descendants of these children.

96. This line is said to have been researched by Mrs. Virginia Farnell for the Clan Ferguson files.

97. Their names are listed in the paper compiled by Dr. Ferguson c. 1912, 3.

98. According to the papers of Mrs. Rozella McLeod.

99. Ibid.

100. Ibid.

101. In 1980 I had correspondence from Mrs. Shirley Ferguson Doran of Charleston, S.C., who as Genealogist of Clan Fergusson Society of North America was collecting considerable information on the families we have mentioned here plus several others.

102. This court action is copied in full in Douglas F. Kelly, *Scottish Blue Family,* 788-790.

103. Jo White Linn, C.G., *Drake, Arrington, White-Turner, Linn-Brown and Two Dozen Related Southern Lines* (privately published in Salisbury, N.C., 1984), 416-427.

104. Ibid., 419.

105. Ibid., 423-427.

106. His dates come from Kenneth L. Kelly, op. cit., 261.

107. Ibid., 261-266.

108. See Linn, op.cit., 417.

109. All of my information on this family comes from the papers of the late Mrs. Rozella McLeod of Eureka.

7

Skye Families in Moore County

IF OUR SUGGESTION BE TRUE that Moore is the most Scottish county in North Carolina, then it may well also be true that it is families from the Isle of Skye who form the largest proportion of this most Highland population in the state. In the last chapter we looked at one prominent Skye family who appeared early in Moore County, the Bethunes. In this present chapter we shall look at nothing but Skye families.

Martin Family

One of the earliest of the Skye families in Moore County, and one of the wealthiest, were the Martins. They were also important in the Revolutionary politics of the upper Cape Fear. The father, Captain John was a leader of the Tories and had been in the Loyalist Legislature, while his son, William, on the other hand, was in the Revolutionary Legislature. After the War, the son worked to protect the rights of any Tories who would take an oath of loyalty. According to some reports, Captain John died in Scotland (says J. McN. Johnson) but others say Nova Scotia (Angus W. McLean[1]). Nolan K. and Peggy C. Moran of Jonesboro, Arkansas have in recent years done considerable research on the Scottish ancestry of this family, and I make use of it here.

According to J. McN. Johnson:

> Flora Martin was a daughter of John Martin. Mrs. Faucette believes John Martin's wife was Miss Sallie McLeod, sister of Dr. McLeod who lived in Scotland [See the research of the Morans below, which corrects this point]. John Martin was married before leaving Scotland, he came over just before the Revolutionary War. He was a rich man, a land owner in Scotland; when the war broke out he would not fight against the crown and returned to Scotland, and died shortly after returning, before he could get his family back.
>
> His children were Murdock Martin, John Martin, William and Katie who married Kinney Murchison, Sallie who married a Martin, I think his name was Alec, and he moved to Tennessee, Flora who married Archibald Black. Flora was the youngest child, 6 weeks old when they crossed the ocean. Mrs. Martin was sick on the ship, and Rev. John B. McIver's mother nursed Flora as they came over. Mrs. Martin died about 6 months after coming over to this country. Grandmother Flora was about six years old when the war was on.
>
> Murdock Martin married a Miss Bethune. To them were born four children, two sons, Angus and Farquar, two girls, Polly and Peggy. Angus married Miss Anne Harris of Montgomery County and they had four boys, Howell, Cyrus, Jim and John, and one girl who married Cal Pemberton, who lived in Arkansas. Farquar married a Miss Stanback and had one son who lives near Mt. Gilead, John Martin died a bachelor. Mrs. Pemberton's name was Flora. Kate married Kinney Murchison, had one daughter Isabella and one son, Roea (*sic*) Murchison, he married in S.C. and had several children. One of his girls married Daniel McCaskill [Johnson's text is unclear here.]
>
> William Martin married a McQueen, Miss Flora. The children were Margaret who married a Wilcox, her daughter married Professor Alex McIver, Sallie married a Brooks, Sophia married a Buchanan and went to Tennessee. Capt. William Martin, father of John Martin, grandfather of Lena Martin was killed in the war [i.e. Between the States].[2]

The research of Nolan and Peggy Moran corrects and adds to the earlier work of Johnson in certain details. They have documented Capt. John Martin's wife as having been Marion MacLeod (b. c. 1720) dau. of William Macleod III of Crackinish & I of Feorlig and wife Margaret Bethune, dau. of Angus of Dunelirich and wife Florence MacLeod of Gesto, dau. of John MacLeod X of Gesto, all belonging to the Isle of Skye. They have also taken these lines back into the history of the chiefs of the MacLeods.

I have also done some research on this family in the Moore County *Book of Wills B*: the will of William Martin (proved May Term 1819) and the will of John Martin (proved May 1824). From all of these sources we can reconstruct the following incomplete and preliminary genealogy:

Captain John Martin and Marion MacLeod came to Cumberland (now Moore) County in 1771 and lived near what is now Carthage. They returned to Scotland, but left six grown children in Moore County. Their children:

I. WILLIAM
II. MURDOCH
III. JOHN Jr.
IV. FLORA
V. MARGARET
VI. CATHERINE

I. WILLIAM MARTIN b. 1768, d. 1819, m. Flora MacQueen. They had (according to William's will):

A. John Martin (III)
B. William Martin (II)
C. Margaret Martin m. ______ Willcox and had (at least) Mary Ann Willcox b. 1832, who m. Prof. Alex McIver.[3]
D. Sarah Martin m. ______ Brooks
E. Catherine Martin
F. Sophia Martin m. ______ Buchanan and went to Tennessee.

William Martin also had (according to his will) two natural daughters:

G. Betsey Martin
H. Polly Martin

II. MURDOCH MARTIN served in the North Carolina House of Commons 1796-1800. He was executor of his brother John's estate in 1824. He m. ______ Bethune and is said to have left descendants in Moore County. According to research of the late William McC. Blue and wife Mazie McLean Blue of Eagle Springs, N.C., it appears that one of Murdoch's daughters was Margaret Martin b. 1800, d. 1888, buried at Bensalem Presbyterian Church, who m. John C. Buie of upper Moore County. I am not absolutely certain however that this identification is definite.

III. JOHN MARTIN JR. d. 1824. According to J. McN. Johnson he was single, and his will indicates this, as nephews, brothers and sisters. are mentioned, but no wife or children.

IV. FLORA MARTIN m. Archibald Black. Their family is traced under the Blacks, and the work of the Morans has further, well-researched information on their line.

V. MARGARET MARTIN no further information.

VI. CATHERINE MARTIN m. Kinney Murchison. They had (at least):
- A. Donald Murchison
- B. Isabella Murchison

McIver Family

One of the larger Highland connections of Moore County is the McIver family of the Parish of Sleat, Isle of Skye, who emigrated to North Carolina between the years 1772 and 1802 (Duncan McIver, son of Kenneth, was the first to come in 1772,[4] and Duncan McIver, son of Evander, son of Kenneth, was the last to come in 1802[5]).

Built in the late seventeenth century, old Kilmore, the parish church of Sleat in the southern part of the Isle of Skye, was abandoned in the mid-nineteenth century when a new structure was built not far away. Dr. Samuel Johnson and Boswell visited this building, and this also is where Flora and Allan MacDonald at times worshipped. In its vast cemetery, many Carolina Scots' surnames are represented: McIver, McIntosh, McGillivray, McDonald, Kelly and scores of others.

This vast family has been traced by Kenneth L. Kelly in *McIver Family of North Carolina* (already mentioned). The whole family is descended from Kenneth McIver, who was b. and d. in Scotland during the eighteenth century. We do not know his wife's name. They lived in the Parish of Sleat in Skye and had:

I.	DUNCAN	IV.	EVANDER
II.	NANCY	V.	JOHN
III.	RODERICK	VI.	DAUGHTER

I. DUNCAN MCIVER emigrated to North Carolina in 1772. He m. a McIver (her first name is unknown) in Scotland. The first four, or possibly all five of their children were b. in Scotland:

A. Alexander "Money-Making" McIver b. 1761, d. Oct. 5, 1810 in Moore County, m. Effie McIver b. in Scotland, d. 1836 in Moore County. They had eight children.[6]

B. "Blacksmith" Daniel McIver b. 1763, d. 1847 in Moore County, m. 1796 Mary McLeod b. 1767, d. 1851. They had seven children.[7]

C. "Wealthy Miller" Duncan McIver b. 1769, Scotland, d. 1844, buried in Scotch Ever Cemetery in Moore County, m. Jane Dalrymple, b. 1770, d. 1844. They had one daughter.[8]

D. Angus McIver may have settled in South Carolina, no information.

E. Katherine McIver m. Robin McIver and had three children.[9]

II. NANCY MCIVER b. in Scotland, d. in Moore County, m. Donald McSween in the Isle of Skye, who d. in Moore County. They lived two miles west of the present Eureka community. They had:

A. Murdock McSween b. in Moore County, m. Margaret Jackson b. 1756 in Waxhaw, South Carolina. They moved to New Port, Tennessee and had seven children.[10]

B. Margaret McSween m. Duncan Ray b. in Richmond County, N.C. They lived near Eureka community. No information.

C. Daughter m. J. Wadsworth. No information.

D. Nancy McSween d. 1844/5, m. Daniel McDonald. They lived between Union Presbyterian Church and Carthage, N.C. They had five children.[11]

E. Elizabeth McSween d. 1844, m. Archibald Ray, b. in Scotland (son of John Ray), emigrated to Moore County, N.C., before the Revolution. He was granted land in the present Eureka community in 1790, which is still inhabited by his descendants. They had four daughters.[12]

III. RODERICK MCIVER b. 1727 in Scotland, d. 1810 in Moore County, emigrated about 1775, m. Nancy ______ , who d. 1836. Both are buried in the Roderick McIver Cemetery in Moore County. They had:

A. Kenneth McIver b. 1762, d. 1836, was a tailor, no further information.
B. Catherine McIver b. 1759, d. 1800, buried Becky Murchison Cemetery, m. Kenneth Murchison. They had twelve children.[13]
C. Duncan McIver b. 1771 in Scotland, d. 1830 in Moore County, m. 1815 Flora Nicholson b. 1788 in Scotland, d. 1863 in Moore County. They had six children.[14]
D. "Big Daniel" McIver d. 1842, m. Mary Wicker d. 1857. They lived in Moore County and had ten children.[15]
E. Margaret McIver b. 1774, d. 1858, m. William Buie. They lived in Chatham County and had four children.[16]
F. Isabella McIver b. 1773, d. 1824, buried Roderick McIver Cemetery, m. Murdock McIntosh. They lived in Moore County and had nine children.[17]
G. "One-Eye" John McIver b. in Scotland, d. in North Carolina. He m. ______ in North Carolina and they had fourteen children.[18]
H. "Little Daniel" McIver d. 1845, m. 1794, Margaret Monroe. They lived in Moore County and had eight children.[19]

IV. EVANDER MCIVER b. c. 1712 in Scotland, d. in Chatham County, N.C., m. in Scotland (wife's name unknown). They had (all born in the Isle of Skye):

A. Daniel McIver m. in Scotland ______ . They had four children, all born in the Isle of Skye.[20]
B. Kenneth McIver b. in Scotland, m. ______ in Scotland. They had three children, all born in the Isle of Skye.[21]
C. John Ban McIver b. 1743, Isle of Skye, d. 1820 in Moore County, N.C., buried in Scotch Ever Cemetery, m. Nancy McDonald b. 1748 in Scotland, d. 1797 in Moore County; also buried in Scotch Ever Cemetery. They came to North Carolina in 1775. He was a member of the North Carolina House of Commons and supported the Whig side in the Revolution. He was a charter elder of Buffalo Presbyterian Church. They had eight children.[22]

D. Duncan McIver b. 1744 in the Isle of Skye, emigrated to Chatham County, N.C., in 1802, sailing from Liverpool on "Duke of Kent" and landing in Wilmington, N.C., 30 October 1802, where he was met by John Ban McIver (Jr.). He m. in Scotland Catherine Robertson b. 1750 in the Isle of Skye, d. 1839 in North Carolina, buried at Union Presbyterian Church. They had ten children.[23]

E. Mary McIver b. in Scotland, d. in North Carolina, m. John McIntosh, b. in Scotland, d. 1820 in North Carolina, buried in the Scotch Ever Cemetery. They had two children.[24]

V. JOHN MCIVER b. in Scotland, no information.

VI. DAUGHTER MCIVER m. a McDonald, no information.

McGilvary Family

The McGilvary family of upper Moore and the lower part of present Lee County intermarried with the McIvers. Some material is found on them in Kenneth L. Kelly's *McIver Family of North Carolina*[25] and even more in Col. Harold A. and Doris Steiner's *The MacGillivrays of Skye* (1985).[26]

According to Steiner, one Charles MacGillivray of Teangue, Parish of Sleat, Isle of Skye, b. perhaps c. 1720-30, had five known sons:[27]

I. MARTIN b. Skye c. 1750
II. CHARLES b. Skye c. 1755
III. ARCHIBALD b. Skye 1763
IV. ANGUS b. Skye 1765
V. ALEXANDER b. Skye before 1775

Of these, three emigrated to the Cape Fear Valley of North Carolina.

I. MARTIN MACGILLIVRAY (spelled MCGILVARY in America) came first in 1789, bringing with him his wife, Mary Dalrymple, whom he m. c. 1770 in Skye, b. Skye c. 1755, d. Moore County, N.C., before 1820. They lived in Moore County, where Martin d. by 1800. They had five children, all born before they left the Isle of Skye:

A. Martin McGilvary b. 1772

B. Daniel McGilvary b. 1774

C. John McGilvary b. 1776, d. 1830-37, Christian County, Kentucky, m. 16 July 1809 in Edenton, N.C., Ruth Owens b. c. 1780, N.C., d. 1837, Christian County, Ky. Their children are partially traced in Steiner.[28]

D. Malcolm Dalrymple McGilvary b. 1778, Parish of Sleat, Isle of Skye, d. 1841 in Moore County, N.C., buried at Scotch Ever Cemetery. He m. Catherine McIver b. 1787, d. 1828 (dau. of Little John and Mary Monroe McIver; Little John was the son of Evander b. c. 1712—see McIver section of this volume). Steiner deals with this branch of the family[29] as does Kenneth Kelly, according to whom they had:

1. JOHN MARTIN MCGILVARY b. 1812, d. 1878 in Texas, m. Eleanor McIver b. 1817, d. 1852. Their children are traced by Kenneth Kelly.[30]
2. EVANDER MCGILVARY b. 1815, d. 1897, buried at Buffalo Presbyterian Church near present Sanford, N.C., m. Mary Ann McIver b. 1816, d. 1903 (dau. of Duncan and Flora Nicholson McIver). They had one son.[31]
3. ARCHIBALD MCGILVARY b. 1817, d. 1818.
4. ALEXANDER MCGILVARY b. 1819, d. in Corsicana, Texas, m. 1854 Sarah Jane Irvine, d. 1907. They had four children.[32]
5. MARY MCGILVARY b. 1822, d. 1897, m. 1856 Abram Helm, d. 1860. They had no children and d. in Navarro County, Texas.
6. ANGUS MCGILVARY b. 1825, d. 1863 in the Confederate Army. He was single and his place of death and burial is unknown.
7. REV. DANIEL MCGILVARY b. 1828 in Buffalo Parish of Moore County, d. 1911 in Chiang Mai, Siam, where he was a missionary with the Presbyterian Church (the first missionary to Laos, Cambodia and Siam). He m. 1860, in Siam, Sophia Royce Bradley b. 1839, d. 1922/3. A graduate of University of North Carolina and Princeton Theological Seminary (1853), he wrote an autobiography, which discusses some of the history of the McGilvary family, *A Half Century Among the Siamese and the Lao, An Autobiography* (New York: Fleming H. Revell Co.). Daniel and Sophia had five children.[33]

E. Nancy McGilvary b. c. 1780.

III. ARCHIBALD MACGILLIVRAY emigrated from Skye along with the Duncan McIver family in 1802 to North Carolina. He m. c. 1800 on Skye, Sally MacDonald b. c. 1770, Skye, d. Moore County, N.C., by 1850.

Archibald d. 1851, Moore County, N.C. They had five children: the first was born in Skye and the others in Moore County, N.C.:

A. John McGilvary b. 1802, d. June 15, 1874, Rusk County, Texas, m. Mar. 15, 1844, Louisa Bass (who was first married to Jessie Choice) Hancock County, Georgia. Their two children are listed in Steiner.[34]

B. Jenny McGilvary b. 1810.

C. Nancy McGilvary b. 1811, d. after 1882 in Moore County, N.C., m. by 1840 Matthew Morris b. c. 1820, d. 1848, Moore County. Their two children are listed in Steiner.[35]

D. Daniel McGilvary b. 1813, d. by Dec. 1893, Rusk County, TX., m. 1845 in Moore County, Nancy McIver b. 1815, Moore County, N.C., d. by 1880, Rusk County, TX. Their five children are listed by Steiner.[36]

E. Alexander McGilvary b. 1815, d. Mar. 1, 1874, Moore County, N.C., m. c. 1854 Sarah Morris b. Apr. 5, 1835, Moore County, d. Mar. 27, 1912, Moore County. Their six children are traced in Steiner.[37]

IV. ANGUS MACGILLIVRAY b. 1765, Isle of Skye, d. c. 1857, Moore County, N.C., m. c. 1797, Isle of Skye, ______ McIver, b. 1765, Skye, d. 1840-50, Moore County, N.C. Their daughter:

A. Jennet McGilvary b. 1799, Skye, d. 1888, Moore County, N.C., m. George McRae b. Jan. 25, 1787, Skye, d. Nov. 3, 1870, Moore County, N.C. Their seven children are traced in Steiner.[38]

Other McGilvary Families of the Cape Fear Valley

In addition to those who came to Moore County, other McGillivray families came from the Isle of Skye to other parts of North Carolina. Harold Steiner has some information on them, but their possible relationship to the Moore County McGilvarys is unknown at present.

Daniel (Donald) McGilvary Family of Cumberland County, North Carolina

Daniel (or Donald) McGilvary was b. Spr. 20, 1772, Isle of Skye, and d. Dec. 28, 1854, Fayetteville, N.C. He m. Anna ______, b. c. 1774, Isle of Skye, d. after 1860, N.C. Their children:

I. FLORA MCGILVARY b. 1809, N.C., m. Feb. 23, 1825, Daniel McLeod.

II. JAMES MCGILVARY b. Mar. 1, 1818, Cumberland County, N.C., d. by 1903, Cumberland County, m. first Mar. 10, 1840, Elizabeth Tyson b. 1822, Moore County, N.C., d. Feb. 23, 1844, Moore County. Their one son is listed by Steiner.[39]

Secondly, he m. Aug. 14, 1851, Hannah Whitfield b. Aug. 1827, N.C., d. after 1910, N.C. Their seven children (all born in Cumberland County, N.C.) are listed in Steiner.[40]

III. CATHERINE MCGILVARY b. c. 1820, N.C., m. Jan. 11, 1842 Alexander Bethune.

IV. DANIEL MCGILVARY b. 1825-39, N.C.

V. UNIDENTIFIED FEMALE MCGILVARY b. 1825-30, N.C.

The Daniel McGilvary Family of Richmond County, North Carolina

Daniel McGilvary b. 1759, Isle of Skye, d. by July 1815, Richmond County, N.C., m. c. 1784 on the Isle of Skye, Catherine ______, b. before 1765 on Skye, d. after 1820, Richmond County, N.C. They had:

I. ALEXANDER MCGILVARY b. 1785, Isle of Skye

II. JOHN MCGILVARY b. 1791, Isle of Skye

III. MARINE MCGILVARY b. c. 1794, Isle of Skye

IV. ARCHIBALD MCGILVARY b. c. 1800, Isle of Skye

V. MARTIN MCGILVARY b. 1802, Isle of Skye, d. 1855-60, Alabama, m. first c. 1828, (?) who was b. 1800-10, d. c. 1836, by whom he had three children who are listed in Steiner.[41] He m. secondly c. 1837, Sarah Gillies b. 1817, N.C. Their seven children are listed in Steiner.[42]

VI. MARY MCGILVARY b. c. 1804, Isle of Skye.

Another Daniel McGilvary Family of Richmond County, North Carolina

Daniel McGilvary b. 1758, Isle of Skye, d. by 1830, Richmond County, N.C., m. c. 1786, Skye, Christian ______, b. Skye c. 1768, d. after 1840, N.C. They had:

I. MALCOLM MCGILVARY b. 1787, Isle of Skye, d. by Jan. 1822, Rich-

mond County, N.C., m. c. 1811 in N.C., Mary ______, b. 1785, Isle of Skye, d. by 1870, Barbour County, Alabama. Their five children are listed by Steiner.[43]

II. JAMES MCGILVARY b. 1789, Isle of Skye, d. by 1863, Barbour County, AL.

III. UNIDENTIFIED FEMALE MCGILVARY b. c. 1795, Isle of Skye

IV. ANGUS MCGILVARY b. 1800, Isle of Skye, d. by 1836, Richmond County, N.C., m. c. 1830 Jane ______, b. Isle of Skye, d. after 1860, Richmond County, N.C. Their three children are listed by Steiner.[44]

V. CHRISTIAN MCGILVARY b. 1805, N.C., d. after 1860, m. Malcolm Blue b. c. 1810.

The John and Alexander McGilvary Families of Richmond County, North Carolina

John McGilvary b. 1760, Isle of Skye, d. 1835, m. by 1788 Sarah Buckhannon (Buchanan?) b. Isle of Skye. They and their son and his wife emigrated to North Carolina c. 1803 or 1804. Their son:

I. ALEXANDER MCGILVARY b. 1788, Isle of Skye, d. 1871, Perry County, MS., m. c. 1812, Mary Elizabeth McLeod b. 1794, Isle of Skye, d. 1860, Perry County, MS., dau. of Murdock McLeod and Christian McSwan. Their six children are listed in Steiner.[45]

Daniel Kelly Family

A second large family closely connected to the McIvers was that of Daniel Kelly. The Kellys and McIvers lived near each other in the Parish of Sleat, Isle of Skye. Their children tended to intermarry, and many of them came to the same locality in Moore County, near Union Presbyterian Church community. Indeed, it was the McIvers, particularly Duncan who came in 1802, and prepared the way for their cousins, the Kellys to come in 1803—a particularly difficult year in Skye on the MacDonald estate, as we have already discussed.

The head of this family was Daniel Kelly b. 1725 in Sleat, Isle of Skye and d. 1819 in Moore County, buried at Union Church. He m. 1765 Catherine Bethune of Sleat, b. 1750, d. 1795 in Skye, buried at Kilmore Church, Sleat. They had ten children. After her death, Daniel m. secondly Catherine Robertson. They had no children, and she d. before

Daniel and children emigrated to Moore County, N.C., in 1803. Daniel and Kate Bethune Kelly had:

I.	ALEXANDER	VI.	JOHN
II.	BARBARA	VII.	PETER
III.	DANIEL	VIII.	NANCY
IV.	JAMES	IX.	HUGH
V.	DANIEL or 'DONALD'	X.	JOHN BETHUNE

I. ALEXANDER KELLY b. in the Parish of Sleat, Isle of Skye, m. _____, and had children, of whom one was Peter. Alexander was crippled and was a tailor. He alone remained in Scotland of all the children of Daniel Kelly. We do not know how many children he had, except for:

A. Peter Kelly b. and d. Isle of Skye, m. ______ and had children. His son was Neill, and from him the Kellys who remain in the parishes of Strath and Sleat in Skye are descended.[46]

II. BARBARA KELLY b. 1767, d. 1849 in Moore County, buried at Union Church, m. Duncan McLeod in Scotland sometime before 1803. Duncan was b. 1761, d. 1838. No further information, although some material may be available in "Dates of Interest Connected with the Family of Daniel Kelly" by Rev. Angus McQueen and Miss Cornelia Shaw (privately compiled in the early 1900s and unpublished). I have part of this work, but not all of it. Also, Kenneth L. Kelly, of Southern Pines, N.C., collected much data on the Daniel Kelly family for many years, and may have some material on Barbara and the others who will be listed here.

III. DANIEL KELLY JR. b. 1770, d. 1829, buried at Union Church in Moore County. He m. Catherine McIver (dau. of Duncan) and their children are traced in K.L. Kelly (290ff).

IV. JAMES KELLY b. 1772, d. 1825, buried at Union Church, m. in Scotland Penelope McKinnon, who is also buried at Union. No further information presently, but see the sources mentioned under II. BARBARA.

V. DANIEL or DONALD b. 1773, d. 1855, buried at Union Church. No information at present, but see sources under II. BARBARA.

VI. JOHN KELLY b. 1778, d. 1836 in Marion County, South Carolina, and buried at the Stewartsville Cemetery in Scotland County, North

Carolina. He m. Catherine Chisholm b. 1783, d. 1859. They lived in Marion County and had:

A. Catherine	F. Penelope
B. Margaret	G. Roderick
C. Nancy	H. Christian
D. Alexander C.	I. Margaret
E. Daniel Jr.	J. John A.

VII. PETER KELLY b. 1780, d. 1853, m. in Skye Catherine McIntosh (dau. of John McIntosh) b. 1786, d. 1838. They emigrated with elder Daniel in 1803, and both are buried at Union. Daniel lived in their home (which still stands—a two-storey log structure, shaped very much like a typical tacksman's house in the Highlands). They lived north of Union Church on what became known as the John McLean Place. They had:

A. Kate Kelly b. 1807, d. 1879, m. Malcolm McLean b. 1807, d. 1879. They lived in Moore County and had no children.

B. Alexander Kelly b. 1810, d. 1872, m. Sarah McLeod b. 1816, d. 1854. They lived in Moore County northwest of Carthage. Alexander was Sheriff of Moore County and also a State Senator and was the largest slaveholder in Moore County. His house (built in 1842) still stands and is a registered historic landmark (pictured on p. 95). Their children are traced in McQueen and Shaw.[47]

C. Angus Robertson Kelly (I) b. 1812, d. 1887 in Marion, Alabama. He graduated from the University of North Carolina and was a lawyer, first in Moore County, then in Alabama. He wrote many letters from his student days onwards, which have been preserved in the family of his older brother, Sheriff Alexander. Angus m. first Ann Margaret McEachin b. 1832, d. 1862, secondly Mary McRae d. 1882. He had children.[48]

D. Duncan Kelly b. 1813, d. 1830, single.

E. Malcolm Kelly b. 1814, d. 1896, m. first Nancy McDonald, secondly Mary Ann Ferguson (dau. of Daniel Ferguson and Mary McIver, q.v. p. 235) b. 1833, d. 1901. By his first wife Malcolm had a daughter who died at childbirth along with her mother. By his second wife he had nine children.[49]

F. Margaret Kelly b. 1818, d. 1888, m. John Robertson b. 1816, d. 1847.[50]

G. Christian Kelly b. 1821, d. 1902, was single and lived in the home of Alexander Kelly after the death of her mother in 1854.

H. Daniel Kelly b. 1824, d. 1892 in Moore County, m. Mary Ann McNeill; no children.

I. Flora Kelly b. 1826, d. 1907 in Moore County, m. John McLean who was b. in Scotland. They lived on the old Peter Kelly homeplace and had children.[51]

J. Rebecca Kelly b. 1829, d. 1907, m. 1853 Peter Cornelius Shaw of Moore County, b. 1826. They both taught at Floral College in Robeson County and had children.[52]

K. Ann Kelly b. 1832, d. 1901, m. Kenneth Campbell Chisholm b. 1813, d. 1855.[53]

VIII. NANCY KELLY b. 1782, d. ?, m. _____ McKinnon.[54]

IX. HUGH KELLY b. 1784, d. 1851, m. Nancy McKinnon b. 1784, d. 1851 (the same years as her husband). They lived in the Bensalem area of western Moore County, where they are buried. They had children.[55]

X. JOHN BETHUNE KELLY b. 1789, d. 1847. He m. first Margaret S. McIver b. 1802, d. 1825, secondly Mary Ann Rowan b. 1811, d. 1842, thirdly Isabelle McLean. He and his three wives are all buried at Union Church. He was a prosperous lawyer and investor. In *The History of Moore County, Part II* by Blackwell Robinson, it is stated that Andrew Johnson, who later became President of the United States after Abraham Lincoln, was once a tailor in Carthage, N.C., and made a suit for John B. Kelly. By Mary Ann Rowan he had:

A. Hamilton Rowan b. 1834, d. 1836

B. Daniel b. 1835, d. 1857

C. Catherine Jane b. 1839, d. 1855

D. John Bethune b. 1840

McIntosh Family

My information is scanty on this large Moore and Cumberland County connection. Shortly after 1900 the Rev. Angus McQueen and Cornelia Shaw compiled an unpublished work, *Dates of Interest Connected with the Shaw, Ray and Kelly-McIntosh Families*, which has considerable material on some lines of the McIntoshes, especially that of John McIntosh d. 1820, who m. Mary McIver (dau. of Evander McIver). Kenneth L. Kelly in *McIver Family of North Carolina* fills this line out to

some extent[56] and Douglas F. Kelly makes reference to it in *Malcolm Kelly Family*.[57] For several years, work has been in progress on a national genealogy of the McIntosh Clan, but I do not know how much has been collected on the Moore and Cumberland County McIntoshes.[58] I currently have information only on the John McIntosh family.

The John McIntosh family came on the same ship with the related Daniel Kelly family from the Parish of Sleat, Isle of Skye to Wilmington, and then Moore County in 1803.[59] They had been neighbors in Sleat and were also neighbors in Moore County. John McIntosh was b. in Skye and d. 1820 in Moore County, N.C., and m. Mary (dau. of Evander McIver) in Skye and had at least two children there, and none (of whom we have any record) in North Carolina. John is buried in the Scotch Ever Cemetery in Moore County. Their two known children were:

I. MURDOCK MCINTOSH b. Isle of Skye, d. Moore County, m. Isabella McIver b. 1773, d. 1824, buried Roderick McIver Cemetery (dau. of Roderick McIver). They had:

- A. Roderick McIntosh b. 1788, m. ____ Morgan and is said to have had three children (names unknown).[60]
- B. Polly McIntosh d. 1848, m. first John Cole d. 1820, secondly in 1820 Jesse Spivey, d. 1865. She had six children by her first husband and four by her second.[61]
- C. Katherine McIntosh b. 1792 in Moore County, N.C., d. 1861, buried Scotch Ever Cemetery, m. first Kenneth McIver, buried Scotch Ever Cemetery (dates illegible on his tombstone). She m. secondly Matthew Wicker, who lived to be 106 years old (b. 1766, d. 1872). By her first husband she had two children and none by the second.[62]
- D. Nancy McIntosh d. 1879, m. Neill McDuffie and had children.[63]
- E. Margaret McIntosh d. 1879, m. 1830 Henry Coffer d. 1857. They had four children.[64]
- F. Kenneth McIntosh, no information
- G. John McIntosh, no information
- H. Daniel McIver McIntosh b. 1802, d. 1886, buried Buffalo Church near Sanford, N.C., m. Margaret McIver b. 1806, d. 1888 (dau. of Big Daniel McIver). They had six children.[65]
- I. Flora McIntosh b. 1804, d. 1860, buried Roderick McIver Cemetery, m. (as his third wife) Duncan Dodridge McIver b.

1801, d. 1876 (son of Big Daniel McIver). They had seven children (Duncan had none by his first wife and one by his second, and none by his fourth wife).[66]

II. JOHN MCINTOSH b. in Isle of Skye, d. in Moore County, m. in Scotland ______, who is believed to have d. before the family emigrated in 1803 (possibly in childbirth with their sixth child in 1803?) They had six children, whom I list here not in their correct order of birth, but as Kenneth L. Kelly lists them.[67]

A. Rev. John McIntosh b. 1799, d. 1871, m. S.J. McIver (dau. of Edward Evander and Sarah McIver) b. 1826, d. 1902, buried at Camp Ground Methodist Church near Fayetteville, N.C. They had children whose names were unknown to K.L. Kelly.

B. Murdock McIntosh is believed to have m. Nancy _____ who is buried at Union Presbyterian Church, b. 1789, d. 1862. Her will does not mention any children.[68]

C. Evander McIntosh b. 1792, d. 1856, was sheriff of Moore County, buried McIntosh Cemetery in Moore County. He m. Margaret McIver b. 1792, d. 1860 (dau. of John Ban and Nancy McDonald McIver). They had six children. All six are traditionally said to have died young.[69]

D. Catherine McIntosh b. 1786 in Scotland, d. 1838 in Moore County, buried at Union Presbyterian Church with her husband, Peter Kelly b. Isle of Skye 1780, d. Moore County in 1858 (son of emigrant Daniel—see Kelly section of this volume, p. 257). They had eleven children.[70]

E. Margaret McIntosh b. 1800 in Scotland, d. 1889 in Moore County, buried at Union Presbyterian Church, was single.

F. Mary McIntosh b. 1803, d. 1872 in Moore County, buried at Union, was single.

McLeod Family of Tuckahoe and Horses Creek

The McLeods who lived first at Tuckahoe Creek (in the present Fort Bragg Reservation) and then at Horses Creek in lower Moore County were and are a well known Moore County family. The head of this family was Neill McLeod who emigrated to North Carolina from the Isle of Skye about 1777 (and thus would have been one of the relatively few who managed to make the journey after the Revolution started). He had been twice married in Scotland and both of his wives had died before he left, bringing his four sons with him.

According to Mrs. Rozella M. McLeod:

> Neill McLeod and his four sons first lived together in Cumberland County, N.C., about twenty miles northwest of Fayetteville near Little River and near where Tuckahoe Creek empties into Little River. The farm they first lived on was known as the Morris Cameron place, now occupied by his son, Dougald Cameron. A few years after they came to North Carolina, Neill McLeod and his sons, Norman, Alexander and John, moved up into what is now Moore County on Horses Creek. Daniel remained in Cumberland County, while Neill purchased a 30-acre tract of land from Neill McLean in the Roseland area on Horses Creek about four miles west of Aberdeen, N.C.
>
> About four years after they arrived in North Carolina, Neill McLeod sent his two younger sons, Alexander and John, to a neighbor's home, the Kenneth Clark place near Drowning Creek. When they arrived, they found a group of neighbors hilling up rows of soil about 10 or 12 inches high to set potato plants. This was done with hoes rather than with plows. Alexander McLeod was killed here by Culp, [tough leader of the Whig forces,] and his men. This was known as the "Revenge of Piney Bottom." It is discussed in *History of Moore County* by Blackwell Robinson (pp. 70, 71) and Caruther's *Revolutionary Incidents* (pp. 382-396).[71]

Neill McLeod had by his first marriage:

I. MARY who m. and remained in Scotland

II. DANIEL

III. NORMAN

By his second marriage:

IV. ALEXANDER

V. JOHN

II. DANIEL MCLEOD b. 1746 in Scotland b. 1839 in North Carolina, buried in McLeod Tuckahoe Cemetery in Cumberland County, m. Martha McKinnon b. 1753 in Scotland, d. 1826 in Cumberland County, buried at Tuckahoe. They had:

A. Margaret McLeod b. 1785 in America, m. c. 1802 Daniel McNeill b. 1778 in Scotland. They had nine children.[72]

B. Sarah McLeod b. 1787, d. 1872, single, buried at Union Church.

C. Neill McLeod b. 1789, d. 1870, m. Sarah Cameron b. 1806, d. 1881, buried at Tuckahoe.

D. Catherine McLeod b. 1790, d. 1869, m. Duncan McLauchlin, buried at Union Church.

E. Mary (Polly) McLeod d. as a young girl, buried at Tuckahoe.
F. Daniel McLeod b. 1796, d. 1870, single, buried at Tuckahoe.
G. William McLeod b. 1800, d. 1856 in Coosa County, Alabama, m. 1830 in Cumberland County Margaret Kelly (dau. of Angus Kelly) b. 1803 in Scotland, d. 1877 in Alabama.
H. John McLeod was killed in Mississippi by a neighbor. He was single.
I. Norman McLeod, single.
J. Alexander McLeod, single.

III. NORMAN MCLEOD b. in Scotland, d. 1823 in Montgomery County, N.C. He was a saddler. No further information.

IV. ALEXANDER MCLEOD b. 1762 in Scotland, d. 1781 at "the Revenge of Piney Bottom."

V. JOHN MCLEOD b. 1770 in Scotland, d. 1863 on Horses Creek near Aberdeen, N.C. He was known as "Squire John" and was a Justice of the Peace, a Mason (Pansophia Lodge) and Clerk of the Session at Bethesda Presbyterian Church. His old home on Horses Creek is still standing and is inhabited by a descendent, Martha McLeod. Squire John m. first c. 1796 Christian Clark (sister of Kenneth), and secondly Nancy McKinnon (dau. of John McKinnon of South Carolina) b. 1822, d. 1889 in Moore County. By his first wife John McLeod had:

A. Dr. Neill McLeod b. 1798, d. 1854 in Moore County. He practiced medicine in the McLeod home for the entire area.
B. Kenneth McLeod b. 1800 in Moore County, d. in Bladen County, where he was Clerk of the Court for one or two terms. He m. Ann McMillan. They lived in Elizabethtown, N.C. No children.

By his second wife, John McLeod had:

C. John Alexander McLeod b. 1858 at Horses Creek, d. 1948 at his home in Eureka community, Moore County, buried at Bethesda Church. He m. 1878 Margaret Union McDonald (dau. of Allen C. McDonald) b. 1861 in Eureka community, d. 1948 at Eureka, buried at Bethesda. They first lived at the old McLeod home on Horses Creek, but in 1887 moved to her deceased father's home in Eureka, where they brought up their family of eleven children.[73]
D. William Neill McLeod b. 1856 and d. 1923 at the old McLeod home on Horses Creek. He was single and is buried at Bethesda.

John McLeod Family of Mineral Springs

We do not know whether there was any relationship between the Neill McLeod family of Tuckahoe and the John McLeod family who lived at Mineral Springs in western Moore County. Nor is it known who were the parents of the head of this family, John McLeod, who was b. c. 1790 and d. 1848. He was a soldier in the War of 1812 from Moore County. His people are said to have come from "Skinniden" in the Isle of Skye (date unknown). John McLeod m. 1813/14 Nancy Campbell b. 1791 or earlier and d. between 1852 and 1866 (probably the latter). Nancy was the daughter. of Angus Campbell, and lived on Drowning Creek, where her father died in 1791. This family has been traced by Kenneth A. McLeod, Jr. with help from several others.[74] All of my information comes from this work.

John McLeod and Nancy Campbell lived in Mineral Springs township near Drowning Creek on what is now the Richard Hurley Farm on what is known as the Loop Road. They had:

I. DANIEL
II. ANGUS
III. MARGARET
IV. CATHERINE (KATE)
V. JOHN ALEXANDER
VI. JANE
VII. ANNA (ANNIE)

I. DANIEL MCLEOD m. Margaret Thomas of Moore County and moved to Rockingham, N.C. He drowned in a flood and left no children. His wife m. secondly _____ Garrett.

II. ANGUS MCLEOD m. E. _____ b. 1816/17, apparently in Tennessee. He m. her on his way west to Mississippi. They had one son:

A. John William (Billy) McLeod b. 1846/7 m. A. ____ E. ____ b. 1847/8. They were both born in Mississippi. Billy was a bookkeeper in Oxford, MS. in 1870 and his father is believed to have died before that date. They had at least one son and one daughter who lived in Oxford.

III. MARGARET MCLEOD b. 1820 was single and lived her last years with John Wilson and family, distant relatives.

IV. CATHERINE MCLEOD b. 1823 was single and lived her last years with Kenneth A. and Mary P. McLeod. She is buried at Mineral Springs Presbyterian Church.

V. JOHN ALEXANDER MCLEOD b. 1835, d. 1887, m. Euphemia (Effie) McAskill (McCaskill) b. 1832, d. 1919, of Montgomery County, near

Drowning Creek, Rocky Springs Township. Her home was what is now the Kenneth McLeod home place. Her father was Hector McAskill of the Isle of Skye (or of the Isle of Eigg?) in Scotland. They had:

A. Sarah Ann McLeod b. 1862, d. 1930, m. 1888 H.S. Poole b. 1862, d. 1950. They had children (traced in *The Descendants of John McLeod and Nancy Campbell*, as are the children of all the others with issue).

B. Hector Rufus McLeod b. 1864, d. 1932, m. first in 1890 Henrietta Wooley b. 1871, d. 1904, and secondly Anna Harding d. 1950. He had five children by his first wife.

C. Angus Johnson McLeod b. 1866, no issue.

D. Kenneth Alexander McLeod b. 1868, d. 1941, m. Mary Agnes Patterson b. 1874, d. 1944. They had ten children.

E. James John (Jim) McLeod b. 1875 d. 1901, no issue.

F. Murdock Marshall McLeod b. 1875, d. 1901, no issue.

VI. JANE MCLEOD b. 1838, d. 1908, was single, her fiancé having been killed in the War Between the States. She lived for a while in Oxford, Mississippi with her brother, Angus, and later returned to Moore County, N.C., and lived with Hector R. and Henrietta McLeod.

VII. ANNA (ANNIE) MCLEOD b. 1840, d. 1904, was single and spent her last years with H.S. and Sarah Ann Poole. She is buried at Mineral Springs Church.

Keith Family

The Keiths were another Moore County Highland Scots family, though not quite so large as some of the others. My information on them comes from the papers of Mrs. Rozella McLeod of Eureka, one of their descendants. William Keith and wife Elizabeth Cameron of the Isle of Skye, Scotland had six children, of whom four came to America c. 1803. Their children:

I. JAMES
II. GEORGE
III. HUGH
IV. PEGGY
V. GENNETH (the oldest daughter, remained in Skye)
VI. EFFIE JANE drowned as a young girl in Skye

I. JAMES KEITH settled in Wilmington, N.C., and had:

A. John Keith
B. Duncan Keith
C. Elizabeth Keith m. ____ Patrick
D. Phoebe Keith remained single

II. GEORGE KEITH landed in New York and had one son and ten daughters. We have information only on the son:

A. John Keith who m. and had a daughter, Mary who m. ______ McKinnon, whose descendants are said to live in Michigan.

III. HUGH KEITH b. 1772, d. 1860, emigrated to Wilmington c. 1803. Around 1805 he came to Moore County, N.C., and purchased about 500 acres on Crane's Creek approximately three miles northeast of Vass, N.C. The next year he worked on the Cape Fear River from Fayetteville to Wilmington. He had been a weaver in Scotland, and was a farmer and fisherman in Carolina. He made his home on Crane's Creek and was a member of Cypress Presbyterian Church. He m. 1808/9 Catherine McCallum (dau. of Col. Duncan McCallum, who tried to prevent the death of the little McLeod boy at the revenge of Piney Bottom during the Revolution). Hugh and Catherine had twelve children, only eight of whom lived to be adults:

A. William Keith b. 1810 d. 1902
B. Duncan Keith b. 1812, d. 1885
C. Elizabeth Ann Keith b. 1814, d. 1903
D. Nancy Keith b. 1816, d. 1910
E. Margaret Keith b. 1818, d. 1880
F. Catherine Keith b. 1820
G. James Keith b. 1822
H. Archibald Keith b. 1824
I. Effy Jane Keith b. 1826, d. 1864
J. Hugh Keith b. 1828, d. 1863
K. John Keith b. 1830, d. 1909
L. Isabelle Keith b. 1833

IV. PEGGY KEITH emigrated to North Carolina and m. John McDougald (McDougle). They had no children, but reared Sandy Johnson. They lived on "the Scotch Sandy Johnson" place, where they are buried, near Little Crane's Creek and the Murchison Road close to Cameron in Moore County.

McCaskill Family

Another smaller, but well known Moore County Highland family was that of McCaskill. Kenneth A. McLeod Jr. deals very briefly with the family of emigrant Hector McCaskill (or McAskill) who lived on the border of western Moore and Montgomery Counties.[75] We do not know what their relationship may have been (if any) to the Angus Alexander McCaskill family of central Moore County, which we cover here (from the papers of Mrs. Rozella McLeod of Eureka). James Vann Comer also includes some information on this family in *Ancestors and Descendants of Kenneth Henderson Worthy* (Published by Ruby Vann Crumpler McSwain: Sanford, N.C., 1996).

Angus Alexander McCaskill, according to his tombstone in the "Old Scotch" Graveyard some five miles west of Carthage, N.C., was b. 1769 in the Isle of Skye and d. Mar. 14, 1807 in Moore County, N.C. His wife's name is unknown. Angus Alexander McCaskill had a son, whose name was also Angus Alexander. According to his tombstone, which is near that of his father, he was b. in Moore County in 1806, and d. June 26, 1853. He m. Elizabeth Worthy (daughter of James Worthy), b. 1813, d. 1878, also buried in the "Old Scotch" Graveyard. They first settled on Governor's Creek and later moved some three miles south of Carthage, where his trade was making hats, so that he was known as "Hatter John." Angus and Elizabeth had five children:

I. JANE
II. CELIA
III. CATHERINE
IV. JOHN WORTHY
V. MARY ELIZABETH

I. JANE MCCASKILL (or, according to James Comer, op. cit., 28—Jennet), b. 1835, m. James Wesley McLeod b.c. 1831, d. between 1880-1894. They had:

A. John McLeod
B. Worthy McLeod
C. Mandy McLeod
D. Barbara McLeod

II. CELIA MCCASKILL b. 1837, m. John B. Ray and lived near what is now Thagard's Pond (Whispering Pines), where they are both buried. They had:

A. Niven Ray
B. Mack Ray
C. John Ray

III. CATHERINE MCCASKILL b. 1840 d. after Sept. 26, 1860, m. John F. McDonald. They had:

A. Alex McDonald
B. Kate Martin McDonald
C. John McDonald
D. Virginia McDonald
E. James McDonald
F. Mary Elizabeth McDonald b. 1873, d. 1964

IV. JOHN WORTHY MCCASKILL b. 1842, d. 1915, m. three times. First to Mary Jane McKenzie b. 1842, d. 1878, secondly to Catherine Emeline McDonald (Kittie) b. 1859, d. 1891, and thirdly to Nancy Underwood (Nannie) b. 1851, d. 1938. He had no children by his third wife.
By his first wife he had:

A. Kenneth Worthy McCaskill b. 1868, d. 1943, m. Flora Ann Stewart
B. Hugh Martin McCaskill b. 1871, d. 1938 m. Lydia Alice Blue
C. Angus Alexander McCaskill
D. Mary Annie McCaskill
E. Betsy Jane McCaskill

By his second wife he had:

F. Anna Bell McCaskill
G. Margaret Elizabeth McCaskill b. 1886
H. Catherine Montgomery McCaskill b. 1888
I. Johnnie McCaskill b. 1890, d. 1892
J. infant son b. 1891

V. MARY ELIZABETH MCCASKILL b. 1844, m. Chester Hales and lived in Hope Mills, N.C. They had:

A. Lillie Hales
B. Susan Hales
C. Giles Hales
D. Bessie Hales
E. Lucy Hales

McKenzie Family

Another large Scots family of Moore County is the McKenzie connection. Good genealogical work was done on this family in 1940 by Duncan James McKenzie: *A Comprehensive Record of the McKenzie Family From the Immigration of Hugh McKenzie to America From Scotland About the Year 1750 and Continuing Through the Present*, and this work was updated and enriched in the late 1970s by the late Mrs. Estelle McKenzie Wicker of Pinehurst, N.C. I have both of these works in my possession, and most of what will be given here on the McKenzies comes from these two works.

According to Duncan James McKenzie, Hugh McKenzie was born in the Isle of Skye and emigrated between 1745 and 1750 to North Carolina, settling in what is now Moore County on Mill Creek, near the present Knollwood Airport (some four miles from Southern Pines). Hugh m. a Miss Nicholson, who was from what is now Richmond County, N.C. He served in the Continental Army of General Greene during the Revolution and was made lieutenant. While in service, he became sick and died, and is buried in Greenville, South Carolina.

Hugh McKenzie and wife had (at least):

I. JOHN
II. POLLY
III. NANCY

I. JOHN MCKENZIE m. Nancy McNeill in the early nineteenth century and lived near Thagard's Mill on Little River in Moore County, not far from the home of Hugh and wife. They had twelve children:

A. Katherine McKenzie b. 1814, m. Daniel Webster McKinnon. They had four sons and four daughters.[76]
B. Alexander (Alexandria) McKenzie b. 1815, m. Betsy Seawell. They had five children.[77]
C. Hugh McKenzie b. 1816 m. Belle Black (dau. of Hugh and Polly Johnson Black). They had six sons and five daughters.[78]
D. Margaret McKenzie b. 1816 was a school teacher and m. William Von Cannon, a blacksmith. No children.
E. Jeanette McKenzie b. 1817, was single. She left a daughter, Jane, who m. W. A. McDonald of Rockingham, N.C.
F. John McKenzie b. 1817, m. first Margaret McNair and secondly Mandy Clark. By his first wife he had four children and five by his second.[79]
G. Nancy McKenzie b. 1819, m. William Seawell and had two daughters.[80]
H. Christian McKenzie b. 1824, m. Wesley Seawell. They had three sons and three daughters.[81]
I. Daniel McKenzie b. 1824, m. Margaret Ann Black (dau. of John M. Black). They had six sons and four daughters.[82]
J. Polly McKenzie b. 1825, was single.
K. Belle McKenzie b. 1825 m. John Caddell. She died at the birth of her first child, who also died.
L. Lovedy McKenzie b. 1827, m. Simon Seawell. They had two sons and two daughters.[83]

II. POLLY MCKENZIE m. Allen McDonald an emigrant from Scotland,

about whom Duncan McKenzie writes: "He had been married in Scotland before coming to America and was the father of seventeen sons. While his eldest son remained in Scotland, the others immigrated to Canada and the northern part of the United States, where they made their homes. Out of this group came several Presbyterian ministers."[84]

Allen and Polly McKenzie McDonald settled on Mill Creek near Knollwood Airport, where Daniel P. Kelly later lived. They had four sons and five daughters, including:

A. Hugh McDonald b. 1782, m. Catherine Ray (dau. of Archibald Ray and Elizabeth McSween). They settled at New Gilead four miles west of Pinehurst on Deep Creek. Hugh served in the War of 1812 and was a school master. They had ten children.[85]

B. John McDonald m. Christian Black (dau. of Dougald Black). They had three sons and nine daughters.[86]

C. Randolph (Randall) McDonald m. Mary Blue (dau. of John Campbell Blue). Their children are traced under the John C. Blue section of this volume, (pp. 228-9).

D. Daniel McDonald m. Miss Clark from near Jackson Springs, N.C. They had no children.

E. Peggy McDonald

F. Sarah McDonald m. Edward Patterson. They had five sons and five daughters.[87]

G. _____ McDonald married ______ Black, according to Duncan McKenzie and left one daughter, Mary, who died single.[88]

III. NANCY MCKENZIE m. ____ Medlin and moved to Tennessee. No further information.

Kenneth Murchison Family

Kenneth Murchison, Sr. emigrated from the Isle of Skye to Moore County, North Carolina (then Cumberland County) in 1774. This family is dealt with in *Ancestors and Descendants of Kenneth Henderson Worthy: Sheriff of Moore County, North Carolina 1850-1856, 1860-1872* by James Vann Comer (Published by Ruby Vann Crumpler McSwain: Sanford, Sanford, N.C., 1996), and a number of the descendants are also traced in Kenneth I. Kelly's *McIver Family of North Carolina.*

Kenneth Murchison, Sr. was born in the Isle of Skye c. 1753, and died in Moore County, N.C. July 6/7, 1834. His father was Simon Murchison of the Isle of Skye. Kenneth was buried in the Becky Murchison Cemetery in Lee County, N.C. (which was then Moore County). He married first Catherine McIver, b. c. 1759 in the Isle of Skye, and d. Moore County, Aug. 17, 1800. She is buried also in the Becky Murchison Cemetery. She was the daughter of Roderick McIver and his wife, Nancy. Their twelve children are listed in Comer, op. cit., 22, and some of them are traced in Kelly, op. cit., 103-116. They were:

I.DUNCAN MURCHISON, Esquire, b. June 1776 in Cumberland County, N.C. (now Moore), d. Sept. 27, 1857; buried in Becky Murchison Cemetery. He. m. first, Isabella McQueen (daughter of Murdoch McQueen). She was b. Sept. 17, 1797, d. Oct. 12, 1847: no children. He m. secondly on Oct. 24, 1848, Fanny (Frances) Roberts (daughter of Thomas Roberts) b.c. 1828, d. after 1853.

II. MARGARET MURCHISON, b. in Cumberland County, d. after July 4, 1853, buried in Becky Murchison Cemetery. She m. in 1810 Peter Sinclair, and they had five children (traced in Kelly, op. cit., 104-105).

III. JOHN MURCHISON b.c. 1781 in Cumberland County, d. after Aug. 15, 1856.

IV. WILLIAM MURCHISON b. Cumberland County, d. after July 4, 1853, m. Nancy Worthy.

V. JENNET MURCHISON b. c. 1787 in Moore County, d. after Aug. 27, 1820, m.c. 1812, James Worthy.

VI. NANCY MURCHISON b. c. 1789 in Moore County, d. before 1864; buried in Becky Murchison Cemetery. She m. c. 1805, John B. Murchison b. Jan. 12, 1774, d. Aug. 26, 1847.

VII. COL. RODERICK MURCHISON b. c. 1789 in Moore County, d. Dec. 23, 1823; buried in Coosa County, Alabama.

VIII. COLIN/COLON MURCHISON b. Moore County, d. after July 4, 1853; buried in Becky Murchison Cemetery. He m. Nancy Torrance.

IX. ISABELLA MURCHISON b. Moore County, d. Apr. 4, 1831, m. May 18, 1812, William Thomas England b. c. 1787, d. May 19, 1852.

X. MARY ('POLLY') MURCHISON b. June 22, 1798, Moore County, d. Dec. 27, 1887, m. Cornelius Tyson b. Apr. 16, 1786, d. Dec. 10, 1866.

XI. KENNETH B. MURCHISON, JR., b. c. 1800, Moore County, d. after

Oct. 21, 1852, and buried at Euphronia Presbyterian Church in Lee County, N.C. He was a lawyer.

XII. DANIEL/DONALD MURCHISON b. Moore County, d. before June 18, 1834.

Kenneth Murchison, Sr., married Secondly, Catherine Campbell b. c. 1785 in North Carolina, d. Aug. 24, 1866 in Moore County; buried in Becky Murchison Cemetery. They had ten children who are listed in Comer, op. cit., 23. They are:

XIII. MURDOCH/MURDOCK b. c. 1801, Moore County, m.c. 1847 Jane (?). He moved to Texas in the 1840s.

XIV. CATHARINE MURCHISON b. Moore County, m. Daniel Curry.

XV. FLORA MURCHISON b. Moore County, b. ______ McLendon.

XVI. ALEXANDER MURCHISON b. Moore County.

XVII. DANIEL MURCHISON b. Moore County.

XVIII. REBECCA 'BECKY' MURCHISON b. c. 1817, Moore County, d. Dec. 5, 1895. She was single.

XIX. LYDIA MURCHISON b. c. 1817, Moore County, d. Sept. 5, 1899, buried in Becky Murchison Cemetery. She was single.

XX. JENNOT MURCHISON b. Moore County, buried in the Martin Family Cemetery.

XXI. CHRISTIAN MURCHISON b. Mar. 5, 1825, Moore County, d. June 27, 1914; m. ______ McDonald.

XXII. AARON MURCHISON b. Moore County, m. June 21, 1850, Celia Cole. He d. in 1853, and is buried in Burleson County, Texas.

Alexander McDonald Family

As would be expected with a large clan like MacDonald, there were many families of this name in the Cape Fear section. But as seems to be the case with the McNeills and McMillans, for instance, the McDonald genealogies do not appear to have been so well researched and published. Hence my information here is limited.

Paul McDonald of Southern Pines, N.C., is presently researching the Alexander McDonald family, and will publish it as *MacDonalds of Moore 1750-1850.* Alexander came to Moore County from the Isle of Skye between 1781 and 1800. His wife's first name was Sarah ______. They had at least one son: Daniel Patterson McDonald b. c. 1808 near Deep Creek in Moore County. He married and left a large number of descendants which will be included in the book mentioned above.

Information on another large family of McDonalds can be found in the McKenzie section immediately above, taken from Duncan James McKenzie's work done in 1940, which includes material on the descendants of Allen McDonald and Polly McKenzie of central Moore County, N.C.

McCrummen/McCrimmon Families

Perhaps the most well known musical family in all of Scotland were the McCrummens, pipers to the McLeods. Indeed this family for generations operated a piping college near Dunvegan, in the north of Skye. Various descendants of this family came to Moore County in the late eighteenth century. Among these were the McCrummens who settled in the western part of the county, and the supposedly unrelated McCrimmons in eastern Moore County. They came at different times from Scotland and were not aware of any close kinship. As for their names, McCrummen is closer to the original Gaelic, while McCrimmon is the more generally used Anglicized version.

There is not a great deal of collected information on either of these families. Douglas Kelly deals somewhat with the western Moore McCrummens,[89] and Alex Patterson deals with the eastern Moore McCrimmons.[90] Some of the letters of Dr. A.C. Bethune and Rev. W. A. McLeod also deal with these families.[91] A good source of material on the western McCrummens is found in the session minutes of old Mineral Springs Presbyterian Church, which this family helped found in 1819. These minutes have recently been published with other related historical material.[92]

A book of limited genealogical value, but of considerable historical musical interest has been published in Australia on the history of the Isle of Skye McCrummens (MacCrimmons) insofar as their piping is concerned.[93] At present, Rory MacLeod of Edinburgh, Scotland is doing research on the McCrummens/MacCrimmons who emigrated to America.

The head of the western Moore County McCrummens was Malcolm McCrummen b. 1771 in the Isle Of Skye, emigrated after the Revolution to North Carolina. He was listed as a member of Bethesda Presbyterian Church in 1812 (where he is buried) and then was a founding elder of Mineral Springs Presbyterian Church in western Moore in 1819 (by which time he had moved from what is the present town of Southern Pines, N.C., to land near present West End, N.C.) He was also a member of the Pansophia Masonic Lodge near Bethesda Church in the early nineteenth century along with other emigrant Scots of the region.

Malcolm McCrummen m. first Katie Graham, by whom he had children, and secondly Margaret McNeill by whom he had children. I am not presently certain which children belonged to which wife, but if the tradition handed down from Malcolm's granddaughter, Mrs. Mary McCrummen Blue (Mrs. Patrick A.) of Eureka (b. 1856, d. 1936) is correct, then this is the situation:

Malcolm had by his first wife (order of birth not certain in either of the two marriages):

I. LUCINDA MCCRUMMEN m. Daniel Washington McDonald and had five children who are traced in the history of Duncan James McKenzie:[94]

- A. Hugh Malcolm McDonald was single
- B. Charles Randolph McDonald b. 1862 near Jackson Springs in western Moore County, d. 1932, buried at Union Presbyterian Church, m. 1891 Sarah Anne Blue b. 1862, d. 1935 (dau. of Malcolm J. Blue, son of John McMillan Blue of Eureka). Their six children are traced in *Scottish Blue Family* (415-423).
- C. Christian Catherine McDonald m. D.W. McKenzie
- D. Mary Eliza McDonald m. D.J. McKenzie
- E. Lucinda Anne McDonald m. J.F. Patterson

II. ISABELLA MCCRUMMEN was single and taught a dame school in the mid nineteenth century in her brother's home near West End, N.C. She d. in the 1890s and is buried at Culdee Presbyterian Church near Eastwood, N.C. in Moore County.

III. ELIZA MCCRUMMEN was single and lived in Malcolm's home. She also taught school.

IV. NANCY (ANN) MCCRUMMEN was single and lived in Malcolm's home. She d. in the late 1890s and is buried at Culdee Church.

V. NORMAN MCCRUMMEN b. 1813, d. 1869 (dates from his tombstone at Bethesda, where he is buried). He m. _____, and according to family tradition his widow and children moved to Alabama.

Also according to family tradition, Malcolm McCrummen had by his second wife:

VI. MALCOLM MCCRUMMEN, according to Rozella McLeod's

research, b. 1821, d. 1916, m. Martha McLauchlin (dau. of Duncan and Catherine McLeod McLauchlin) b. 1825, d. 1890. They had five children:

A. Franzena McCrummen b. 1854 and is buried at Union Presbyterian Church in Moore County.
B. John McCrummen b. 1860, d. 1865, buried at Union Church.
C. Duncan McLauchlin McCrummen b. 1856, d. 1940, buried at Union Church.
D. Martha Ann McCrummen b. 1862, d. 1940, buried at Union Church.
E. Malcolm Daniel McCrummen b. 1858, d. 1943, m. 1891, Margaret Adina Caddell b. 1870, d. 1944. Both are buried at Union Church. They had five children.[95]

VII. CHARLES C. MCCRUMMEN who with his brother Neill was a census taker in Moore County in 1850. This writer possesses a few pieces of his set of plate silver with his initials engraved on it. He is buried at Bethesda Presbyterian Church. He was single.

VIII. NEILL MCCRUMMEN was also an 1850 census taker and was single. He is buried at Bethesda.

IX. JOHN MCCRUMMEN b. 1831, d. 1897, buried at Culdee Church. He served as Treasurer of Moore County and lived near West End, N.C. His home was burned by Sherman's army, but the house he built back is still standing. He m. Regina Buie b. 1834 in Moore County, d. 1924 and is buried at Culdee. They had only two daughters:

A. Margaret McCrummen m. Neil Pierce McKenzie of Moore County. They lived at the old McCrummen homeplace near West End, N.C. and helped found Culdee Presbyterian Church in 1886. Their ten children are traced by Duncan James McKenzie.[96]
B. Mary McCrummen b. 1856, d. 1936, buried at Bethesda. She m. 1876 Patrick A. Blue b. 1839, d. 1904, buried at Bethesda (son of John McMillan Blue) of Eureka in Moore County. Their nine children are traced in *Scottish Blue Family* (491-514).

To the best of my limited information (taken directly from Admiral Patterson's *The Monroes of the Upper Cape Fear*), the head of the eastern Moore County McCrimmons seems to have been Angus McCrimmon and his wife Margaret, "who in early life may have lived in Moore

County, but latterly lived in Cumberland County."[97] Angus d. intestate in Cumberland in 1819 or 1820 and Margaret d. 1841 in Cumberland, leaving a will naming her children and some grandchildren (in Cumberland County Wills, 1757-1869, C. R. 029. 301. 14 in Division of Archives and History, Raleigh, N.C.). Their children (not necessarily in correct order of birth):

I. RODERICK MCCRIMMON b. 1802, d. c. 1862, m. Lovedy Ann Monroe b. 1835, d. c. 1875 (dau. of Neill and Mary (Priest) Monroe). Their children are traced in this volume under the Lovedy Ann Monroe section, (pp. 282-3).

II. JOHN MCCRIMMON, no further information

III. DUNCAN MCCRIMMON, said in his mother's will to have moved West, no further information

IV. KENNETH MCCRIMMON moved to Louisiana, m. Charlot ____, and wrote letters home to his brother Roderick in 1829 and 1830; no further information.[98]

V. CHRISTIAN MCCRIMMON m. ____ McDonald

VI. JANET MCCRIMMON m. ____ McLeod

VII. FLORA MCCRIMMON (single at time of her mother's death)

VIII. EFFIE MCCRIMMON m. ______ McMillan (see discussion of this by Alex Patterson[99]) and had these children listed in their grandmother's will:

A. Mary Ann McMillan
B. Margaret Elizabeth McMillan
C. Christian Neal McMillan
D. John McMillan

Notes

1. A.W. McLean, op. cit., 664.
2. Johnson, op. cit., 19. Johnson says his information was obtained from Mrs. Lydia Faucette, dau. of Mrs. Jane Curry, formerly Miss Jane Black, dau. of Archibald Black of Moore County, who married Flora Martin. I have not checked any of this information.
3. See Kenneth L. Kelly, op. cit., 16ff. on this family.
4. Kenneth L. Kelly, *McIver Family in North Carolina*, 7.

5. Ibid., 290.
6. Traced in ibid., 15-43.
7. Traced in ibid., 43-60.
8. Traced in ibid., 60-67.
9. Traced in ibid., 67-68.
10. See ibid., 68.
11. Listed in ibid., 69.
12. Traced in ibid., 69-103.
13. Traced in ibid., 103-116.
14. Traced in ibid., 117-125.
15. Traced in ibid., 125-174.
16. Traced in ibid., 174-178.
17. Traced in ibid., 178-191.
18. Traced in 191-208.
19. Traced in ibid., 208-234; see also p. 235 of the present work.
20. Traced in ibid., 234-257.
21. Traced in ibid., 257-260.
22. Traced in ibid., 260-290.
23. Traced in ibid., 290-304.
24. Traced in ibid., 304-315.
25. 241-250.
26. Especially Part Four and Appendix A and B. It can be ordered from the Steiners, P.O. Box 12354, Las Vegas, NV 89112.
27. Ibid., B-l.
28. Ibid., B-2ff.
29. Ibid., B-6, and B-18ff.
30. Kenneth L. Kelly, *McIver Family,* 242-250.
31. Traced in ibid., 117.
32. Traced in ibid., 250.
33. Traced in ibid., 250-253.
34. Steiner, op. cit., B-22.
35. Ibid., B-23.
36. Ibid., B-23, 24.
37. Ibid., B-25 to B-43.
38. Ibid., B-44 to B-47.
39. Ibid., B-49.
40. Ibid., B-49.
41. Ibid., B-51.
42. Ibid.
43. Ibid., B-53.
44. Ibid.
45. Ibid., B-54.
46. See Douglas F. Kelly, *Malcolm Kelly Family,* 13, 14, 28.
47. Angus McQueen and Cornelia Shaw, "Dates of Interest Connected with the Family of Daniel Kelly" unpublished, compiled in the early 1900's.

48. See Douglas F. Kelly, op. cit., 32 and McQueen and Shaw, op. cit.
49. Traced in Douglas F. Kelly, op. cit., 34-66.
50. For offspring see D.F. Kelly, op. cit., 32 and McQueen and Shaw, op. cit.
51. See McQueen and Shaw, op. cit.
52. Ibid.
53. Ibid.
54. See D.F. Kelly, op. cit., 29 and McQueen and Shaw, op. cit. for offspring.
55. See McQueen and Shaw, op. cit.
56. K.L. Kelly, op. cit., 304-315.
57. p. 33.
58. One can contact: "Genealogy of Clan McIntosh, USA," Mary Lou Combs, R.R. 4, Box 694, Bloomfield, Indiana 47424.
59. Kenneth L. Kelly, op. cit., 304.
60. Ibid., 179.
61. Traced in ibid., 179-189.
62. Traced in ibid., 189, 190.
63. Only one of them is listed in ibid., 191.
64. Traced in ibid., 191.
65. Traced in ibid., 171-174.
66. Traced in ibid., 141-160.
67. Ibid., 304.
68. Ibid.
69. Listed in ibid., 290.
70. Traced in ibid., 304-315.
71. Rozella M. McLeod, *McLeods of Tuckahoe & Horses Creek* (1981), 6.
72. See R. M. McLeod, op. cit., 26.
73. Ibid., 83-110.
74. Kenneth A. McLeod, Jr. with help from Lelia McLeod, Ethel McLeod, Geneva McLeod, Clarence Poole and others (The John Alexander McLeod Association: 1960, revised 1968, 1979), with an introduction by Marshall Watson McLeod.
75. See Kenneth A. McLeod, Jr. and others, op. cit., 10.
76. Traced in Duncan McKenzie, op. cit, 3 and Estelle Wicker, op. cit., 2.
77. Traced in McKenzie, op. cit., 3, 4.
78. Traced in ibid., 4-9.
79. Traced in ibid., 11.
80. Traced in ibid., 11, 12.
81. Traced in ibid., 9.
82. Traced in ibid., 10.
83. Listed in ibid.
84. Ibid., 12.
85. Traced in ibid., 13-15.
86. Traced in ibid., 15, 16.
87. Traced in ibid., 17-20.
88. Ibid., 16.
89. *Scottish Blue Family*, 472-477.

90. *The Monroes of the Upper Cape Fear Valley,* chapter 9.

91. CORRESPONDENCE and DOCUMENTS Pertaining to the BETHUNE, KEAHEY, MCLEOD, MCFARLAND, PATTERSON and Other Related Scottish Highlander Families of North Carolina, 5. 01, 5. 24, 5. 33.

92. A Sketch of the History, Chronicles, and Records of Mineral Springs Church transcribed and indexed by Marie Smith Gordan, 1988. It can be order from Ms. Gordan, Route 12, Box 886, Laurel, Mississippi 39440.

93. The Piobaireachd of Simon Fraser with Canntairechd compiled and edited by Dr. B.J. Maclachlan Orme (Spectrum Publications: Burwood, Victoria, Australia, 1985 second edition).

94. *A Comprehensive Record of the McKenzie Family From the Immigration of Hugh McKenzie to America About the Year 1750 and Continuing to the Present,* compiled by Duncan James McKenzie, 1940, unpublished, p. 14, 15.

95. Traced in Rozella McLeod, op. cit., 67-69.

96. Duncan J. McKenzie, op. cit., 8.

97. Patterson, *The Monroes of the Upper Cape Fear Valley,* 98.

98. Ibid.

99. Ibid.

8

Families of Western Cumberland, Robeson and (Present) Hoke Counties

WE MUST NOW MOVE FURTHER down the Cape Fear Valley south of Moore County in order to look at some Highland Scots families who settled in the area now know as Hoke County, as well as in adjoining sections of the older counties of Cumberland and Robeson.

Monroe Families

Rear Admiral Alex M. Patterson compiled a significant history of several of the Cape Fear Valley Monroe families in 1976.[1] Among them he included the families of:

Neill Monroe (Munroe)

Neill Monroe b. 1790, d. 1851, m. Mary (Polly) Priest. They lived on Piney Bottom Creek near the Morganton Road in the present Fort Bragg Reservation, some five miles south of present Southern Pines, N.C. In his will he left over 1,000 acres of land to his wife and children. His ancestry is not definitely determined. Neill and Mary (Polly) Munroe had the following children (all of whom—with the exception of John—changed their names from Munroe to Monroe, according to Admiral Patterson[2]):

I.	JOHN W.	V.	CATHERINE
II.	GILBERT	VI.	ELISHA
III.	MARY	VII.	LOVEDY ANNE
IV.	MALCOLM	VIII.	JANE

I. JOHN W. MUNROE b. 1810, d. c. 1875, m. Mary Ann ____ b. 1820. They had:

A. William David Munroe b. 1848, m. first Malvina Jackson, secondly Annie E. ___ b. 1865. By his first wife he had three children.[3]

B. Mary Margaret Munroe b. 1849, m. 1871 Robert R. Matthews and lived in Carver's Creek Township. No record of issue.

II. GILBERT MONROE b. 1819, d. 1901, m. 1841 Margaret Matilda McColeman b. 1816, d. 1894. They lived in Cumberland County, N.C., near Galatia Presbyterian Church. He served in the Confederate Army. By his first wife he had:

A. Mary Monroe b. 1842, d. 1919, taught school in Moore and Cumberland Counties, was single.

B. Sarah Amanda Monroe b. 1844, d. 1926, m. Roderick McMillan b. 1937, d. 1918. He served in the Confederate Army and was sheriff of Robeson County during the years of the Lowery gang of Lumbee Indians in the 1870s and '80s. No children.

C. Hariett Ann Monroe b. 1846, d. 1931, was single and is buried at Galatia Presbyterian Church.

D. Frances (Fannie) Monroe b. 1848, d. 1928, was single and is buried at Galatia.

E. William Monroe b. 1852, d. 1938, m. Cynisca English Davis b. 1858, d. 1838. They lived in the Galatia Community and had four children.[4]

F. Henry Thomas Monroe b. 1860, d. 1965, m. Alice Troy Davis b. 1866, d. 1936, lived near Rockfish in Cumberland County. They had eight children.[5]

III. MARY MONROE b. 1823, d. 1900, m. Cornelius ("Tailor") Priest

b. 1808, d. 1900. They lived in upper Cumberland County, south of present Vass and Lakeview, and are buried in Moore County at Lakeview, N.C. They had:

A. John Hector Priest b. 1853, d. 1928, m. Catherine Ferguson b. 1853, d. 1918. They had four children.[6]

B. Mary Catherine Priest b. 1856, d. 1925, m. Angus McNeill. They lived south of Lakeview and had no children.

C. Jane Ann Priest b. 1858, d. 1927, single.

D. Elisha Neill Priest b. 1860, d. 1935, m. Mary Elizabeth (Molly) Cameron b. 1871, d. 1917. They lived near Vass, N.C., and had nine children.[7]

E. Flora Margaret Priest b. 1865, m. Thomas Holder. They lived near Vass, N.C. and had five children.[8]

IV. MALCOLM MONROE b. 1829, d. 1898, m. Margaret Ann Patterson b. 1841, d. 1875. This family is traced under the Patterson section in this volume.

V. CATHERINE MONROE b. c. 1826, was single.

VI. ELISHA MONROE b. 1827, d. 1915, m. Ann Eliza Cheek b. 1858, d. 1909. They lived in Cumberland County and were members of Sandy Grove Presbyterian Church now on the Fort Bragg Reservation. They had:

A. Mary Monroe b. 1879, d. 1879 in infancy

B. Elisha Neill Monroe b. 1880, d. 1913, m. Mary Jane Holder b. 1887, d. 1942. All their children died young.

C. Margaret Ann Monroe b. 1882, d. 1948, m. Albert Alphonso Barnard b. 1888, d. 1943. They lived in Raeford, N.C. No children.

D. Lydia Jane Monroe b. 1885, d. 1941, m. Lonnie James Dorman, b. 1879, d. 1973. They moved to Chesterfield, S.C., and had four children.[9]

E. James Brantly Monroe b. 1888, d. 1958, m. Lueola Shaw b. 1892, d. 1950. They lived in Cumberland (now Hoke) County and were buried at Philippi Presbyterian Church. They had eleven children.[10]

F. John Gilbert Monroe b. 1890, d. 1893, buried in Sandy Grove Church Cemetery.

G. Sarah Catherine Monroe b. 1893, d. 1896, buried at Sandy Grove.

H. Lonnie Martin Monroe b. 1896, d. 1961, m. Flonnie Mae Thompson b. 1904. They lived in Southern Pines, N.C., and had two children.[11]

I. Hugh Murdock Monroe b. 1900, d. 1963, lived in Fayetteville and was single.

VII. LOVEDY ANN MONROE b. 1835, d. c. 1875, m. Roderick McCrimmon (McCrummen) (son of Angus and Margaret McCrimmon of Cumberland County) and lived in James Creek in northwestern Cumberland County, near present Southern Pines, N.C. Roderick McCrimmon was first married to Flora McIver (or according to Kenneth L. Kelly, her name was Janet McIver, dau. of Little Daniel and Margaret Monroe McIver[12]) b. 1809 (according to Kelly, but 1801 according to Patterson[13]), d. 1845 (according to Kelly).

Roderick and his first wife Janet (or Flora?) had:

A. Angus McCrimmon b. 1843, d. 1864 in the Confederate Army of pneumonia. He was single.

B. Daniel McCrimmon b. 1845, d. 1905, m. 1878 Martha Jane Black (a descendant of Kenneth Black of Moore County), b. 1853, d. 1926. They lived in the James Creek section of Cumberland County and had six children.[14]

Roderick McCrimmon and his second wife, Lovedy Ann Monroe had:

C. Kenneth McCrimmon b. 1857, d. 1931, m. Frances Eliza McQueen Ferguson (dau. of John and Catherine (Priest) Ferguson) b. 1857, d. 1940. They lived in the Piney Bottom section of northern Cumberland County, south of Southern Pines and had six children.[15]

D. Neill Monroe McCrimmon b. 1859, d. 1933, m. 1885 Mary Eliza Guiton (Guin?) b. 1864. Both were born in Cumberland County, N.C., lived for a time in Mississippi, and eventually returned to North Carolina. They are buried in Bethesda Cemetery near Aberdeen. They had ten children.[16]

E. John McCrimmon b. 1861, d. 1939, m. first Eliza Cummings and secondly Doretta Ann Fry b. 1895, d. 1932. He had one child by his first wife and six by his second.[17]

F. William McCrimmon b. 1870, d. 1929, m. 1892 Mary William Wood b. 1872. They lived near Vass, N.C., and had eleven children.[18]

G. Mary Jane McCrimmon b. 1870, d. 1930, m. George Robert Morrison b. 1860, d. 1928. They lived in Moore County and are buried at Bethesda Cemetery. They had six children.[19]

H. Elisha McCrimmon b. 1875, d. 1914, m. 1899 Emma Kennedy b. 1888, d. 1928. They lived near Southern Pines, N.C., where he farmed, and are buried in Tuckahoe cemetery on the Fort Bragg Reservation. They had six children.[20]

VIII. JANE MONROE b. 1837, m. Edmond Andrews. They are believed to have lived near Durham, N.C., and to have had at least two children.[21]

"Scotch Monroe" Family

Admiral Patterson deals with this family which consisted of at least three brothers, who were somehow related to the Neill Monroes, though the degree is uncertain.[22] The three "Scotch Monroe" brothers were:

I. PETER
II. MALCOLM
III. DUGALD

I. PETER MONROE b. 1812, d. 1888, m. first Isabella Jane Cameron b. 1818, d. 1886, secondly Amanda Cameron, both from the Cameron Hill section of present Harnett County. He first lived in Montgomery County, and then after 1850 in Cumberland County near where the old Plank Road crossed Nicholson's Creek fifteen miles west of Fayetteville. He was a well known building contractor and while in Montgomery County, according to Admiral Patterson, built the county courthouse and jail, Pee Dee Presbyterian Church, and Spring Hill Baptist Church. In Cumberland he built several Presbyterian Churches: Montpelier near Wagram (1852), Bethel near Raeford (1852), Sandy Grove in present Fort Bragg, Galatia between Fayetteville and Raeford (1862), and Laurinburg Academy (1852). He was an organizing elder at Sandy Grove and sent all of his children to college except one who was killed in the War between the States.[23] By his first wife he had six children, and none by the second:

A. Evander Monroe b. 1842, d. 1865, d. in Confederate Hospital in Raleigh, N.C. Was single.

B. Colin Alexander Monroe, D.D. b. 1844, d. 1919, m. Mary Jane Stokes b. 1847, d. 1941, served in the Confederate Army and graduated from Davidson College and Union Theological Seminary. He served various Presbyterian Churches in North Carolina. They had four children.[24]

C. Dugald Monroe b. 1846, d. 1924, m. Nancy (Nannie) McRaney Buie b. 1850, d. 1938. He served in the Confederate

Army and graduated from Davidson and Union Theological Seminary. He served Presbyterian Churches in Tennessee and North Carolina. No children.

D. Edmund Marshall Monroe, D.D., b. 1849, d. 1923, m. first Emma Rae, secondly Sallie McLean. He also graduated from Davidson and Union and served churches in Arkansas and Texas, where he died. His children are traced in part by Admiral Patterson.[25]

E. Archibald Cornelius Monroe b. 1852, d. 1920, single. He attended Davidson College without graduating and was a school teacher in Cumberland County. He is buried at Sandy Grove.

F. Margaret Jane (Maggie) Monroe b. 1855, d. 1934, m. Malcolm James Blue b. 1849, d. 1917 (son of Malcolm M. Blue of near Bethesda in Moore County, discussed under the Blue section). They had seven children.[26]

G. John Peter Monroe, M.D. b. 1857, d. 1940, was single. He graduated from Davidson College and University of Virginia Medical School. He was president of North Carolina Medical College in Charlotte and practiced medicine there for many years.

II. MALCOLM A. MUNROE b. 1820, d. 1871 m. Martha Pemberton b. 1828, d. 1888. They lived near Little River on the road from Troy to Biscoe in Montgomery County. He was a carpenter and later became a millwright and operated a grist mill on Little River. They had nine children:

A. Calvin Spencer Munroe b. 1847, d. 1910 m. Mary Campbell. They lived near Rockingham, N.C., and had 8 children.[27]

B. Samuel D. Munroe b. 1849, d. 1910, m. ____ Hurley. They lived near Hoffman, N.C. He was killed in a fall from a wagon.

C. John Munroe b. 1851 m. Lutie Freeman.

D. David P. (Tug) Munroe b. 1854, d. 1915, wife's name unknown.

E. Tamar Jane Munroe b. 1856, d. 1926, m. Sam J. Smitherman, who served as sheriff of Montgomery County. They lived in Troy, N.C., and had children, of whom only one was known to Admiral Patterson.[28]

F. George H. Munroe m. Fannie Shaw and lived in Troy, N.C.

G. Malcolm A. Munroe Jr. b. and d. 1862.

H. Martha Pat Munroe m. A.R. (Spike) Morris and lived in Raeford, N.C. They had two children.[29]

I. Neill E. Munroe b. 1867, d. 1936 m. Ursula Dolberry. They lived in Biscoe, N.C., and had five sons and two daughters.[30]

III. DUGALD MUNROE b. 1832, d. 1867, m. Jane ____. Based upon the settlement of his estate (in Cumberland County Administrative Bonds, MaP, C.R.29.501.3, Box 9 Division of Archives and Records, Raleigh, N.C.) his wife predeceased him and there were no children. He is traditionally believed to have died during the War Between the States.[31]

John Munroe Family

Admiral Patterson discusses in careful detail the possible (but as yet unproved) relationships between this and the other Monroe families.[32] What is clear is that John Monroe, who d. 1841, m. 1803 Sarah McCall b. 1773, d. 1855 and lived in upper Cumberland County, a few miles southeast of present Southern Pines. They had nine children:

I. DUGALD MUNROE, wife unknown, was left one dollar in his father's will (Cumberland County *Record of Wills*, B, 357) in 1841. Patterson thinks that Dugald may have been the father of Peter Monroe, the architect (mentioned in the previous section) but this is not documented.

II. NEILL MUNROE, wife unknown (may have been Mary Priest?)

III. ISABELLA MUNROE b. 1809, presumed to have been single.[33]

IV. MARY MUNROE m. John Cameron. According to the 1850 census, Mary was deceased and apparently left a daughter Sarah Cameron who was living with her father John.[34]

V. NANCY MUNROE m. ____ Priest. She appears to have died shortly before the 1850 census, and to have left these children:[35]

A. Nancy Priest b. 1828
B. John Priest b. 1832
C. Ann Priest b. 1834
D. Ellen Priest b. 1850

VI. HUGH MUNROE mentioned in his father's will, but not in the 1850 census.

VII. PETER MUNROE mentioned in his father's will and was living at home at that time.[36]

VIII. SARAH MUNROE b. 1815, was living with her mother in 1850, no record of marriage.

IX. CATHERINE MUNROE b. 1817, was also living with her mother in 1850, no record of marriage.

Malcolm Patrick Monroe Family

Another family of probable, but uncertain relationship to the other Monroes is that of Malcolm Patrick Monroe. According to Admiral Patterson, Malcolm Patrick Monroe was b. 1747 in Scotland and d. 1818 in Cumberland County, N.C. "By land grant No. 1082, dated 20 October 1794, he obtained 200 acres of land on Stewart's Creek, probably between Fayetteville and Fort Bragg."[37] He m. Margaret McNeill (dau. of "Big Neill" McNeill, a son of Daniel McNeill and Sarah McKay, sister of Alexander McKay, who opposed the Revolution). He is buried at Longstreet Presbyterian Church. One child is known:

I. PETER MUNROE b. 1790, d. 1872, m. 1819 Catherine Johnson b. 1792. In later life they lived on Flat Creek, about twelve miles west of the present Pope Air Force Base, and to distinguish him from other Peter Munroes in Cumberland County, he was called "Flat Creek Peter." He was a farmer and miller. She was the daughter of Alexander Johnson, sheriff of Cumberland County.[38] They had ten children:

A. Flora E. Munroe b. 1815, d. 1867, single

B. Patrick Daniel Patterson Monroe b. 1816, d. 1895, m. 1857 Mary Katherine McKethan b. 1832, d. 1886 (dau. of Alexander and Elizabeth Ann (Geddie) McKethan). "They lived on the Flat Creek estate of his father until later life when they moved down to Stewart's Creek and built a house which is still (1975) standing. He was a building contractor and farmer, and he owned a sawmill and gristmill."[39] Admiral Patterson notes that "about this time members of the family began spelling their name 'Monroe.' "[40] They had four children.[41]

C. Mary Margaret Monroe b. 1821, d. 1895, m. 1847 John A. McDonald b. 1823, d. 1869. They had five children.[42]

D. Duncan J. Monroe b. 1833, d. 1865, m. 1861 Isabella Murphy Monroe b. 1837, d. 1917. They had three children.[43]

E. Catherine Johnson Monroe b. 1825, d. 1900, single and was buried at Longstreet Church.

F. Alexander John Monroe b. 1827, d. 1898, m. Mary E. Ray b.

1836, d. 1878. They had five children.[44]

G. Malinda A. Monroe b. 1828, d. 1900, single and was buried at Longstreet.

H. Effie Monroe b. 1829, d. 1884, single and was buried at Longstreet.

I. Sarah W. Monroe b. 1831, d. 1900, single and was buried at Longstreet.

J. Edward William Monroe b. 1834, d. 1853, no record of marriage. He was buried at Longstreet.

John Alexander Monroe Family

John Alexander Monroe b. c. 1790, m. 1820 Margaret McLaurin b. c. 1800. They lived in Cumberland County, N.C. They had seven children:

I. NEILL L. MONROE b. 1821, d. 1907, single

II. MARY ANN MONROE b. 1824, d. 1852, single

III. GEORGE MCDUFFIE MONROE b. 1825, d. 1845, single

IV. DUNCAN L. MONROE b. 1827, d. 1908, m. 1860 Martha Hilliard. They had:

A. Robenia Monroe b. 1865, d. 1956, single

B. Joseph McArthur Monroe b. 1869, d. 1962, single

V. FLORA P. MONROE, single

VI. ISABELLA MURPHY MONROE b. 1837, d. 1917, m. Duncan J. Monroe b. 1833, d. 1865 (see Malcolm Patrick Monroe section above).

VII. JOHN ALEXANDER MONROE JR. b. 1842, d. 1887, m. Amanda McKethan b. 1839, d. 1887. They had:

A. Kenneth Hubert Monroe b. 1877, d. 1946, m. Ida Cornelia Leslie b. 18810, d. 1963. They lived in Fayetteville, N.C., and had seven children.[45]

B. John Alexander Monroe III m. Lillie King

C. Clarence Leroy Monroe m. first Anna Jackson, secondly Minnie Lindsay.

Archibald Monroe Family

Archibald Monroe b. c. 1799, m. 1820 Mary Campbell. They lived in Cumberland County. According to Admiral Patterson, Mary had at least two brothers, John and Colin Campbell.[46] Archibald and Mary had five children:

I. FLORA MONROE b. 1824, m. John Ellis Jr., no children.

II. NEILL C. MONROE b. 1826, d. 1876, m. 1858 Elizabeth Ann Graham, b. c. 1840, d. 1896. They had:

A. Archibald Monroe b. and d. 1864
B. Mary Ann Monroe b. 1866, d. 1887, single
C. William D. Monroe b. 1867, d. 1901, single
D. Catherine Elizabeth Monroe b. c. 1869, m. 1892, Alexander McDougald and had one child.[47]
E. Sarah Margaret Monroe b. 1876, d. 1946, m. Neill Patrick Monroe b. 1865, d. 1932 (See Peter Monroe/Catherine Johnson section on p. 286).
F. Isabella Monroe b. c. 1877, d. 1889, single

III. DANIEL C. MONROE b. 1828, single

IV. SARAH JANE MONROE b. 1832, m. 1862 Angus McGill. They had:

A. Rebecca McGill b. 1863, d. 1921, m. John Alexander Patterson b. 1853, d. 1926. They first lived in Cumberland County, N.C. and later in Dillwyn, Virginia. They had five children.[48]

V. MARY ANN MONROE b. 1836, single

Bensalem Monroe Family

The relationship of the Monroes who lived near Bensalem Presbyterian Church in western Moore County to the other Monroes is unknown. Little is known about the progenitor of this family, who is believed by Rassie Wicker and Alex Patterson to be Malcolm Monroe, who m. Margaret Patterson, although Miss Alberta Monroe believed his name was Daniel or Donald, rather than Malcolm.[49]

Malcolm Monroe and his wife, Margaret Patterson (dau. of Archibald and Mary Patterson Patterson) had at least two children:

I. DANIEL MONROE m. Isabel Patterson (dau. of John and Isabel McDuffie Patterson—see under Isabella McDuffie section of this volume).

II. MALCOLM MONROE b. 1774 in North Carolina, d. 1859 in Alabama, m. 1802 Margaret Black b. 1774 in North Carolina, d. in Alabama. She was the widow of Colin Black. They moved to Talladega County, Alabama before the 1850 census, where Malcolm was listed as a blacksmith.[50] They had seven children:

A. Colin A. Monroe b. 1795 in North Carolina, d. (in Alabama?)[51] They had at least three children.[52]

B. Archibald Monroe b. 1897 in North Carolina, d. in Alabama, where he seems to have moved about 1841. He was a farmer and m. Terry Cochran b. 1804 in N.C., and d. in Alabama. They had ten children.[53]

C. John M. Monroe b. 1802 in N.C., d. in N.C., lived in the Bensalem area of Moore County. He m. Mary (Polly) Deaton b. 1808 in N.C. and d. in N.C. They had nine children.[54]

D. Duncan Monroe b. 1806 in N.C., d. 1896 in Georgia, m. first Sarah Phillips, secondly, Elizabeth Phillips b. 1816, d. 1868 in Alabama, and thirdly m. Matilda Morris. When Duncan and family moved to Georgia is not known, and which wives were the mothers of his nine children is also unknown.[55]

E. Francis Monroe b. 1804, d. 1864 in N.C., m. first Amanda Deaton b. 1804, d. 1831 in N.C., and secondly m. Catherine Dowd b. 1814, d. 1888. They lived near Bensalem Presbyterian Church in Moore County. He had two children by his first wife and five by the second.[56]

McKeithan (McKeithen, McKethen, McKicchan) Families

A number of McKeithan families emigrated from the Hebridean Islands of western Scotland to the middle and upper Cape Fear Valley over a period of several decades from approximately 1740 to the early 1780s. Since in this volume we are discussing the emigrant families by approximate geographical areas, we will look at the McKeithan families who arrived later, because they are the ones who went further upstream to the area of Carolina now under surveillance: present day Hoke County and surrounding territory in lower Moore, western Cumberland and upper Robeson Counties. Later in this volume we will look at the McKeithan families who came earlier and settled further east in lower Bladen County, but first we must cover a number of other settlements in between Hoke and lower Bladen.

This family name has a number of variations, partly owing to the difficulty of transliterating Gaelic into English. All of the standard histories of the McKeithans rightly state that the various spellings all refer to the same family groups, since often the same family will spell its name two different ways within one or two generations. Hence we are not to think that McKeithan, McKeithen or even (the earliest attempts in lower Bladen to transliterate it into English) McKicchan refer to different clans.

Neill McKeithen Family

According to the research of Evelyn F. Smith, Neill McKeithen Sr. was b. c. 1752 in the Isle of Uist in the Outer Hebrides.[57] The late E.T. McKeithen of Aberdeen had papers which indicated that Neill Sr. emigrated to North Carolina between 1780 and 1782.[58] He d. 1835 in Cumberland County, and is buried at Longstreet Church. He m. 1785 Mrs. Lovedy McLauchlin McMillan b. c. 1748, d. 1823, who was the widow of Archibald McMillan and mother of two children by him: Daniel and Catherine. Before their marriage Neill Sr. worked for Mrs. McMillan as a shepherd and then farm overseer at her estate on Crain's Creek in Cumberland County. Her children by Archibald McMillan are dealt with in *Scottish Blue Family* by D. F. Kelly.[59]

According to Evelyn Smith (following records of historian E.T. McKeithen of Aberdeen, N.C.), Neill McKeithen Sr. and Lovedy McL. McMillan had:[60]

I. DOUGALD
II. JOHN
III. DANIEL
IV. NEILL
V. MARY JANE
VI. MARGARET R.
VII. MARY "POLLY"

I. DOUGALD MCKEITHEN b. 1786/7 in N.C., d. in Georgia, m. c. 1815 Nancy Wadsworth. They moved to Georgia about 1820. Their five children are traced by Mrs. Smith.[61]

II. JOHN MCKEITHEN b. 1788 in N.C., m. c. 1805/06 Margaret (Peggy) Blue b. 1783 in N.C. (dau. of John C. Blue and first wife). See John C. Blue section of this volume for a reference to their three children, (p.228).

III. DANIEL MCKEITHEN b. 1792 in N.C., d. 1865 in N.C., m. c. 1815 Cyntha Yarber (or Yarboro) b. 1794, d. 1822 in N.C. His will was probated January 1866 in Moore County (*Book C*, p. 128). He was a merchant, farmer and Presbyterian. His eight children are traced by Mrs. Smith.[62]

IV. NEILL MCKEITHEN JR. b. 1793 and d. 1830 in N.C., buried at Longstreet Church, m. 1819 Sarah Smith b. 1790, d. 1865, buried at Cypress Church (dau. of Daniel and Ann McKay Smith). Their seven children are traced by Mrs. Smith.[63]

V. MARY JANE MCKEITHEN b. 1831, mentioned in Lovedy Smith's will.[64] No further information.

VI. MARGARET R. MCKEITHEN, no further information.

VII. MARY "POLLY" MCKEITHEN b. in N.C., m. 1811 in Cumberland County John Daniel McMillan b. and d. in N.C. After her husband's death, she went to Alabama to live with her son, Neill McMillan in Wilcox County. Mary McKeithen and John Daniel McMillan had five children.[65]

We will look at three other McKeithen families when we reach lower Bladen County.

Currie Family

Slightly to the west of the general area inhabited by the Monroes and McKeithens lived the Currie family in what is today Hoke County. The Rev. William Angus McLeod of Cuerco, Texas, wrote the history of this family in the 1930's, and from it I take the following genealogical outline.

Archibald Currie came from Kintyre, Scotland, with his wife and year old daughter, Flora, in 1775 to what is now Hoke County (then, Bladen and later Robeson).[66] He is thought to have died before the 1790 census. Young Flora was living with her brother Randall (spelled Raynald in the census) in 1790. Flora m. c. 1797 Angus Currie, who had emigrated from the Isle of Colonsay in Scotland with his elderly mother in 1791.[67] He settled about three miles northeast of the present Antioch Presbyterian Church between Red Springs and Raeford on what is now called "the Burder Conoly place." He became a founding elder of Antioch Church in 1833, and is buried with his wife in the old McEachern cemetery, six miles south of Raeford.

Angus and Flora Currie had six children:

I.	ISABELLA	IV.	ARCHIBALD C.
II.	MARY	V.	ANGUS R.
III.	JOHN C.	VI.	FLORA

I. ISABELLA CURRIE b. 1798, d. 1846, single. She d. of typhoid fever and is buried near her mother's old home "Randallsville."

II. MARY CURRIE b. 1800, became the second wife of Gilbert Gilchrist c. 1823/24 (son of John Gilchrist Sr. and Effie McMillan) b. 1780 in Robeson County, N.C. He was an elder for twenty years in Laurel Hill Presbyterian Church and held large lands in upper Robeson County (later sold to Archibald McEachern). Gilbert was first m. to Nancy McPherson (whose sister Mary was the wife of Gilbert's brother Archibald) by whom he had at least nine children. According to W.A.

McLeod, about 1826 Gilbert and all of his family except for three daughters and one son moved to Barbour County, Alabama, where he died in 1857. Mary Currie d. 1879. They had nine children:

A. Charner H. Gilchrist b. 1825/26, d. 1864, d. single in the Confederate Army. He held lands in East Texas.

B. John McIntyre Gilchrist b. 1827 in Robeson County, N.C., d. 1887 in Butler County, Alabama. He was a Captain in the Confederate Army and a state legislator. He m. Dorinda Calhoun at Seale, Alabama in 1852 (great-niece of John C. Calhoun). She d. 1904. They had twelve children, and they are traced by W.A. McLeod.[68]

C. Caroline Isabelle Gilchrist b. 1829, d. 1864, m. 1856 James W. Blakey d. 1909. They lived at Midway, Alabama and had four children.[69]

D. Nancy McPherson Gilchrist b. 1831, d. 1888, m. Joseph Thigpen and had no children. She is buried in Bullard Cemetery near Tyler, Texas.

E. Angus Jackson Gilchrist b. 1833, d. 1888. He lived at Wills Point, Texas and m. Kate Douglass b. 1849, d. 1924. They had eight children.[70]

F. Gilbert Scotland Gilchrist II b. 1836 in Barbour County, Alabama, d. 1912 in Texas to which he moved in 1857. He m. in 1861, Zilpha Ann Blow b. 1843, in James County, Georgia. They had eleven children.[71]

G. Adoline M. Gilchrist b. 1838 in Barbour County, Alabama, d. 1913 and is buried in Panola, AL. She m. John Hook, a farmer in Crenshaw County, AL. They had three children.[72]

H. Amanda Gilchrist b. 1840, d. 1843.

I. Jemima Gilchrist b. 1842, d. 1843.

III. JOHN C. CURRIE b. 1803 in what is now Hoke County on what is known in the twentieth century as "the Burder Conoly Place." He was a well known school teacher and had an excellent knowledge of Gaelic. In 1854, he helped organize Sandy Grove Presbyterian Church on the present Fort Bragg Reservation. He m. one of his pupils in 1836, Margaret Keahey (dau. of John Keahey and Elizabeth Patterson, who by this time were dead. Margaret was living with her grandfather, "Buffalo Daniel" Patterson in Cumberland County). John C. and Margaret lived near the present site of Raeford, N.C. John C. d. 1888 and Margaret in 1893. They had eleven children.[73]

A. Elizabeth Caroline Currie b. 1837, d. 1876 m. Captain John M. Graham (son of Alexander and Anna McFarland Graham), b. in Cumberland County and a Confederate veteran. She d. 1876. They had three children.[74]

B. Archibald Keahey Currie d. in childhood.

C. Flora Ann Currie d. in childhood.

D. Mary Jane Currie d. in infancy.

E. William Jackson Currie b. 1846, was a Confederate veteran and elder in Sandy Grove Presbyterian Church before moving to Shoe Heel (now Maxton) in Robeson County, N.C. He was a N.C. legislator from Robeson and m. Catherine Smith of Wakulla, near Red Springs. He d. 1929 in Maxton, and she d. 1934. They had five children.[75]

F. John Calvin Currie (older of twins) b. 1848, d. 1902. He was a farmer and N.C. State legislator and an elder in Shiloh Presbyterian Church. He m. Mary (Mollie) McLean (dau. of William and Almena McLeod McLean of present Scotland County, N.C.). They lived at Turnpike Bridge over Lumber River, and had ten children.[76]

G. Angus Doddridge Currie (twin to John C.) b. 1848, d. 1938. He was a singing teacher and was in the turpentine business and served as a N.C. State legislator. He moved to Sumter, South Carolina in 1874 and m. 1877 Ida Gertrude China. They d. in Montgomery County, Georgia, at their daughter's home. They had four children.[77]

H. Isabella Amanda Currie b. 1850 near present Raeford, N.C., and lived through Sherman's Raid in March, 1865. She m. 1873 John Daniel McLeod (son of Angus and Serena McPhatter McLeod). She moved with her family to Leggett, Polk County, Texas in 1897. She d. 1898 near Leggett. They had eight children.[78]

I. James Burder Currie b. 1852 on Mountain Creek in North Carolina. He m. first Flora Chisholm (dau. of Kenneth Chisholm of Montgomery County, N.C.), and secondly Catherine Elizabeth Stewart (dau. of Malcolm Stewart of Richmond County, N.C.). By his first wife he had a child who d. in infancy and by his second wife three children.[79]

J. Newton Bethune Currie d. 1931, was single and is buried at Shiloh Presbyterian Church.

K. Margaret Jane Currie b. 1858 on Mountain Creek and d. 1936. She m. Murdoch McLeod (son of Archibald and Isabella Graham McLeod and grandson of "Sailor Murdoch McLeod" who emigrated from Isle of Skye to Rockfish Creek, Cumberland County). Margaret and Murdoch had eight children.[80]

IV. ARCHIBALD C. CURRIE b. c. 1806 and attended Donaldson Academy in Fayetteville, N.C. He m. 1833 Isabella McNeill (dau. of Daniel and Elizabeth McNeill of Rockfish). They moved soon after marriage to Kemper County, Mississippi and had nine children.[81]

V. ANGUS R. CURRIE b. 1813, d. 1846 according to family tradition of typhoid and is buried at Randallsville. He m. Jane McLean (dau. of Dr. Hector McLean of near present Raeford). They had two children.[82]

VI. FLORA CURRIE b. 1817, d. 1896, m. Adam Currie b. 1815, who was her mother's brother. They lived near the old Archibald Currie place near Raeford. They had three children.[83]

Johnson Family

It is impossible to give a formal genealogy of the Johnson family at this time. This family, though smaller than many of the other Highlander groups, was very influential in what is now Hoke and then in Moore County. James McN. Johnson wrote a short history of some members of this family in the early 1900s, and a biographical sketch of Johnson was composed by Judge H.F. Seawell in 1918 in Carthage, N.C., which has been reprinted in *Argyll Colony Plus* (Vol. 3, No. 2., 63-66), with more recent information and bibliographical help by Louise Rourke of Citrus Heights, California. There are also some letters and documents relating to the Johnson family in *CORRESPONDENCE and DOCUMENTS Pertaining to the BETHUNE, KEAHEY, MCLEOD, MCFARLAND, PATTERSON and other Related Scottish Highlander Families of North Carolina*, section 25.00.

In brief, we may note from the *Argyll Colony Plus* article that the emigrant head of this family was Peter Johnson, who is said to have arrived with his sons about 1759 (though no documentation is given of the date) and to have settled near Philippi Presbyterian Church in what is now Hoke County (then Cumberland). Most of the Seawell article deals with the descendents of Peter's son, Daniel Johnson (but not in a way that can be organized into a family chart).

McPhaul Family

One of the older families of present Hoke County, N.C., was that of John McPhaul and his son Neill, who settled near the "Mill Prong" or "Little Raft Swamp" and soon gave their own name to the area as McPhaul's Mill. Today it is generally known as the Antioch community between Raeford and Red Springs. The history of this family was written by John Henry McPhaul and published (privately) by John A. McPhaul in 1959. Most of my information is taken directly from this sixteen page booklet. I also refer to John Edwin Purcell's *Lumber River Scots,* which traces some parts of this family.

Sometime before 1761 John McPhaul came to Cross Creek (now Fayetteville) with his son, Neill, traditionally from one of the Hebridean Islands, after his wife had died in Scotland. Sometime between 1767 and 1770[84] John and his son settled at what became McPhaul's Mill. According to John H. McPhaul, John and Neill McPhaul arrived in the Mill Prong of the Raft Swamp:

> Here they found a tiny settlement around a tavern kept by a widow and her comely daughter—Ann Perkins and Mary Perkins. It was here that they also found contentment for in time Ann Perkins became the wife of John McPhaul and 'Pretty Molly' Perkins married Neill McPhaul. Thus was founded the McPhaul family in North Carolina.
>
> Ann Perkins was granted fifty acres of land 'lying on a branch of the Raft Swamp' by patent dated April 20, 1767 and John McPhaul was granted one hundred acres 'lying on the mill prong of the Raft Swamp' by patent dated December 22, 1770. The grant to John McPhaul reveals that the two tracts of land were adjacent.
>
> Old John McPhaul had been a miller in the old country and had brought his mill stones with him. He and his son, finding the run of the Little Raft admirably suited to their purpose, soon built a grist mill which drew customers from far and near among the many Scottish Emigrants who eventually settled thickly there between the waters of the Cape Fear and Pee Dee Rivers. With the passing years, the mill and tavern became a gathering place for the community.[85]

Like most of the emigrant Scots of this area, the McPhauls were Loyalists to the Crown, and a battle occurred between the Tories and the Americans led by General Rutherford at McPaul's Mill in October of 1781, which is described in E. W. Carruthers *Revolutionary Incidents and Sketches of Character Chiefly in the Old North State* (1854).

Neill McPhaul, son of John by his first wife (name unknown) m.

Mary Perkins and had six children, which are traced by John H. and John A. McPhaul as follows:

I.	DANIEL	IV.	MARGARET
II.	CATHERINE	V.	JOHN
III.	SARAH	VI.	MARY

I. DANIEL MCPHAUL b. 1762, d. 1844, m. Flora Patterson b. 1758, d. 1825. They had:

A. Neill McPhaul m. Margaret (Kelly) McPhatter. They had three children.[86]
B. John McPhaul, moved to Florida.
C. Daniel McPhaul m. Jane McKay and had ten children.[87]
D. Duncan McPhaul m. Mary Fadden and had six children.[88]
E. Malcolm McPhaul, moved to Mississippi.
F. Mary McPhaul m. Archibald Smith and had ten children.[89]
G. Catherine McPhaul m. Sion Alford, who lived near Rowland, N.C. They had five children.[90]
H. Effy McPhaul m. John McLean and had four children.[91]
I. Sarah McPhaul m. James L. Alford and had twelve children.[92]
J. Alexander McPhaul m. Mary McNeill and had six children.[93]

II. CATHERINE MCPHAUL b. 1763, d. 1851, m. John McArthur b. 1764, d. 1800. They had:

A. Margaret McArthur m. ____ Currie and had two children.[94]
B. Peter McArthur
C. John McArthur m. first Christian Gordon, and secondly Sarah Ann McNeill. He had five children by his first wife and eight by his second.[95] He m. thirdly Mary Jane Barfield, but had no children by her.
D. Duncan McArthur m. Sarah McNeill. They had seven children.[96]
E. Archibald McArthur, no further information
F. Alexander McArthur m. Jane Love and had eight children.[97]
G. Neill McArthur, no further information

III. SARAH MCPHAUL m. _____ McNeill and had:

A. Mary McNeill
B. John McNeill
C. Lydia Betsy McNeill
D. George W. McNeill
E. Rhode McNeill[98]

IV. MARGARET MCPHAUL d. 1846, m. David Torrey d. 1827. This family is traced in John Edwin Purcell's *Lumber River Scots* (311-335),

and I use that source to give the following outline. According to Purcell, David Torrey was b. in Scotland and accompanied his parents to the Fayetteville section of North Carolina. He d. in Mississippi. The Torrey family first moved from Fayetteville to lower Robeson during the Revolutionary conflict, and later moved to upper Robeson, until 1817, when David moved to Mississippi. He m. first Anna McDuffie (dau. of Archibald McDuffie of Cumberland Co., N.C.), and secondly m. Margaret McPhaul. He was on the Whig side during the Revolution. His will is recorded in Jefferson County, Mississippi.[99]

He had three sons by Anna McDuffie[100] and ten children by Margaret McPhaul. These are the children of the second marriage:

A. Nancy (or Emily C.) Torrey b. 1796, m. Alexander Willis 1819. No further information.

B. Neill Torrey b. 1798, d. 1843, was single and d. in Mississippi.

C. Elizabeth Torrey b. 1800, d. 1833, m. A. Longaree 1831.

D. Mary Torrey b. 1802 in North Carolina, m. Huston L. Tucker 1843 in Jefferson County, Mississippi, d. 1892 at her home near Ebenezer in Jefferson County, MS. They had two children.[101]

E. Margaret Torrey b. 1810, d. 1882 m. 1832 Joel Hullum b. 1800, d. 1865. They had eleven children.[102]

F. Sarah Torrey b. 1813 in North Carolina, d. c. 1846 in Fayette, Mississippi. She m. first John Pipes in 1835, and secondly John Young in Fayette, MS., in 1838. There were four children by the second marriage.[103]

G. James Torrey b. 1815, d. 1833.

V. JOHN MCPHAUL b. 1770, d. 1820, m. Margaret Gilchrist b. 1775, d. 1834 (dau. of John Gilchrist), both are buried in the McEachern Cemetery at Mill Prong in Hoke County, N.C. This family is traced by John E. Purcell whom we follow here. They had eight children (the exact order of birth is not certain, according to Purcell, who uses the Robeson County will of Margaret G. McPhaul and other information[104]):

A. Daniel McPhaul b. 1801, d. 1865, m. 1829 Catherine McArn of Richmond County, N.C., b. 1814, d. 1882. They had eleven children.[105]

B. William McPhaul b. in Robeson County, N.C. No further information.

C. Neal McPhaul b. in Robeson County, no further information.

D. John McPhaul II b. in Robeson County, m. Katherine Blue

and had at least two children. Purcell was uncertain about the information on this family.[106]

E. Archibald McPhaul b. in Robeson County, is said to have been killed by being thrown from a horse.

F. Malcolm McPhaul b. 1816, d. 1857, m. 1834 Christian McArn of Richmond County, N.C., b. 1818, d. 1855. They lived near Antioch Presbyterian Church and are buried there. They had nine children.[107]

G. Effie McPhaul b. in Robeson County is believed to have m. a Johnson and moved to Florida. Other reports say her husband was a Singletary, and in the *McPhaul* history, the name Graham is used. No children.[108]

H. Mary Gilchrist McPhaul b. in Robeson County, and known as "Pretty Mary." She m. John McMillan (son of Archibald), who was her cousin. They moved to Florida, where he was known as "Florida John McMillan." They both d. there. They had nine children.[109]

VI. MARY MCPHAUL b. 1772, d. 1848, m. Duncan McArthur and had seven children:

A. Mary McArthur m. Neill Baker. They had five children.[110]
B. Duncan McArthur
C. Margaret McArthur m. John McCormick
D. Nancy McArthur m. Alexander McKay
E. Christian McArthur was single
F. Effy McArthur m. Alexander McLean
G. Catherine McArthur m. Daniel Blue. They had eight children.[111]

Conoly Family

The Rev. W.A. McLeod in his *The Curries and Their Kin* states that "The Conoly family was an old one in the Highland section [i.e. of the upper Cape Fear]."[112] This family owned large tracts of land in what is now Hoke County. Part of the Conoly connection is traced in W.A. McLeod's work, and others of them are traced in John E. Purcell's *Lumber River Scots,* and still others in Alex M. Patterson's *Highland Scots Pattersons.* Brief reference is made to them in Isabel C. Patterson's *Builders of Freedom and Their Descendants.* I also have access to the family Bible of Cordelia Currie Conoly of Hoke County, N.C., which has a number of relevant names, dates and places of birth of the Conolys. Even with these sources, I can give only a brief and incomplete

outline of the genealogy of this strong family.

The head of this family was Daniel Conoly, b. in the Isle of Islay, Scotland, who m. Nancy (Ann) or Jane Campbell of the Isle of Islay.[113] I do not know the date of their emigration to North Carolina, but apparently they had been in upper Robeson County several years before their son James was b. at St. Pauls in 1798 (according to the family Bible of Cordelia Conoly) of their children, I have limited information only on three (order of birth is uncertain):

I. JAMES
II. WILLIAM
III. MALCOLM

I. JAMES CONOLY b. 1798 in St. Pauls, N.C., m. Mary Currie b. 1800 at Randallsville near present Antioch in Hoke County (dau. of Randall Currie and Nellie Johnson—see Currie section of this volume). Of their children I have information only on two:

A. Henry James Conoly b. 1826 in Robeson County, m. Margaret Ann McPhaul (dau. of Malcolm McPhaul and Christian McArn) b. 1835, d. 1912. They and all of their children moved to Poulan, Georgia from 1882-1885. Their nine children were all born in Robeson County.[114]
B. George Burder Conoly b. 1832 at Lumber Bridge, N.C., m. Flora C. Currie (dau. of Angus R. Currie and Janie McLean) b. 1843 at Antioch, N.C.[115] In later years they lived in Red Springs, N.C. They had nine children.[116]

II. WILLIAM CONOLY b. 1803, d. 1854, m. Ann Patterson b. 1814, d. 1889 (dau. of Alexander Patterson I and his third wife Sarah Mathews (Mathis)).[117] According to research of Admiral Alex Patterson, William Conoly and Ann Patterson had:

A. John A. Conoly b. 1834, d. 1904, m. Sarah McNish Currie and had six children.[118]
B. William Scott Conoly b. 1836, d. 1919, m. Sarah Patterson Currie. They had six children.[119]
C. Sarah Caroline Conoly b. 1839, d. 1906, m. Simeon Carlyle b. 1831, d. 1904. They had two children.[120]
D. James Wallace Conoly b. 1840, d. 1922, m. Polly Ann Prevatt. Issue not known.
E. Ann Elizabeth Conoly b. 1845, d. 1919, m. William Joseph Prevatt, b. 1840, d. 1920. They had six children.[121]
F. Sidney Franklin Conoly b. 1847, m. Laura Tolar.

III. REV. MALCOLM CONOLY is mentioned by W.A. McLeod as having moved to Texas and having left descendants there, one of whom he names—Judge Graham Gillis, a grandson.[122]

Notes

1. Alex M. Patterson, *The Monroes of the Upper Cape Fear Valley* (Miami, Florida: McAskill Publ. Co., 1976).
2. Ibid., 19.
3. Listed in ibid., 21.
4. Traced in ibid., 58,59.
5. Traced in ibid., 63-66.
6. Traced in ibid., 67-70.
7. Traced in ibid., 71-74.
8. Traced in ibid., 74-76.
9. Traced in ibid., 92, 93.
10. Traced in ibid., 93-96.
11. Traced in ibid., 96.
12. See Kenneth L. Kelly, op. cit., 234.
13. Patterson, op. cit., 98.
14. Traced in ibid., 99.
15. Traced in ibid., 99-101.
16. Traced in ibid., 101-111.
17. Traced in ibid., 111-114.
18. Traced in ibid., 114-118.
19. Traced in ibid., 118-121.
20. Traced in ibid., 122, 123.
21. Listed in ibid., 22.
22. Ibid., 24, 25.
23. Ibid., 26.
24. Ibid., 26-29.
25. Ibid., 30, 31.
26. Traced in ibid., 31-35.
27. Traced in ibid., 35, 36.
28. Ibid., 36.
29. Listed in ibid.
30. Two of them are listed in ibid.
31. Ibid., 37, 38.
32. Ibid., 39-41, 44.
33. Ibid. 40.
34. Ibid.
35. Ibid.
36. Ibid.
37. Ibid., 41.
38. Ibid.
39. Ibid.

40. Ibid.
41. Traced in ibid., 41, 42.
42. Traced in ibid., 43, 44.
43. Traced in ibid., 46.
44. Traced in ibid.
45. Traced in ibid., 48.
46. Ibid., 49.
47. Ibid.
48. Traced in ibid., 49, 50.
49. See ibid., 50, 51 for discussion.
50. Ibid., 51.
51. See ibid. for discussion of their possible movements.
52. See ibid. for names.
53. Listed in ibid.
54. Listed in ibid., 52.
55. Listed in ibid., 52, 53.
56. Traced in ibid., 53-55.
57. E.F. Smith, op. cit., 220.
58. Ibid.
59. D.F. Kelly, op. cit., 276-278, 281-286.
60. Smith, op. cit., 220-238.
61. Ibid., 220-222.
62. Ibid., 223-231.
63. Ibid., 231-238.
64. Ibid. 238.
65. Listed in ibid.
66. Flora's tombstone in the old McEachern cemetery six miles south of Raeford states that she was born in Kintyre ("Cantyre"), according to William Angus McLeod, *The Curries and Their Kin,* 4.
67. W.A. McLeod, op. cit., 2, 4.
68. Ibid., 9-20.
69. Traced in ibid., 13-15.
70. Traced in ibid., 16.
71. Traced in ibid., 17.
72. Traced in ibid., 19, 20.
73. Traced in ibid., 22-36.
74. Traced in ibid., 23.
75. Traced in ibid., 24, 25.
76. Traced in ibid., 26, 27.
77. Traced in ibid., 28-31.
78. Traced in ibid., 32-35.
79. Traced in ibid., 36.
80. Traced in ibid., 37-38.
81. Traced in ibid., 39, 40.
82. Traced in ibid., 41-44.
83. Traced in ibid., 45.

84. *McPhaul* by John H. McPhaul and John A. McPhaul (1959), 3.
85. Ibid., 2, 3.
86. Listed in ibid., 9.
87. Listed in ibid.
88. Listed in ibid.
89. Listed in ibid., 9, 10.
90. Listed in ibid., 10.
91. Listed in ibid.
92. Listed in ibid., 10, 11.
93. Listed in ibid., 11.
94. Listed in ibid.
95. Listed in ibid., 11, 12.
96. Listed in ibid., 12.
97. Listed in ibid.
98. No further information on any of these in ibid.
99. Extracts are given in J.E. Purcell, op. cit., 312, 313.
100. Traced in ibid., 313-321.
101. Traced in ibid., 321, 322.
102. Traced in ibid., 322-326.
103. Traced in ibid., 326-335.
104. Ibid., 526.
105. Traced in ibid., 526-547.
106. Ibid., 548.
107. Traced in ibid., 549-561.
108. Ibid., 562 and McPhaul, op. cit., 16.
109. Traced in ibid. (without dates), 562-566.
110. Listed in McPhaul, op. cit., 16.
111. Listed in ibid.
112. W.A. McLeod, op. cit., 41.
113. This information from the Bible of Cordelia Conoly, bearing the date Nov. 17, 1910.
114. Traced in J.E. Purcell, op. cit., 549-557.
115. This information from the Bible of C. Conoly.
116. Traced in W.A. McLeod, op. cit., 41-44.
117. This line is mentioned in Isabel C. Patterson, *Builders of Freedom,* 38 and is traced more fully in Alex M. Patterson, *Highland Scots Pattersons,* 433, 434.
118. Traced in Patterson, op. cit., 433, 434.
119. Listed in ibid., 434.
120. Listed in ibid.
121. Traced in ibid.
122. W.A. McLeod, op. cit., 41.

9

Families of the Longstreet Church Area of Cumberland County

McFadyen Family

THE MCFADYEN FAMILY ORIGINALLY SETTLED in what is now the Fort Bragg Reservation of Cumberland County, near Longstreet Presbyterian Church, but in later years many of them spread over into present Hoke County in the general direction of the last few families we have considered. Most of my information on this numerous family comes from a thirteen page typed manuscript, sent to me by Mr. and Mrs. D.B. McFadyen of Raeford, N.C. Unless I state otherwise, it can be assumed that all names, places and dates come from this paper on the McFadyen family.

The head of this family was Archibald McFadyen, son of Daniel McFadyen, b. 1754 on the Isle of Islay, Scotland. He landed at Wilmington, N.C., 1785, and settled in Cumberland on what came to be called

The ruins of this medieval church in the Isle of Islay shows (to the right of the building) the perfectly preserved 8th century Kildalton Celtic Cross. Tombstones around this old church bear the names of many of the families who emigrated to Cumberland County, N.C.: McFayden, McEachern and Gillis, as well as others.

McFadyen Springs. He was a fuller and made hats. He m. first in1790 Mary Buie (dau. of Archie and Catherine Shaw Buie) d. 1800, and secondly in 1806 Nancy McNeill (dau. of James McNeill), d. 1825. He and his two wives are buried beside each other at Longstreet Church.

By his first wife he had:

I.	DANIEL	VII.	ISABELLA
II.	JOHN	VIII.	NEILL
III.	ARCHIE BUIE	IX.	ELIZABETH
IV	FLORA	X.	MARY ANN
V.	CATHERINE	XI.	DOUGALD
VI.	JAMES		

I. DANIEL MCFADYEN b. 1791, m. 1829 (according to Monroe Bride Index in Cumberland County) Effie Monroe. He is buried near Manchester. No further information.

II. JOHN MCFADYEN b. 1794, no further information.

III. ARCHIE BUIE MCFADYEN b. 1795, m. Christian McNeill of the Bridge McNeill family (see that section in this volume) b. 1810, d. 1889, buried at Big Rockfish Presbyterian Church Cemetery. The descendants of their grandson, William M. McFadyen and wife, Lena Blue of Raeford, N.C., are traced by Alex Patterson.[1]

IV. FLORA MCFADYEN b. 1797, d. 1851 in Alabama, m. Daniel Monroe Turner.

V. CATHERINE MCFADYEN b. 1799, m. Daniel Monroe, buried at Longstreet in Cumberland County.

By his second wife he had:
VI. JAMES MCFADYEN b. 1807, d. 1811

VII. ISABELLA MCFADYEN b. 1809, d. 1872, m. Archibald Cameron, buried at Cypress Presbyterian Church. Their ten children are traced under the Merchant John Cameron family of this volume, in the section on John Cameron and Pollie Johnson, pp. 213-215.

VIII. NEILL MCFADYEN b. 1814, m. Mary Jane Bethune (dau. of Lauchlin Bethune and Annie Patterson), buried in the McFadyen Cemetery in Hoke County, N.C. Alex Patterson states that they had ten children, whose names were unknown to him.[2] The McFadyen history names one of them as Mary Eliza McFadyen.[3]

IX. ELIZABETH MCFADYEN b. 1816, m. ___ McBryde and went to San Antonio, Texas.

X. MARY ANN MCFADYEN b. 1818, m. Dr. Duncan McBryde and went to Arkansas or Texas.

XI. DOUGALD MCFADYEN b. 1821, d. 1892, m. 1860 Annie Black Lindsay, born mid-ocean, May 16, 1839 en route to Wilmington, N.C., from the Isle of Islay (dau. of John Lindsay and Mary Black). Annie d. 1925. Dougald was a teacher at Montrose and at Longstreet Schools and was also a farmer and deacon in Longstreet Presbyterian Church. They had eleven children:

A. John Fleetwood McFadyen b. 1861, d. 1937, buried at Raeford, m. first Urzula Howard d. 1910, and secondly Mary Parker d. 1943. They had ten children who are traced in the McFadyen history.[4]

B. Daniel Graham McFadyen b. 1862, d. 1927, m. Sarah Jane Cameron (dau. of Daniel Edward and Margaret McLeod Cameron) d. 1949. Both are buried in Cypress Church Cemetery. They had six children.[5]

C. Archie Buie McFadyen b. 1864, d. 1936, m. Jennie McDiarmid (dau. of Archibald and Catherine McArthur McDiarmid) d. 1950, buried at Raeford. They had seven children.[6]

D. Catherine Ann McFadyen b. 1866, m. Charles Hugh Graham and lived in the Fayetteville area. They had five children.[7]

E. Neill Lindsay McFadyen b. 1868, d. 1947, m. Annie Laurie McDougal b. 1870, d. 1926 (dau. of Dr. Alexander McDougal and Harriet Newell Graham).[8] They are buried at McPherson Presbyterian Church, Fayetteville, N.C. Their five children are traced by J.E. Purcell in more detail than in the McFadyen history.[9]

F. James Vance McFadyen b. 1870, d. 1935, buried at Cross Creek Cemetery in Fayetteville, was single.

G. Duncan Black McFadyen b. 1873, d. 1948, m. Jessie Stubbs (dau. of Angus Priest Stubbs and Isabel Bullock) d. 1942. Both are buried in Raeford Cemetery. They had ten children.[10]

H. Mary Isabella McFadyen b. 1874, d. 1953, was single and is buried at Cross Creek Cemetery in Fayetteville.

I. Elizabeth Jane McFadyen b. 1876, d. 1917 m. Neill D.M. Clark (son of Neill Alexander and Margaret McNeill Clark) d. 1945. Both are buried at Cross Creek Cemetery in Fayetteville. They had ten children.[11]

J. Effie Turner McFadyen b. 1879, d. 1950, m. Alex A. McDiarmid (son of Archibald and Catherine McArthur McDiarmid) d. 1969. Both are buried at LaFayette Cemetery, Fayetteville. They had eight children.[12]

K. Dougald Alexander Stephens McFadyen b. 1883, d. 1950, buried at Cypress Church, m. Fannie Stewart (dau. of Neill Stewart and Sarah Catherine Morrison) b. 1896. They lived near Lobelia, N.C., and had three children, whose descendants are traced in *Scottish Blue Family.*[13]

Lindsay Family

Another family in the Longstreet area, which like the McFadyens

tended to move over into Hoke County was that of the Lindsays. This family was apparently one of the very last to emigrate to the upper Cape Fear, not coming until 1839, exactly a century after the arrival of the first Argyll Colony. My information on them mainly comes from the previously quoted McFadyen history (into which family some of them married), plus some material from Admiral Patterson's two volumes and Major-General Roderick L. Carmichael's *The Scottish Highlander Carmichaels of the Carolinas,* as will be indicated.[14]

According to the McFadyen history, John Lindsay m. Mary Black on the Isle of Islay in Scotland. They emigrated to the upper Cape Fear in 1839, during which voyage their daughter, Annie Black was born.[15] They settled near Longstreet Presbyterian Church section of Cumberland County. Their children:

I.	ANNIE BLACK	VI.	NEILL
II.	KATIE	VII.	ISABELLA
III.	SALLIE	VIII.	JENET
IV.	DUNCAN	IX.	MARY
V.	ARCHIE		

I. ANNIE BLACK LINDSAY b. mid-ocean May 16, 1839, d. 1925, m. Dougald McFadyen 1860. Their children are traced under the previous McFadyen section, p. 305.

II. KATIE LINDSAY m. ____ Blue and was buried at Bethel Presbyterian Church near Raeford. No further information in the McFadyen history.

III. SALLIE (SARAH) LINDSAY b. 1850 in Cumberland County, d. 1910 in Cumberland, m. Alexander Leslie b. 1849 in Cumberland and d. 1932 in Hoke County. Both are buried at Galatia Presbyterian Church. They lived many years in Seventy-First Township of Cumberland County, where he was superintendent of the County Home, and later moved to Rockfish community where he farmed. They joined Galatia Presbyterian Church. This family is traced by Alex M. Patterson.[16] They had:

A. Mary Black Leslie b. 1872, d. 1935, m. John Archie Campbell b. 1857, d. 1923 (his second wife). They lived near Raeford, N.C., where he was a farmer and are buried at old Sandy Grove Presbyterian Church on the Fort Bragg Reservation. Her children are traced by Patterson.[17]

B. Flora Scott Leslie b. 1876, d. 1903 in Cumberland County, m. John Archie Campbell (same as above). She was his first wife.

She is buried at Sandy Grove. They had four children.[18]

C. Sallie Isabel Leslie b. 1876, d. 1955 in Cumberland, m. John David Burton, b. 1869, d. 1951 in Cumberland. They lived near Galatia Presbyterian Church and are buried at LaFayette Cemetery in Fayetteville. Patterson notes that since Flora and Sallie Leslie are both listed as b. 1876, there must be an error.[19] They had eight children.[20]

D. Emily Florence Leslie b. 1878, d. 1949 in Cumberland, m. _____ Johnson (his second wife). They lived in Raleigh, Dunn and elsewhere. She is buried at Galatia Church. No children.

E. Ida Cornelia Leslie b. 1880, d. 1963 in Cumberland, m. Kenneth Herbert Monroe b. 1877, d. 1946 in Cumberland (son of John Alexander and Amanda McKeithan Monroe). He was superintendant of the Cumberland County home for the indigent. They are buried at Cross Creek Cemetery in Fayetteville. They had seven children.[21]

F. Daniel Alexander Leslie believed to have lived in Florida and to have been married. No information was known to Admiral Patterson.

G. Nettie Lee Leslie b. 1888, d. 1911, was single, d. in N.C. State Tuberculosis Sanatorium at McCain, N.C., buried at Galatia.

H. John Thomas Leslie b. 1892, d. 1922 in Cumberland County, was single. He was a veteran of World War I and is buried at Galatia.

I. Annie May Leslie b. 1893, d. 1904 in Cumberland, buried in Sandy Grove Cemetery.

IV. DUNCAN LINDSAY m. ____ Love. No more information.

V. ARCHIBALD LINDSAY m. Flora McDougald. According to Alex Patterson, they moved for a time to Chesterfield, South Carolina.[22] Of their children, I have information only on one:

A. John Duncan Black Lindsay, who according to Rozella McLeod, was b. 1866, d. 1933, m. 1896 Florence Cameron (dau. of Daniel and Margaret McLeod Cameron) b. 1877, d. 1920.[23] According to Patterson, John Duncan and family lived briefly in Arkansas, where he was killed in a sawmill accident.[24] Their six children are traced by Rozella McLeod.[25]

VI. NEILL LINDSAY m. Mary Jane Carmichael, who—according to

Roderick L. Carmichael—was b. 1835, d. 1920 (dau. of John B. Carmichael and Nancy Carmichael Carmichael, who lived first in South Carolina, and later in Rockfish, N.C., in Cumberland County, where their children were reared).[26] They had six children.

A. Dougald Lindsay b. 1869, m. first Ann Wintz, and secondly Schelpt Johnson. They lived at Jacksonville, Florida. No children.[27]
B. Gilbert Lindsay b. 1871, m. 1906 Jane King. They lived in Perkinstone, Mississippi and had eight children.[28]
C. Kate Lindsay b. 1872, m. 1901 James Walter Townsend. They lived at Rockfish, N.C., and had six children.[29]
D. Alexander Lindsay b. 1875, m. 1911 Marjorie Hammond. They lived at Rockfish, N.C., and had seven children.[30]
E. Calvin Lindsay b. 1878, m. 1916 Jean McGregor. They lived at St. Pauls, N.C., and had three children.[31]
F. Mary Portia Lindsay b. 1881, m. 1919 Frank Bethea. They lived at Rockfish, N.C., and had no children.

VII. ISABELLA LINDSAY m. John Holt. According to the McFadyen history, they lived in Galatia community and then moved to Durham. They are buried at Galatia.[32]

VIII. JENET LINDSAY m. Neil Ray. They lived in Cumberland County and are buried at Galatia.

IX. MARY LINDSAY m. _____ McLean. They lived in Harnett County and had no children.[33]

Gillis Family

The Gillis family lived in the same general area as the McFadyens and Lindsays, in western Cumberland County and in present day Hoke County, where many of their descendants still live. Clayton G. Metcalf has included a section on the genealogy of this part of the Gillis clan in *The Gillis Family in the South.* Most of my information comes directly from that source, as will be indicated.

The head of the Cumberland County Gillis family was John Gillis, who was born in Scotland, and came to North Carolina about 1783-85. He settled in what is now Hoke County on Cabin Branch, just off Rockfish Creek, and thus his family has been known as "the Cabin Branch Gillises." According to Metcalf, John Gillis had been a soldier in the British Army before coming to America. His wife is said to have had the maiden name of Black.[34]

They had six known children:

I. COLONEL RODERICK D. GILLIS b. c. 1783, Scotland, d. Mar. 29, 1872, buried near the Turnpike Bridge in Hoke County, N.C. He was m. three times; first, to Mary Patterson, dau. of "Buffalo" Daniel Patterson and Margaret Graham. They had:

A. Flora Ann Gillis m. Daniel Leslie and had two children, listed in Metcalf.[35] See also the Patterson family in this volume, p. 203.

B. Margaret Gillis m. _____ Johnson and moved to Florida and had children.

Secondly, Roderick Gillis m. Margaret Graham, dau. of Squire Alex Graham and Margaret McFarland. They had two children:

C. John Alexander Gillis m. Catherine J. Blue, dau. of Neill McK. Blue and Elizabeth T. Smith. Their children are traced in Kelly's *Scottish Blue Family.*[36]

D. Mary Gillis m. a widower—McLeod, and d. within a year of their marriage.

Thirdly, Roderick Gillis m. Nancy Campbell by whom he had eight children:

E. Duncan J. Gillis b. Oct. 8, 1848, d. Feb. 18, 1933; was single. He served as an officer in Sandy Grove Presbyterian Church in Cumberland County, N.C.

F. Murdock A. Gillis m. Mary (Mollie) Clark from near Fayetteville, N.C., sister of Sandy and Neal Clark. They moved from Sandy Grove to Raeford, N.C., and had six children, who are listed in Metcalf.[37] Some of their descendants are also traced in Kelly's *Scottish Blue Family.*[38]

G. Neill Whitfield Gillis b. Jan. 25, 1852, d. Jan. 13, 1933, m. Dec. 9, 1896 Isabella McNeill, dau. of Lauchlin McNeill and Margaret Ann Hughes. Their six daughters and one son are traced in Metcalf.[39]

H. Evander Gillis b. May 6, 1860, d. June 5, 1892.

I. Roderick A. Gillis b. Oct. 20, 1853, d. Apr. 16, 1932, m. Flora Blue b. Nov. 25, 1867, d. Aug. 25, 1898, and had one son, Jasper Gillis, who d. young.

J. Malcolm Gillis b. June 16, 1859, d. Feb. 8, 1937; was single.

K. Jonathan Gillis b. Oct. 6, 1855, d. Nov. 23, 1921; was single.

L. Sarah (Sallie) Jane Gillis b. Nov. 19, 1862, d. Apr. 22, 1900; was single.

II. DANIEL GILLIS m. Catherine McKinney b. 1824, N.C. They moved to Bullock County, Alabama. They had three sons:

A. John Gillis; no information.

B. William Andrew Gillis b. May 25, 1854, d. Nov. 7, 1900, buried at Inverness, Ala. He m. Flora Ann Elizabeth McMillan b. Sept. 27, 1854 at Inverness, AL., d. Oct. 20, 1920, Selma, AL. Their eight children are listed in Metcalf.[40]

C. Martin Columbus Gillis b. June 5, 1858, m. first Martha (Mattie) V. Norris by whom he had four children who are listed in Metcalf, and secondly m. Alice Viola Hall by whom he had three children, also listed in Metcalf, and thirdly m. Matilda Hall by whom he had three children, listed in Metcalf.[41]

III. MURDOCK GILLIS no information.

IV. JOHN GILLIS no definite information, though he may have bought land in Pike County, AL., in 1835 and 36.[42]

V. MARY GILLIS ("POLLY") was single and remained at her parents' homeplace in Cumberland County, N.C.

VI. JANET GILLIS was single and lived at her parents' homeplace.

McInnis Family

Another family which spread from the Longstreet Church section of Cumberland County to present Hoke County was the McInnis clan. My information on them is taken directly from a paper written by N. McInnis from the 1930 Reunion of the McInnis Clan at Mr. J.C. Campbell's, near Raeford, N.C. This paper was recopied by Mary N. Doggett of Greensboro, N.C., in 1952 and was given to me with handwritten notations added by Mrs. Lee McCaskill of Eureka Community in Moore County, N.C.

The head of this family was Angus McInnis, b. Feb. 15, 1785, near Inverlussa, Isle of Jura. His first wife was Mary Shaw of Jura. He was a sailor until he left Scotland for America sometime between 1815 and 1820. Angus McInnis emigrated with his wife and three children: Duncan, Isabel and John. They were accompanied by his wife's sister, Flora Shaw.

They came first to Quebec, then to New York, and thence by ship to Wilmington, N.C., and on up river to Fayetteville. Angus McInnis purchased land one mile west of Fayetteville and there farmed and raised his children. By his first wife he had five children:

I.	DUNCAN	IV.	FLORA
II.	ARCHIBALD	V.	JOHN
III.	ISABEL		

After his first wife's death, Angus m. Margaret McEachern of near St. Paul's in Robeson County, N.C. She d. Nov. 22, 1873, aged 76. They had six children:

VI.	ANNIE	IX.	DANIEL
VII.	NEILL	X.	ANGUS
VIII.	MALCOLM	XI.	JAMES

I. DUNCAN MCINNIS m. and lived in Robeson County, N.C.

II. ARCHIE MCINNIS m. and lived in Marlboro County, S.C.

III. ISABEL MCINNIS m. Sandy Johnson and lived in Robeson County, N.C.

IV. FLORA MCINNIS was single and lived with her brother, Archie in Marlboro County, S.C.

V. JOHN MCINNIS lived in Robeson County, N.C., m. first Ruth Ann McMillan b. 1823, d. 1859 by whom he had:

A. John Frank	C. Ellen
B. Mary Elizabeth	D. Florence

John m. secondly Eliza Livingston, by whom he had:

E. Harriette	G. Julia Isabel
F. Charlie	H. (hard to decipher: Sarah?)

VI. ANNIE MCINNIS b. Nov. 13, 1828, m. Lod Gillis and lived in (present) Hoke County, d. Mar. 1, l907. They had several children (not listed in the McInnis paper).

VII. NEILL MCINNIS b. Feb. 18, 1830, served in the War Between the States at the Arsenal in Fayetteville, N.C. He m. a Miss McDougald, by whom he had one daughter, Neallie, who was b. after his death on Sept. 18, 1865.

VIII. MALCOLM MCINNIS b. Mar. 12, 1832, served at the Arsenal also. He m. Sarah Shaw McPhail and lived in Cumberland County, N.C. After his wife's death, he and two of his sons, a daughter and son-in-law moved to Alabama, where he d. Sept. 5, 1899.

IX. DANIEL MCINNIS b. May 4, 1834, m. Mar. 5, 1868 Ann Catherine

McFadyen, daughter of Neill McFadyen, b. Mar. 2, 1846. This family lived on the old Angus McInnis homestead in Cumberland County, where Daniel d. Dec. 10, 1886, leaving his wife with six sons and one daughter (not listed in the McInnis paper).

X. ANGUS MCINNIS b. Apr. 22, 1836, served with the Confederate Army until he fell in battle at Gain's Mill near Richmond, Va. on June 26, 1862. He is buried at Galatia Presbyterian Church, Cumberland County, N.C.

XI. JAMES MCINNIS b. Mar. 15, 1838, d. Apr. 9, 1840, buried at Galatia Church.

McDiarmid Family

Another family of this same East Cumberland and Hoke County region is that of William McLeod McDiarmid, b. in Isle of Islay, Scotland in 1797 and d. Oct. 16, 1877 in Cumberland (now Hoke) County, buried in McDiarmid Family Cemetery. His wife was Elizabeth A. McKinnon b. Oct. 23, 1807 in Scotland and d. July 12, 1855 in present Hoke County. My information on this family is limited to material extracted from the John Currie McLean Family Bible by Harold McDiarmid, originally of Raeford, N.C., now of Jackson, Mississippi. It is as follows.

The children of William and Elizabeth McDiarmid (all b. in Cumberland, now Hoke County, N.C.):

I. CATHERINE A. MCDIARMID b. Mar. 22, 1825, d. Feb. 14, 1885, m. John Peterson.

II. EFFIE MCDIARMID b. 1826, d. Apr. 12, 1900, m. John McNair McNeill.

III. MARTHA JANE MCDIARMID b. May 24, 1830, d. Nov. 22, 1900, m. John Currie McLean.

IV. CHRISTIAN E. MCDIARMID b. Dec. 14, 1834, d. May 15, 1891, m. Duncan Keith.

V. DAVID ALEXANDER MCDIARMID b. Apr. 8, 1840, d. May 2, 1891, m. Oct. 17, 1867 Mollie E. Bostick of Richmond County, N.C.

VI. DANIEL A. MCDIARMID b. Dec. 22, 1846 (twin) d. Oct. 19, 1848.

VII. MARGARET R. MCDIARMID b. Dec. 22, 1846 (twin) d. Aug. 23, 1847.

VIII. SCOTT MCDIARMID, Presbyterian minister, founder of "The Robesonian" Newspaper of Lumberton, N.C. Drowned in Lumber River.

IX. WALLACE MCDIARMID, Editor of "The Robesonian."

X. CALVIN MCDIARMID, Medical Doctor, moved to Alabama.

XI. WILLIAM MCDIARMID

XII. INFANT DAUGHTER b. and d. 1848.

McRackan Family of Fayetteville, North Carolina

Most of the Highland families we have covered in Cumberland County have generally been located in the outlying rural areas, as would be expected in an agrarian economy. But there were a number of Scots in the town of Fayetteville itself, and one of these families was the McRackans. Their history has been compiled and carefully documented by Ada McRackan Allen in *James McRackan and His Descendants* (privately published for the family c. 1983). All of my information comes directly from this source.

The head of this family was James McRackan of Galloway, Scotland, who with his wife, Margaret and their two oldest children emigrated to North Carolina between 1775-78. The U. S. Census of 1790 gave James McRackan as the head of the household, which was made up of seven persons and one slave. A slip of paper which James carried in his wallet (presently in the possession of Ada Allen) gives the ages of James and Margaret McRackan's children. Their children:

I. JAMES MCRACKAN Jr., b. in Galloway, Dec. 6, 1773, and d. in Fayetteville, N.C., Oct. 26, 1812, and is buried in Old Cross Creek Cemetery in Fayetteville. He m. on Nov. 14, 1812, Marianne Wingate in Fayetteville, b. Dec. 1782, d. July 10, 1822, also buried at Old Cross Creek. James was a merchant in Fayetteville, and his family were members of the First Presbyterian Church there. Their four children are traced by Mrs. Allen:

A. James McRackan b. July 24, 1804, d. July 25, 1814, buried at Old Cross Creek.
B. Robert Maxwell McRackan b. Oct. 31, 1806 in Fayetteville, and d. Feb. 12, 1883 in Columbus County, N.C., and is

buried in the Western Prong Cemetery. He was educated in Connecticut and was a well known scholar. He built a school in Columbus County and represented his county in the N.C. Legislature in 1836. He was married four times: (l) to Sarah Ann Baker b. Apr. 14, 1807, d. Mar. 20, 1836, by whom he had four children; (2) to Mariah Marsh Ward b. July 22, 1808, d. Sept. 11, 1839, by whom he had two children; (3) to Emily Helen Shipman b. Jan. 9, 1822, d. Apr. 20, 1853, by whom he had three children; (4) to Mary McMillan Kelly Toon b. Apr. 10, 1818, d. Apr. 7, 1884, by whom he had three children. All of these are traced by Ada Allen in the volume on the McRackans.

C. Ann Elizabeth McRackan, m. a Judge Jordan and moved to Arkansas.

D. William Wallace McRackan b. June 19, 1811, d. Aug. 15, 1832 at his brother's home at Smithville in Brunswick County. He was single.

II. ROBERT MCRACKAN b. in Scotland May 8, 1775, and d. Fayetteville, May 15, 1819. He was single.

III. THOMAS MCRACKAN b. Sept. 13, 1781; was single.

IV. ELIZABETH MCRACKAN m. a McPherson; no further information.

Notes

1. Patterson, *The Monroes,* 31.
2. Patterson, *Highland Scots Pattersons,* 425.
3. p. 1.
4. p. 4.
5. Traced in McFadyen history, p. 5.
6. Traced in ibid., 6.
7. Traced in ibid., 7.
8. Her dates are taken from Purcell, op. cit., 129.
9. Purcell, op. cit., 129, 130, and McFadyen history, 8.
10. Listed in McFadyen history, 9.
11. Traced in ibid., 10.
12. Listed in ibid., 11.
13. D.F. Kelly, op. cit., 843-845.
14. Printed privately in 1935 and reprinted in 1978 by The R. L. Bryan Co.: Columbia, S.C.
15. McFadyen history, 2.

16. In *Highland Scots Pattersons,* chapter 22.
17. Traced in ibid., 394-396.
18. Traced in ibid., 396, 397.
19. Ibid., 398.
20. Traced in ibid., 398-404.
21. Traced in ibid., 404-407.
22. Patterson, *The Monroes,* 58.
23. In her *McLeods of Tuckahoe & Horses Creek,* 54.
24. Patterson, op. cit., 58.
25. McLeod, op. cit., 54-58.
26. Roderick L. Carmichael, *The Scottish Highlander Carmichaels of the Carolinas,* 115, 116.
27. Ibid., 116.
28. Listed in ibid., 117.
29. Traced in ibid., 117, 118.
30. Listed in ibid., 117.
31. Listed in ibid.
32. McFadyen history, 2.
33. Ibid.
34. Clayton Metcalf, *The Gillis Family in the South* (Enterprise, Ala., 1975), 334.
35. Ibid., 335.
36. Douglas Kelly, *Scottish Blue Family,* 748-750.
37. Metcalf, op. cit., 336.
38. Douglas Kelly, op. cit., 834-838.
39. Metcalf, op. cit., 337.
40. Ibid., 338, 339.
41. Ibid., 339.
42. Ibid.

10

Families of Upper Robeson and Scotland [Richmond] Counties

We must move somewhat south and east of Cumberland and Hoke Counties to the neighboring vicinity of Robeson and Scotland (formerly part of Richmond) Counties. These counties were also heavily populated by Highland Scots, though there was a good mixture of English and others, especially as the nineteenth century wore on. We will look at several of these Scots families.

It is appropriate here to refer to some helpful articles on the Highland Scots composition of the Robeson County population in *The Robeson County Register,* edited in Charlotte, North Carolina by Dr. Morris F. Britt. In an article dealing with the 1850 Census of Robeson County, Dr. Britt notes that, " . . . the largest ethnic group reported themselves as natives of Scotland . . . ." Among those forty-eight names listing Scotland as their birth place were the following:

Black, Blue, Brown, Campbell, Chisholm, Currie, Evans, Frasier,

Galbreath, Gilchrist, Graham, Gunn, Harrison, Johnson, Lamont, Leach, Livingston, McArthur, McBryde, McDonald, McDougald, McDuffie, McGill, McGoogan, McInnis, McIntyre, McKay, McLauchlin, McLean, McLeod, McNair, McNeill, McPhatter, McPhaul, McQueen, McRae, McRainey, McRimmon, Molloy, Monroe, Patterson, Ross, Shaw, Smith, Saintclair [Sinclair], Sullivan, Walker, and Wilkinson.

> Generally those of Scottish descent settled primarily in the northern and western portions of Robeson, those areas covered in the northern district of the 1850 census. They also found thick settlements of 'Macs' in contiguous portions of present Richmond, Hoke, Harnett, Cumberland, Bladen and Moore Counties.[1]

Lists of Robeson County family surnames for which some type of history is preserved in the Hoyland Livermore Jennings Genealogy Room of the Robeson County Public Library of Lumberton, North Carolina, are found in *The Robeson County Register,* Vol. I, No. 1, 5-13 (Kate Britt Biggs Collection) and Ibid., 27, 28 (Henry Hodgin Cabinet). Further material on "Family and Individual Histories" is found in the same publication, Vol. I, No. 2, May, 1986, 50-53 (Genealogical Manuscripts and Books, Genealogy Filing Cabinet, Robeson County Library).

Another useful resource for some of the Highland families of upper Robeson is found in *Argyll Colony Plus,* Vol. 2, No. 2, Spring 1987, 57-63, "Early Elders of St. Paul's Presbyterian Church, Robeson County, North Carolina." These sketches were written in 1899 by John Daniel McGeachy, and include information on: Duncan McNair, John Malloy, James Stevens, Thomas McMillan, Archibald Little, Duncan Crawford, Neill McAlpin, John Matthews, Alexander McGeachy, Jessie Jackson, Malcom McNair, Andrew Sinclair, John McNair, Neill McNeill, Neill McArthur, Archibald McDonald, Alexander Johnson, Duncan Campbell, John McKinnon, John Caldwell, Duncan Bethune, Duncan McNair (son of John, grandson of Duncan), Archie Malloy, Neill Ronald McGeachy, Daniel H. McMillan.

McNair Family

Branches of this family name were located both in the St. Paul's area of Robeson County, not far from the Cumberland County line, and also some thirty or so miles south and west near present Maxton (Robeson County) and present Laurinburg (now in Scotland County). Most of the published information on this family which I have seen deals with the St.

Paul's branch, and so we will make most of our reference here to that large group.

Various publications have dealt with these (and, in some cases, other) McNairs. Several pages of careful work were devoted to them in Jo White Linn's (C.G.) *Drake-Arrington, White-Turner, Linn-Brown And Two Dozen Related Southern Lines* (Privately Published: Salisbury, North Carolina, 1984), as did the much earlier work by Isabel C. Patterson, *Builders of Freedom and Their Descendants: A Genealogy of Related Families Whose Ancestors Were Champions of liberty And Among The Early Settlers of America.* Another, more general and rather less valuable work was *McNair, McNeer and McNeir Genealogies,* which seems to have been put out in several supplements (Chicago, 1923; Chicago, 1929; Los Angeles, 1955). Also James A. Sinclair of Fayetteville, N.C., carefully copied out five pages of material from "a ledger book of family records of Misses Louise and Reva McGoogan of Shannon, N.C., on March 25, 1967." This material, to which I have access, contains much documented information not only on the McNairs, but also on McGoogans, Graham, Patterson, Smylie, McNeill and McMillan.

Unless otherwise stated, all of the genealogical information I shall mention here is directly taken from Jo White Linn's work (pp. 415-427).

Duncan McNair, a native of Kintyre in Argyllshire, m. Catherine McCallum. They emigrated from Kintyre to America in 1786, and settled in Robeson County, near St. Paul's. Duncan was the first ruling elder at the Presbyterian Church in St. Paul's, and d. Sept. l, 1801. He and his wife are buried in the McNair Cemetery, McAlpine Grove near St. Paul's.[2] They had seven children:

I. JOHN MCNAIR of St. Paul's, N.C., b. Jan. 1, 1786, d. May 1, 1873, m. Polly Graham b. Apr. 5, 1787, d. Aug. 6, 1872. They had ten children and are buried at St. Paul's Presbyterian Church.

II. MALCOLM MCNAIR, b. c. 1787, d. Sept. 9, 1823, buried at McAlpine Grove with his parents. He m. Margaret Dalrymple, daughter of Col. Archibald Dalrymple of Moore County (listed in the Dalrymple section of this book, pp. 240-41). They had four children traced by Jo White Linn.[3]

III. ROBERT MCNAIR, b. c. 1790, d. before 1850, m. first Prudence Dalrymple, daughter of Col. Archibald Dalrymple. She d. Sept. 25, 1817, age 25. Robert m. secondly, Betsey Patterson of Robeson County, N.C., and lived some five miles from Red Springs, N.C. Betsey was the daughter of

Alexander Patterson and Margaret McLaughlin, his second wife. They had five sons. According to Jo White Linn, "One of their descendants, James McNair of Columbia, S.C., was a governor of S.C."[4]

IV. MARY MCNAIR b. c. 1792, d. 1875, m. Neill McArthur of Cumberland County. They had seven children.

V. ISOBELLE MCNAIR, d. young.

VI. KATHERINE MCNAIR b. 1797, d. Nov. 3, 1865, m. Aug. 20, 1818 Neill McGeachy, b. 1793, d. Nov. 12, 1861, son of Alexander and Sarah (McCoulsky) McGeachy, who lived near Brown Marsh Church in Bladen County, N.C. They had twelve children.[5]

VII. DUNCAN MCNAIR b. Sept. 25, 1800, d. Sept. 21, 1831, buried McAlpine Grove, m. Dec. 24, 1825 Elizabeth McNair, dtr. of Roderick and Mary McGill McNair. Three sons. [6]

McNair Family of Scotland County

I do not know what, if any, was the relationship between the St. Paul's and Scotland County McNairs, nor did Jo White Linn know it.[7] The papers of Misses Reva and Louise McGoogan (as copied by J.A. Sinclair) include some information on this branch of the McNairs, which I include here.[8]

John McNair, according to Jo White Linn[9], b. 1735 in Argyllshire, Scotland, and according to the Misses McGoogan papers, emigrated to North Carolina in 1770 with his son Roderick, then five years old, and a younger daughter, and settled in Robeson County.[10] He was an elder of Centre Presbyterian Church. According to the McGoogan papers, John McNair was b. in Kilkenney Parish of Argyll, the youngest son of Neil and Sallie McNair.[11] A brief article in *The Robeson County Register*, Vol. I, No. 3, August 1986, includes useful information on both the Scottish ancestry and Carolina descendants of John McNair, and particularly of his son, Rev. Malcolm McNair.[12]

According to these papers, John first married Jennet Smylie, who d. 1769, before he came to America. They had three children:

I. RODERICK MCNAIR b. 1764, d. 1839, m. Mary McGill. According to the McNair Family Bible (printed in1816, and owned in the 1960s by Rory McNair of near Maxton, N.C.), they had these children:

A. Neill McNair b. 1795
B. Jennet McNair b. 1797

C. Margaret McNair b. 1799, m. John Smith
D. Elizabeth McNair b. 1801, m. Duncan McNair son of Duncan and Catherine McCallum McNair (see above).
E. Mary McNair b. 1803, m. Neill McDonald
F. Sarah Ann McNair b. 1805
G. John McNair b. 1808, m. Anabelle McNair (dau. of Rev. Malcolm McNair)
H. Evander McNair b. 1811. He was a Presbyterian minister of Fayetteville Presbytery in North Carolina. He was minister of Bethesda, Longstreet and Cypress Churches, and later moved to Texas and Alabama. He was a chaplain in the Confederate Army.[13]

II. BETSEY MCNAIR b. 1766

III. NEILL MCNAIR b. 1768, d. 1769.

John McNair came to North Carolina in 1770, and m. secondly, Catherine Buie McFarland in 1772, dau. of John Buie McFarland of Dura, Scotland.[14] They had:

IV. SALLIE MCNAIR b. 1773, m. Peter Wilkinson and moved to Mississippi.

V. MALCOLM MCNAIR b. 1776, d. 1822. He was a Presbyterian minister, and served Ashpole, Center and Laurel Hill Churches (and other charges as well). He m. Jennett _____ in 1809. They had:
A. Eliza Jane McNair
B. Kate Buie McNair b. 1812, d. 1883, m. Archibald Sellers McKay
C. Murphy McNair b. 1818, d. 1881, graduated from Davidson College, m. Margaret Elizabeth Stubbs, b. 1830, dau. of Rev. Campbell Stubbs.
D. Howard Campbell McNair

McNair Family of Richmond County, North Carolina

Another family of McNairs lived in Richmond County, N.C., and attended Mineral Springs Presbyterian Church near Jackson Springs in Moore County, N.C. I do not know what, if any, may be the relationship between this and the other McNair families previously traced.

These Richmond County McNairs have been traced by Nancy McNair Yingling in *John and Nancy McFarland McNair of Richmond County,*

N.C., Vol. I in 1982.[15] According to her information:

John McNair was b. 1770 in North Carolina and Nancy McFarland, his wife, was b. in the late 1770s in North Carolina. They were members of Mineral Springs Presbyterian Church, and are listed in its Session Minutes, which have recently been copied. They had six children, who are traced by Mrs. Yingling:

I. ARCHIBALD MCNAIR b. c. 1808, d. 1840 in Mississippi. He m. Judith Ann Powell.

II. ISABEL MCNAIR b. c. 1814 in Richmond County, N.C., d. 1856 in North Carolina.

III. MARY MCNAIR d. young

IV. SARAH MCNAIR b. c. 1815, d. 1894 near Ellerbe, N.C. She m. 1841 Duncan McLean b. 1815, d. 1856.

V. NANCY (ANN) MCNAIR b. 1821, d. 1901 in Ellerbe, N.C.

VI. JOHN NELSON MCNAIR b. 1824, d. 1865 in Richmond, Va. He m. 1849 Clementine Love Baldwin.

McKinnon Family of St. Pauls Area of Robeson County

Some information is included in the work of Jo White Linn on the St. Paul's McKinnons, to which I make reference here. Dr. William C. Powell, a descendant of this family, who lives in Fayetteville, N.C., has done much work on this line as well as on that of the McNairs.[16]

Kenneth McKinnon, "the immigrant, father of John McKinnon, was b. 1760 in Scotland on the Isle of Skye and d. 25 Feb. 1848 in Robeson County, NC testate, leaving to his son John seven negroes. Catherine (Munn) McKinnon was b. 1762 in Scotland and d. 27 May 1844 in Robeson Co., N.C. They are buried at St. Pauls Churchyard. Catherine Munn's brother's tombstone at St. Pauls Church cemetery says he was born in Glasgow, Scotland. Neill McKinnon and children Hector, Kenneth, and John and perhaps others from Isle of Skye came c. 1772 to the Rockfish Creek area of Cumberland Co., N.C. Kenneth McKinnon moved in the early 1790's about 8-10 miles away to St. Pauls in Robeson Co., N.C."[17]

Kenneth and Catherine (Munn) McKinnon had:

I. ANNE MCKINNON b. Jan. 31, 1788, d. Aug. 11, 1845, m. c. 1810 Duncan Galbreath

II. MARY MCKINNON b. Oct. 30, 1789, single

III. MARGARET MCKINNON b. Nov. 18, 1791, m. a Wilkerson

IV. CATHERINE MCKINNON b. Nov. 18, 1793, d. c. 1881, m. William C. Bain

V. NEILL MCKINNON b. c. 1796, d. Mar. 5, 1860, m. 1818 Jennet Sinclair

VI. DANIEL L. MCKINNON b. Mar. 15, 1797, d. Feb. 7, 1865, m. Dec. 23, 1823 Flora McDonald McKinnon

VII. CHRISTIAN MCKINNON b. July 13, 1800, d. Mar. 13, 1886, m. Dec. 5, 1827 Duncan Campbell

VIII. ANGUS MCKINNON b. July 12, 1802, d. Dec. 31, 1852, m. Feb. 14, 1832 Jane C. McNeill

IX. JOHN MCKINNON b. Dec. 4, 1804, d. Oct. 26, 1866, m. Catherine Gaster McNair (dau. of Malcolm and Margaret Dalrymple McNair) b. 1814, d. Aug. 21, 1854. Their children are listed by Jo White Linn.[18]

X. HECTOR MCKINNON b. 1807, d. Feb. 19, 1846, m. Sept. 28, 1837 Margaret Graham Patterson (dau. of Archibald and Sallie McEachern Patterson) b. May 24, 1818, d. Sept. 3, 1901.

McKinnon Family of Richmond [now Scotland] County

A Sketch of this family was written by Angus C. McKinnon for the 1926 McKinnon Family Reunion in Maxton, N.C. A copy of it has been made available to me by Hon. Henry McKinnon of Lumberton, N.C. All of my information on this branch of the McKinnons comes directly from this Sketch. Judge Henry McKinnon is presently doing further research on this family.

The head of this family was Daniel McKinnon, a native of Kintyre in Scotland, who immigrated to America with his wife, Grace Currie, and their oldest son, Peter, about 1788 on the ship "Industry." They landed in Charleston, South Carolina, and went from there to Richmond County, North Carolina [now Scotland County]. They first lived on a farm which was later occupied by Mrs. Mary Ann Blue. A year later

Daniel McKinnon bought two tracts of land about two miles south of the first location, and moved his family there. A few years later he built another house on a sand hill near what is known as the "Duck Pond," where he lived until his death.

Daniel and Grace Currie McKinnon had six sons and six daughters. Only the first son was born in Scotland. Their children were:

I.	PETER	VII.	DANIEL
II.	CHRISTIAN	VIII.	MARGARET
III.	MARY	IX.	FLORA
IV.	KATIE	X.	ALEXANDER
V.	DUNCAN	XI.	JOHN
VI.	JEANNE	XII.	MURDOCK

I. PETER MCKINNON b. in Scotland sometime before 1788; no further information.

II. CHRISTIAN MCKINNON b. about 1788 during the voyage to America, about six days from land. She m. John McDonald Shaw Apr. 1, 1817 and had:

A. Angus Currie Shaw
B. Harriet Shaw (twin)
C. Sophronia Shaw (twin)
D. Francis Woodbury Shaw
E. Catherine McKay Shaw
F. Daniel Adams Shaw
G. Joseph Whitfield Shaw

III. MARY MCKINNON was single, d. 1868.

IV. CATHERINE (KATIE) MCKINNON m. Robert Murphy and had one daughter:

A. Catherine Love m. John Hector McLean

V. DUNCAN MCKINNON was single and was crippled. He d. 1843.

VI. JEANETTE MCKINNON m. Archibald C. McCormick in 1817. They had:

A. Christian McCormick, who d. 1897
B. Margaret McCormick
C. Jeanette McCormick, who d. at age 83
D. Archibald McCormick
E. Daniel McCormick
F. Murdock McCormick
G. Duncan McCormick
H. Catherine McCormick
I. John McCormick
J. Dougald McCormick
K. Nathaniel L. McCormick

VIII. DANIEL MCKINNON m. Margaret McKoy. They had:

A. Archibald M. McKinnon
B. Catherine McKinnon
C. Harriet McKinnon
D. Mary Ann McKinnon
E. Margaret McKinnon
F. Daniel Patrick McKinnon
G. John M. McKinnon
H. Luther McKinnon
I. McKoy McKinnon

IX. MARGARET MCKINNON m. Edward McMillan. She d. in 1866, leaving two children.

X. ALEXANDER CURRIE MCKINNON, b. 1800, d. Jan. 13, 1870 in present Scotland County, N.C. He m. first Sarah L. McMillan, who d. without children. Next he m. Charlotte Cameron, who d. 1843, leaving three children:

A. Cameron McKinnon
B. Daniel McKinnon
C. Sarah McKinnon

He m. thirdly, Mrs. Sarah McQueen Currie. They had:

D. Archibald McKinnon
E. Martin McQueen McKinnon
F. Alexander James McKinnon
G. Catherine McKinnon
H. Angus Currie McKinnon

The descendants of this family are traced to the 1930s in the paper of Angus Currie McKinnon, from which all of my information is taken.

XI. JOHN MCKINNON d. about 18 years old.

XII. MURDOCK MCKINNON m. first, Ester McMillan, who d. 1837, leaving four children:

A. An infant
B. Sarah McKinnon, who d. in infancy
C. Daniel Paisley McKinnon
D. Gilbert McMillan McKinnon

Murdock m. secondly Mary Blue in 1838. They had:

E. Margaret Sophronia McKinnon
F. John Blue McKinnon
G. Murdock Milton McKinnon
H. Catherine McKinnon
I. Alexander Murphy McKinnon
J. Angus McKinnon
K. Finley Currie McKinnon
L. Mary Jane McKinnon
M. Calvin McKinnon
N. Flora McKinnon
O. Sarah Martha McKinnon
P. Martin Luther McKinnon
Q. Evander William McKinnon

The descendants of this family are traced in Douglas F. Kelly's *Scottish Blue Family,* pp. 171-179.

The MacQueen Family of Queensdale (Robeson County, North Carolina)

This large family has been carefully and eloquently traced by Mrs. Annabella Bunting MacElyea of Queensdale (near Maxton, N.C.) in 1916, in a volume: *The MacQueens of Queensdale: A Biography of Col. James MacQueen And His Descendants.* This valuable genealogy was reprinted in the 1970s. Since it is widely available, I will give only the briefest outline of the major branches of this family here.

Col. James MacQueen was born c. 1760 in the Isle of Skye, son of Archibald MacQueen and Flora MacQueen (born MacDonald). He emigrated to North Carolina c. 1772, landing at the port of Brunswick or Wilmington, and settled first in Anson County, N.C., where he taught school for several years.[19] He later moved to Queensdale in Robeson County, N.C., where he d. June 21, 1824, and is buried in Stewartsville Cemetery in present Scotland County, N.C. He represented Robeson County in the North Carolina Legislature in 1794, 1802 and 1803, and was Deputy Clerk of the Superior Court of Robeson County, Colonel of a Militia Regiment and Acting Justice of the Peace.

He m. Ann MacRae, b. in Kintyre, Scotland c. 1770, daughter of John and Mary MacRae. She, along with other children, accompanied her parents to America, through the port of Charleston, S.C. They first lived in Anson County, N.C., where she attended the school of James MacQueen, whom she m. c. 1790. A few years after their marriage, they moved to Maxton, N.C. (Queensdale), and her parents also moved to the section. According to the Family Bible, she d. Aug. 14, 1855 and is buried at Stewartsville Cemetery.

They had twelve children:

I. ARCHIBALD MACQUEEN, b. 1791, d. 1851, a Presbyterian minister. He m. first Margaret Stewart by whom he had three children and secondly, Julia Ann MacLeod, by whom he had three children. Thirdly, he m. Mary MacLeod, and by her had three more children.[20]

II. FLORA MACDONALD MACQUEEN, b. 1793, d. 1845, m. Col. Richard Bunting. They had seven children.[21]

III. MARGARET MACQUEEN, b. 1794, d. 1810, was single.

IV. KATHERINE MACQUEEN, b. 1796, d. 1862, m. Col. Donald MacQueen. They had thirteen children.[22]

V. SARAH (SALLY) MACQUEEN, b. 1797, d. 1829, m. Col. Archibald MacEachin, son of Patrick (Para Ban) MacEachin. They had four children.[23]

VI. EDMUND MACQUEEN, a physician, b. 1804, d. 1858, m. Susan Moore. They had ten children.[24]

VII. ANNABELLA MACQUEEN, b. 1803, d. 1869, m. first Col. Archibald MacEachin, after the death of her sister Sarah (Sally). Col MacEachin had two children by Annabella.[25] Secondly, she m. William Stewart (no children by this marriage).

VIII. NEILL MACQUEEN, b. 1805, d. 1835, m. Mary Stewart. They had two children.[26]

IX. JOHN MACQUEEN, a General, b. 1807, d. 1867, m. first Sarah Rogers by whom he had one child, and secondly, Sarah Pickens, by whom he had five children.[27]

X. JAMES HUGH MACQUEEN, b. 1809, d. 1878, m. Maria (Campbell) Coit. They had two children.[28]

XI. MARIA MACQUEEN, b. 1810/11, d. 1891, m. Peter MacEachin, son of John MacEachin and grandson of Patrick (Para Ban MacEachin). They had twelve children.[29]

XII. CHARITY [CHATTIE] ANNE LEE MACQUEEN, b. 1813, d. 1884, m. Duncan MacCallum. They had five children.[30]

Malcom McRae Family of Western Robeson County

Another Highland Scottish family which settled in the Maxton area of Robeson County, N.C., not far from the McQueens was the Malcolm McRae clan. Mrs. Anna Henderson Parham has traced this family, largely based on information received from Lee Ray McFarland and Hoyt Lamm of Maxton, and also from *The McRae History* by Sarah McRae Polk. All of my material comes from Mrs. Parham's *"My Family" The Hendersons of the Carolinas and Their Connections* (privately printed: Latta, S.C., 1994).

Malcolm McRae was born in Scotland c. 1755/56, and died in Robeson County, N.C., Mar. 8, 1830. He is buried in McLeans Cemetery near Maxton, N.C. None of the material indicates the year of their emigration from Scotland to North Carolina (though it had to have occurred before 1801, when his wife died and was buried in Robeson County). He married first:

Katherine McDonald, b. in Scotland and d. 1801 in Robeson County. They had:

I. DANIEL MCRAE
II. CHRISTIAN MCRAE
III. WILLIAM MCRAE

Malcolm married secondly Sarah Margaret McDuffie b. 1755 in Scotland, d. 1825 in Robeson County, N.C. They had:

IV. "POLLIE" MARY MCRAE
V. JOHN A. MCRAE (BLACKSMITH JOHN) MCRAE
VI. NANCY MCRAE
VII. ARCHIBALD MCRAE
VIII. EFFIE MCRAE

I. DANIEL MCRAE b. 1791, d. July 2, 1854, buried in McLeans Cemetery near Maxton, N.C. He married Katherine McRae b. June 7, 1802, d. Dec. 5, 1892, the daughter of Norman McRae and Mary Lytch. Their children:

A. Effie McRae b. June 7, 1822, d. Nov. 26, 1851, m. Alexander McLean. Some of the descendants of their daughter, Isabel McLean, who m. Norman Stewart are traced by Parham.[31]
B. Capt. Peter P. McRae b. July 1825, d. July 11, 1902. He m. first Miss Patterson, and secondly, Mrs. McKinnon. His five children are listed in Parham.[32]
C. John A. McRae b. Mar. 15, 1827, d. Feb. 1, 1907. He m. on Oct. 12, 1858 Jane Gilchrist. Their nine children are listed in Parham.[33]
D. Malcolm Hugh McRae ("Make") b. 1835
E. Margaret Ann McRae b. 1836, m. on Sept. 12, 1867 Dr. James R. McRae. Their four children are listed in Parham (p. 65).
F. Christian McRae b. 1838
G. Flora Ann McRae b. 1845, m. John A. McLean. Their four children are listed in Parham (p. 65).
H. Mary McRae m. on May 23, 1853 Squire Billy McRae (of the Richmond County McRae family, son of John McRae and Christian McDonald). Their four children are listed in Parham (65).
I. Sarah McRae m. on Feb. 25, 1856 the widower of her sister, Effie: Alexander McLean. Their six children are listed in Parham (65).
J. Catherine McRae m. John Artemus McLean. Their five children are listed in Parham (65).
K. and L. died in infancy.

II. CHRISTIAN MCRAE (daughter of Malcom McRae and Katherine McDonald) b. 1793, was living still in 1850). She married John McRae of the Richmond County McRaes (son of emigrant William McRae).[34] Their son:

A. William McRae "Squire Billy" m. Mary McRae (daughter of Daniel and Katherine McRae—see immediately above—I.H.).

III. WILLIAM MCRAE (son of Malcolm and Katherine McDonald McRae) b. Oct. 1801, d. Mar. 24, 1881. His mother died when he was born. He lived near Shoe Heel (now Maxton, N.C.), and was known as "Billy the Miller", since he operated a grist mill on a stream by his home. He m. Flora McRae b. Dec. 16, 1805, d. May 1, 1852, daughter of Norman McRae and Mary Lytch.[35] They had eleven children:

A. Mary Catherine McRae b. 1832, m. John W. Carmichael. Their five children are listed in Parham (66).
B. Abigail McRae b. 1834, m. Neil Douglas; no children.
C. Christian Ann McRae b. 1836
D. Malcolm John McRae b. 1839, unmarried.
E. Margaret Flora McRae b. 1842,[36] m. on June 26, 1867 John Andrew Henderson b. June 4, 1842, d. May 22, 1900. Their six children are traced in Parham (9-59).
F. Hector McRae b. 1845, m. Panola McKay b. 1847. Their four children are listed in Parham (76).
G. Daniel H. McRae b. 1848, unmarried.
H. Sara Jane McRae, first m. John McCall, and secondly, m. Ben Smith. No children by either marriage.
I. Norman McRae, unmarried.
J. and K. died in infancy.

IV. "POLLIE" MARY MCRAE (daughter of Malcolm McRae and second wife, Sarah M. McDuffie) b. 1812, d. 1881. She first m. Daniel Stewart and secondly, James Stewart. Mrs. Parham lists her two children (without stating by which husband):[37]

A. Sara Jane Stewart
B. Archibald Stewart

V. JOHN A. MCRAE (son of Malcolm McRae and Sarah M. McDuffie) b. 1809, d. May 2, 1885, m. Isobel Sutherland on Feb. 2, 1836, daughter of Roderick and Sallie Chisholm Sutherland. They had eight children:

A. Sarah Catherine McRae b. Mar. 11, 1837, d. 1921, unmarried.
B. Flora Ann McRae b. Apr. 4, 1838, m. Archie Ray. Their five children are traced in Parham (67).

C. Roderick S. McRae b. Jan. 17, 1840, died at Gettysburg.
D. Malcolm Lafayette McRae b. Nov. 17, 1842, m. Nancy Jane Graham. Their daughter is listed in Parham (67).
E. Margaret Elizabeth McRae b. Aug. 27, 1843, m. Dec. 23, 1868 John E. Hinson.
F. Henriette McRae b. Apr. 21, 1845, d. Nov. 1921.
G. Effie Jane McRae b. Mar. 25, 1847, d. May 31, 1849.
H. John Murdock McRae b. Sept. 12, 1850, d. Dec. 28, 1897, m. Mary McDonald McLean b. Apr. 16, 1857, d. Mar. 22, 1889 (daughter of Daniel and Sarah McLean). Their three children are listed in Parham (67, 68).

VI. NANCY MCRAE (daughter of Malcolm McRae and Sarah M. McDuffie) b. 1814, d. 1903, m. Alexander Morrison. They had nine children:

A. Margaret Jane Morrison
B. Sarah Ann Morrison
C. Daniel A. Morrison
D. Catherine Annabelle Morrison
E. Malcolm John Morrison
F. Catherine A. Morrison m. George C. Fisher
G. Mary N. Morrison
H. Harriet McRae Morrison m. D. M. "Bud" Currie
I. Anne Christian Morrison m. James Riley Johnston. Their eight children are traced in Parham (68).

VII. ARCHIBALD MCRAE (son of Malcolm and Sarah M. McRae) b. 1807, d. Nov. 8, 1883, m. Mary McRae (daughter of Norman McRae and Mary Lytch[38]), b. Apr. 3, 1812, d. May 31, 1881. They had seven children:

A. Norman D. McRae, unmarried
B. Anne Elizabeth McRae, unmarried
C. Sarah McRae, unmarried
D. Mary Catherine McRae m. on Apr. 14, 1887 Daniel McLean
E. Flora Jane McRae, unmarried
F. Daniel M. McRae, unmarried
G. Malcolm William McRae m. first, Mary Katherine McCall d. 1870, and secondly, Nannie McCall. By his first wife he had two children, and by his second wife, six children, all of whom are listed in Parham (68, 69).

VIII. MALCOLM MCRAE (son of Malcolm and Sarah M. McRae) m.

Flora Morrison on Oct. 19, 1842. They had eight children:

A. Daniel Arch McRae, unmarried
B. Mary Jane McRae, unmarried
C. Angus McRae
D. Sarah E. McRae, unmarried
E. Margaret C. McRae
F. Malcolm McRae, unmarried
G. Effie Ann McRae m. Frank Humphrey (one of twin brothers). Their two children are listed in Parham (69).
H. John W. McRae m. Alyce Sanderson. Their six children are listed in Parham (69, 70).

IX. EFFIE MCRAE (daughter of Malcolm and Sarah M. McRae) m. Robert McLean. Their seven children are listed in Parham (70):

A. Maggie McLean m. Tom Monroe. Their seven children are listed in Parham (70).
B. Effie McLean
C. Mary J. McLean
D. John D. McLean m. Jessie Owens and had two children.
E. Sion McLean
F. Douglas McLean
G. Malcolm McLean m. Sadie Phillips and had two children.

McRae Family of Richmond County, North Carolina

Another McRae family is traced here along with other Scottish emigrants of Western Robeson County. Actually this family settled in Richmond County, N.C., (in that part of the county that later became Scotland County and borders western Robeson County). Some of this McRae group did move into western Robeson County, though most of them remained in Richmond/Scotland County. This family tended to intermarry with the other McRae families (both the one in Maxton, N.C., and the one in Dillon County, S.C.). William McRae was the emigrant head of this group. He was born in the Isle of Skye, Scotland, in 1745, and emigrated to North Carolina with his family as well as that of Daniel Lytch in 1801.[39] William McRae died Sept. 15, 1802 and is buried in Stewartsville Cemetery in Scotland County, N.C. His wife is believed to have died in Scotland sometime before he and his four children came to North Carolina. His four children were:

I. NORMAN MCRAE b. 1771 in Scotland, d. Dec. 7, 1850 in North Carolina, m. Mary Lytch (daughter of Daniel and Jane Lytch). Mary was b. in Argyllshire, Scotland in 1787, and d. in North Carolina Jan. 11, 1856. Norman and Mary are buried in Stewartsville Cemetery with her father. According to Norman McRae's will (made Oct. 1, 1850 and probated in Robeson County, N.C.), they had twelve children:

A. Catherine McRae b. June 7, 1802, d. Dec. 5, 1892, m. Daniel McRae (son of Malcolm and Katherine McDonald McRae—see previous section, p. 328 for their descendants).

B. Flora McRae b. Dec. 16, 1805, d. May 1, 1852, m. "Billy the Miller" McRae (son of Malcolm and Katherine McDonald McRae—see previous section, p. 328, for their descendants).

C. Mary McRae b. Apr. 3, 1812, d. May 31, 1881, m. Archibald McRae (son of Malcolm and Sarah McDuffie McRae—see previous section, p. 330 for their descendants).

D. Christian McRae b. Apr. 5, 1814, d. 1872, m. James Stewart b. 1817, d. 1879. Their two children are listed in Parham (72).

E. William L. McRae b. June 16, 1816, d. Nov. 29, 1885, unmarried.

F. Archie L. McRae b. 1818, d. Feb. 14, 1878, unmarried.

G. Daniel L. McRae b. Mar. 21, 1820, d. May 21, 1851, unmarried.

H. John McRae m. Mary Nancy Stewart. They moved to Mississippi and died there. Their three children are listed in Parham (72).

I. Norman McRae, Jr., b. Nov. 11, 1822, d. Oct. 13, 1859, unmarried.

J. Nancy McRae b. Oct. 23, 1825, d. Feb. 18, 1888. She m. first Archie Fairley, and secondly John Lytch. The children of her daughter (by her first husband) are listed in Parham (72).

K. James Q. R. McRae b. Mar. 11, 1828, d. May 16, 1871, unmarried.

L. Sarah McRae b. Sept. 14, 1831, d. May 29, 1872, m. Daniel McLean b. 1831, d. 1896. Descendants of their five children are traced in Parham (72, 73).

M. Margaret McRae m. Duncan McRae.

II. JOHN MCRAE (son of William) b. in the Isle of Skye, d. in North Carolina before Feb. 19, 1827, m. Christian McRae (daughter of Malcolm and Katherine McDonald McRae—see previous section pp. 328-29 for descendants).

III. CHRISTIAN MCRAE (daughter of William), born 1785 in the Isle of Skye, died in N.C. Jan. 5, 1813, and is buried by her father in Stewartsville Cemetery.

IV. NANCY MCRAE (daughter of William), born in the Isle of Skye, died in North Carolina.

The McArn Family of Richmond [Scotland] County, North Carolina

Another Highland Scottish family of the Scotland (originally Richmond) County area of North Carolina was that of Daniel McArn, who came from Knapdale, Argyllshire in the very late eighteenth century. Daniel McArn died in North Carolina in 1799. He married first, Katie McMillan, and secondly, Mary Catherine McAlpine (daughter of Mary Smith and Malcolm McAlpine of Richmond County, N.C.).

Daniel McArn and Katie McMillan had:

- I. JOHN MCARN
- II. ARCHIBALD MCARN
- III. KATIE MCARN

Daniel McArn and Mary Catherine McAlpine had:

- IV. HUGH MCARN
- V. MARGARET MCARN
- VI. SARAH MCARN

I. JOHN MCARN, born in Scotland, emigrated as a child to North Carolina with his father, and then moved to Fayette, Mississippi, where he d. 1819. He m. Kate Blue, who died after 1819.[40] They had nine children:

- A. Mary McArn
- B. Sarah McArn
- C. Catherine McArn
- D. Flora McArn
- E. Efffie McArn
- F. Daniel McArn
- G. Neil McArn
- H. Duncan McArn
- I. John McArn, who died in Mississippi in 1850, leaving a large family. He m. Lizzie Powers. Two of their children are listed by Parham (74).

II. ARCHIBALD MCARN b. in Scotland 1774, d. Jan. 11, 1836, m. 1792 Sarah Blue b. 1774, d. Apr. 25, 1857[41]. (John and Archibald married sisters). They had eleven children:

- A. Margaret McArn b. May 1, 1773, d. June 1, 1865, m. Daniel McBryde. Their seven children are listed in Parham (74, 75).

B. John McArn b. Nov. 1794, d. at the Presbyterian Hospital in Philadelphia, PA, Apr. 7, 1845, as the result of a train accident. He lived in Fayetteville, N.C.

C. Mary McArn d. at age 18, unmarried.

D. Katherine McArn b. Mar. 15, 1799, d. May 8, 1877, m. Malcolm Graham.

E. Sarah McArn b. 1801, d. 1869, m. Angus McBryde (not related to Daniel). Their four children are listed in Parham (75).

F. Christian McArn d. at age 87, m. Malcolm Buchanan. Their four children are traced in Parham (75).

G. Effie McArn b. 1806, d. Nov. 1866, m. Daniel Campbell. Their six sons (three of whom died in the War Between the States) are listed in Parham (75).

H. Daniel Blue McArn b. Apr. 1809, d. Oct. 1867 in New York, m. Nannie Hunter of Florida. Their three children are traced in Parham (76).

I. Archibald McArn d. in Hannibal, MO., unmarried.

J. Malcolm McArn b. 1813, m. Mary Reed in Montgomery, Alabama, where he died.

K. Hugh McArn (twin to Malcolm) b. 1813, d. 1883 in Montgomery, Alabama.

III. KATE MCARN (daughter of Daniel) b. in Scotland, d. before 1828 in North Carolina, m. Allen McGill. They had:

A. Margaret McGill
B. Mary McGill
C. Betsy McGill
D. Christian McGill
E. Isabella McGill
F. Flora McGill m. a Cameron
G. Daniel McGill

IV. HUGH MCARN (son of Daniel) b. in Scotland, 1784, d. in North Carolina June 27, 1830, m. Sallie McNeil b. 1788, d. June 25, 1877. They had four children:

A. Catherine McArn b. Jan. 20, 1814, d. Aug. 20, 1882, m. on Jan. 25, 1829 Daniel McPhaul (son of John McPhaul and Margaret Gilchrist), b. July 20, 1801, d. July 20, 1865. Their eleven children are traced in J.E. Purcell, *Lumber River Scots,* 526-547.

B. Nancy McArn b. 1817, d. Apr. 21, 1877, m. first, John Carmichael Henderson. Their three sons are traced in

Parham (7-59). Nancy McArn Henderson m. secondly, William McKay. Their five children are traced in Parham (76, 77).

C. Christian McArn b. 1818, d. Oct. 1855, m. Malcolm McPhaul b. 1816, d. July 31, 1857. Malcolm was brother to Daniel McPhaul, who married Christian McArn's sister, Catherine. According to Purcell (op. cit., 549), they lived near Antioch Presbyterian Church (between Red Springs and Raeford, N.C.) and are both buried in its cemetery. Their nine children are traced in Purcell (549-561).

D. Daniel McArn m. Amy McKay. Their two children are listed by Parham (76).

V. MARGARET MCARN (daughter of Daniel McArn and Mary C. McAlpine) m. Edward McMillan.

VI. SARAH MCARN (daughter of Daniel McArn and Mary C. McAlpine) m. Robert Campbell.

Other Interconnected Highland Scots Families of the General Area Around Robeson, North Carolina

Mrs. Mable S. Lovin of Red Springs, N.C., has carefully compiled with considerable documentation several valuable (largely hand-written) volumes on a number of inter-connected families of the Robeson County area. These unpublished volumes are available in the Robeson County Public Library of Lumberton, N.C. These volumes are as follows:

Volume I, The Children of Our Clans, Descendants and Collateral Lines of Catherine McCallum and Duncan McNair

Catherine McCallum was b. in Scotland and d. in Robeson County in 1844. She m. before 1786 Duncan McNair, b. in Scotland, and d. in Robeson County in 1800. They had seven children who are traced in the above volume:

I. JOHN MCNAIR b. 1786, d. 1873, m. c. 1811 Mary Graham, b. 1787, d. 1872.

II. MALCOLM MCNAIR b. before 1790, d. 1823, m. 1812 Margaret Dalrymple, b. 1787, d. 1883.

III. ROBERT MCNAIR b. before 1790, d. before 1850, m. c. 1821 Elizabeth (Betsy) Patterson, b. 1801.

IV. MARY (POLLY) MCNAIR b. 1792, d. 1875, m. before 1822, Neil McArthur, b. 1788, d. 1864.

V. CATHERINE (CATTIE) MCNAIR b. 1798, d. 1865, m. 1818, Neill McGeachy, b. 1793, d. 1861.

VI. DUNCAN MCNAIR b. 1800, d. 1831, m. 1825 Elizabeth McNair, b. 1801, d. 1832.

VII. ISABELLE MCNAIR b. before 1800, d. before 1810.

Volume II, Descendants and Collateral Lines of Mary McCormick and Alexander Graham

Mary McCormick was b. in Knapdale, Scotland in 1745 and d. 1826 in Cumberland County, N.C., daughter of John McCormick and Sallie McLeod. She m. Alexander Graham, b. in Knapdale, 1739, and d. Cumberland County in 1794, son of Daniel Graham and Christian Munn. Mary McCormick and Alexander Graham had nine children who are traced in the above volume:

I. ISABELLA GRAHAM b. 1770, d. 1841, m. before 1800 Thomas McMillan

II. JOHN GRAHAM m. first Effie McGoogan and secondly, Mary Finlayson

III. DANIEL GRAHAM m. first Belle Crawford and secondly, in 1814, Nancy Black

IV. DUNCAN GRAHAM b. 1777, d. 1798

V. SARAH (SALLIE) GRAHAM b. 1778, d. 1867, m. 1799, Neil McNeill, b. 1791, d. 1858

VI. MARGARET GRAHAM b. after 1781, m. Archibald McKellar

VII. FLORA GRAHAM

VIII. CHRISTIAN GRAHAM m. Duncan McKellar

IX. MARY GRAHAM b. 1787, d. 1872, m. c. 1811, John McNair, b. 1786, d. 1873.

Volume III, Descendants and Collateral Lines of Mary Buie and Hugh Brown

Mary Buie was b. in Scotland in 1725, and d. before 1810 in Robeson County, N.C. She m. in 1738/9 in present Cumberland County,

Hugh Brown, b. 1716 in Scotland, d. 1794 in Robeson County, N.C. They had ten children who are traced in the above volume. This family has also been traced in the volume *The Family Buie Scotland to North America* by T.R. Buie and Scott Buie.[42] According to the research of Mrs. Lovin in Volume III, these ten children were:

I. DANIEL BROWN b. 1740

II. PETER BROWN b. 1745

III. NEILL BROWN b. 1748, d. 1835, m. 1776 Ann Smith, b. 1752, d. 1839

IV. JOHN BROWN b. 1751, d. 1794, m. 1781 Ada Bennett, b. 1762, d. 1837

V. CATHERINE BROWN b. 1753, m. c. 1775/6 Archibald Smith

VI. WILLIAM BROWN b. 1755, d. 1826, m. c. 1783 Mary Campbell, b. c. 1760 in Cumberland County, N.C., d. c. 1825 in Robeson County.

VII. MARY BROWN b. 1758, d. 1839, m. c. 1784 John Fort, b. 1762, d. 1840.

VIII. HUGH BROWN JR., b. 1762, d. 1851, m. 1789, first Catherine Fort b. 1768, d. 1838, and m. secondly, Catherine Smith.

IX. ANN BROWN b. 1765, m. George Ikner, who d. before 1830

X. DUNCAN BROWN b. 1771, d. 1861, m. Susan Frierson

Volume IV, Descendants of Jane Campbell and William McNeill

Jane Campbell was b. in Scotland and d. in Robeson County, N.C. She m. c. 1750, William McNeill, b. in Scotland and d. before 1774 in present Robeson County. According to General William Curry Harllee in *Kinfolks: A Genealogical and Biographical Record* (Seearcy & Pfaff, Ltd.; New Orleans, La., 1934), Jane Campbell McNeill is buried somewhere near Ashpole Presbyterian Church in Robeson County, N.C., though her grave is unmarked (Vol. I, p. 866). They had five children who are traced both in *Volume IV: Descendants of Jane Campbell and William McNeill* and in Harllee's *Kinfolks* (Vol. I, 865-866):

I. HECTOR ("Fiddler") MCNEILL b. 1756, d. 1830, m. first Unice McNeill, who d. before 1791, and secondly in 1791, Ayles [*sic*] McNeill, b. 1774, d. 1840. Harllee records Revolutionary War Pension Claim, W. 18501, showing that Hector was a lieutenant in the North Carolina troops, and other vital statistics.[43] According to Harllee,[44] the children of

Hector and Ayles McNeill were:

A. Elizabeth McNeill b. June 23, 1792

B. Hector McNeill b. July 25, 1794

C. Elizabeth McNeill b. June 26, 179-. Harlee believes that the first Elizabeth died young. This Elizabeth m. Mr. Munn.

D. Margaret McNeill b. Mar. 9, 1799

E. William C. McNeill b. Mar. 21, 1801

F. James McNeill b. Sept. 5, 1803

G. Simon P. McNeill b. Aug. 4, 1805, m. Dec. 28, 1837, Mary Jane McNeill (daughter of Malcolm and Katie Torrey McNeill b. Dec. 1, 1816. Their six sons and one daughter are listed in Harlee (888).

H. Jane (or Jean) McNeill b. Mar. 16, 1811, m. Mr. Elmore.

I. Nancy McNeill b. Dec. 3, 1813, m. Mr. Coward.

II. ARCHIBALD MCNEILL b. 1760, d. 1834, m. four times: first, Rebecca Cameron in 1780; secondly, Barbara Patterson in 1788; thirdly, Rebecca Cameron, and fourthly, Effy McEachern in 1830.

III. NANCY MCNEILL m. before 1790 Hector McNeill

IV. ELIZABETH MCNEILL

V. ____died at sea, 1774.

Volume V, Descendants and Collateral Lines of Jane Campbell McNeill and Neill McNeill

Jane Campbell McNeill (see Vol. IV above) m. secondly, Neill McNeill, b. in Scotland, d. in Robeson County, N.C. By his first wife, Neill McNeill had four children:

I. MALCOLM MCNEILL, mentioned in Col. Harllee's *Kinfolks.*[45]

II. HECTOR MCNEILL

III. NEILL MCNEILL II

IV. ELIZABETH MCNEILL, who m. a Mr. Hogg

Jane Campbell and Neill McNeill had:

V. DANIEL MCNEILL b. 1778, d. 1852, m. Mary (Polly) Buie Brown, b. 1786, d. 1852. According to Harllee, they had children and lived in Robeson County, N.C.

VI. JOHN MCNEILL, m. first a Miss Baker, and secondly, Mary Harrell. According to Harllee, John raised a family and died and was buried near Great Marsh in Robeson County, N.C.

Daniel McCallum Family of Lower Robeson County

The Daniel McCallum Family of lower Robeson County had some connections by marriage with some of the previously mentioned families of central Robeson. The Daniel McCallums were traced in 1946 by Col. Louis Farrell and Flora Hamer Hooker in *McCallums: Daniel McCallum and Isabel Sellars: Their Antecedents, Descendants and Collateral Relatives: a Compilation.*[46] This family is also discussed in Harllee's *Kinfolks,* Vol. II, 1422-1425.

Daniel McCallum was b. 1740 in Kintyre, Scotland, and m. first c. 1760 (unknown). According to Harllee, Daniel's parents were Archibald McCallum b. c. 1690, d. 1750 (Kintyre, Scotland) and Effie McCarter b. c. 1695, d. 1770 (Kintyre). They are said to have had several sons, all of whom died young, and a daughter (no information). Their only son who lived to be grown was Daniel.

Daniel and his wife emigrated to Wilmington in 1770 with three or four children. By 1771 his wife and all their children had died (according to Harlee, of yellow fever). He settled near Ashpole Presbyterian in lower Robeson County (near present Rowland, N.C.) by 1779, where he d. in 1807. He m. Isabel Sellars in 1773, b. in Argyll in 1745 and d. in Robeson County Feb. 3, 1814. Daniel d. Feb. 7, 1807 in Robeson County, N.C.

Daniel and Isabel McCallum's children are traced in the volume by Farrell and Hooker, as well as by Harllee (1422-1425). Here I list only the first generation.

I. ANGUS MCCALLUM b. 1774, m. Rebecca Brown, daughter of Angus Brown and Mary McFarland of Kintyre, Scotland

II. ARCHIBALD MCCALLUM b. 1775[47]

III. CATHERINE MCCALLUM b. 1777

IV. DANIEL MCCALLUM JR. b. 1779, d. 1830

V. EFFY MCCALLUM b. 1780

VI. MARY (Polly) MCCALLUM b. 1783, was single

VII. JOHN MCCALLUM b. 1785

VIII. ELIZABETH MCCALLUM b. 1787

IX. ISABEL MCCALLUM b. 1789, was single

McMillan Families of Robeson County

Recent work has been done on the large McMillan families of Robeson County from various quarters. Mrs. Mable S. Lovin of Red Springs, N.C., has compiled (an unpublished) volume: *The Scottish Connection: The Story of Robeson County Families Descending From John McMillan I and his wife, Margaret McMillan, daughter of John McMillan I.*[48] She deals with their six children:

I. ARCHIBALD MCMILLAN d. before 1825, m. Mary "Polly" McArthur

II. MALCOLM MCMILLAN b. 1772, d. 1852, m. Flora Patterson, b. 1769, d. 1871

III. HECTOR MCMILLAN b. 1776, d. 1836, m. Barbara Patterson, b. 1776, d. 1851

IV. CHRISTIAN MCMILLAN b. 1777, m. Alexander McMillan b. 1776

V. MARGARET MCMILLAN b. 1781, d. 1864, m. John McNeill b. 1775, d. 1850

VI. SARAH "SALLIE" MCMILLAN b. 1788, d. 1860, m. Neil Crawford

Robert H. McMillan Jr. has traced part of the McMillan family in *Record of McMillan and Allied Families.*[49] He deals with the children of Malcolm McMillan and wife, Catherine McArthur, whom he found on a ship's list from Scotland to North Carolina in 1774. Malcolm McMillan was b. in Scotland in 1716 and d. in Cumberland County, N.C., where his will was probated in 1805. His wife was b. c. 1716 in Scotland. Robert H. McMillan traces their sons:

I. JOHN MCMILLAN b. 1744

II. MALCOLM MCMILLAN b. 1746

III. DANIEL MCMILLAN b. 1750

IV. ARCHIBALD MCMILLAN b. 1758

V. GILBERT MCMILLAN b. 1764

I have fuller information the Archibald McMillan line in a letter written by Mrs. James A. Graham of Red Springs, N.C., on June 10, 1989.

Family of Gilbert and Chriosdaidh Ban McMillan

A numerous progeny is descended from Gilbert and Christian (in Gaelic, *Chriosdaidh Ban*) McMillan. I am unaware of what the relationship of Gilbert may have been to the previously listed McMillans. At least they all came from the Kintyre area of Scotland. *Chriosdaidh Ban* (or "Fair Christian"—owing to her fair hair) was believed by J.E. Purcell to have been descended from a McBryde who was married to a McCormick.[50] An old document in the possession of Mrs. Janie Peterkin McNiel of Dillon County, South Carolina, a descendant of Chriosdaidh Ban, definitely indicates that she was a Taylor rather than McBryde.[51] She was b. 1727 in Scotland, and d. June 15, 1811 in Robeson County, N.C.[52] She m. Gilbert McMillan, b. 1723, the son of Donald McMillan and Margaret McMillan of Drumore, Kintyre. He was baptized at Campbeltown, Feb. 7, 1731. He d. in 1771, just two years after they emigrated to Robeson County, N.C.[53]

Chriosdaidh Ban was famous in colonial Robeson County as a woman of wise advice in family and business matters, as well as going far and wide to help the sick and dying. "On her little gray pony it was the usual thing for her to ride from five to twenty-five miles to see sick people. It is known that she was at times called away from home for a distance of sixty miles or more."[54]

Christian and Gilbert McMillan had one son and seven daughters:

I. EFFIE MCMILLAN b. 1748, d. 1794. Married John Gilchrist Sr.

II. BARBARA MCMILLAN m. Angus McAllister and moved to South Carolina.

III. FLORA MCMILLAN m. Daniel McKay.

IV. MARGARET MCMILLAN m. first, Daniel Taylor, and secondly, D. McEwen.

V. CHRISTIAN MCMILLAN m. Sam Brown of Tennessee.

VI. ARCHIBALD MCMILLAN m. a Miss McArthur.

VII. MARY MCMILLAN m. Archibald Sellars.

VIII. A DAUGHTER, died in infancy.

Purcell traces descendants of three of these eight children: Effie

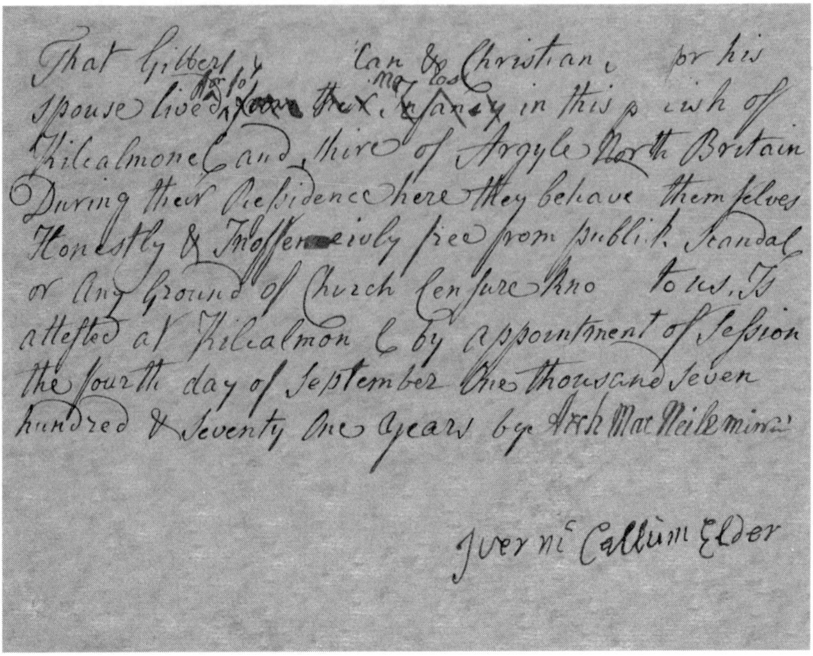
That Gilbert [illegible] Can & Christian [illegible] or his
spouse lived [illegible] in this parish of
Kilcalmonel and shire of Argyle North Britain
During their Residence here they behave themselves
Honestly & Inoffensively free from publick Scandal
or Any Ground of Church Censure kno to us. Is
attested at Kilcalmonel by appointment of Session
the fourth day of September One thousand seven
hundred & Seventy One years by Arch MacNeill min:

Iver mc Callum Elder

A letter of recommendation in behalf of Gilbert and Christian McMillan sent from the Kilclmonell Parish Church in Clachan in 1771. The letter was discovered in an old trunk belonging to Flora McMillan McKay, a daughter of the McMillans, and a sister of Effie McMillan Gilchrist. The letter provided evidence that Christian McMillan's maiden name was Taylor.
The letter reads:

THAT GILBERT AND CHRISTIAN T[AYLOR] HIS SPOUSE LIVED IN THIS PARISH OF KILCALMONEL AND SHIRE OF ARGYLE NORTH BRITAIN. DURING THEIR RESIDENCE HERE THEY BEHAVED THEMSELVES HONESTLY AND INOFFENSIVELY FREE FROM PUBLICK SCANDAL OR ANY GROUNDS OF CHURCH CENSURE KNOWN TO US. IS ATTESTED AT KILCALMONEL BY APPOINTMENT OF SESSION THE FOURTH DAY OF SEPTEMBER ONE THOUSAND SEVEN HUNDRED AND SEVENTY ONE YEARS BY ARCH MCNEILL MIN[ISTER].

IVER MCCALLUM ELDER
JOHN CAMPBELL SESS: CLK

NOTE: Mr. Ian McDonald of Clahan has stated that in a clearer copy of this certificate the words: "from their infancy" were marked out, and written in was: "for fourt(een) years from May last." This would indicate that the McMillans came to reside in Kilcalmonell Parish in the year 1757 in the month of May. This would indicate that they had a small farm, in that May was one of the two months in Scotland when farming tenancies began.

McMillan and John Gilchrist Sr.,[55] Mary McMillan and Archibald Sellars,[56] and Archibald McMillan, who m. a McArthur.[57]

Notes

1. Dr. Morris Britt, "The Origin of Robesonians" in *The Robeson County Register,* Vol. I, No. 3, August, 1986, 82, 83.
2. Jo White Linn, op. cit., 415.
3. Ibid., 423-427.
4. Ibid., 417.
5. Ibid.
6. Ibid., 418.
7. Ibid., 417.
8. See papers of the McGoogans as copied by J.A. Sinclair, 4, 5.
9. Linn, op. cit., 417.
10. Papers of the McGoogans as copied by Sinclair, 4.
11. Ibid., 5.
12. "John and Robert McNair of Early Robeson," submitted by Patricia Nicholson Edwards, p. 116, editor, Dr. Morris F. Britt.
13. Papers of the McGoogans, 4.
14. Ibid., 5.
15. This unpublished information is available in the Robeson County Public Library in Lumberton, N.C.
16. Jo White Linn, op. cit., 423.
17. Ibid., 424, 425.
18. Ibid., 425.
19. Annabella B. MacElyea, *The MacQueens of Queensdale,* 1916, p. 16.
20. This family is traced in MacElyea, op. cit., 29-54.
21. Traced in MacElyea, op. cit., 55-60.
22. Traced in MacElyea, op. cit., 63-123.
23. Traced in MacElyea, op. cit., 125-148.
24. Traced in MacElyea, op. cit., 149-169.
25. Traced ibid., 161-163.
26. Traced ibid., 165-167.
27. Traced ibid., 169-191.
28. Traced ibid., 193-199.
29. Traced ibid., 201-214. Further research was done on this family by Mrs. John Q. Anderson of College Station, Texas in 1959 in a six page booklet entitled "MacQueen-McEachin."
30. Traced in MacElyea, op. cit., 215-227.
31. Parham, 64.
32. Ibid.
33. Ibid.
34. See Parham, 71.
35. Parham 66 and 71.
36. On p. 66 of Parham, it states that she was born in 1842, but on p. 9, that she was

born Mar. 15, 1838, d. July 21, 1922.

37. Ibid., 67.

38. Ibid., 71.

39. Ibid., 71.

40. See Douglas F. Kelly, *Scottish Blue Family,* 51 for Kate Blue's ancestry.

41. See Douglas F. Kelly, *op. cit.,* 51 for Sarah Blue's ancestry.

42. T.R. Buie and Scott Buie, Compilers, *The Family Buie Scotland to North America* (Chelle-Kirk Printing: Arlington, Texas, 1983), 267-270.

43. Harllee, *Kinfolks,* Vol I, 866-867.

44. Ibid., 867.

45. Ibid., 866.

46. Williams Printing Company: Spartanburg, S.C. This volume is available in Robeson County Public Library, Lumberton, N.C.

47. Some of the descendants of Archibald McCallum are traced in J.E. Purcell, *Lumber River Scots,* 361-373.

48. Available in Robeson County Public Library, Lumberton, N.C.

49. Penisular Publishing Co.: Tallahassee, Florida, 1973.

50. J.E. Purcell, *Lumber River Scots And Their Descendants,* 742.

51. The document is a church recommendation for Gilbert McMillan and wife, Chriosdaidh Taylor, who were members in good standing of the Parish Church of Kilcalmonel in Kintyre. It is dated 4 Sept. 1771, and is signed by Archibald McNeill, minister and John Campbell, Session Clerk. This old letter was found in the trunk of a great-aunt of Mrs. McNiel.

52. Purcell, ibid.

53. Ibid., 743.

54. Ibid.

55. Ibid., 467-700.

56. Ibid., 338-414.

57. Ibid., 745-746.

11

"Lumber River Scots": Robeson County and Lower Cape Fear

PROBABLY THE FINEST SINGLE GENEALOGY of Highland Scots families in the Robeson County area (or anywhere else in the Carolinas, for that matter) is *Lumber River Scots And Their Descendants* by John Edwin Purcell II, to which we have frequently referred in this volume. Principally, Purcell deals with five main families, who tended to be inter-related: the McLeans, the Torreys, the Purcells, the McIntyres, and the Gilchrists. Incidentially, he deals with scores of other connected Carolina Scots families—some of them in considerable detail. Of these five major families, all of them are from Scotland, except for the Purcells, who were Irish, but are properly listed here, since they are so closely intermarried with the other Highland families.

This tremendous piece of genealogical research and cultural history was first published in 1942, and after being out of print for decades (and widely sought after), it was reprinted in 1986. Because of its present wide availability, I will give here only a very brief outline of its main sections.

The McLean Family

This family was headed by John McLean of the Isle of Mull, who sailed from Greenock, port of Glasgow, to Wilmington, N.C., on the Brig Mallyy, Sept. l, 1792, arriving on Oct. 16, 1792. He came to upper Robeson County, near Patrick McEachin's Bluff, later called McEachin's Bridge. In fact, McEachin was an old friend from Scotland. McLean bought lands on the north side of Buck Pond, in what is now Hoke County, and is known as the Allen McLean place. After arriving in America, he married Effie McLean, daughter of Hector and Jennet Murphy McLean. She was born Nov. 20, 1781, and d. Dec. 20, 1849. He d. May 15, 1846 aged 76, and was buried on his plantation. They had five sons and two daughters:

I.	HECTOR	V.	CHRISTIAN
II.	NEILL	VI.	ALEXANDER
III.	ALLEN	VII.	JENNET
IV.	ANGUS DUART		

I. HECTOR MCLEAN, b. Aug. 18, 1807, d. July 3, 1889. He attended Donaldson Academy in Fayetteville, N.C., taught school and then graduated from Union Theological Seminary in Virginia. He was licensed to preach in 1832, becoming pastor of the Presbyterian Church at Antioch and of Philadelphus in upper Robeson. Later he served churches in the Pee Dee area of South Carolina. He m. Jan. 17, 1833, Susanna Brown, dau. of Rev. Daniel Brown, b. July 13, 1809, d. Dec. 10, 1890, see p. 383.

II. NEILL MCLEAN b. 1808, d. Sept. 24, 1839 and was single.

III. ALLEN MCLEAN b. Mar. 12, 1812, d. June 5, 1889 and was single.

IV. ANGUS DUART MCLEAN b.1814, d. June 20, 1869. He graduated from Jefferson Medical College, Philadelphia, Pa., and practiced medicine and surgery in his home territory near Floral College, Robeson County, where he was a ruling elder in the Presbyterian Church. He helped incorporate Floral College. Sherman's army did much damage to his plantation during the War. He married twice: first, Mary Jane McEachin, dau. of Col. Archibald McEachin and Sarah (Sallie) McQueen McEachin (see the McQueen section, pp. 326-27). Secondly,

Dr. McLean m. Mary (Polly) McCallum, dau. of Archibald McCallum and Margaret Wilkinson McCallum.

By his first wife, Angus McLean had six children, who are traced by Purcell[1]:

A. James Dickson McLean b. Jan. 17, 1841, d. June 17, 1888
B. Archibald Alexander McLean, b. Apr. 10, 1844, d. Mar. 5, 1906
C. Sallie McLean b. Dec. 15, 1847, d. Mar. 5, 1906
D. John Allen McLean b. Aug. 16, 1851, d. Feb. 11, 1932
E. Hector McLean b. June 10, 1854, d. June 25, 1921
F. Peter McLean b. Junl 2, 1856, d. Sept. 20, 1880

By his second wife, Angus McLean had three children who are traced by Purcell:[2]

G. Mary Jane McLean b. Nov. 11, 1864, d. Sept. 8, 1865
H. Anna McLean b. July 15, 1867, d. June 10, 1939 (twin)
I. Margaret McLean (Maggie) b. July 15, 1867, d. June 15, 1869 (twin)

V. CHRISTIAN MCLEAN b. Oct. 14, 1817, d. Apr. 20, 1837, single.

VI. ALEXANDER MCLEAN b. c. 1820, d. June 23, 1856, studied law and was a ruling elder in First Presbyterian Church, Lumberton, N.C., which he helped to organize. He was single.

VII. JENNET MCLEAN died Aug. 30, 1851, before reaching maturity.

The Purcell Family

Although this family was of Irish origin, they are closely connected to the Scots of the upper Robeson County area. J.E. Purcell, in his work, traces the descendants of John Purcell I and his wife Mary Gilchrist (widow of Col. Archibald McKay). She was the oldest child of John Gilchrist Sr. and Effie McMillan, dau. of Chriosdaidh Ban McMillan (already mentioned in this volume, p. 341). The descent of the seven children of John Purcell and Mary Gilchrist (McKay) is given by Purcell:[3]

I. MALCOLM PURCELL b. Sept. 15, 1799, d. June 9, 1878

II. EFFIE PURCELL b. Oct. 4, 1801

III. JOHN PURCELL II b. Jan. 29, 1804, d. Oct. 7, 1874

IV. ELIZABETH PURCELL b. May 1, 1806, d. Jan. 13, 1888

V. ALEXANDER TORREY PURCELL b. Apr. 19, 1808, d. May 21, 1882

VI. MARY GILCHRIST PURCELL b. Apr. 10, 1810, d. Mar. 19, 1877

VII. ARCHIBALD PURCELL b. Aug. 12, 1812, d. Jan. 22, 1884.

The McIntyre Family

The head of this family, Revd. John McIntyre, was the son of Catherine Ann Stuart and John (or Donald) McIntyre, and born on a farm called Kenlochlaish in the Parish of Lismore and Appin in Argyllshire, Scotland, in Aug. 21, 1750. He d. Nov. 17, 1852, at one hundred and two years of age. While employed as a shepherd in the Highlands, he m. Catherine Ann McCallum on Dec. 15, 1789. They had one child before leaving Scotland, and then on Aug. 10, 1791, they sailed from Appin to Wilmington, N.C., arriving Nov. 11, 1791. Sadly, their little girl died and was buried at sea, shortly before their arrival in North Carolina. He and his wife settled about fifteen miles west of Fayetteville, N.C., near Philippi Church in Cumberland County. Revd. John McIntyre was married four times, and his children are traced by Purcell[4]:

Children of John McIntyre and Catherine Ann McCallum:

I. INFANT DAUGHTER, buried at sea.

II. ANN CATHERINE MCINTYRE b. Cumberland County, N.C., in 1792, d. in Jacksonville, Ala., March, 1857.

Children of John McIntyre and Mary Wright:

III. INFANT child, dying soon after birth.

IV. INFANT child, dying soon after birth.

Children of John McIntyre and Jane McColman:

V. JANE SARAH MCINTYRE b. July 21, 1802, d. July 14, 1883.

VI. A DAUGHTER, probably dying in infancy.

Children of John McIntyre and Mary McNeill (Graham):

VII. MARY AMANDA MCINTYRE b. Jan. 2, 1814, d. July 6, 1889.

VIII. HARRIET NEWELL TURNER MCINTYRE b. July 17, 1817, d. Apr. 17, 1896.

IX. JOHN CALVIN MCINTYRE b. May 14, 1819, d. Dec. 31, 1862.

The Torrey Family

The head of this family was John Torrey, who is believed to have come from Paisley, Argyllshire, Scotland via Philadelphia about 1765, finally settling near Fayetteville, N.C.[5] His wife was Margaret, and they had three sons and three daughters. This family name no longer exists in the Cape Fear section of North Carolina, but there are numerous descendants of this couple there.

According to Purcell, John and Margaret Torrey had:

I. JAMES TORREY	IV. BEATRICE TORREY
II. GEORGE TORREY	V. ELIZABETH TORREY
III. DAVID TORREY	VI. MARY TORREY

Purcell traces the descendants of a number of these children, many of whom moved to Mississippi.[6] However, a large part of the descendants of this family remained in Carolina, including: IV. BEATRICE TORREY, who married first Malcolm Purcell, and secondly, Daniel McEachern, whose descendants are traced by Purcell,[7] as are those of V. ELIZABETH TORREY, who married John Sillers of Sampson County, N.C.,[8] and VI. MARY TORREY, who married "Red" Hector McNeill of Cumberland County, N.C.[9]

The Gilchrist Family

The head of this large family was John Gilchrist Sr., who came to America in 1770 from Kintyre in Scotland, with his wife, Effie McMillan. Illustrating the fact that often many from the same Scottish community made the decision to emigrate to the same area, he had a sister, Mary Gilchrist, who had emigrated with her husband, John McBryde of Kintyre, to North Carolina some seven years earlier, while his wife, Effie, was dau. of Gilbert and Chriosdaidh Ban McMillan who also emigrated to Robeson County at that time.[10] (We have discussed them earlier, under the McMillan section of this volume, p. 341-42).

They m. in Kintyre, Scotland, on Feb. 12, 1770, and eventually settled in Robeson County on Mill Prong Swamp (now Hoke County), where they became vast landholders, owning perhaps 200,000 acres.[11] Their old Gilchrist home is currently being carefully restored (see p. 97). John was a member of the N.C. Legislature in 1792, 1793-1796 and 1797. Effie d. 1794, aged 46, and John m. secondly, Flora Currie. John Gilchrist Sr. died in Robeson County in May, 1802, aged 62.

The children of John Gilchrist Sr. are traced by Purcell as follows. John Gilchrist and Effie McMillan had nine children:[12]

I. MARY GILCHRIST b. 1771, d. Nov. 20, 1843. Married first Col. Archibald McKay, and secondly, John Purcell.

II. ANGUS GILCHRIST b. 1773, d. Oct. 2, 1834. Married first Margaret McKay, and secondly, Mrs. Elizabeth McNeill (Graham).

III. MARGARET GILCHRIST b. 1775, m. John McPhaul.

IV. ARCHIBALD GILCHRIST b. 1777, m. Mary McPherson. (J.E. Purcell notes a difficulty in the dates of birth of ARCHIBALD and his brother, MALCOLM).[13]

V. MALCOLM GILCHRIST b. c. 1777/78, d. Mar. 17, 1850/51, m. Anny Galbraith.

VI. GILBERT GILCHRIST b. 1780, d. 1857, m. first, Nancy McPherson, and secondly, Mary Currie.

VII. FLORA GILCHRIST b. 1782, d. Oct. 29, 1843, m. Dougald Torrey.

VIII. JOHN GILCHRIST II b. 1785, d. Dec. 6, 1868, was single.

IX. LINLIE GILCHRIST.

John Gilchrist Sr. married secondly, Flora Currie from near Turnpike Bridge on Lumber River. She is buried in the old McIntosh Cemetery in present Scotland County, N.C., and d. Dec. 5, 1847, aged 87. They had one child:

X.EFFIE GILCHRIST b. June 21, 1796, d. Dec., 1866. She m. John Blue II, b. in North Carolina, Sept. 28, 1776, d. May 3, 1831. The descendants of their ten children are traced by Purcell.[14]

The sister of John Gilchrist Sr., Mary Gilchrist, who as we have said, had emigrated with her husband to North Carolina in 1763, was older than her brother, and had been married several years when they came to America.[15] Her husband, John McBryde, was her first cousin, and they were married in 1759. Mary Gilchrist and John McBryde are buried at the McEachern Cemetery at Mill Prong in Hoke County, N.C., John McBryde d. 1785, and Mary d. 1792. They had five children, who are traced by Purcell[16]:

I. DUNCAN MCBRYDE b. in Kintyre, Scotland, 1762, d. Dec. 11, 1838.

II. JOHN MCBRYDE II, d. single

III. ANGUS MCBRYDE d. single

IV. ARCHIBALD MCBRYDE, married and first lived in Richmond County, N.C., and then moved to Alabama.

V. MARY MCBRYDE m. Archibald Smith and moved to Chesterfield District, S.C.

A More Recent Gilchrist History

It should be noted here that further research has been done on the Gilchrist family by Robert W. Gilchrist of Titusville, Florida, which includes considerable information on both the Scottish and American sides not found in the earlier work of Purcell. It is entitled: *The Gilchrists of Kintyre, Scotland,* and was published privately in 1987 and again in 1997. It contains four chapters.

I. The Origin of the MacGilchrists of Western Scotland
II. The MacGilchrists of 17th and 18th Century Kintyre
III. The Arrival of John and Malcolm Gilchrist in North Carolina
IV. The Gilchrists in South Alabama

McLeod Family

This family, which has been well known in Robeson County for over a century, lived for many years in Moore County, N.C., to which their emigrant ancestor, Alexander McLeod first came from Scotland. Their family history has been compiled by the Revd. James B. MacLeod of Lumberton, N.C., and published privately for the family in 1985, under the title: *Patriarchal Papers: Vol. 7: The Descendants of Alexander McLeod (?-1815).* All of my information on the McLeods comes directly from this volume.

The head of this family, Alexander McLeod, is believed to have been born on the Isle of Skye, where he married Nancy Ann McDonald. They had five children born in Scotland, and had entered a land grant application in (then) Cumberland County, N.C., in 1783.[17] They lived on the banks of Upper Little River (now in Moore County) and acquired a tract of 815 acres by the time of Alexander's death in 1815. They attended Buffalo Presbyterian Church, near present Sanford, N.C. Alexander and his wife were buried on the family plantation in what became known as the McLeod-McIver Cemetery in present Lee County. This cemetery was rediscovered by the family in 1983.[18]

Alexander McLeod d. May 30, 1815, and Nancy d. May 22, 1833. They had five children born in Scotland, and one born in North Carolina:

I. DANIEL MCLEOD
II. ANGUS MCLEOD
III. MARY MCLEOD
IV. KATHERINE MCLEOD
V. FLORA MCLEOD
VI. JOHN MCLEOD

I. DANIEL MCLEOD lived in Moore County, d. single in 1852

II. ANGUS MCLEOD, no information

III. MARY MCLEOD b. 1767 on the Isle of Skye, buried McLeod-McIver Cemetery in Lee County, N.C. She m. Daniel McIver I and had seven children (see the McIver section of this volume, and refer to Kenneth L. Kelly's *McIver Family of North Carolina*).

IV. KATHERINE MCLEOD, lived in Robeson County. It is uncertain whether or not she married.[19]

V. FLORA MCLEOD b. on the Isle of Skye, m. in Moore County David McNeill. They had five children:

A. Nancy Catherine McNeill
B. Maggie McNeill
C. Mary McNeill
D. Robert McNeill
E. Claude McNeill

VI. JOHN MCLEOD, the only one of the Alexander McLeod children to be born in America, was born—according to census records—in 1783. He d. in Moore County in 1853. He went from the Upper Little River section of then Moore County (now Lee County) to the Lick Creek section of Moore to teach school. He married a widow, Elizabeth Hinton Brewer, born 1788. She had four children by her first marriage to Brewer: Drake, Patsy, Delilah and Sackfield.[20] By her second marriage to John McLeod:

A. Louis Hinton McLeod b. Mar. 23, 1826, d. Mar. 27, 1863, m. Eliza Jane Walker and lived near Broadway, N.C. They had five children who are traced by J. B. MacLeod.[21]
B. Nancy Ann McLeod b. 1828, d. Aug. 31, 1888, m. James D. Pullen. They lived in Raleigh, N.C., and had three children.[22]
C. Alexander Hamilton McLeod b. Jan. 27, 1830, d. Sept. 25, 1904, was the progenitor of the Robeson County McLeods. He moved to the Marietta district of Robeson County to pursue the mercantile business. Later, after his father's estate

in Moore County was settled, he moved to Lumberton, N.C., where he m. Emily Sarah Blount on Aug. 16, 1855. She was age 15. They had seven children, several of whom died with diphtheria. The descendants of these are traced by J.B. MacLeod:[23]

1. John Blount McLeod b. Sept. 9, 1856, d. Aug. 25, 1890
2. Fannie Hinton McLeod b. Sept. 10, 1858, d. Oct. 22, 1864
3. George Badger McLeod b. June 22, 1860, d. Jan. 1, 1943
4. Ida McLeod b. Dec. 22, 1861, d. Nov. 1, 1864
5. Sallie Neill McLeod b. Aug. 13, 1864, d. Dec. 13, 1864
6. Alpheus Hinton McLeod b. Oct. 9, 1869, d. Oct. 15, 1918
7. Alexander Hamilton McLeod b. Apr. 13, 1874, d. Apr. 10, 1952

Fairly Family of Robeson County

The John Fairly Family has been traced recently by Clarice G. Fairly (Mrs. Kenneth W. Fairly) of Brandon, Mississippi. Her five page work (unpublished) on this old Robeson County family (much of which migrated to the Southwest) is carefully documented and is in my possession. All of my information comes directly from this work. Mrs. Fairly has extensive genealogical material on these lines and is glad to correspond with interested researchers.

John Fairly b. 1717, d. 1798, and his wife, Margaret Stewart, b. 1719, d. 1781, came from Kintyre, Scotland sometime after 1764 and before 1772 with four sons and two daughters to Wilmington, N.C. They settled on Drowning Creek in present Robeson County, and were buried in a family cemetery about one quarter mile north of Centre Presbyterian Church, near Maxton, N.C. All of their children were born in Scotland:

I. ARCHIBALD FAIRLY
II. MARY FAIRLY
III. ALEXANDER FAIRLY
IV. DANIEL FAIRLY
V. ROBERT FAIRLY
VI. JOHN FAIRLY
VII. ANN FAIRLY

I. ARCHIBALD FAIRLY b. 1749, d. 1807, m. Mary McRae. They had:

A. John Fairbanks Fairly b. 1777, d. 1867, m. Isabelle McNair. He d. in MS.

B. Alexander Fairly
C. Peter Fairly b. 1782, m. Margaret Little. He d. in MS.
D. Archibald Fairly b. 1794, m. Margaret Carmichael. He d. in MS.
E. Angus Fairly

II. MARY FAIRLY b. 1751, d. 1834, m. Patrick McEachin. They are buried in the Fairly Cemetery near her parents. Their dau. Margaret Fairly, b. 1783, d. 1823, m. Hon. James Stewart. She is buried in Stewartsville Cemetery near Laurinburg, N.C. There were probably other children.

III. ALEXANDER FAIRLY b. 1753, d. 1827, m. in 1791 Effie McLaurin in Richmond County, N.C.(who left from Port Appin, Scotland, with her brothers in 1790). All of their children were born in North Carolina:
A. Archibald Fairly b. 1792, d. 1831, m. Eliza McLean.
B. Peter Fairly b. 1793, d. 1852, m. Mary McLaurin, dau. of "Piper" Hugh McLaurin and Mary McColl. They had four children born in Richmond County, N.C., and then three children born in Jefferson County, MS., to which they had moved in 1834.
C. Margaret Fairly m. Daniel McNair. They came to MS.
D. Nancy Fairly m. Peter McEachin. They came to MS.
E. Catherine Fairly was single and came to MS.
F. Mary Fairly m. Daniel McMillan and came to MS.
G. John McLaurin Fairly b. 1805, d. 1862, m. Margaret McLaurin. They are buried on the Jim Walter McLaurin Farm between Hasty and Johns, N.C. This family remained in North Carolina with their five children.
H. Daniel Fairly b. 1806, d. 1831, m. Mary "Polly" McArthur. The are buried in the McLaurin Cemetery near Johns and Hasty, N.C. Their daughter, Katie Fairly m. J. R. McLaurin.

IV. ROBERT FAIRLY b. 1760, d. 1821, m. Effy Peterson. They are buried in the Fairly Cemetery near Center Presbyterian Church, Maxton, N.C. They had a son named John Fairly.

V. JOHN FAIRLY b. 1763, d. 1854, m. Katherine Carmichael. They went to Miss. in the 1820's and died in Perry County, MS. All of their eleven children were born in North Carolina between 1797 and 1822.

VI. ANN FAIRLY b. c. 1764, d. before 1795, m. Angus McGill. They had children whose names are unknown.

Brown Marsh Families

Most of the Scots families of Carolina tended to be inland from the point of arrival in Wilmington, settling in the areas towards Fayetteville and beyond to the northwestward, or on the Lumber River in Robeson County. However, a number of Highland families settled in the Brown Marsh section of the lower Cape Fear River in Bladen County at an early date. While these families were not so numerous as the upcountry Scots, they tended to control very large areas of land, and many of them in later years married into the upper Cape Fear and Lumber River Scots families.

The center of this settlement was Brown Marsh Presbyterian Church. We know that it served the early settlements, because it was visited by Revd. Hugh McAden in 1756, but its Session Minutes are defective and go back only to 1792. This Church was described in an article in the

Black River Presbyterian Church, a few miles from Brown Marsh near Ivanhoe, N.C., was founded by early Scottish emigrant members of the Argyll colony some time after 1740. This particular building was constructed in 1859. The building committee consisted of James Kerr, Daniel McAlister, William Colvin, James McDuffie, Cornelius Johnson, George Bannerman, James Ennis, and William Robinson.

North Carolina Presbyterian, April, 1858, which has been recently reprinted in *The Robeson County Register.*[24]

Several of the Brown Marsh Scots emigrant families have been written about in Lionel Dane Melvin's *Lest We Forget: Our Melvins and Kin,* particularly, the MacKeithans, McColls (McCalls), Iver McKays.[25] Ada McRackan Allen has written concerning the Ronald McMillan and James McRackan families, and mention has been given to the Daniel McNeill of Gigha family in *The McNeill's Ferry Chronicle and Campbell University* by Everett McNeill Kivette.[26]

We will briefly list basic information concerning some of these Brown Marsh families. There is not sufficient material presently available to me to trace the Daniel McNeill family or the Iver McKay family. I deal with the McRackan family at the end of the Cumberland County section, since they were there many years before some of them came to Brown Marsh.

McKeithan (McKiechan) Families of Bladen County

All of my information on these families is taken from Lionel Melvin's *Lest We Forget.*

There are several McKeithan families in this vicinity. According to the information compiled by Melvin, they do all appear to be descended from Donald McKeithan (McKiechan) b. c. 1680, Isle of Uist, Scotland, d. 1750 in Bladen County. Donald received land grants in Bladen in 1740 and 1746, thus showing that he was one of the earlier Scots emigrants to Carolina, appearing immediately after the 1739 Argyll Colony.[27] He held land in Brunswick, Bladen and Cumberland Counties. His wife's name is unknown. They had seven children:[28]

I. ALEXANDER MCKEITHAN (listed in a 1746 New Hanover County, N.C. land deed)[29]

II. SARAH MCKEITHAN (listed in her brother, Dugald's will of 1750)[30]

III. DUGALD MCKEITHAN made his will on Jan. 21, 1750/51 in Bladen County, and named: "father, Donald; brothers, James and Duncan; sisters, Nancy McLauchlin and Sarah McKeithan (McKicchan) . . . "[31] He is believed to have been born c. 1700, Isle of Uist. His second wife, Mary, was with child when he made his will, and he provided for the unborn child or twins.[32] By a former marriage:

A. Mary McKeithan m. Robert Hilliard of North Hampton County, N.C., son of John and Mary Hilliard. They had one son, Robert, and three daughters, Mary, Martha (Patsy), and Pharaby.

IV. NANCY MCKEITHAN m. _________ McLauchlan.

V. JAMES MCKEITHAN b. c. 1710, will probated in 1794, m. 1740. They had: "Blind John" McKeithan, who m. Grisella, dau. of Col. Alexander McAlester, James McKeithan, Donald McKeithan, Ann McKeithan, and Sarah McKeithan.

VI. DONALD MCKEITHAN (?). According to the 1750 will of Dugald, Donald had a son Duncan.[33]

VII. DUNCAN MCKEITHAN SR. He is listed in the 1750 will of his brother, Dugald. His own will was written in 1775 and names:

- A. Duncan McKeithan Jr. b. 1725, d. 1778, m. Isabella McKay and had:
  - 1. Daniel McKeithan b. 1750, d. 1829, m. Mary Coll and had four sons and one daughter (listed in his will).[34]
- B. Margaret McFatter
- C. Elizabeth McDaniel

McColl (McCall) Family of Brown Marsh

The emigrant ancestor of this family is unknown. His two sons and two daughters were well known in the Brown Marsh area:[35]

I. ALEXANDER MCCOLL b. 1750, d. 1824, m. Flora Blue.

II. MARY (MOLLY) MCCOLL b. 1757, d. 1821, said to have m. Daniel McKeithan.[36]

III. DUNCAN MCCOLL (MCCALL) b. 1760, d. 1841, m. Christian McCoulskey, dau. of Neil McCoulskey and Mary Clark, dau. of John Clark, who was a member of Gov. Gabriel Johnston's Council of State. Neil McCoulskey came over from the Isle of Jura, Scotland, with his father, Duncan, c. 1746, and settled in the Brown Marsh area.[37] Duncan McColl and Christian McCoulskey had:

- A. Neill McColl, b. May 8, 1789 at Brown Marsh, d. Mar. 30, 1826, and buried in McColl-McCoulskey Cemetery near Brown Marsh. He m. Aug. 29, 1816 Mary McNeill.
- B. Catherine McColl, b. Nov. 4, 1790 at Brown Marsh, m. John Munn.

C. Mary McColl, b. June 12, 1792 at Brown Marsh, d. Sept. 3, 1832 at Brown Marsh, m. in 1819 Dougald McKeithan, son of Daniel McKeithan and Mary McColl (see previous page).

D. Archibald McColl

E. John McColl b. Feb. 14, 1788 at Brown Marsh, d. May 1, 1877, m. Apr. 6, 1820 Ann McNeill. He m. twice after the death of Ann on Sept. 3, 1822.[38]

F. Ann McColl b. Apr. 4, 1794 at Brown Marsh, d. Feb. 22, 1881, and buried at Mt. Horeb Presbyterian Cemetery, Bladen County. She m. at Brown Marsh on Feb. 18, 1823, John McKeithan, son of Daniel McKeithan of Hammond's Creek in Bladen County.

Ronald McMillan Family of Brown Marsh

This family has been carefully researched by Ada McRackan Allen in *Ronald McMillan and His Descendants 1784-1985* (privately printed for the family). All of my information comes from this source.

The head of this family was Ronald McMillan of Southend, Kintyre, Scotland, who was living on Knockmorran farm in 1770. He had a sister, Flora McMillan Clarke, who lived in Campbeltown, and a brother, Iver, who lived at Inveresk near Edinburgh. Iver McMillan was a man of wealth, commander of the Honourable East India Company ship, "Valentine," whose will (executed after his death in 1807) left a large estate to the surviving children of his brother, Ronald McMillan, who had emigrated to North Carolina in 1784.

Ronald McMillan came to North Carolina with his wife and eight children in 1784, and received various grants of land in Bladen County on Horseshoe Swamp, Middle Swamp and Baptist Neck. He died without a will in 1823. The family possesses an original document from the Parish of Southend, giving the birth dates of their eight children. The children of Ronald McMillan Sr. and wife:

I. MARY MCMILLAN b. Feb. 10, 1770, m. Daniel Shaw of Bladen County, N.C. She d. 1825 and was buried in Shaw Cemetery in Bladen County.

II. ALEXANDER MCMILLAN b. Dec. 21, 1771. According to the research of Mrs. Ada McR. Allen, Alexander never came to America. He

served as an officer in the 26th Cameronian Regiment, until he sold out his commission on 7 March 1814.

III. IVER MCMILLAN b. Sept. 2, 1773. He lived in Bladen County and is buried at Old Brown Marsh Church. According to his tombstone, he m. Mary _____, who d. July 26, 1840 aged 64 years. Iver represented Bladen County in the North Carolina House of Commons nine times: 1824-1833 and in the Senate in 1834-1835. Their children:

A. Daniel McMillan, who d. Jan. 13, 1840, aged 5 years and is buried with his parents
B. Dougald McMillan
C. Ronald McMillan
D. Iver McMillan
E. Archibald McMillan

IV. BETTY MCMILLAN b. Sept. 14, 1775, d. May, 1814; she was single.

V. ARCHIBALD MCMILLAN b. July 20, 1777, d. Sept. 12, 1823; was single. He made trips to London and Scotland to assist in the settlement of his Uncle Iver's estate in 1815 and 1816.

VI. RONALD MCMILLAN b. Apr. 21, 1780, d. July 20, 1838, buried in the Western Prong Cemetery (Bladen County). He m. Mary (Polly) McKay, b. Nov. 20, 1782, d. June 17, 1832. They had two daughters:

A. Margaret McMillan b. 1815, d. 1874, buried in Whiteville Cemetery. She m. William Baldwin, b. 1810, d. 1897. They had eleven children, who are traced in the volume of Ada Allen.
B. Mary McMillan b. Apr. 10, 1818, d. Apr. 7, 1884, buried in Western Prong Cemetery. She was m. three times: first, to John R. Kelly; secondly, to Anthony F. Toon, and thirdly, to Robert M. McRacken. The descendants of the ten children of these marriages are traced in Ada Allen's volume.

VII. DANIEL (DONALD) MCMILLAN b. Mar. 10, 1782, d. Dec. 12, 1860, and is buried in Western Prong Cemetery. Is believed to have been single.

VIII. DOUGALD MCMILLAN b. June 10, 1784, d. 1822 or 23. Is believed to have been single.

Notes

1. Ibid., 17-55.
2. Ibid., 55-60.
3. Ibid., 73-175.
4. Ibid., 181-224.
5. Ibid., 227.
6. Ibid., 230-335.
7. Ibid., 336-414.
8. Descendants traced in ibid., 414-457.
9. Descendants listed, though not traced, in ibid. 458.
10. Ibid., 465.
11. Ibid., 466.
12. Traced in ibid., 468-700.
13. Ibid., 468.
14. Ibid., 702-735.
15. Ibid., 735.
16. Ibid., 735-742.
17. James B. MacLeod, *Patriarchal Papers,* Vol. 7, (1985), 5, 6.
18. Ibid., 7, 8.
19. Ibid., 16.
20. Ibid., 18.
21. Ibid., 68-83.
22. Listed in ibid., 83.
23. Ibid., 30, 31, 83-90.
24. See Vol. 1, No. 2, May, 1986, submitted by Charles F. McKee.
25. Published 1979 by Media, Inc.: Greensboro, N.C.
26. Published by Yancey Graphics: Burnsville, N.C. 28714.
27. Lionel D. Melvin, *Lest We Forget,* 162, 163.
28. Ibid., 163.
29. Ibid., 160.
30. Ibid.
31. Ibid.
32. Ibid., 163.
33. Ibid., 160.
34. Ibid., 161, 162.
35. Ibid., 182ff.
36. My copy of ibid. has been anotated by hand of Mr. Jack McPhaul of Southern Pines, N.C. with information that changes the name of Molly McColl's husband from Duncan to Daniel on p. 182 of the text
37. Ibid., 182. A history of this family has been written by John K. Clark, *The Double-Branch Clarks.*
38. Melvin, op. cit., 182.

12

Highland Scots in the Pee Dee Area of South Carolina

THIS STUDY IS ENTITLED *Carolina Scots* rather than *North Carolina Scots,* because large numbers of the Cape Fear Valley Scots spilled over into the Marlboro and Marion districts of nearby South Carolina: an area generally known as the Pee Dee Country. No study of Highlanders in Carolina could hope to be complete which did not deal with some of the large and old Scottish emigrant families of this area.

Although technically the Pee Dee area is in South Carolina, in many respects it has always been culturally an extension of the Cape Fear Highland settlement. Indeed, it is not very far from the heart of the Highland community: Fayetteville. As Major-General Roderick L. Carmichael wrote: "From Fayetteville the settlement spread out, and by 1800 covered an area extending about 50 miles in all directions, including portions of Marion, Marlboro and Chesterfield counties in South Carolina. The later arrivals therefore had a considerable distance to go after reaching Fayetteville before reaching their new homes."[1]

This is the oldest Scottish immigrant house in the Pee Dee. It is in the Carolina section of (present) Dillon County, S.C., near the Robeson County, N.C., line. Daniel McKay was born in Kintyre, Scotland, in 1754 and emigranted to the Pee Dee area of South Carolina about 1774. He built this house in the early 1790s. In 1978 it was moved across the road by its present owners, Mr. and Mrs. Robert McNiel. Mrs. McNiel is a descendant of emigrant Daniel McKay.

The Carmichaels

One of the large Pee Dee families is that of Carmichael. Their history was traced in 1935 by Major-General Roderick L. Carmichael, and considerable reference is made to many of this clan in Mary Belle Manning Bethea's *Ancestral Key to the Pee Dee*.[2] The following Carmichael families are traced in Roderick Carmichael's genealogy:

Archibald Carmichael

Archibald Carmichael was born in Scotland in 1749, and with his wife Mary, also born in 1749, and a daughter, Katherine, age 7, sailed from Scotland on September 4, 1775, to Wilmington, N.C., on the ship "Jupiter." He acquired lands by 1784 on Leith's Creek in Richmond (now Scotland) County, N.C., and added more property in the 1790s. By 1802 he acquired lands on the east side of Little Pee Dee River in Marion (now Dillon) County, 'adjacent of lands of his sons.'[3] His wife died between 1820 and '30, and he may have been married twice. According to Roderick L. Carmichael:

After moving to Marion County about 1819, Archibald lived near Little Pee Dee Church, a short distance from his sons Dougald and Neil, and a few miles from his daughter Katherine and his son Duncan. After his wife's death, between 1820 and 1830, he lived with his daughter Katherine, who was a widow after about 1817. He died between 1830 and 1840, and he and his wife are buried in one of the two earliest Carmichael graveyards, about one-half mile NW of Little Pee Dee Church. Archibald was brother of Duncan, of Daniel and of one or more of the other Immigrant Carmichael heads of families of the Scottish Highland group that came to North and South Carolina, and was a cousin of the others.[4]

Archibald and Katherine Carmichael had three children:

I. KATHERINE II. NEIL

III. DUNCAN

I. KATHERINE CARMICHAEL b. 1769 in Scotland, d. 1852 in South Carolina, m. Duncan Carmichael, her first cousin, son of emigrant Duncan, who was brother of Archibald. Duncan was b. 1779 in North Carolina and d. c. 1817 in South Carolina. They had seven children who are traced in R.L. Carmichael's work.[5]

II. NEIL CARMICHAEL b. c. 1776 in North Carolina, d. 1809 in South Carolina, m. his first cousin, Christian Carmichael, daughter of Archibald's brother, Duncan. She was b. 1780 in North Carolina, d. 1856 in South Carolina. They had six children who are traced in R.L. Carmichael's work.[6]

A mill rock and candle stick that were among other effects brought by Daniel McKay from Kintyre to South Carolina in 1774. They are pictured behind the home of Mr. and Mrs. Robert McNiel.

III. DUNCAN CARMICHAEL b. c. 1778 in North Carolina, d. 1836 in South Carolina, m. Mary Monroe, b. 1790 in North Carolina, d. 1857 in South Carolina. They had seven children who are traced in Carmichael's work.[7]

Duncan Carmichael Family

The second Carmichael family traced by Roderick L. Carmichael is that of emigrant Duncan Carmichael, said to be a brother of Archibald Carmichael. Duncan was born in Scotland c. 1750, and d. in North Carolina before 1790. He lived on Leith's Creek in Richmond County, N.C. His wife's name is unknown. They had two known children:

I. DUNCAN CARMICHAEL, whose family is traced under Archibald Carmichael, immediately above, since he married Archibald's daughter, Katherine.

II. CHRISTIAN CARMICHAEL, whose family is traced under Archibald Carmichael, immediately above, since she married Archibald's son, Neil.

Daniel Carmichael Family

Emigrant Daniel is traditionally said to be a brother of Archibald and Duncan Carmichael, but no records confirm this. He came from the Isle of Lismore, Argyllshire, and settled in Richmond (now Scotland) County, N.C., about 1792. Around 1797 he moved to the SW side of Little Pee Dee River at Carmichael's Bridge (named for him), some two miles NW of Fork, S.C., where he d. between 1820 and 1830. Daniel Carmichael was b. c. 1750 and m. Katherine Calhoun, b. in Scotland, and d. in South Carolina between 1820 and 1830. They had three known children:

I. JOHN C. CARMICHAEL b. 1781? or 1785? in Scotland, d. 1857 in Georgia, m. c. 1816 Margaret Morrison, b. 1787 in North Carolina, d. 1850 in Georgia. John C. came from Scotland about 1792 to North Carolina. By 1797 he was in Fork, S.C., and then c. 1831 moved to Sumter County, Georgia. They had seven children who are traced in Carmichael's work.[8]

II. DOUGALD CARMICHAEL b. 1787 in Scotland, d. 1866 in South Carolina, m. 1812 Katherine Carmichael, daughter of yet another emigrant, Dougald Carmichael (see following section). She was b. 1793 in North Carolina, and d. 1853 in Mullins, S.C. They had eleven who are traced in Carmichael's work.[9]

III. MALCOLM CARMICHAEL b. 1792 in North Carolina, d. 1860-70 in Alabama, m. c. 1818 Nancy McDuffie, b. 1850 in Scotland, d. in Alabama. Malcolm lived in (present) Dillon County, S.C., until c. 1833, when he moved to Dale County, Alabama. They had eight children who are traced in Carmichael's work.[10]

Dougald Carmichael Family

Roderick L. Carmichael shows that there were several immigrant Dougald Carmichaels in the Carolinas.[11] This Dougald Carmichael was b. c. 1750 in Scotland, and d. 1820-30 in South Carolina. He m. Flora Monroe, d. 1820-30 near present Dillon, S.C. They are buried in the old Carmichael graveyard, one-half mile NW of Little Pee Dee Presbyterian Church. They had ten children:

I. NEIL CARMICHAEL (SQUIRE) b. 1787 in North Carolina, d. c. 1864 in Texas, m. Mary McCall, b. 1791 in North Carolina, d. in Gonzales County, Texas. They moved from present Dillon County, S.C., to Texas in 1857. They had eleven children who are traced by Carmichael.[12]

II. MARY CARMICHAEL b. 1786 in North Carolina, d. 1859 in Alabama, m. 1801 "Commodore" Dougald Carmichael, b. c. 1768 in Scotland, d. c. 1830 in S.C. They had seven children who are traced by Carmichael.[13]

III. KATHERINE CARMICHAEL, whose family is traced under the Daniel Carmichael section, since she m. Dougald, son of emigrant Daniel.

IV. DANIEL WASHINGTON CARMICHAEL b. 1791 in North Carolina, d. 1860 in South Carolina, m. Agnes Campbell, b. 1801, d. 1875 near present Dillon, S.C. They had seven children who are traced by Carmichael.[14]

V. ARCHIBALD CARMICHAEL b. 1794 in North Carolina, d. 1844 in Mississippi, m. Katherine McQuaig, b. 1794 in Virginia, d. 1882 in Clarke County, Miss. They moved from present Dillon County, S.C., to Mississippi in 1835. They had seven children who are traced by Carmichael.[15]

VI. DOUGALD CARMICHAEL b. 1795 in South Carolina, d. in Arkansas, m. Lucy Fuller, d. 1840-50 in South Carolina. He moved from present Dillon County, S.C., to Arkansas in 1855. They had three children who are traced by Carmichael.[16]

VII. NANCY CARMICHAEL b. 1799 in South Carolina, m. William S. Campbell b. 1801, lived near present Latta, S.C. They had eight children who are listed by Carmichael.[17]

VIII. MALCOLM R. CARMICHAEL b. 1808, d. 1870, m. Katherine Ray, b. 1805, d. 1840 in present Dillon County, S.C. They had four children who are listed by Carmichael.[18]

IX. MICHAEL CARMICHAEL b. 1807, d. 1864, m. Mary Ray, b. 1803, d. 1881 in present Dillon County, S.C. They had eight children who are traced by Carmichael.[19]

X. FLORA CARMICHAEL b. 1801, m. _____ McBryde.

Family of Immigrant Dougald McIntyre and Wife, Christian Carmichael

Christian Carmichael was the sister of Archibald, Duncan and Daniel Carmichael, whose families have just been traced. She was b. c. 1760 in Scotland, and d. in Scotland c. 1820, just before her husband, Dougald McIntyre, whom she m. in 1790, came to America with their children c. 1820/1. Dougald was b. 1753 in Scotland, and d. 1823 in South Carolina, near present Hamer. They had four children. Two of their sons, Duncan and Daniel, came to South Carolina in 1820, and the other two, Dougald and Archibald, accompanied their father to present Dillon County, S.C., by way of Boston, Mass. and Georgetown, S.C., in 1822. They later settled about one mile east of Kentyre Presbyterian Church, near present Dillon, S.C. Their children:

I. DOUGALD MCINTYRE b. 1791 in Scotland, d. 1860 in South Carolina, m. 1819 Lily Campbell, b. 1800 in Scotland, d. 1882 in South Carolina. They had eleven children who are listed by Carmichael.[20]

II. DUNCAN MCINTYRE b. 1793 in Scotland, d. in North Carolina. He was a Presbyterian minister in North and South Carolina.

III. ARCHIBALD MCINTYRE b. 1798 in Scotland, d. 1854 in Alabama, m. Effie McCallum. They moved to Alabama in 1836.

IV. DANIEL MCINTYRE b. 1800 in Scotland, d. 1878 in South Carolina, m. 1825, Mary (Polly) Carmichael, daughter of "Commodore" Dougald Carmichael. She was b. 1802, d. 1869. They had three sons who are traced by Carmichael.[21]

Family of Immigrant Duncan Carmichael

Duncan Carmichael was b. in Scotland before 1755 and is said to have sailed from Edinburgh in 1788 with two sons and one daughter. They are supposed to have lived first in New York State, and in 1797 to have moved to Richmond County, North Carolina. Duncan made a will in 1814 in which he names his son John, his daughter Mary Carmichael McColl and his grandson, Duncan McColl.[22] Duncan and his wife (name unknown) had three children, of whom two are known:

I. MARY CARMICHAEL b. in Scotland, m. Alexander McColl of Marlboro County, South Carolina. They probably had several children, but only Duncan McColl is listed in his grandfather's will.

II. JOHN CARMICHAEL b. 1790, d. 1865, m. Katherine McCormick, b. 1793, d. 1877 near Laurinburg, N.C. Katherine was the daughter of Duncan McCormick and wife, Katherine Carmichael (parentage unknown). John and Katherine Mc C. Carmichael had nine children who are traced by Carmichael.[23]

Family of Immigrant John Carmichael

John Carmichael is said to have been b. in Scotland in 1755 and d. 1837 in North Carolina. He immigrated to Carolina before 1799, when he purchased land in Richmond (now Scotland) County. He is said to have originally been a sailor, and to have been known as "John Ban." [Ban in Gaelic means "fair".] He m. Nancy, daughter of John McKeichen of Mederlock, Scotland. She was b. 1765 in Scotland, and d. 1838 in North Carolina. John is believed to have come from Appin. They lived near Laurinburg, N.C., and had nine children:

I. JOHN CARMICHAEL b. c. 1790 in North Carolina, d. c. 1860 in Georgia, m. first Sarah McRae, d. 1830, and secondly Miss Calhoun. They moved to Rockmart, Georgia, and had eight children who are traced by Carmichael.[24]

II. ARCHIBALD CARMICHAEL b. in North Carolina, went to Louisiana c. 1830.

III. HUGH CARMICHAEL b. 1804 in North Carolina, d. 1881, m. Tamar Wilkinson. They lived in Lauderdale, Mississippi, and had eight children, some of whom are traced by Carmichael.[25]

IV. DUNCAN M. CARMICHAEL b. 1807, d. 1859, m. Nancy Hasty, lived at Laurinburg, N.C., no children.

V. JEANNETTE CARMICHAEL b. 1794, d. 1862 at Laurinburg, N.C., was single.

VI. EFFIE CARMICHAEL b. 1795, d. 1854 at Laurinburg, N.C., was single.

VII. KATHERINE CARMICHAEL b. 1796, d. 1849 at Laurinburg, N.C., was single.

VIII. MARGARET CARMICHAEL b. 1801, d. 1880 at Laurinburg, N.C., was single.

IX. MARY CARMICHAEL b. 1790, d. 1835, m. John McIntyre, b. 1767 in Scotland, d. 1854 at Laurinburg, N.C. They had ten children who are traced by Carmichael.[26]

Family of Daniel Carmichael of Richmond County, North Carolina

This Daniel Carmichael is said to have been b. in Richmond County in 1804. He moved with his family first to Alabama and then to Mississippi, where he d. 1889 at Union Church, a largely Scottish settlement. He m. Nancy McCormick b. 1801, d. 1876. They had ten children:

I. KATHERINE JANE CARMICHAEL b. 1830, d. 1876, m. 1856 Archibald McIntyre; lived at Union Church, Mississippi. They had four children.[27]

II. EVANDER JOSEPH CARMICHAEL

III. MARY MARGARET CARMICHAEL

IV. NANCY ANN CARMICHAEL

V. REBECCA CARMICHAEL b. 1836, d. 1921, m. 1860 Archie Fairly, b. 1794, d. in Mississippi. They are listed in this volume under the family of John Fairly and wife, Margaret Stewart, pp. 353-55. They had six children, some of whom are traced by Carmichael.[28]

VI. DOUGALD CARMICHAEL

VII. FLORA CARMICHAEL b. 1839, d. 1906, m. 1867 Josiah Garrett, d. 1928, Union Church, Mississippi. They had seven children who are listed by Carmichael.[29]

VIII. DUNCAN CARMICHAEL

IX. JOHN BROWN CARMICHAEL b. 1842, d. 1920, m. Mary Parker, lived at Union Church, Mississippi. They had four children who are traced by Carmichael.[30]

X. DANIEL WASHINGTON CARMICHAEL

McLaurin Family of Pee Dee

The large and widespread McLaurin family has been more fortunate than many of the Scots emigrants in having carefully preserved many of its early pre-emigration records, as well as having talented writers who have recorded much of its post-emigration genealogy. Bert McLaurin published a history of the McLaurins, *Seannachie,* in 1971 (printed privately in Rockingham, N.C.), and later in the 1970s, Gordon G. McLaurin of Dillon, S.C., published (privately, in Dillon) *G.G. McLaurin and Some of His Kin: Sketches and Genealogy.* In addition to these two excellent sources of information, there are references to the McLaurins in Rev. Thomas' *History of Marlboro County*[31] and more contemporary genealogical information will be found in Mary Belle M. Bethea's *Ancestral Key to the Pee Dee.*

Gordon G. McLaurin has researched the pre-emigration genealogy of the Pee Dee McLaurins to Daniel McLaurin I, b. c. 1610, who m. an Appin Stewart.[32] His son was John McLaurin I, b. c. 1645, who m. a Cameron and had four children, one of whom was John McLaurin II ("Culloden John"), b. c. 1680 in Argyllshire and killed at the Battle of Culloden in 1745. By his first wife (name unknown) he had a son, Neill, b. 1723, and by his second wife, a Miss Buchanan (?), whom he m. c. 1730, he had three sons:[33]

I. DANIEL MCLAURIN II, from whom the Pee Dee McLaurins are descended. Most of this section on the McLaurins is to be given to his descendants, after we briefly mention the second and third sons of Daniel I.

II. HUGH MCLAURIN, who d. before maturity

III. DUNCAN MCLAURIN, b. 1740 in Argyllshire, emigrated to Carolina via Charleston, S.C., in 1770, and settled in Richmond (now Scotland) County, N.C. He fought with the American forces under Captain William Meer during the Revolution. After the War he first m. a Miss McPhater, by whom he had a daughter, Catherine, who never married. Secondly, he m. in 1790 Catherine McLaurin, who had recently arrived from Glasgow. They had four sons and one daughter:

A. Neill McLaurin b. 1792, d. 1856, m. Jane McColl. Gordon G. McLaurin traces some of the descendants of Neill McLaurin, most of whom lived in Mississippi.[34]

B. Duncan McLaurin b. 1794, d. 1845, a medical doctor; was single.

C. John McLaurin, d. young

D. Hugh McLaurin b. 1800, d. 1856, single

E. Christian McLaurin m. Henry Howard

I. DANIEL MCLAURIN II m. Margaret McLaurine, sister of Episcopalian minister, Robert McLaurine. They had:

A. Hugh McLaurin

B. Daniel McLaurin

C. John McLaurin

Gordon G. McLaurin summarizes the movements of these ancestors of the Pee Dee McLaurins:

> Hugh, known to our family and his descendants as "Piper" Hugh and to John Roy McLaurin as "Captain" Hugh, and his brother Daniel probably came to this country during the early stages of the Revolutionary War, while still in their 'teens.' Their younger brother, John (great-grandfather), was to follow the next year, but the war prevented his reaching this country until 1783 or 1784. It is believed that 'Piper' Hugh and his brother, Daniel, landed in Charleston and went directly to Richmond County, North Carolina, where their uncle, Duncan McLaurin, had already settled. . . .
>
> It is believed that Margaret, the wife of Daniel McLaurin II, died in either 1785 or 1786, and soon thereafter Daniel came to this country. The date of his arrival is not known to me, but all agree that he landed in Wilmington, N.C., went up the Cape Fear River to Fayetteville...and from there, eventually came to Marlboro County and settled near the home of his youngest son, John, (great-grandfather).[35]

While Bert and Gordon McLaurin in their genealogies largely devote their attention to the descendants of the youngest son, John III ('Surly' John), Gordon McLaurin does give some information on the two older sons as follows.

A. Hugh "Piper" McLaurin b. c. 1760 in Argyllshire, and came to Richmond County, N.C., during the first stages of the American Revolution along with his brother Daniel. He m.

Mary McColl of Richmond County, and later lived in Marlboro County, S.C. They had seven children all of whom, except possibly the youngest, were born in Richmond or Marlboro Counties. According to Gordon McLaurin:

> About 1806, it is said, Piper Hugh sold everything he owned except his slaves and moved to the Caseyville section of Mississippi. He established his home in that community and lived there until he was well up into his nineties. He is buried in the McLaurin or Blue Cemetery near Caseyville.[36]

Their children:

1. Daniel McLaurin b. 1793, d. 1850, m. Mary (Polly) McLaurin, b. 1793, d. 1893, daughter of Lauchlin McLaurin and Sarah Anne McColl of Marlboro County, S.C. They had seven children who are listed by G. G. McLaurin.[37]
2. Mary McLaurin b. 1794, d. 1860, m. Peter Fairly[38] b. 1793, d. 1852.[39] They moved to Mississippi in the early 1800s and had seven children who are listed both by McLaurin and Fairly.[40]
3. Peter McLaurin b. 1795, d. 1845, m. Margaret (Peggy) McLaurin b. 1790, who was born en route to America. She was the sister of the wife of Daniel McLaurin (b. 1793), her husband's brother. Their two children are listed by McLaurin.[41]
4. Lauchlin McLaurin b. 1796, d. 1858, m. Miss Pittman; had several children whose names are unknown.
5. Ann McLaurin (called Nancy) b. 1797, d. 1842, m. Archibald (or Daniel) Cameron. They had two sons and two daughters, three of whom are listed by McLaurin.[42]
6. John McLaurin b. 1802, single. He was in the shipping business out of Mobile, Alabama and may have been lost at sea.
7. Duncan McLaurin b. 1806, m. Rebecca Gillis. They had a daughter who m. a Mr. Cates.

B. Daniel McLaurin III b. c. 1762 in Argyllshire, and emigrated to Carolina in the mid 1770s. Traditionally he is said to have joined a whaling expedition out of Portsmouth, Maine, and to have been lost at sea, although one theory holds that he has descendants in Canada, though without documentation.[43]

C. John McLaurin III ("Surly" John or Big John) b. Dec. 9, 1765, d. Oct. 31, 1848. He was b. in Scotland and came to South Carolina via Georgetown in 1783 or 84. He first settled near his uncle Duncan in Richmond County, N.C., and later took land in Marlboro County, S.C., between present Clio and McColl. He m. Mary McNair b. 1769, d. Feb. 4, 1847. They had four children:

1. Daniel N. McLaurin b. Oct. 15, 1808, d. April 10, 1886, m. Anne Elizabeth Buie of the Union Church section of Mississippi, to which he had previously moved. He and his family later lived in McComb, Mississippi, and are buried in Brookhaven. They had five children who are partially traced by Gordon McLaurin.[44]
2. Margaret McLaurin b. April 28, 1811, d. when about two years old.
3. Lauchlin Leroy McLaurin b. April 14, 1813 near McColl, S.C., d. 1888, buried in McColl, m. Effie Ellen McColl, b. 1816, d. 1897, daughter of "Steady Hugh" McColl. They had ten children whom we list here, since the majority of the present Pee Dee McLaurins are descended from them (most of the descendents of the other McLaurin progeny now live in different parts of the country):

   a. Mary Jane McLaurin b. June 5, 1840, d. Apr. 29, 1869, m. Capt. John R. Parker and had one child who d. in infancy.
   b. John Franklin McLaurin b. Oct. 17, 1841, d. Nov. 26, 1906, m. Kittie Hubbard b. May 22, 1849, d. June 26, 1931, daughter of Peter Hubbard. They had eight children who are traced by Gordon McLaurin.[45]
   c. Hugh Laughlin McLaurin b. Dec. 16, 1843, d. Nov. 18, 1926, m. Flora Jane Calhoun b. June 6, 1845, d. Apr. 1, 1914. They had seven children who are traced by Gordon McLaurin.[46]
   d. Daniel Washington Mclaurin b. Dec. 16, 1843, d. July 13, 1928, m. Martha Colin (Mattie) McLucas b. Feb. 15, 1846, d. Mar. 15, 1924; no children.

e. Margaret Ann (Maggie) McLaurin b. Dec. 10, 1845, Aug. 6, 1869, m. John C. McCaskill. They had one child who died young.

f. James Alexander McLaurin b. Mar. 11, 1848, d. Jan. 9, 1889, m. Nancy Della McIntyre b. Dec. 9, Dec. 9, 1855, d. Sept. 3, 1933. They had five children who are traced by Gordon McLaurin.[47]

g. Albina McLaurin b. Jan. 27, 1850, d. Sept. 16, 1898, m. J. Furman Willis, b. Mar. 17, 1849, d. Dec. 14, 1920. They had four children who are traced by Gordon McLaurin.[48]

h. Effie Ellen McLaurin b. Feb. 11, 1857, d. Apr. 10, 1904, m. Roderick S. McLucas b. Mar. 10, 1842, d. Mar. 23, 1902. They had eight children who are traced by Gordon McLaurin.[49]

i. Luther McLaurin b. Aug. 20, 1857, d. Apr. 1, 1933, m. first Annie McKinnon b. Dec. 25, 1862, 1862, d. June 17, 1896, and m. secondly, Elizabeth (Liza) Covington b. Oct. 11, 1872, d. Sept. 14, 1956. He had two children by his second wife who are traced by McLaurin.[50]

j. Walter Bishop McLaurin b. Dec. 10, 1859, d. Apr. 18, 1925, m. Julia A. Terry b. Sept. 12, 1863 d. July 19, 1920. They had ten children who are traced by McLaurin.[51]

4. John J. McLaurin, youngest child of "Surly" John McLaurin III, b. Jan. 19, 1816, d. July 17, 1892, m. Belinda McLaurin b. Apr. 5, 1828, d. Nov. 15, 1878, daughter of Daniel C. McLaurin. He served in the Confederate Army and lived in McColl, S.C. They had ten children, three of whom d. young, and only three of whom married:

a. Mary Ellen (Molly) McLaurin b. Feb. 11, 1847, 1847, d. Oct. 20, 1913, m. James M. McIntyre b. Feb. 2, 1851, d. Mar. 5, 1920. They had three children who are traced by McLaurin.[52]

b. Eliza McLaurin b. Dec. 11, 1848, d. Sept. 28, 1921, was single.

c. Sidney Cameron McLaurin b. July 21, 1850,

d. Mar. 13, 1898, m. Flora Willie Henderson, and had three children who are listed by McLaurin.[53]

d. John D, McLaurin b. May 15, 1854, d. Apr. 18, 1909, m. first, Flora E. Willis b. Jan. 14, 186? d. Dec. 31, 1885, and had two children who are listed by McLaurin, and m. secondly Cattie Parker b. Oct. 6, 1863, d. Aug. 12, 1940, by whom by whom he had seven children who are listed by McLaurin.[54]

e. Atalia Mclaurin b. Apr. 2, 1856, d. July 5, 1857.

f. D.J. McLaurin b. June 3, 1858, d. Sept. 14, 1858.

g. Cary McLaurin b. Sept. 29, 1859, d. Mar. 16, 1896, was single.

h. Hugh T. McLaurin b. Mar. 21, 1865, d. May 17, 1936, was single.

i. Lauchlin McLaurin b. Mar. 6, 1868, d. Feb. 12, 1891, was single.

j. William G. McLaurin b. Aug. 24, 1882, d. Aug. 6, 1885.

McIntyre Family of Pee Dee

Gordon G. McLaurin has given considerable information on the McIntyre family of the Pee Dee area in his volume on the McLaurins,[55] and they have been more briefly dealt with in Roderick L. Carmichael's work on the Carmichaels.[56] Many of them are listed in Mary Belle M. Bethea's *Ancestral Key to the Pee Dee.* Nearly all that I relate here comes directly from Gordon G. McLaurin.

The head of this family was Archibald McIntyre, Sr., who emigrated to America in 1794. He was the son of Daniel McIntyre and his wife Christian Munro, who were born and died in Scotland. Archibald brought his family with him to America, including his wife, Catherine McKay and four, or possibly all five of his children. He died Dec. 19, 1836, and his wife died Dec. 12, 1835. They lived in Marlboro County, S.C., on the waters of Beaver Dam Creek and White Oak Creek.

Their children:

I. DANIEL MCINTYRE lived and died in Marlboro County, was single.

II. DUNCAN MCINTYRE is believed to have married, had children and to have lived in Marlboro County.

III.HUGH MCINTYRE is believed to have married and moved to Georgia.

IV. CHRISTIAN MCINTYRE m. Angus McIntyre and had children.

V. ARCHIBALD MCINTYRE, JR. m. Martha Jane Turnage when he was some fifty years old. They had seven children:

A. John Turnage McIntyre b. Jan. 19, 1845, d. Mar. 6, 1865, was single. He was wounded in the Confederate Army and died in Elmira Prison, Elmira, N.Y.

B. Catherine (Katy) McIntyre b. Aug. 9, 1846, d. Oct. 21, 1885, m. J.P. Bunch b. Aug. 7, 1839, d. May 24, 1919. They had three children who are traced by McLaurin.[57]

C. Daniel Luke McIntyre b. Sept. 12, 1848, d. Jan. 31, 1899, single.

D. James M. McIntyre b. Feb. 2, 1851, d. Mar. 5, 1920, m. Mary Ellen (Molly) McLaurin b. Feb. 11, 1847, d. Oct. 20, 1913, daughter of John J. McLaurin. They had three daughters who are traced by McLaurin.[58]

E. Archibald Kay McIntyre b. Feb. 1, 1853, d. July 18, 1927, m. Eliza Jane Fletcher b. Aug. 25, 1855, d. Apr. 15, 1939, and had two children who are listed by McLaurin.[59]

F. Nancy Della McIntyre b. Dec. 9, 1855, d. Sept. 3, 1933, m. James Alexander McLaurin b. Mar. 11, 1848, d. Jan. 9, 1899, and had five children who are traced by McLaurin.[60]

G. Hugh Bishop McIntyre b. Apr. 26, 1862, d. Oct. 16, 1946, m. first Sally McKinnon b. Feb. 16, 1868, d. May 13, 1899; m. secondly, Valeria Welch b. May 20, 1882, d. Sept. 26, 1955, and had one child whose offspring are traced by McLaurin.[61]

McColl Families of Pee Dee

A number of McColl families emigrated into Marlboro County, S.C., or neighboring Richmond County, N.C., in the 1790s. The relationship between them (other than intermarriage) is not necessarily clear. It is not possible for me to give a full genealogy of most of these families, but some good source material is available on them, as we shall see. Gordon G. McLaurin has traced the family of "Steady" Hugh McColl of Marlboro County, son of Daniel McColl as follows.

"Steady" Hugh McColl Family of Marlboro

"Steady" Hugh McColl was the oldest son of Daniel and Nancy

Gordon McColl.[62] Daniel and Nancy McColl also had Daniel McColl Jr., Dugald McColl and Christian McColl. "Steady" Hugh was born in Appin, Scotland in 1777, and died in Marlboro County, S.C., on Aug. 9, 1845. He m. Mary McColl McColl, who was b. in Appin, Scotland in 1785, and d. in Marlboro County, Dec. 22, 1853. Both are buried in the old Stewartsville Cemetery in present Scotland County, N.C. They had four children:

I. MARGARET (PEGGY) MCCOLL b. June 15, 1809, d. Jan. 20, 1886, m. David McColl, b. Oct. 22, 1813, d. Jan. 17, 1899. They had four children:

- A. Penelope McColl m. A.A. McLean and had six children, who are traced in Gordon McLaurin[63] and in Mary Belle M. Bethea.[64]
- B. Duncan Donald McColl b. Apr. 23, 1842, d. Mar. 10, 1911, m. Deborah Thomas, b. Apr. 29, 1846, d. Dec. 6, 1917, daughter of J.A.W. Thomas. They had seven children who are traced in McLaurin and Bethea.[65]
- C. Hugh W. McColl b. 1844, d. 1870, lived in Hornsby or Webberville, Texas; was single.
- D. John M. McColl b. Mar. 26, 1846, d. May 4, 1907, m. Mary Louise Roberts, b. Aug. 28, 1848, d. Apr. 4, 1935. They had one child.[66]

II. NANCY MCCOLL b. Apr. 15, 1811, d. May 29, 1857, m. Solomon L. McColl, b. Apr. 3, 1811, d. Dec. 25, 1857. They had eight children:

- A. James W. McColl b. Dec. 2, 1835, d. Dec. 4, 1866, was single.
- B. Mary C. McColl b. Jan. 20, 1838, d. May 15, 1911, was single and helped rear her younger brothers and sisters.
- C. Martha J. McColl b. Sept. 19, 1841, d. May 30, 1901, m. Silas McColl b. Mar. 7, 1838, d. Mar. 10, 1908. They had six children, who are traced by McLaurin and Bethea (although Bethea spells their name McCall, rather than McColl).[67]
- D. John H. McColl b. Aug. 22, 1843, d. Apr. 4, 1860, single.
- E. Hugh Spencer McColl, b. Nov. 19, 1845, d. Oct. 10, 1864, served in Confederate Army, and died in the Elmira, N.Y., prison camp.
- F. Lucy E. McColl b. Oct. 23, 1848, d. ____ 1917, m. John Wesley Roper, b. Apr. 15, 1830, d. July 23, 1894. She was his second wife. They had seven children, who are traced by McLaurin and Bethea.[68]

G. Narcissa McColl b. Sept. 9, 1852, d. Apr. 23, 1964, m. Alfred Hargrove. They had one child, listed by McLaurin and Bethea.[69]

H. Menardie McColl b. Feb. 2, 1857, d. Dec. 10, 1929, was single.

III. JOHN B. MCCOLL b. 1814, d. 1894, m. three times: first, Mary Ann Crawford, b. Jan. 15, 1816, d. Sept. 14, 1845, by whom he had four children, who are traced by McLaurin and Bethea (although she spells it McCall):[70]

A. Flora McColl b. May 18, 1843, d. July 22, 1913, m. Eli Willis b. May 25, 1839, d. Sept. 28, 1923, served in the Confederate Army and was wounded at the Battle of Cold Harbor. They had eight children.

B. Hugh S. McColl b. 1840, served in the Confederate Army (S.C. Volunteers), and died in Federal Prison.

C. Crawford McColl b. 1841, served in S.C. Volunteers and was killed at Gettysburg, July, 1863.

D. John T. McColl b. 1844, settled near Webberville, Texas, m. Ella Dawson; no children. He d. 1916. John B. McColl m. secondly Katherine Shaw b. July 16, 1825, d. Apr. 9, 1857; no children. He m. thirdly Jo Anne Salmon b. 1837, d. 1924, by whom he had eight children, who are listed in McLaurin:[71]

E. Mary Ruth McColl b. 1860, d. 1945, single.

F. Margaret McColl b. 1862, m. Kirk York.

G. Hugh C. McColl b. 1864, d. 1936, m. Lorena Merietta McQueen.

H. Belle McColl b. 1866, m. William Wright and had several children.

I. Anna C. McColl b. 1868, m. Dennis Dew and had four children.

J. John B. McColl Jr., m. Lonie McCormick and had six children.

K. Ellial McColl m. and had children.

L. Lois V. McColl m. J. B. Newberry and had several children.

IV. EFFIE ELLEN MCCOLL b. Nov. 10, 1816, d. Jan. 14, 1897, m. Lauchlin LeRoy McLaurin, traced under the McLaurin family in this volume.

John McColl Family of Marlboro County

This family is mentioned in J.A.W. Thomas's *A History of Marlboro County, S.C.*,[72] and is partially traced in Bethea, (who spells the name as McCall), as follows:[73]

John McColl (or according to Bethea, McCall) came from Appin,

Scotland, in 1791. He was b. 1773, and d. 1858. He first stayed with his kinsman, David McColl, who lived near the N.C. State line, and later moved to Tatum, S.C. In 1810 he m. Mary Currrie, b. 1775, d. 1853, daughter of Rev. Lauchlin Currie. They had four children:

I. JOHN L. MCCOLL (MCCALL) d. 1856, m. Nancy Sinclair (daughter of Archie Sinclair of the Isle of Islay). They had six children:

A. C.S. McColl (McCall)
B. T. Dickson McColl
C. J.G.B. McColl
D. John McColl
E. Pocahontas McColl
F. Kate McColl

II. SOLOMON L. MCCOLL ("BIG SOLOMON") m. Nancy McColl, daughter of David McColl. They had three children who are listed by Bethea[74] and mentioned by J.A.W. Thomas also:[75]

A. Hugh McColl
B. David McColl
C. Peter McColl, d. 1871, Clerk of Court in Marlboro County.

IV. DANIEL MCCOLL m. Nellie McRae, daughter of Farquar McRae.[76]

V. SAMUEL ALLEN MCCOLL b. 1815.

McRae Families of the Pee Dee

The genealogy and history of the numerous McRaes of the Pee Dee area has never been adequately compiled. Mrs. Betty McRae Hamrick of Florida is presently working on a complete genealogy of the Pee Dee McRaes. When her research is finished, it should fill a large gap in Pee Dee genealogy. The best I can do at present is to present a very incomplete outline of the original McRae emigrants and their children. This family is dealt with in J.A.W. Thomas[77] and in Mary Belle M. Bethea.[78] Mrs. Robert L. McNiel (Janie Peterkin) of Dillon, S.C., has sent me a number of copies of McRae documents from various sources, as will be indicated. More recently, Anna McIver Henderson Parham has traced part of the McRae connection, and I rely heavily upon her work here.[79]

This is a tentative outline of the original McRae emigrants to Marlboro County. It is taken from the sources mentioned above, and I am not able to vouch for its accuracy:

The head of this family was Finlay (or Ian) McRae b. 1700, d. 1780, a native of Kintail, Scotland, as were all of his eleven children who accompanied him to South Carolina c. 1776, (or, according to Anna Parham, he emigrated with his family in 1780, and died on shipboard,

and was buried at sea.[80]) He is said to have been the first son of Farquhar MacRae, and to have married a MacRae. His children (order of birth is uncertain) were:

I. CHRISTOPHER MCRAE m. Sarah McRae (according to Bethea[81]) and lived on a plantation in Marlboro County, later known as the Charles Crossland place. He is buried at Salem Churchyard, Bennettsville, S.C.[82] They had at least the following children (according to Bethea and the papers from Mrs. R.L. McNiel, as well as Mrs. Anna Parham):

A. John L. McRae
B. Alexander McRae m. Ann Farwell
C. Colin McRae, unmarried
D. Sallie (Sarah) McRae (1809-1865), m. Dr. Job Weatherly
E. Polly McRae m. ____ McRae
F. Katie McRae m. ____ Battle
G. Barbara McRae (1801-1857) m. James Peterkin
H. Christian McRae m. William Bristow

II. MURDOCK MCRAE

III. JOHN MCRAE m. Mary McInnis. His will was filed in Lumberton, N.C. Feb. 2, 1844 (Will Book of Robeson County, No. 1, p. 438). The papers from Mrs. R.L. McNiel list these children:

A. John McRae Jr. b. Nov. 20, 1820, d. June 21, 1870, a graduate of Davidson College in North Carolina. He m. Emma Walpoole of Huntsville, Alabama. They had six children, three of whom died in Alabama. Later they moved back to Robeson County, N.C., where their three surviving children lived, married and reared families (listed in the papers from Mrs. McNiel).
B. Murdock McRae, who lived near Red Bluff in Marlboro County, S.C., and wrote a letter about the McRae and McInnis history to Mrs. L. W. McKinnon on Nov. 30, 1898 (which survives among the McNiel papers, and came from Hugh McLucas).
C. Alexander McRae of Red Bluff
D. James McRae
E. Catherine McRae m. Neil Southerland
F. Martha Jane McRae m. Paisley Alford (?)
G. Margaret McRae m. James McQueen
H. Mary Ann McRae m. Hector McKay

IV. ALEXANDER MCRAE d. 1824, m. Catherine Douglas (daughter of Daniel Douglas), and had, according to Bethea:[83]

A.Roderick Alexander McRae (1795-June 15, 1869) m. Christian Chisholm (1796-Aug. 10, 1857).[84]

B. Margaret McRae, unmarried

C. Isabella McRae, unmarried

D. Mary McRae m. John McGee. They had four children, none of whom married.[85]

V. DUNCAN MCRAE m. a MacLeod (according to Julia Clare Pate[86]), and had Bea Isabella McRae b. 1781, according to Bethea.[87] Bea Isabella (d. Mar. 11, 1872) m. Shockley Adams b. 1779-Oct. 3, 1824). Both are buried in Bethea Crossroads Cemetery in Marlboro County, S.C. Their eight children and spouses are listed by Pate.[88]

VI. COLIN MCRAE, whose line has been recently researched by Mrs. Earnest B. Meynard of Columbia, S.C. Her work (passed on to me by Mrs. R.L. McNiel) indicates that Colin was b. 1763 in Bundalloch, Kintail Parish in Scotland, and d. 1832 in Marion County, S.C. He m. c. 1788 Elizabeth Campbell, b. 1770 Augusta County, VA., d. 1830 in Marion County, S.C. The part of Marion County in which they lived is now Dillon County, S.C. They had eight children, according to papers written by their son, Archibald McRae of Texas, in the possession of Mrs. Meynard of Columbia, S.C.:

A. Colin McRae Jr. b. Mar. 1789 in Marion County, S.C., d. Nov. 26, 1832 in Appalachicola, Florida, m. Grace Denley.

B. Archibald McRae b. 1792, Marion County, S.C., d. Feb. 24, 1851 in Victoria, Texas, m. in Mobile, Alabama on May 31, 1821, Vincey Williams b. 1800 in Tar River, N.C., d. Mar. 2, 1894 in Lamar, Texas.

C. Alexander McRae

D. Christopher McRae

E. John L. McRae

F. Murdoch McRae, lived in Holmes Valley, Florida

G. William McRae, lived in Holmes Valley, Florida

H. Sarah McRae m. ____ Brewer and moved to Texas c. 1830.

VII. RODERIC(K) MCRAE, b. 1765 and d. Apr. 8, 1850, according to Bethea,[89] and m. Margaret McRae, b. 1777, d. Aug., 1842, according to Parham. Their known children:

A. John D. McRae b. 1797, d. 1853, m. Elizabeth McInnis (1799-1867). Their children are listed by Bethea[90] and are traced in some detail by Parham.[91]

B. Duncan D. McRae b. Apr. 9, 1803, d. Jan. 14, 1859.

C. Nancy McRae b. Dec. 24, 1799, d. Feb. 24, 1846. According to Parham, she married a McRae.[92]

D. Catherine McRae b. Feb. 1, 1801, d. May 14, 1838. She married Joseph Alford and had two children (listed by Parham).[93]

E. Sarah (Sallie) McRae b. Apr. 13, 1809, d. Sept. 3, 1839, first wife of Jesse A. Peterkin b. Mar. 7, 1800, d. July 20, 1844, according to the papers from Mrs. McNiel and Mrs. Parham's book. The descendants of their son, James Alexander Peterkin are traced by Mrs. Parham.[94]

F. Margaret McRae b. 1806, d. 1858, m. David Spears.

G. Christian McRae m. John Meekins d. 1858.

H. Mary McRae b. 1807, d. 1866, m. Hugh McLucas b. 1807, d. 1848, and had five children listed in Bethea.[95]

VIII. MALCOM MCRAE d. before Feb. 5, 1810.

IX. DONALD MCRAE

X. CHRISTIAN MCRAE b. 1766 in Kintail, d. Aug. 16, 1856 in Marlboro County, S.C. Buried in the Martin/McRae Cemetery near Johns, N.C. (from which these dates are taken). She m. James McRae, and from information taken from tombstones in the Martin/McRae Cemetery, we know they had at least the following children:

A. Catherine McRae d. Apr. 8, 1872, aged 74.

B. John C. McRae d. Aug. 10, 1873, aged 68.

XI. MARY MCRAE

Henderson Family of Pee Dee

Mrs. Anna McIver Henderson Parham of Latta, South Carolina, has traced the Henderson family of the Pee Dee area (part of which moved to Mississippi) in *"My Family" The Hendersons of the Carolinas and Their Connections* (privately printed: Latta, S.C., 1994). The emigrant head of this family was Manasseh Henderson of Scotland. The dates of his life, death and emigration are unknown. He had two known children:

I. ARCHIBALD II. CATHERINE

I. ARCHIBALD HENDERSON married Sarah Carmichael, daughter of Daniel Carmichael (b. 1736, d. Jan. 5, 1822) and Sallie McCall (b. 1752, d. Sept. 28, 1840). This family moved to Mississippi from Carolina (sometime before the 1840 census). They had:

A. Daniel Carmichael Henderson b. 1806, d. Nov. 1869, a graduate of Hampden-Sydney College in Virgina, and of Union Theological Seminary in Virginia in 1831. He was an ordained minister of the Presbyterian Church, and served most of his ministry in Mississippi and Louisiana. He married Sarah Gilchrist, daughter of Archibald and Mary McPherson Gilchrist. Their two children are listed and traced in Parham (5, 6). After the death of his first wife, he married Anna Jane Torrey b. 1812, d. 1883, daughter of Dougald Torrey and Flora Gilchrist. Their four children are traced in Purcell's *Lumber River Scots* (277-280) and in Parham (6).

B. John Carmichael Henderson b. 1810, d. after 1844, m. Nancy McArn b. 1817, d. Apr. 21, 1877, daughter of Hugh McArn and Sarah McNeill McArn. He attended Hampden-Sydney College in the class of 1828. Their three children are traced in Parham (7-59).

C. Malcolm Carmichael Henderson b. c. 1813, d. Mar. 10, 1843 in Mississippi. The 1840 census shows him and three sons living in Panola County, Mississippi. They are listed in Parham (5).

II. CATHERINE HENDERSON, daughter of Manasseh Henderson, b. c. 1770, and married in Aug. 31, (1815?) Adam McKay (sometimes spelled Mackey). They had a son (no further information) and a daughter who died single. According to Mrs. Parham (60), there is some material on this family in *The Mackeys and Allied Families of North Carolina* (I do not know the name of the author, nor publisher).

Family of Rev. Daniel Brown

Mrs. Janie Campbell McEachern, of Hamer, S.C., wrote *A Sketch of the Descendants of Rev. Daniel Brown, John McLean and Neill McEachern* (October, 1945, privately printed). From it we take the following information concerning the progenitors of a number of Brown/McLean/McEachern descendants in the Pee Dee Area of South Carolina.

Rev. Daniel Brown b. 1776 in Robeson County, N.C., son of Neill

Brown and Sarah McPhaul of Raft Swamp Presbyterian Church section (near present Red Springs), was a Presbyterian minister, a graduate of David Caldwell's Academy in Guilford County, N.C., and licensed to preach at Barbeque Church in (then) Cumberland County on Mar. 27, 1801. He served in Williamsburg District, S.C., and died Aug. 18, 1815, while visiting his father in Robeson County, N.C. He is buried at Philippi Presbyterian Church, near Raeford, N.C. He m. Oct. 14, 1806, Catherine McPherson, b. 1787, d. Nov. 3, 1868, daughter of Daniel McPherson and Sarah McNeill.[96] They had:

I. GEORGE BURDER BROWN b. Sept. 29, 1807, d. Sept. 16, 1881.

II. SUSANNAH BROWN b. Jan. 13, 1809, d. Dec. 10, 1890, m. Rev. Hector McLean on Jan. 17, 1833; no heirs, see p. 346.

III. JOHN WITHERSPOON BROWN b. Mar. 17, 1811, d. Nov. 30, 1834.

IV. NEIL WASHINGTON BROWN b. May 10, 1812, d. May 6, 1827.

V. SARAH JANE BROWN b. Feb. 3, 1814, d. Nov. 8, 1885, m. May 21, 1835, Archie McLean d. 1845, aged 43, son of John and Margaret McLean McLean, natives of Scotland, and residents of the Antioch section of Robeson County, N.C.[97] After Archie's death, Sarah Jane Brown McLean m. secondly, Daniel B. Smith, Feb. 4, 1847 and had two daughters and one son, all of whom remained single.

Sarah Jane Brown and first husband, Archie McLean had six children:

A. Susanna Haseltina McLean b. June 6, 1836, d. Apr. 3, 1901, m. Daniel S. Morrison, Mar. 2, 1854. They had ten children who are traced by McEachern.[98]

B. Catherine Ann Newell McLean b. Dec. 25, 1837, d. June 30, 1891, m. Jan. 10, 1861, Brown McCallum. They had four children who are traced by McEachern.[99]

C. Margaret Jane Frances McLean b. Mar. 22, 1839, d. Mar. 22, 1915, m. D. B. McLaughlin. They had nine children who are traced by McEachern.[100]

D. Daniel Brown McLean b. June 16, 1840, d. Sept. 10, 1906, m. Feb. 3, 1869, Ellen McKay. They had one son whose line is traced by McEachern.[101]

E. Mary Cameron McLean n.Jan. 16, 1842, d. Oct. 29, 1897, m. Archie McGoogan, Apr. 28, 1870. They had six children who are traced by McEachern.[102]

F. Sarah Archie McLean b. June 28, 1843, d. June 10, 1929, m.

May 18, 1865, Hugh A. Campbell. They had eight children who are traced by McEachern.[103]

Neill McEachern Family of the Pee Dee

The work of Janie Campbell McEachern also includes a section of the McEachern family of present Dillon County, S.C. (originally part of old Marion District).[104]

According to Mrs. McEachern (quoting from W.W. Seller's *History of Marion County, S.C.)*, the head of this family was Neill McEachern, who emigrated from Scotland with his family to Marion County, S.C., in the early nineteenth century. According to his tombstone in the McEachern Cemetery in present Dillon County, his name was spelled Neal rather than Neill. He m. in Scotland Effie McKellar. They had four sons and two daughters, of whom four are said to have been born in Scotland. Their children:

I. DUNCAN MCEACHERN m. Peggy McInnis and lived and d. in Marlboro County, S.C.

II. DANIEL MCEACHERN, a native of Kintyre in Scotland, b. July 13, 1814, d. Jan. 18, 1881, m. Mary Ann McGill b. Aug. 29, 1826, d. Feb. 22, 1906, daughter of Archie McGill and Katie McCallum. They had:

- A. Catherine Margaret McEachern b. Oct. 23, 1845, d. Oct. 26, 1917, was single.
- B. Neill McEachern b. July 21, 1846, d. Oct. 11, 1918, was single.
- C. Archibald McEachern b. 1850, d. 1853.
- D. Effie Eugenia McEachern b. Oct. 20, 1851, d. Jan. 2, 1934, m. Feb. 29, 1878, Richard H. Braswell, who d. Aug. 8, 1922. Their three children are traced in McEachern.[105]
- E. Louisa McEachern b. June 8, 1853, d. July 19, 1936, m. Dec. 16, 1880, W. D. Carmichael, who d. June 15, 1942. Their three children are traced by McEachern.[106]
- F. Sallie McEachern b. July 13, 1855, d. 1909, m. John R. Jackson. They had two children who are traced by McEachern.[107]
- G. Joseph A. McEachern b. Feb. 28, 1858, d. Jan. 19, 1930, m. Jan. 7, 1885, Donnie Legette, who d. Sept. 27, 1894. They had two sons who are traced by McEachern.[108]
- H. John B. McEachern b. Oct. 25, 1864, d. Feb. 26, 1910, m. Oct. 30, 1894, Mary Jane McEachern. Their two children are traced by McEachern.[109]
- I. Duncan E. McEachern b. June, 1871, d. June, 1915, m. Lily

Grimes (in Daisy, Georgia). They had one son listed by McEachern.[110]

John and Peter McEachern Families

General Harllee deals with the families of the emigrant brothers, John and Peter McEachern of Scotland, whose descendants lived on the border of North and South Carolina in the Richmond (now Scotland) and Robeson County areas of North Carolina and just over the line in the Pee Dee area of South Carolina (now Dillon County). Neither Mrs. Janie Campbell McEachern nor General Harllee indicate whether there is any known relationship between this family and the Neill McEacherns.

According to Harllee, John and Peter (or Patrick) McEachern came to this region from Scotland "in early youth."[111]

John McEachern Family

John McEachern was born in Scotland about 1740, came as a young man to North Carolina, and here married Mary Currie, who was born about 1750 and died at the age of 87. John died at age 74.[112] They had seven children:

I. MARGARET MCEACHERN b. 1776, d. 1809, married in 1799 in Richmond County, N.C. (now Scotland County) Angus McNeill b. 1762, d. 1835. They had:

A. Daniel McNeill (known as "Calder Daniel") b. 1800, d. Feb. 15, 1868 m. Feb. 7, 1828, Ann McNeill, daughter of Malcolm McNeill and Kate Torrey (Malcolm was the son of the Scots emigrants, Godfrey W. and Killie McDougald McNeill[113]). Their four children are traced in Harllee (871-892).

B. John ("Major Jack") McNeill b. 1801, 1879. m. first Catherine McKay, sister to William and Archie McKay and Mrs. Daniel McKinnon. She d. 1840 after having three children (listed in Harlee[114]). He m. secondly, Elizabeth Buchanan, daughter of John Buchanan, the gun smith. Their four children are listed in Harllee (871).

C. Mary McNeill b. 1803, d. 1856 m. John McCallum, son of Archibald and Margaret Wilkinson McCallum, and lived near Ashpole Presbyterian Church, Robeson County, N.C. (See Daniel McCallum Family of Lower Robeson County in chapter 10 of *Carolina Scots*). Their two sons and two daughters are traced in Harlee (872-873).

D. Hector McNeill ("Preacher McNeill") b. 1805, d. 1872, m. Mary Purcell, daughter of John Purcell. Their two sons and two daughters are listed in Harllee (872).

E. Flora McNeill b. 1807, d. 1872, m. William C. McNeill and had five children, who are traced in Harllee (872-873).

F. Lauchlin McNeill b. 1809, at whose birth his mother died. He d. 1893. He m. Mary McEachern, daughter of Col. Archie McEachern (son of Daniel McEachern and Beatrice Torrey (Purcell) and Effie Sellars. Their six sons and two daughters are traced in Harllee (873-874, 883-884).

II. JAMES MCEACHERN b. 1790, d. 1868, m. Effie Purcell, daughter of John and Mary Gilchrist (McKay) Purcell, b. 1794, d. 1843. They had nine children:

A. John McEachern
B. Archie McEachern
C. Calvin McEachern
D. Purcell McEachern
E. Mary McEachern
F. Jane McEachern
G. Margaret McEachern
H. Elizabeth McEachern
I. Harriet McEachern

III. EDWARD MCEACHERN m. Mrs. Mary Johnson. They had:

A. Daniel (Major) McEachern
B. Evander McEachern
C. Jane McEachern
D. Annie McEachern
E. Eliza McEachern
F. Amanda McEachern

IV. PETER MCEACHERN m. Miss Fairley. They had:

A. Margaret McEachern who m. Mial Wall of Anson County, N.C.

V. NANCY MCEACHERN m. Hector and had two sons and four daughters.

VI. FLORA MCEACHERN b. 1785, d. Jan. 15, 1862, m. Archibald Lytch d. May 20, 1848, aged 65. They lived and died one mile from Laurinburg, N.C.,[115] and had:

A. Mary Lytch d. Oct. 10, 1888, single.

B. John Lytch d. June 1892, age 64 years. He m. Mary Patterson

and had two children (listed in Harlee, 893).

C. William Lytch d. July 1881, age 56 years, m. Catherine McNair and had two sons and four daughters.

D. Angus Lytch d. March 1881, age 61 years, m. Sarah Ann McDonald, who d. 1846, age 23 years with no children. He m. secondly, Jane McLaurin of South Carolina, who d. c. 1885, age 75 years. Their one son is listed in Harllee (893).

E. James Lytch m. Sarah James Shaw. Their eight children are listed in Harlee (893).

VII. MARY MCEACHERN b. 1779, d. 1856, m. Angus McLean. They had:

A. Angus McLean
B. Giles McLean
C. Eliza McLean

Peter McEachern Family

Peter (or Patrick) McEachern, brother and fellow Scottish emigrant of John, lived near his brother John in North Carolina. General Harllee writes about him:

> He was reputed to have been a very strong man. He was a blacksmith by trade. It is said he could take an anvil of two hundred pounds weight by the horn in his right hand and set it off or up on the block. He was afraid the tories might capture his shop and destroy his outfit, so he buried his anvil near the shop and seven years later when peace was declared he found it with great difficulty. The anvil had sunk several feet deep in the soft sand.[116]

Peter McEachern m. Mary Fairley (or Fairly) b. 1751, d. 1834. They are both buried in the Fairly Cemetery near her parents (one quarter mile north of Center Presbyterian, near Maxton, N.C.). Information is given on the ancestry of Mary Fairley under "The Fairly Family" (Chapter 11 of *Carolina Scots*). They had:

I. JOHN MCEACHERN m. (wife's name unknown) and had:

A. "Little Peter" McEachern, who m. Maria McQueen and had Mary, who m. James McLean.

II. PETER MCEACHERN m. Sarah Malloy and had:

A. Peter McEachern m. Mrs. Gunter

B. Mary McEachern m. Benton Prince (father of Dr. Daniel Malloy Prince of Laurinburg, N.C.)

C. Charles McEachern married in Alabama.

III. ARCHIBALD MCEACHERN (he seems to have changed the spelling of his last name to McEachin) m. first, Sarah (Sally) McQueen, daughter of Col. James Queen and Ann McRae of Queensdale. Sarah (Sally) was born 1797, d. 1829. Archibald is called "Colonel Archibald McEachin" in McElyea's *The MacQueens of Queensdale* (63). Their four children are traced in McElyea (125-148). See 'The MacQueens of Queensdale' in Chapter 10 of *Carolina Scots* for more on this family. They had:

A. Ann Eliza McEachin C. Flora McEachin
B. Mary Jane McEachin D. Margaret McEachin

Archibald McEachern (McEachin) m. secondly, Annabella (Nephsie) McQueen sister of his first wife. Annabella McQueen b. 1803, d. 1869. They had two children (traced in McElyea, op.cit., 161-163). After the death of Archibald McEachin, Annabella m. William Stewart (no children by this marriage).

IV. MARGARET MCEACHERN m. James Stuart

V. Another sister (name unknown to Harllee-892) who m. W.W. Carmichael.

MacDonald Family of Cumberland County, N.C. and Dillon County, S.C.

Another Highland Scots family that we shall survey in the Pee Dee area of South Carolina is part of the larger McDonald connection which lived between Longstreet and Galatia Presbyterian Churches in the original Cape Fear settlement of North Carolina. Most of my information on this family comes from a booklet on the MacDonald Family written in the early 1920s, owned by Jeanette MacDonald Stone, and available in the Genealogy Vertical File in the North Carolina State Library in Raleigh, N.C. Information on the Dillon County branch of this family can also be found in Mary Belle M. Bethea's *Ancestral Key to the Pee Dee.*

The head of this family was Neil MacDonald, who with his wife and three sons, emigrated from the Isle of Skye to North Carolina in 1802. They settled about nine miles north of Fayetteville, near Galatia Church in Cumberland County. His wife was a Finlayson. They had:

I. JOHN MACDONALD m. ____ McNeill and lived near Sandy Grove Presbyterian Church in Cumberland County. They had three children:

A. Neill N. MacDonald b. Mar. 12, 1828, d. Apr. 1, 1908[117] m. Ann Woodly and had several children.

B. Angus MacDonald m. Sarah MacCaskill; no children. He d. in the War Between the States.

C. Sarah MacDonald m. Archie Ray and lived on her father's homeplace in Cumberland County. They had three sons, listed in the MacDonald booklet.[118]

II. MALCOLM MACDONALD b. 1785, d. Feb. 16, 1857, m. Mar. 19, 1818, Mary MacQuaige in Cumberland County. She d. Feb. 23, 1862. They moved from the Longstreet Church section (where they were members) to Blue's Bridge on Lumber River, and later sold out and moved to Marion District, South Carolina, now Dillon County, near Carolina Presbyterian Church. He was one of the original elders in Carolina Church, which was organized in 1850. They had seven children:

A. Annie MacDonald b. May 5, 1819, d. Apr. 27, 1882, m. Benjamin L. Alford.[119] According to Mary Belle Bethea, she was Alford's second wife.[120] They had one child, listed in MacDonald and Bethea.[121]

B. Alexander J. MacDonald b. July 5, 1820, d. Apr. 23, 1902, m. Katherine McInnis of the Carolina section of present Dillon County, b. Dec. 9, 1838, d. Apr. 23, 1899. Their six children are traced in the MacDonald booklet[122] and information on many of them can also be found at various places in Bethea. The present Dillon County MacDonalds are descended from this couple. Mrs. Anna Henderson Parham includes considerable information on some of the descendants of Alexander J. and Katherine McInnis MacDonald's son, Malcolm (particularly the eight children of Mr. "Mac" [Kate McLaurin MacDonald]—one of the sons of Malcolm—and his wife, Mary Alene McQueen: Malcolm John MacDonald, Roderick MacDonald, James MacQueen MacDonald, Flora Louise MacDonald, Charles Brown MacDonald, Alexander MacRae MacDonald, Donald Francis MacDonald, and Robert McLaurin MacDonald.)[123]

C. Jennette MacDonald b. Nov. 16, 1822, d. Apr. 20, 1852, single.

D. Catherine MacDonald b. Feb. 12, 1824, d. Nov. 22, 1882, single.

E. Neill Q. MacDonald b. Nov. 9, 1825, d. May 25, 1882, single.

F. Christian MacDonald b. Mar. 19, 1827, d. July 15, 1892, single.

G. Daniel W. MacDonald b. May 11, 1831, d. June 26, 1862, single.

McLellan Family of the Kentyre Community in Dillon County, South Carolina

The large McLellan family of Dillon County is descended from Alexander and Mary McKinnon McLellan, natives of Scotland, who emigrated first to North Carolina, and soon afterwards came to the Kentyre section of Dillon County (then, Marion District), South Carolina, around the year 1800. Their history is recorded in *Meet the Macs: Genealogical Record of Descendants of Timothy Rogers McLellan* (privately printed, Dillon, S.C. First edition, 1963 by Morris Campbell, Cecil Carmichael, Jimmie Hayes, Ruby Coleman, Sara Jane Currin, Cora Lee Coleman, Sylvia McLellan, Alva McLellan; second edition, 1980 by Morris Campbell, Ann McLellan Braswell, Thad W. Carmichael, Jimmie Carmichael Hayes, Alva McLellan, Fay McLellan Sloan). All of my information is taken from this source (unless otherwise indicated).

Emigrants Alexander and Mary McKinnon McLellan were married in Scotland, and had several infants buried there. They lived about one mile directly in front of Kentyre Church, and were prosperous farmers. They are buried in the Lock (sometimes called McDuffie or McLellan) Cemetery. According to their tombstones, Alexander McLellan died Apr. 17, 1839, aged 77 years, and Mary McK. McLellan died at age 42. They had five children who reached maturity:

I. FLORA MCLELLAN
II. DANIEL MCLELLAN
III. DUNCAN MCLELLAN
IV. ARCHIE K. MCLELLAN
V. COLIN MCLELLAN

I. FLORA MCLELLAN b. 1798, d. 1877, m. Dougald B. Carmichael (son of Duncan and Catherine Carmichael) b. 1808, d. 1857. They lived near Kentyre Church. The history of their seven children is traced in R.L. Carmichael, *The Scottish Highlander Carmichaels of the Carolinas* (80-84):

A. Mary Ann Carmichael b. 1825, d. 1900, m. Neil McDuffie b. 1818, d. c. 1901, lived near Kentyre (Hamer, S.C.). Their twelve children are listed in R. L. Carmichael (81).

B. Katherine Carmichael b. 1828, m. Neil B. McQueen, lived in Dillon, S.C. Their three children are listed in Carmichael (81).

C. James Alexander Carmichael b. 1831, d. 1863, was single and killed during the War Between the States.
D. Duncan Calvin Carmichael b. 1834, m. first Sarah McKinnon b. 1842, and secondly, Lemantha Walters. They lived near Hamer, S.C. By his first wife he had three children, and four by his second wife. They are listed in Carmichael (81).
E. Daniel A. Carmichael b. 1837, d. 1863, single and was killed during the War Between the States.
F. Malcolm Colin Carmichael b. 1839, d. 1922, m. Amanda Carmichael, lived at Hamer, S.C. Their eight children are listed in Carmichael (81).
G. John L. Carmichael b. 1841, d. 1862, was single and killed during the War Between the States.

Thus, this one family lost three sons in the Confederate Army.

II. DANIEL MCLELLAN, son of Alexander and Mary McK. McLellan, lived on his father's homestead and was a teacher. He was single.

III. DUNCAN MCLELLAN, son of Alexander and Mary McLellan, lived on his father's homestead and was single.

IV. ARCHIBALD KINNON MCLELLAN, son of Alexander and Mary McLellan, m. on Dec. 4, 1833 Harriet Rogers, daughter of Sarah Bethea and Timothy Erasmus Rogers, at her father's home (the site is where the Fitzhugh Bethea home now stands). They lived in the Kentyre Community and had five daughters and nine sons. Much earlier (in 1935), General Harllee included some information on the descendants of Archibald in *Kinfolks* (Vol. II, 2305-2306).They are listed in *Meet the Macs* as follows (without dates of birth and death):

A. Sarah McLellan
B. Flora Jane McLellan
C. Miranza McLellan
D. Margaret McLellan
E. Mary Ann McLellan
F. Malcolm McLellan
G. Alexander McLellan
H. Timothy Rogers McLellan
I. Daniel McLellan
J. John B. McLellan
K. Archie K. McLellan, Jr.
L. F. Tristram McLellan
M. Duncan McLellan
N. Robert McLellan

Meet the Macs gives further information only on three of these:

E. Mary Ann McLellan m. Archibald McC. Stuart from near Rowland, N. C., and had several children.
H. Timothy Rogers McLellan (to whose descendants the major-

ity of the book is devoted) b. Feb. 26, 1836, d. Apr. 9, 1895, m. on Feb. 4, 1866 Flora Amanda McCormick b. July 10, 1847, d. June 3, 1922. They lived in the Kentyre Community and are buried at Kentyre Presbyterian Church. They had five sons and four daughters, whose families are traced down to 1980. They are:

1. Alexander McLellan m. Ann Murphy Carmichael and had five children
2. Harriet Drusilla Carmichael m. Joel R. Carmichael and had six daughters
3. Sarah Katherine m. Archibald McIntyre and had one son.
4. Archie Kenneth McLellan m. Isla Byrd Faulk and had five sons and four daughters.
5. James McCormick m. first Cora Carmichael and had six children, and secondly, m. Hattie Vera Gaddy (McIntyre), and had two children.
6. Malcolm Robert McLellan m. first Cordelia McIntyre: no children. Secondly, m. Hattie Lee Carter and had three children.
7. Flora Margaret McLellan ("Fobie") m. George Brown Campbell. They had ten children.
8. Martin Brearly McLellan died in infancy and buried at Kentyre Church.
9. Lou Ellen McLellan m. Duncan Archibald Carmichael and had nine children.

V. COLIN MCLELLAN, son of Alexander and Mary McK. McLellan, m. Rebecca Bethea. He d. at age 48. They had children, and some of their descendants live around Rowland, North Carolina, according to *Meet the Macs* (1).

McDaniel Family of Kentyre Community, Dillon, South Carolina

Another Scottish emigrant family which lived in the Kentyre area of Dillon County, S.C. (near the border of Robeson County, North Carolina) is that of James A. DcDaniel, Sr. According to information given to me by Mrs. Ruth Norris of Dillon, S.C., James A. McDaniel Sr. was born Feb. 2, 1801 and d. June 2, 1892, m. Martha Ann Edwards b. Aug.

13, 1810, d. Jan. 2, 1882, daughter of Margaret (Peggy) Cameron and Husband, Colin Edwards, in whose house the first services of Kentyre Presbyterian Church were held. James A. and Martha Ann McDaniel are buried in the Lock Cemetery, near Kentyre. They had twelve children:

I. JAMES A MCDANIEL, JR. b. Mar. 24, 1836, d. after 1900.

II. JOSEPH MCDANIEL b. Feb. 10, 1838, d. Aug. 20, 1862.

III. NANCY JANE MCDANIEL b. Nov. 1, 1841, d. Jan. 15, 1882.

IV. WILLIAM C. PRESTON MCDANIEL b. Jan. 18, 1843, d. Jan. 3, 1862 during the War Between the States at Sullivan Island, near Charleston, S.C., and is buried in the Lock Cemetery near Kentyre.

V. BENJAMIN F. MCDANIEL b. Dec. 23, 1845, d. Feb. 18, 1918.

VI. ROBERT C. HAMER MCDANIEL b. Feb. 18, 1851, d. July 19, 1933.

VII. GEORGE MCDUFFIE MCDANIEL b. Mar. 3, 1853, d. May 17, 1947.

VIII. SARAH E. MCDANIEL b. Mar. 2, 1855, d. Feb. 24, 1948.

IX. LUCY ANN MCDANIEL b. Nov. 4, 1856, d. Feb. 8, 1946.

X. ALEXANDER MCDANIEL b. Sept. 24, 1832, d. June-Aug. 1863, during the War Between the States in the "Liberty Guards", and is buried near Tupelo, Mississippi.

XI. JOHN W. MCDANIEL b. June 20, 1834, d. ?

XII. MARY CATHERINE MCDANIEL b. July 1, 1848, d. Aug. 9, 1866 of typhoid fever.

Notes

1. Roderick L. Carmichael, *The Scottish Highlander Carmichaels of the Carolinas* (R.L. Bryan: Columbia, S.C., 1978 reprint of 1935 original), 23.
2. Mary Belle Manning Bethea, *Ancestral Key to the Pee Dee* (R.L. Byran Company: Columbia, S.C., 1978).
3. Carmichael, op. cit., 63.
4. Ibid., 64.
5. Ibid., 80-84.
6. Ibid., 64-79.
7. Ibid.
8. Ibid., 85-99.
9. Ibid.

10. Ibid.
11. Ibid., 100-101.
12. Ibid., 101-112.
13. Ibid., 119-120.
14. Ibid., 101-112.
15. Ibid.
16. Ibid.
17. Ibid., 102.
18. Ibid.
19. Ibid., 102, 104.
20. Ibid. 113-114.
21. Ibid., 119-120.
22. Ibid., 121.
23. Ibid., 121-123.
24. Ibid., 125-128.
25. Ibid., 125, 126.
26. Ibid., 125-129.
27. Ibid., 130.
28. Ibid., 130, 131.
29. Ibid.
30. Ibid.
31. Thomas, *History of Marlboro County, S.C.*
32. Gordon G. McLaurin, *G.G. McLaurin and Some of His Kin: Sketches and Genealogy* (privately printed in Dillon, S.C. in the 1970s), 1.
33. Ibid., 1-6.
34. Ibid., 126, 127.
35. Ibid., 7.
36. Ibid., 123, 124.
37. Ibid., 124, 125.
38. In ibid., 125, Fairly is misprinted as "Fairless."
39. These dates are from the Fairly History by Clarice Fairly, previously referred to, p. 2. See the Fairly section of this volume.
40. See G.G. McLaurin, op.cit., 125 and Clarice Fairly, op. cit., 2.
41. McLaurin, op. cit.
42. Ibid.
43. Ibid., 122, 123.
44. Ibid., 118, 119.
45. Ibid., 49-55.
46. Ibid., 55-58.
47. Ibid., 21-48.
48. Ibid., 61-63.
49. Ibid., 63-66.
50. Ibid., 66-67.
51. Ibid., 68-70.
52. Ibid., 84-85.
53. Ibid., 121.

54. Ibid., 121, 122.
55. Ibid., 71-87.
56. R.L. Carmichael, op. cit., 54.
57. Gordon McLaurin, op. cit., 81-83.
58. Ibid., 84-85.
59. Ibid., 85-87.
60. Ibid., 21-48.
61. Ibid., 87.
62. Ibid., 97.
63. Ibid., 110.
64. Bethea, op.cit., 436, etc.
65. McLaurin, 110, 111, 112; Bethea, 436, etc.
66. See McLaurin, 112; Bethea, ibid.
67. McLaurin, 113; Bethea, 438.
68. McLaurin, 114; Bethea, 639.
69. McLaurin, 114; Bethea, 321.
70. McLaurin, 114, 115; Bethea, 437, etc.
71. Ibid., 116.
72. J.A.W. Thomas, *A History of Marlboro County, S.C.* (Baltimore: Regional Publishing Company, 1971, reprint of 1897 edition), 138, 139.
73. Bethea, op. cit., 437, 441, 444, etc.
74. Ibid., 444.
75. Thomas, 139.
76. See Bethea, 441.
77. Thomas, 152ff.
78. Bethea, 496, 497, etc.
79. Anna McI. H. Parham, *"My Family" The Hendersons of the Carolinas and Their Connections* (privately printed, Latta, South Carolina, 1994).
80. Ibid., 96.
81. Bethea, 496.
82. Parham, 96.
83. Bethea, 496.
84. According to Parham, 96. Mrs. Parham traces the descendants of Roderick A. and Christian Chisholm MacRae, 96-99.
85. Ibid., 96.
86. Julia Clare Pate, *Pate, Adams, Newton and Allied Families Principally in Richmond, Scotland and Robeson Counties in North Carolina and Marlboro County, South Carolina* (privately printed, Red Springs, N.C., 1958), 106.
87. Bethea, 497.
88. Pate, 106.
89. Bethea, 498.
90. Ibid., 497.
91. Parham, 99-100.
92. Ibid., 100.
93. Ibid.
94. Ibid.

95. Bethea, 487.

96. Janie Campbell McEachern, *A Sketch of the Descendants of Rev. Daniel Brown, John McLean and Neill McEachern* (privately printed: 1945), 3, 4.

97. Ibid., 5.

98. Ibid., 7-9.

99. Ibid., 10, 11.

100. Ibid., 12, 13.

101. Ibid., 13, 14.

102. Ibid., 14.

103. Ibid., 15-19.

104. Ibid., 19-23.

105. Ibid., 20.

106. Ibid., 21.

107. Ibid., 21, 22.

108. Ibid., 22.

109. Ibid., 22, 23.

110. Ibid., 23.

111. Harllee, op. cit., I, 871.

112. Ibid.

113. Harllee includes a "sketch of the McNeill Families" by Cyrus McNeill in op. cit., I, 869-893.

114. Harllee, 871.

115. Ibid., 893

116. Ibid., 892.

117. These dates from his tombstone in Carolina Presbyterian Church Cemetery near Dillon, S.C.

118. Entitled simply "MACDONALD", 2.

119. Ibid., 4.

120. Bethea, op.cit., 3.

121. MacDonald, 4; Bethea, 3.

122. Ibid., 4-8.

123. Parham, 97, 98.

Epilogue

South and West From Carolina

THIS VOLUME CANNOT DEAL WITH A SUBJECT which would require 15 or 20 large volumes—the great migration of the children and grandchildren of the Carolina Scots to the Southwest territory of the developing United States—but it should at least be mentioned. This movement was particularly strong during the first half of the nineteenth century after the American Government moved the Indian tribes westward, thus opening up the lands of Alabama, Mississippi and beyond.

As Roderick L. Carmichael states: "There was at that time no method of renewing the fertility of cultivated soil, and when the virgin productivity of the land was exhausted, new land was brought under cultivation. As a consequence the settlers were usually looking for new and more productive land, and this caused them to change location, and accounts for some of the moves."[1] Another factor that encouraged migration in addition to the desire for new lands and economic betterment, was the large number of children born to the Carolina Scots, which meant that only a few of them could inherit enough farm land from their parents to have a viable living.

Old Pee Dee Presbyterian Church today.

It is now impossible to determine just what percentage of these Carolinians left, but what happened to the membership of Pee Dee Presbyterian Church near Dillon, S.C., is probably typical of the entire region. R.L. Carmichael writes: "The church lost more than half of its membership through emigration to the South and Southwest, 1830-36 and 1845-57."[2]

The trip from North Carolina to Mississippi or Alabama by families with all their belongings through vast forests and across rivers, creeks and swamps must have been, in many respects, as difficult as sailing from Scotland to Wilmington. Dugald McLaughlin of Cumberland County, N.C., for instance, emigrated to Natchez, Mississippi in 1804, along with his parents and sisters and a niece. According to Neil Blue:

> The journey to the newly settled parts of Mississippi from North Carolina was very tedious and dangerous. The route was by the Cumberland river. The emigrants settled in Tennessee the first year and made a crop and there built flat boats for conveying them, their horses and a portion of their crop, down the Cumberland into the Ohio river and thence down that river into the Mississippi and on to Natchez. The family arrived at their destination without any serious difficulties or losses.[3]

Neil Blue also describes the trip his extended family took from Cumberland County, N.C., to Montgomery, Alabama, in February and March of 1819:

> At that early period, the journey from Carolina and other Eastern states to Alabama . . . was long, wearisome and hazardous. It required several weeks, sometimes over a month, for completion, and was made on horseback and in carts and wagons. The route, too, lay across the territory of the Creek, Choctaw and Chickasaw Indians, and serious apprehensions for safety were shared by those not familiar with the Red man. Our emigrating party started about the middle of February, 1819, for their new and distant homes on Pearl River, some on horses and some in light wagons. No unusual incidents occurred on the trip to Montgomery, Alabama. Other emigrants, bound west, joined them at different points with various destinations. They averaged about twenty miles per day, camping out at night and purchasing supplies for themselves and their animals on the road, at high prices. On the 15th day of March, 1819, they arrived at "Alabama Town," just beyond the present city of Montgomery, where they decided to halt for a few days for rest and recruiting, with some old North Carolina acquaintances, located at that point.[4]

T.R. and Scott Buie devote an entire chapter to "Westward Movement" in *The Family Buie Scotland to North America.*[5] In this chapter they include Mrs. Kate McGeachey Buie's description of an 1841 Buie migration from Carolina to Arkansas, which included spending several months en route to make a crop.[6]

Historical marker at Pee Dee Church. The "other congregations" are dotted all over the South.

Work has been done and continues to be done on many of the Carolina Scots families which migrated to the South and West. Carmichael dealt with some of his own kin as did Purcell in *Lumber River Scots* on Gilchrists, Blues and many others. Many of these people concentrated in the Union Church area of Mississippi, near Fayette. Indeed, the Union Presbyterian Church of Mississippi was founded in the first third of the nineteenth century by Carolina emigrants from Union Church in Moore County, N.C., and they extended a call to their former Moore County pastor, Rev. McCallum, who accepted it. Undoubtedly this Gaelic speaking congregation wanted a pastor who was able to preach in Gaelic, as of course McCallum could. T.R. and Scott Buie include much material about Carolina Scots who settled at Union Church, Mississippi in *The Family Buie Scotland to North Carolina,* as will be seen under the Buie section of this volume, Chapter 5, pp. 183-208.

Many Carolina Scots also went to Euchee Valley in Florida from 1820 onwards for about two more decades. Much of their history has been compiled by Clayton G. Metcalf.[7]

One of the best current resources on the Carolina Scots families who came to Alabama and Mississippi and points westward is *Argyll Colony Plus.* Articles or notices of publications of books have dealt with such families as the Smylies,[8] the John McLean family,[9] the McDonalds,[10] the McFarlands,[11] the McEacherns,[12] and many others. I suspect that future studies will reveal that many of the cultural characteristics traditionally ascribed to the deep South states are an adaptation of Carolinian qualities, which must in large part be traced to Highland Scotland.

Whatever else one might say about the basis of the Southern culture and religion, no one can doubt that this Carolina Scottish origin is true of a substantial percentage of the population of the deep South.

Carolina Scots and Scots in Carolina

In September 1953, Dame Flora MacLeod of MacLeod, Chief of Clan MacLeod, visited her kinsmen in Carolina, many of whose families had now been on this side of the water for as much as two centuries. She brought greetings from Dunvegan Castle in the Isle of Skye to the large congregation at the annual homecoming of Old Bethesda Presbyterian Church, near Aberdeen, North Carolina. Dame Flora is behind the pulpit. Seated on her right is the late Talbot Johnson of Aberdeen, distinguished Attorney, Presbyterian elder and great scholar in the history of the Scots in Moore County. On her left is the pastor of Bethesda at that time, the Rev. Jack Ewart. The author remembers being at this service with his extended family.

Notes

1. Carmichael, op. cit., 23, 24.
2. Ibid., 30.
3. Matthew P. Blue, *Genealogy of the Blue Family* embracing a Sketch of Neil Blue (Montgomery, Ala.: Barrett Co., 1886), 8.
4. Ibid., 16.
5. Buie compilers, op. cit., chapter VI, 19-22.
6. Ibid., 20, 21.
7. e.g. Clayton G. Metcalf, *The Gillis Family in the South.*
8. Argyll Colony Plus, 2.1, 29.
9. Ibid., 3.2, 70, 71.
10. Ibid., 2.4, 142.
11. Ibid., 2.1, 27.
12. Ibid., 3.2, 78.

Bibliography

Adam, Margaret I., "The Causes of the Highland Emigrations of 1783-1803" in *The Scottish Historical Review*, Vol. XVII, No. 66, January, 1920

"Eighteenth Century Landlords and the Poverty Problem," in *The Scottish Historical Review*, Vol. XIX, No. 73, October, 1921

"The Highland Emigration of 1770," in *The Scottish Historical Review*, Vol. XVI, 1919

Barkley, Louise B., et al., *1804-1993 Ferguson Descendants*, privately printed: Newton, N.C., 1993

Bethea, Mary Belle Manning, *Ancestral Key to the Pee Dee*, R.L. Bryan Company: Columbia, S.C., 1978

Black, William, Rev., *History of Alexander Black*, Presbyterian Historical Foundation, Montreat, N.C.

Black, George F., Ph.D., *The Surnames of Scotland: Their Origin, Meaning, and History*, The New York Public Library: Astor, Lenox and Tilden Foundations, n.d.

Blue, Matthew P., ed., *Genealogy of the Blue Family, embracing a Sketch of Neil Blue*, privately printed at Montgomery, Alabama, 1886

Boswell, James, *The Journal of a Tour to the Hebrides with Samuel Johnson, Ll.D.*, first Published 1785, reprinted Houghton Mifflin Company: Boston, 1965

Buie, Scott, editor, *Argyll Colony Plus*, 6716 Meadow Haven, Fort Worth, Texas 76132

Buie, T.R. and Buie, Scott, Compilers, *The Family Buie: Scotland to North America* Chelle-Kirk Printing: Arlington, Texas, 1983

Burt, Edward, *Letters from a gentleman in the north of Scotland to his friend in London; containing the description of a capital town in that northern country*; . . . In two volumes. . . . London, printed for S. Birt, 1754. [spelling & spacing *sic.*]

Butler, Bion H., *Old Bethesda*, Grosset & Dunlap: New York, 1933

Campbell, John Francis, *Popular Tales of the West Highlands*, Vol. I, Wildwood House, 1983, first published 1860

Carmichael, Alexander, *Carmina Gadelica: Ortha Nan Gaidheal (Hymns and Chants)*, Vol. I, Oliver and Boyd: Edinburgh, 1928 reprint

Carmichael, Roderick L., *The Scottish Highlander Carmichaels of the Carolinas*, privately published in 1935, republished by The R.L. Bryan Company: Columbia, S.C., 1978

Caruthers, Rev. E.W., *Revolutionary Incidents and Sketches of Character chiefly in the "Old North State"*, Hayes & Zell: Philadelphia, 1854

Clark, Victor, *My Isle of Jura Clarks and McLeans*, privately printed by Lt. Col. Victor Clark, USAF, ret.: Dallas, Tx., 1987

Genealogy of Clarks from the Isle of Jura, Scotland and Allied Families, privately printed by Victor Clark, 1987

Comer, James Vann, *Ancestors and Descendants of Sheriff Kenneth Henderson Worthy of Moore County, North Carolina: 1850-1856, 1860-1872*, published by Ruby Vann Crumpler McSwain: Sanford, N.C., 1996

Cregeen, E.R., "The House of Argyll and the Highlands" in *Scottish Studies*

"The Tacksmen and Their Successors," in *Scottish Studies*

Dial, Adolf L. and Eliades, David K.,*The Only Land I Know*, The Indian Historian Press: San Francisco, 1975

Errington, Linsdsay, 1989 Exhibition Catalogue: *William McTaggart 1835-1910*, National Gallery of Scotland, 1989

Ferguson, Joan P.S., *Scottish Family Histories*, National Library of Scotland: Edinburgh, 1986

Foote, William Henry, *Sketches of North Carolina: Historical & Bibliographical Illustrative of the Principles of a Portion of its Early Settlers* (1846; reprinted by Dr. Harold J. Dudley for the Committee on Historical Matters, Synod of N.C., PCUS and the N.C. Presbyterian Historical Society, 1965)

Fowler, Malcolm, *They Passed This Way: A Personal Narrative of Harnett County History, 1955; Valley of the Scots,* published by Wynona Fowler, 1986, in Raleigh, North Carolina

Froude, James A., "The Influence of the Reformation on the Scottish Character" in *Short Studies on Great Subjects, Vol. I,* Charles Scribners and Sons: New York, 1871

Gillies, W., ed. *Gaelic and Scotland/Alba agus a' Ghaidhlig*, John Donald Publishers, Ltd.: Edinburgh, 1984

Graham, Ian Charles Cargill, *Colonists From Scotland: Emigration to North America 1707-1783*, Cornell University Press: Ithaca, N.Y., 1956

Grant of Rothiemurchus, Elizabeth, *Memoirs Of A Highland Lady*, edited with an introduction by Andrew Tod, Canongate Classics, 1898,1988

Grant, I.F., *Everyday Life On An Old Highland Farm 1769-1782*, Shepheard-Walwyn: London, 1924,1981

Grant, Ian R. and Withrington, Donald J., General Editors, *The Statistical Account of Scotland; Vol. XX The Western Isles,* 1983

Harllee, William Curry, *Kinfolks: A Genealogical and Biographical Record*, Searcy & Pfaff, Ltd.: New Orleans, La., 1934, 3 vols. and general index.

Hume Brown, P., *Scotland: A Short History*, Oliver and Boyd: Edinburgh, 1908, 1961

Hunter, James, *The Making of a Community*, John Donald Publishers: Edinburgh, 1976

Johnson, James McNeill, *History of the Black Family of Moore County, N.C.*

Johnson, Samuel, *A Journey to the Western Islands of Scotland*, first published 1775, reprinted Houghton Mifflin Company: Boston, 1965

Kelly, Douglas F., *Malcolm Kelly Family of Moore County, North Carolina*, Dillon, South Carolina, 1978

The Scottish Blue Family From Carolina to Texas, Dillon, South Carolina, 1982

Kelly, Kenneth L., *McIver Family of North Carolina*, McIver Art and Publications, Inc.: Washington, D.C., 1964

Kennedy, John, *The Days of the Fathers in Ross-Shire*, Christian Focus Publications: Inverness, 1979, reprint of 1861 edition

Lefler, Hugh T. and Powell, William S., *Colonial North Carolina: A History*, Charles Scribners' Sons: New York, 1973

Linn, Jo White, C.G., *Drake, Arrington, White-Turner, Linn-Brown and Two Dozen Related Southern Lines*, privately published in Salisbury, N.C., 1984

Martin, Martin, *A Description of the Western Islands of Scotland*, Glasgow: Thomas D. Morison, 1884, first edition, 1703

McAllister, D.S., *Genealogical Record of the Descendants of Col. Alexander McAllister of Cumberland County, N.C., Also of Mary and Isabella McAllister*, Richmond, Va.: Whittet & Shepperson, 1900

McAllister Family Papers, Cumberland County, North Carolina 1747-1935 North Carolina Archives file PC 1738.1-2, Papers on file in the: North Carolina Archives, 109 E. Jones Street, Raleigh, NC 27601-2807, Finding aid completed by George Stevenson and William C. Fields on 6 July 1990.

McDonald, Fergus, "The Bible Societies in Scotland" in *The Bible in Scottish Life and Literature*, ed. David F. Wright, St. Andrew Press: Edinburgh, 1988

MacDonell, Margaret, *The Emigrant Experience: Songs of Highland Emigrants in North America*

MacElyea, Annabella Bunting, *The MacQueens of Queensdale*, Charlotte, N.C., 1916

MacGilliosa, Domhnall, *An Eaglais Shaor Ann An Leodhas 1843-1900*, Knox: Edinburgh, 1981

McGilvary, Daniel, *A Half Century Among the Siamese and the Lao, An Autobiography*, Fleming H. Revell Company: New York.

McKerral, Andrew, *Kintyre in the Seventeenth Century*, Oliver and Boyd:Edinburgh, 1948

McLean, Angus W., *Highland Scots in North Carolina*, Vol. I (1919), 48 (quoting *North Carolina Colonial Records*, Vol. IV, 447)

MacLeod, John, *Highlanders: A History of the Gaels*, Hodder and Stoughton: London, 1997

MacLeod, John, *Scottish Theology in Relation to Church History Since the Reforma-*

tion, Reformed Academic Press: Greenville, S. C., 1995, reprint of 1943 edition

McLean, J.P., *An Historical Account of the Settlements of Scotch Highlanders in America*, Baltimore: Genealogical Publishing Co., 1978, reprint from 1900 original

McLeod, Kenneth A., Jr., *Descendants of John MacLeod and Wife Nancy Campbell MacLeod*, The John Alexander McLeod Association, 1979, revised

McLeod, Rozella, *McLeods of Tuckahoe & Horses Creek*, printed by Neill McLeod Family of North Carolina: Carthage, N.C., 1981

MacLeod, Ruairidh H., *Flora MacDonald: The Jacobite Heroine in Scotland and North America*, Shepheard-Walwyn Publishers Ltd., 1995

McLeod, W. A., Jr., *The Curries and Their Kin*, unpublished, written in the 1930s in Cuero, Texas

MacSween, Ann, with photographs by John Cooper, *Skye*, Canongate Publishing Ltd.: Edinburgh, 1990

Meek, Donald, "The Gaelic Bible" in *The Bible in Scottish Life and Literature* , ed. David F. Wright, St. Andrew Press: Edinburgh, 1988

Melvin, Lionel Dane, *Lest We Forget: Our Melvins and Kin,* Media, Inc.: Greensboro, N.C., 1979

Metcalf, Clayton, *The Gillis Family in the South*, Enterprise, Ala., 1975

Meyer, Duane, *The Highland Scots of North Carolina 1732-1776*, Chapel Hill: The University of North Carolina Press, 1961

Miller, John F., Clevelly, J. jun., and Miller, James, *Drawings, partly colored, illustrations of Sir Joseph Banks voyage to the Hebrides, Orkneys and Iceland, in 1792*, 4 Vols. Large Folio. (MS in the British Library, 96 Euston Rd,. London NW1 3DB.)

Moran, Flora Ann Black, *History of John Martin Black and Nancy Ray,* Burlington, North Carolina, unpublished

Newsome, A.R., Editor, *Records of Emigrants from England and Scotland to North Carolina 1774-75*, Division of Archives and History: North Carolina Department of Cultural Resources, Raleigh, 1976, reprint of 1934

Oates, John A., *The Story of Fayetteville and the Upper Cape Fear*, 3rd ed., 1981

Parker, William F. , compiler, *Daniel McNeill Parker, His Ancestry and A Memoir of His Life*, printed by Wm. Briggs: Toronto, 1910, as reproduced in an article by Everette McNeill Kivette, "The Unusual Family Heritage of Julia and Esther McNeill of the Saint Pauls Review," in *Argyll Colony Plus*, Vol. 3, No. 4, Fall, 1988

Patterson, Alex M., *The Monroes of the Upper Cape Fear Valley*, Miami, Florida: McAskill Publ. Co., 1976 , and *Highland Scots Pattersons*

Patterson, Isabel C., *Builders of Freedom and Their Descendants*, privately printed

Powell, William S., *North Carolina Through Four Centuries*, The University of North Carolina Press: Chapel Hill and London, 1989

Prebble, John, *Culloden*, Penguin Books, 1967

The Highland Clearances, Penguin Books, 1969

Purcell, John E., McLean, Angus W., et al., *Lumber River Scots and Their*

Descendants, 1942, reprinted 1986, William Byrd Press Inc.: Richmond, Va

Richardson, Emma and Thomas, *History of Aberdeen*, The Malcolm Blue Historical Society: Aberdeen, N.C., 1976

Roberts, John K., *History of Union Presbyterian Church*, Kelly Printing Co.: Carthage, N.C., 1910

Royal Commission on the Ancient and Historical Monuments of Scotland, *Volume I, Kintyre*, Edinburgh, 1971, *Argyll, An Inventory of the Monuments, Volume 3, Mull, Tiree, Coll & Northern Argyll*, Edinburgh, 1980, *Argyll, An Inventory of the Monuments, Volume 5, Islay, Jura, Colonsay & Oronsay*, Edinburgh, 1984, *Argyll, An Inventory of the Monuments, Volume 7, Mid Argyll, Cowal, Medieval and Later Monuments*: Edinburgh, 1992

Royal Commission on the Ancient and Historical Monuments and Constructions of Scotland, *Ninth Report with Inventory of Monuments and Constructions in the Outer Hebrides, Skye and the Small Isles*: Edinburgh 1928

Saint Fond, Faugus de, *A Journey through England, and Scotland and the Hebrides in 1784*

Schaw, Janet, *Journal of a Lady of Quality*, eds. E. W. and C. M. Andrews, New Haven: Yale University Press, 1921

Scotus Americanus, *Information concerning the Province of North Carolina Addressed to Emigrants from the Highlands and Western Isles of Scotland*, Glasgow: James Knox, 1773

Smith, Evelyn Futch, *Charn Cuimhne To Our Scots of North Carolina*, privately printed: Jacksonville, Fl., 1969

Stewart, A.I.B., "The North Carolina Settlement of 1739," first in *The Kintyre Antiquarian & Natural History Society Magazine*, No. 15, and reprinted in *Argyll Colony Plus*, Issue No. 1, April, 1986

Thomas, Barbara McKay, and Fraine, Bettie McKay, *Archibald McKay 1720-1797: Scotland to Cumberland County, N.C.*, 1979

Thomas, J.A.W., *A History of Marlboro County, S.C.*, Baltimore: Regional Publishing Company, 1971, reprint of 1897 edition

Wicker, Rassie E., *Miscellaneous Ancient Records of Moore County, N.C.*, published under the auspices of Moore County Historical Association, 1971

Withers, Charles W. J., *Gaelic in Scotland 1698-1981: The Geographical History of a Language*, Edinburgh University Press, 1989

Additional sources without listed authors:

Argyll Colony Plus, April and October 1986, Issues Nos. 1 and 2; Fall, 1988, Vol. 3, No. 4

Historical Sketch of Antioch Presbyterian Church, Red Springs, North Carolina 1833-1983

Material published by the School of Scottish Studies: University of Edinburgh:
Scottish Tradition 3: Waulking Songs From Barra
Scottish Tradition 6: Gaelic Psalms from Lewis
AnTocher: Tales, Songs, Tradition

Credits

The authors wish to thank the following for permission to reproduce the illustrations:

C. C. Adams
p. 398 Old Pee Dee Presbyterian Church
p. 399 Historic Marker

The Duke of Argyll
p. 53 Island House of Tiree, plans
p. 73 Map of Campbeltown, 1763

Connie Blue
p. 130 Gaelic sermons—in the Historical Room of First Presbyterian Church, Fayetteville
p. 131 Ibid.

Mrs. John Sam Blue
p. 90 Slave cabin in Moore County, North Carolina.
p. 91 Building on the "River Daniel" Blue farm
p. 98 Cooking pot

The British Library
p. 72 Weaver's House near Bowmore on Islay in 1772

Cornell University Press
pp. xvii & 5 "The Highland Line". Reprinted from Ian C.C. Graham: *Colonists from Scotland: Emigration to North America, 1707-1783*. Copyright (c) 1956 by the American Historical Association

Crown Copyright: Royal Commission on the Ancient and Historical Monuments of Scotland
p. 29 Erray House
p. 30 View of a cottage in Mull by W. Watts, c. 1800
p. 32 Cara House, 1733
p. 34 The Marketplace in Inverary
p. 38 Dunvegan Castle, stone in lower corridor, dated 1686
p. 39 Former Manse, Kilchoan
p. 40 Parish Church, Southend
p. 41 Parish Church, Clachan, 1760
p. 42 Old Lowland Church, 1706, Campbeltown
p. 44 17th Century statue of a Skye woman in the Dunvegan Castle courtyard

p. 52 Island House, Tiree, built in 1748 by Archibald Campbell, 3rd Duke of Argyll
p. 55 Killbride Farmhouse and date panel
p. 56 Limecraigs House, Campbeltown, early 18th century
p. 58 Springfield House, Campbeltown
p. 59 Castle Sween on the shores of Loch Sween in Knapdale
p. 64 1815 Pencil Drawing of Tobermory
p. 65 Plans for the new inn at Tobermory in 1790
p. 67 Culloden House, 1745
p. 69 "The Prince's Bed" in Culloden House, an 1874 engraving

Rev. Dr. and Mrs. Frank Gibson
p. 184 Buie Tombstones in Jura
p. 233 Arichonan
p. 304 Kildalton Church and Celtic Cross

Marion Fisher Hartman
p. 355 Old Black River Presbyterian Church

Mrs. Wanda Howard
p. 94 Daniel Kelly's house at Capisdol, Isle of Skye

Keeper of the Records of Scotland
p. 64 1790 sketch of intended development of Tobermory, Mull; original held at the Scottish Record Office, reference number GD9/4, p117.

Martha McCrummen Fraser Kelly
p. 86 Drawing of Barbeque Church
p. 93 "River Daniel" Blue house
p. 94 Daniel Kelly's log house
p. 95 The Sheriff Alexander Kelly house
p. 96 The Malcolm Blue house
p. 97 The Mill Prong House
p. 100 Old Bluff Presbyterian Church
p. 101 Ashpole Presbyterian Church
p. 103 Union Church today
p. 106 Psalm 23 in the "Squire" John McLeod Gaelic Bible
p. 109 Signed Title Page in the "Squire" John McLeod Gaelic Bible
p. 110 Barbeque Church today
p. 113 Bethesda Church
p. 116 The Shaw House

Cary McLeod, Jr.
p. 248 Kilmore Church

John McLeod of McLeod
p. 62 Coat of Arms over Dunvegan Castle

Dan McMillan, MacMillan and MacMillan, Architects, Fayetteville, NC
p. 152 Map showing Bluff, Longstreet and Barbeque Churches

Mr. and Mrs. Robert McNiel
p. 342 Church letter
p. 362 Old Daniel McKay house, photograph by James A. Atkins
p. 363 Candlestick and Millstone, photograph by James A. Atkins

The Trustees of the National Library of Scotland
Front Endpaper—Map of the Isles from *A Description of the Western Islands* by Martin Martin
p. 8 Duart Castle, Mull, 1748
p. 13 Inside of the Cottage of McNab
p. 15 Cart and Piper in Edward Burt, *Letters From the North of Scotland*
p. 16 Market Cross in Inverness, ibid.
p. 21 A House, ibid.
p. 23 Rural Scene, ibid.
p. 26 Women Washing, ibid.
p. 27 Women at Talyskir "waulking," from T. Pennant, *A Tour in Scotland and a Voyage to the Hebrides*, 1774.
p. 43 Highland Dress in Edward Burt, *Letters From the North of Scotland*
p. 50 Women Washing, ibid.

North Carolina Collection, University of North Carolina Library at Chapel Hill
p. 80 Sir Walter Raleigh
p. 81 Map of North Carolina, H. Moll, 1740
p. 82 Governor Johnston's Coat of Arms
p. 84 A Map of North Carolina, 1737
p. 107 "Plate" of the Town of Fayetteville, 1825
p. 121 "New and Accurate Map of North Carolina", 1779
p. 128 Map of North Carolina, *1795*
Back Endpaper—Map of the Carolinas by Mouzon, c 1775

Courtesy of N.C. Division of Archives and History, originals in the British Museum
p. 85 Plan of the Town and Port of Brunswick, 1769
p. 88 Plan of the Town of Cross Creek, 1770
p. 89 Plan of the Town of Wilmington, 1769
p. 124 Flora MacDonald's Silver

Fred Plummer, Fayetteville, NC
p. 83 Gaelic tombstone of Angus McDiarmid
p. 99 Longstreet Church
p. 105 Sandy Grove Presbyterian Church
p. 112 Longstreet Church and graveyard

The Scottish National Portrait Gallery
p. 7 Highland Chieftain, 1660, Sir Mungo Murray, son of Marquis of Atholl, by John Michael Wright

p. 11 John Campbell, 4th Duke of Argyll (c. 1693-1770), by Gainsborough,1766
p. 12 James Boswell, 1765, by George Willison (1741-1797)
p. 37 General Stuart of Garth
p. 48 Alexander, 1st Lord MacDonald (c. 1745-1795) and his brother, Sir James MacDonald (1742-1766) by Jeremiah Davison
p. 51 2nd Duke of Argyll
p. 68 Prince Charles Edward Stewart 1720-1788 by Antonia David (b. 1698)
p. 68 Flora MacDonald, 1747, by Richard Wilson
p. 70 George II, 1755, by John Shackleton

Also: In a private Scottish collection
p. 61 The 2nd Lord MacDonald, by Sir Alexander Wentworth, 1803

Tate Gallery, London/Art Resource, NY
Dust jacket—McTaggart, William, 1835-1910. *The Emigrants*, Oil on Canvas, 1883-9. Tate Gallery, London, Great Britain

R. E. Wicker
pp. 210-211 Map of Moore County

Index

Index

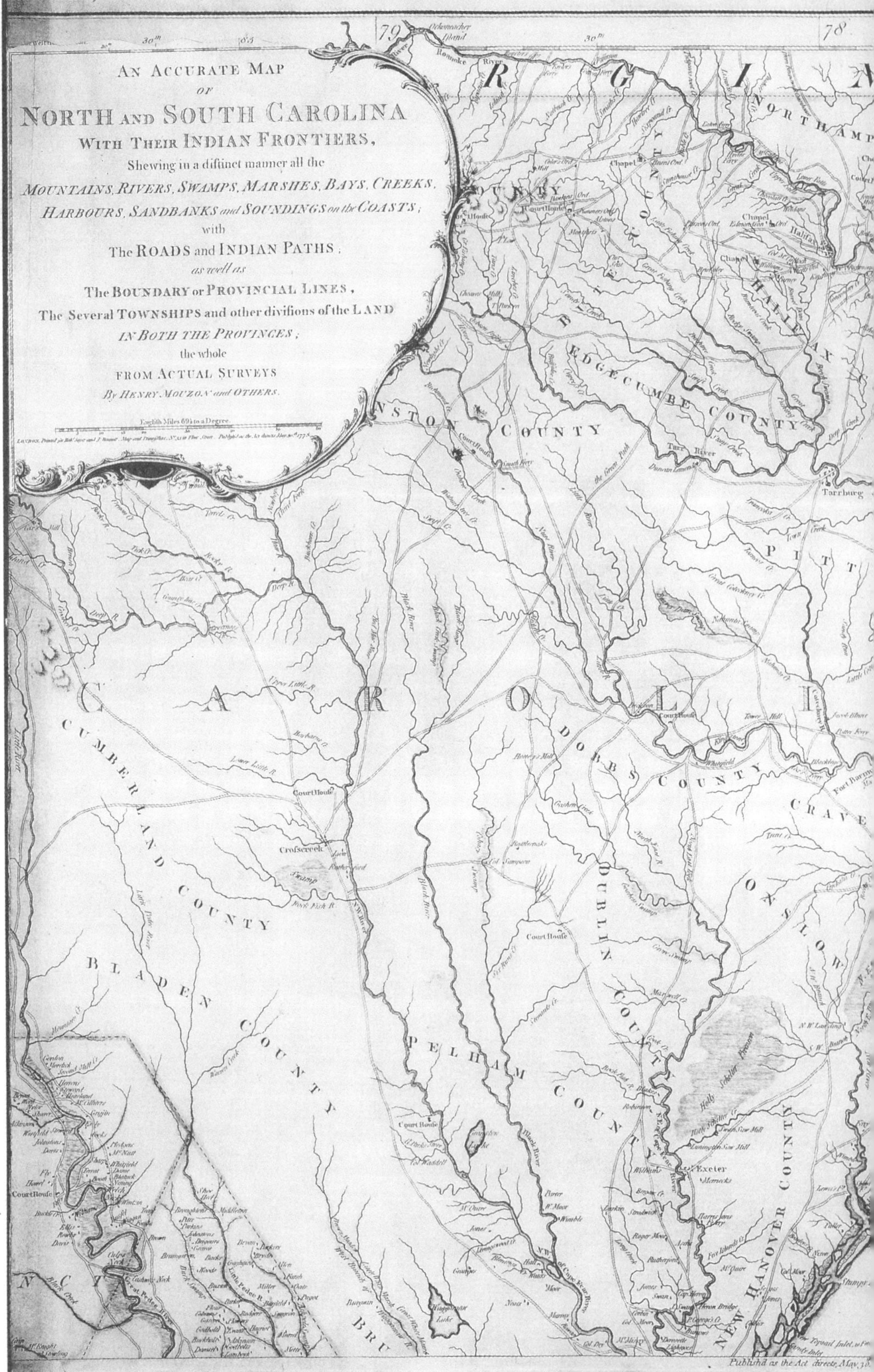
AN ACCURATE MAP
OF
NORTH AND SOUTH CAROLINA
WITH THEIR INDIAN FRONTIERS,
Shewing in a distinct manner all the
MOUNTAINS, RIVERS, SWAMPS, MARSHES, BAYS, CREEKS,
HARBOURS, SANDBANKS and SOUNDINGS on the COASTS;
with
The ROADS and INDIAN PATHS;
as well as
The BOUNDARY or PROVINCIAL LINES,
The Several TOWNSHIPS and other divisions of the LAND
IN BOTH THE PROVINCES;
the whole
FROM ACTUAL SURVEYS
By HENRY MOUZON and OTHERS.
English Miles 69½ to a Degree.
79
78
EDGECUMBE COUNTY
HALIFAX
NORTHAMP
COUNTY
PITT
DOBBS COUNTY
CRAVE
CUMBERLAND COUNTY
BLADEN COUNTY
PELHAM COUNTY
DUBLIN COUNTY
ONSLOW
NEW HANOVER COUNTY
Tarrburg
Crosscreek
Court House
Exeter
Published as the Act directs May 30